PEACE/MIR

Syracuse Studies on Peace and Conflict Resolution
Harriet Hyman Alonso, Charles Chatfield, and Louis Kreisberg
Series Editors

The Russian language edition of this volume,
*Mir/Peace. Al'ternativy voine ot Antichnosti
do knotsa mirovoi voiny. Antologiia,*
is published by Nauka Press, Moscow.

PEACE/MIR

*An Anthology of
Historic Alternatives to War*

VOLUME EDITORS

Charles   *Ruzanna*

Chatfield & Ilukhina

SYRACUSE UNIVERSITY PRESS

Copyright © 1994 by Syracuse University Press
Syracuse, New York 13244-5160
All Rights Reserved

First Edition 1994
94 95 96 97 98 99   6 5 4 3 2 1

This volume is the result of a collaborative project sponsored by the Institute of Universal History, Russian Academy of Sciences, and the Council on Peace Research in History, affiliated with the American Historical Association.

The paper used in this publication meets the minimum requirements of American National Standard for Information Sciences—Permanence of Paper for Printed Library Materials, ANSI Z39.48-1984. ∞™

Library of Congress Cataloging-in-Publication Data
Peace/mir: an anthology of historic alternatives to war / volume
editors, Charles Chatfield and Ruzanna Ilukhina.
p.   cm.—(Syracuse studies on peace and conflict resolution)
Includes bibliographical references and index.
ISBN 0-8156-2601-0 (cloth). —ISBN 0-8156-2602-9 (pbk.)
1. Peace—History—Sources.   I. Chatfield, Charles, 1934–   .
II. Iliukhina, R. M. (Ruzanna Mikhaĭlovna)   III. Series.
JX1937.P43   1994
327.1′72′09—dc20   93-25167

Manufactured in the United States of America

Volume Editors

Charles Chatfield　　　　　　　Ruzanna Ilukhina

Editors

Kyril Andersen　　　　　　　Sandi E. Cooper
Alexei Filitov　　　　　　　　Carole Fink
Victoria Ukolova　　　　　　Lawrence S. Wittner

Contributing Editors

Nelly A. Chaplygina　　　　Alexander Chudinov
Victor M. Heitzman　　　　Valentina Isajeva
Jaroslav N. Schapov　　　　Tatiana I. Telyukova

Consultants

John Whiteclay Chambers II　　William Edgerton
Udo Heyn　　　　　　　　　Karl Holl
Steven Huxley　　　　　　　Nicholas Ivanov
Dorothy V. Jones　　　　　　Helen Nechaeva

David S. Patterson

Contents

Documents

In the English-language version of this volume, current American spelling and punctuation are supplied for all documents in which the text or translation used is from the nineteenth century or later, and some documents have been reformatted. In other respects the original language is retained unless specifically noted.

Generally, the sources cited are published, English-language versions accessible to the reader. A few documents are from foreign-language editions or archives.

Each document listed below is identified by number, author, and a brief title that highlights a theme related to this anthology. In the text this information is supplemented by a reference to the original source and date of the document. The full citation is available in the list of Document Sources. Authors, including institutional authors, are included in the index.

To the Reader

This anthology documents the long search for alternatives to war in order to help students and teachers, scholars and civic-minded people to explore ways of thinking about peace. It is organized chronologically, although documents are grouped thematically within specific periods. The documents are excerpted and are interpreted in their historical contexts. Drawn from many societies and authors, they illustrate approaches to peace that range from absolute to qualified pacifism, from arbitration to international organization, from citizen peace action to state diplomacy.

Some limits are necessary, of course. Our working definition of alternatives to war excludes the approach of unilateral armed defense, or deterrence, although that idea is approximated within the just war tradition and in some of the documents. Our treatment of the evolution of international law on peace and war is oriented more to its philosophical and political dimension than to the body of law. And although the various approaches in this volume represent the western experience from antiquity to 1945, they reflect the modern period most fully.

"Western civilization" refers to what once was called the Occident, a region extending from Russia to North America and from Scandinavia to the northern rim of the Mediterranean. The region was home to the Christian and Jewish religions, and it drew upon the heritage of ancient Israel, Greece, and Rome. By the early nineteenth century, its people had a long shared history and numerous common social, political, economic, and cultural institutions. Western leaders anticipated a common future, and they self-consciously distinguished their civilization from others.

The editors are keenly aware that the ideas of peace in western civilization, for all of their diversity, constitute only one of several great traditions. We hope that this volume will be followed by others clarifying the peace traditions of Asian, African, and indigenous American cultures. Such a series would create the basis for a comprehensive study of global ideas of peace in the second half of the twentieth century.

There are several ways in which this collection can be used. Each requires a word of caution.

On one level, it is possible to follow the evolution of peace concepts in Western history. It is a full and fascinating story. An introduction to each chapter relates key ideas of peace to developments in a historical period. Within the chapter, each central theme is introduced by a brief essay and is illustrated by documents. Given the limits of space, the interpretive essays are highly generalized. They can only point to selective aspects of history. Behind every generalization there is a literature of scholarly analysis and debate. Therefore, the reader is urged to supplement this volume with further study. Moreover, the chronological order should not be taken to imply a linear sequence of historical development. Rather, the selections illustrate varied approaches to peace under changing circumstances. In this respect, it should be noted that one criterion for including a document is its fresh articulation of an idea of peace; a particular approach may well have continued within the western tradition beyond the point where it is documented in this anthology.

On a second level, it is possible to compare various approaches to peace within various historical contexts and to question them. In the table of contents, the reader can identify alternative ideas or periods, which can be compared. The introduction to the whole volume identifies some of the questions and issues about peace that seem important to the editors. Others will occur to the reader. It is vital to remember that the questions which are more important to us are not necessarily those raised by people in another time, and that historical comparisons can be both suggestive and deceptive.

On a third level, the volume can be used to identify specific documents, organizations, or authors. These subjects can be located in the list of documents at the beginning of the volume, or in the index of names at the end. The list of Document Sources in the back identifies the complete citation for the text that has been excerpted. In view of the limitations of space and the range of documents, our excerpts are short and very selective. Much of the richness and resonance of the full documents is lost. We invite our readers to become peace researchers—to read the full documents, to evaluate our selection and interpretation of them, to locate other documents, and, through various networks of citizens and scholars in the United States, Russia, and the rest of the world, to discuss the implications of various ideas for peacemaking.

This collection is the result of cooperation by U.S. and Russian historians. Since 1964, American historians in the Council on Peace Research in History (CPRH) have fostered the history of peace movements and ideas, and increasingly they have worked with colleagues in other nations. In 1985 at the International Congress of Historical Sciences at Stuttgart, there were two Soviet-U.S. panel sessions. Three years later the director of the Institute of Universal History (USSR), Dr. Alexander Chubarian, formally proposed that the CPRH cooperate in a joint project on the ideas of peace in history. We had no idea at the time how much the world would change during our collaboration or how familiar U.S.-Russian joint ventures would become.

Working separately but consulting with each other, the Soviet and American editors developed lists of nearly 400 prospective documents that illustrated historic concepts of peace. Meeting together in Moscow at the Institute of Universal History in June 1990, we narrowed our lists. During the following year we refined our selection and interpretation, which we confirmed during a second joint meeting at Rutgers University in May 1991. The editors drafted essays for each chapter and each group of documents, and annotated the selections. In consultation with the others, the volume editors then finalized the whole manuscript for publication in English and Russian editions. Both editions are the same in content and substance, although there are variations in format and in the length of documents, corresponding to usage in the respective societies.

Those of us who collaborated on this volume are not simply Americans and Russians. More important, we are historians with different areas of expertise and points of view. Our selection of documents and themes evolved from sometimes intense discussion, and it reflects the interaction of historical interpretations rather than of national or ideological perspectives. With the end of the Cold War and the nuclear arms race, it seems especially appropriate to offer this survey of the ideas of peace in western history.

Here are key documents presenting various ideas about peace. They draw on the experience of several western cultures. They reflect major historical movements, such as the rise of the nation state and early industrialism, the growing interdependence of the world, and the global wars of the twentieth-century. They come from individuals and movements, citizens and states, reformers, revolutionaries, and defenders of the status quo. They offer varied explanations for war and alternative solutions to it—the accommodation of national interests, for example, the imposition of authority, the repudiation of violence, the transformation of society, and the formation of world government. They represent efforts to deal with questions of abstract principle and with immediate crises.

All thinking about peace involves underlying assumptions about values and ideals, human and social nature, and the causes of conflict. Modern civic and foreign policy contains layers of ideas laid down in historical contexts that often have been forgotten. In the interest of clarity, it is useful to identify, trace, and distinguish the various ways of thinking about peace that have come to us through history. That is our purpose. This book does not evaluate the merits of alternative ideas. Instead, it opens the diversity and richness of historic thinking about peace in the western tradition for the reader to assess.

Charles Chatfield
Ruzanna Ilukhina

Springfield, Ohio, and Moscow
March 1993

Acknowledgments

Financial support for this project was provided by the Russian Academy of Sciences through the Institute of Universal History and by the United States Institute of Peace. The opinions, findings, and conclusions or recommendations expressed in this volume are those of the editors and do not necessarily reflect the views of the United States Institute of Peace or the Institute of Universal History.

Valuable administrative support was provided by the Institute of Universal History, by the officers and library staff of Wittenberg University, and by John Whiteclay Chambers II and the Center for Historical Analysis, Rutgers University. A travel grant from the International Research and Exchanges Board permitted Russian editors to attend meetings in the United States. Additional support of various kinds was furnished by the Faculty Development Organization of Wittenberg University, the Center for International Service, College of Staten Island, C.U.N.Y., and the Dean of Arts and Sciences, University of North Carolina at Wilmington. Thelma Morris of the Cleveland Public Library provided assistance with League of Nations documents, and Jennifer Swickard was very helpful in assembling documents for the English edition.

Scholarly advice was furnished by Dr. Peter van den Dungen of Bradford University, England, and Dr. Jo Vellacott of Simone de Beauvoir Institute, Concordia University, Canada, in addition to the formal consultants for the project. New translations were provided for some documents, as noted in the list of Document Sources, by Timothy Bennett, Sandi E. Cooper, Emily Darby, Alexander de Grand, Manuela

Dobos, Susan Heuman, Steven Huxley, Ruzanna Ilukhina, Tatiana Telyukova, and Judith Wishnia.

The editors acknowledge their appreciation for this considerable help, and also for the professional services of Syracuse University Press and Nauka Press, which undertook to publish this volume jointly in the United States and Russia. In particular, we are grateful for the dedicated expertise of Bettie McDavid Mason and Joyce Atwood in preparing the English edition.

We reserve a special and personal note of appreciation for our colleague Valentina Isajeva (1945–1991), whose untimely death deprived us of her valuable expertise and vibrant enthusiasm.

Permissions

The editors have tried diligently to obtain permission to reprint material under active copyright, except in clear cases of fair use. If inadvertently we have made omissions, we will appreciate being advised so that they can be corrected in future editions. We gratefully acknowledge the permission of the following publishers to reprint:

Cambridge University Press, from *The Journal of George Fox,* ed. John L. Nickalls (1952), and *The 'Adages' of Erasmus: A Study with Translations,* ed. Margaret Mann Phillips (1964).

The Catholic University of America Press, from vols. 29, 49, and 58 of The Fathers of the Church: Eusebius Pamphili, *Ecclesiastical History,* trans. Roy J. Defarrari (1955); Lactantius, *The Divine Institutes,* trans. Sister Mary Francis McDonald, O.P. (1964); and Gregory of Nyssa, *Ascetical Works,* trans. Virginia Woods Callahan (1964).

Charles Scribner's Sons, an imprint of Macmillan Publishing Company, from *A Source Book for Medieval History,* by Oliver J. Thatcher and Edgar Holmes McNeal. Copyright 1905 Charles Scribner's Sons; copyright renewed 1933 Oliver J. Thatcher.

Eleanor Cousins, for Norman Cousins, "Modern Man Is Obsolete."

Doubleday and Company, Inc., from *An Aquinas Reader,* ed. Mary T. Clark (Image Books, 1972).

Franciscan Herald Press, from *St. Francis of Assisi: Writings and Early Biographies,* ed. Marion A. Habig, fourth rev. ed. (1975).

Victor Gollancz, from Harold Laski, "The Economic Foundations of Peace," in Leonard Woolf, ed., *The Intelligent Man's Way to Prevent War* (1934), and Léon Blum, *For All Mankind* (1943).

Greenwood Publishing Group Inc., from Julius Braunthal, *History of the International,* 2 vols. (Frederick A. Praeger, 1967); and Thomas Nelson & Sons for the world rights to this work.

Hackett Publishing Co., from *Plato's Republic,* trans. G. M. A. Grube (1974, a 1992 edition is available, rev. C. D. C. Reeve).

Harcourt Brace & Company, excerpt from "Thoughts on Peace in an Air Raid" in *The Death of the Moth and Other Essays* by Virginia Woolf, copyright 1942 by Harcourt Brace & Company and renewed 1970 by Marjorie T. Parson, Executrix, reprinted by permission of the publisher.

HarperCollins, Publishers, from *Christianity through the Thirteenth Century,* ed. Marshall W. Baldwin (New York: Harper & Row, 1970), Randolph Bourne, *War and the Intellectuals,* ed. Carl Resek (New York: Harper Torchbooks, 1964), John Foster Dulles, *War, Peace and Change* (New York: Harper & Brothers, 1939), and excerpt from "A Report to the Secretary of War" by James Franck et al., in *The Atomic Age,* ed. Morton Grodzins and Eugene Rabinowitch, © 1963 by BasicBooks. Reprinted by permission of BasicBooks, a division of HarperCollins Publishers, Inc.

Nat Hentoff, from *The Essays of A. J. Muste,* ed. Nat Hentoff (Simon & Schuster, 1970).

Indiana University Press, from *Memoirs of Peasant Tolstoyans in Soviet Russia,* trans. and ed. William Edgerton.

The Johns Hopkins University Press, from *The Hague Peace Conferences of 1899 and 1907,* ed. James Brown Scott (1909), and *Hesiod: Theogony, Works and Days, Shield,* trans. and ed. Apostolos Athanassakis (1983).

The Montessori-Pierson Estates, by kind permission, from Maria Montessori, *Education and Peace.*

The Nobel Foundation, from Frederick W. Haberman, editor, *Nobel Lectures: Peace,* 3 volumes (1906).

Oxford University Press, London, from James L. Brierly, *The Law of Nations* (1938).

Pathfinder Press, from Mary-Alice Waters, ed. *Rosa Luxemburg Speaks* (copyright © 1970 by Pathfinder Press).

Princeton University Press, from Peter Brock, *Pacifism in Europe to 1914* (1972).

The Putnam Publishing Group, from David Hunter Miller, *The Drafting of the Covenant* (1928), and Salvador de Madariaga, *Disarmament* (1929, reprint 1967).

Stanford University Press, from *The Bolsheviks and the World War,* trans. and ed. Olga Hess Gankin and H. H. Fisher.

The University of California Press, from Miriano Picón-Salas, *Cultural History of Spanish America—From Conquest to Independence*, ed. and trans. Irving Leonard (copyright © 1962, The Regents of the University of California), and Robert Kerner and Harry Nicholas Howard, *Balkan Conferences and the Balkan Entent, 1930–1935* (copyright © 1936, The Regents of the University of California).

The University of Chicago Press, from *Virgil's Georgics: A Modern English Verse Translation*, trans. Smith Palmer Bovie (1956).

The University of Massachusetts Press, from *Against Racism: Unpublished Essays, Papers, Addresses, 1887–1961, by W. E. B. Du Bois.* Ed. by Herbert Aptheker (Amherst: University of Massachusetts Press, copyright © 1985.

The University of Minnesota Press, from Harold S. Quigley, *From Versailles to Locarno* (Minneapolis: University of Minnesota Press, 1927).

The University Press of New England, from Inge Scholl, *The White Rose*, trans. Arthur R. Schultz, pp. 73–74, 78–79, 82–84, copyright 1970 by Inge Aicher-Scholl, Wesleyan University Press.

W. W. Norton & Company, Inc., from Sigmund Freud, *Civilization and Its Discontents* (1961).

Editors and Consultants

Volume Editors

Charles Chatfield, Ph.D. Vanderbilt University, is Professor of History at Wittenberg University. His research fields are twentieth-century U.S. history, peace and antiwar movements, and his publications include *For Peace and Justice: Pacifism in America 1914–1941* (1971), *An American Ordeal: the Antiwar Movement of the Vietnam Era* (with Charles De-Benedetti, 1990), and *The American Peace Movement: Ideals and Activism* (1992).

Ruzanna Ilukhina holds the ranks of Ph.D. and Professor with the Faculty of History, Moscow University, and is a senior researcher at the Institute of Universal History. Chief of the Institute's working group on the ideas of peace in history, she specializes in international relations and peace movements and on pacifism in Russia, having written *Give Peace to the Land of the Soviets* (1963), *The League of Nations* (1983), and *Le Pacifisme Russe* (1992). She co-chairs the Peace Society of Russia.

Editors

Kyril Anderson, Ph.D., Faculty of History, Moscow University, is affiliated with the Institute of Universal History. A specialist in eighteenth and nineteenth century utopian socialism in Great Britain, he is the author of *Owenites in Britain* (1989).

Sandi E. Cooper, Ph.D., New York University, is Professor of History at the College of Staten Island, City University of New York. Her fields are European history, women's history, and nineteenth-century peace movements in Europe, and her writings include *Internationalism in Nineteenth Century Europe: The Crisis of Ideas and Purpose* (1976), *The Political Vision of Italian Peace Movements, 1867–1915* (1985), and *Patriotic Pacifism: Waging War on War in Europe, 1815–1914* (1991).

Alexei Filitov holds the rank of Professor, Faculty of History, Moscow University; and is a senior researcher with the Institute of Universal History. *The Cold War Debate in Western Historiography* (1991) reflects his studies of the history of the Cold War and the post–World War II Settlement.

Carol Fink, Ph.D., Yale University, is Professor of History at Ohio State University. Her fields include twentieth-century international relations and European intellectual history. She has written *The Genoa Conference: European Diplomacy, 1921–1922* (1984) and *Marc Bloch: A Life in History* (1989), translated Marc Bloch's *Memoirs of War* (1985), and edited *German Nationalism and the European Response, 1890–1945* (1985).

Victoria Ukolova holds the rank of Professor, Faculty of History, Moscow University, and is vice-director of the Institute of Universal History. Her research in the cultural history of late Rome and Medieval Europe resulted in books such as *The Last Romans and European Culture* (1989), and *The Heritage of Antiquity and the Culture of the Early Middle Ages* (1989).

Lawrence Wittner, Ph.D., Columbia University, is Professor of History at the State University of New York at Albany. Researching the history of U.S. foreign policy, the twentieth-century U.S. peace movement, and the worldwide campaign against nuclear weapons, he has published *Cold War America* (1974), *American Intervention in Greece, 1943–1949* (1982), *Rebels Against War: The American Peace Movement 1933–1983* (1969, rev. 1984), and *One World or None* (1993).

Contributing Editors

Nelly A. Chaplygina, Ph.D. in History, Kishinyov State University, is a researcher at the Institute of Universal History. Her field of history is ancient Rome, and she is the author of *Population of the Dniester and the Carpathian area and Rome in the First to Third centuries A.D.* (1990), *Romans on the Danube* (1991).

Alexander Chudinov, Ph.D., Moscow Institute of Pedagogy is a researcher at Institute of Universal History. Publications such as *The Political Justice of William Godwin* (1990), and *At the Origins of Revolutionary Utopianism* (1991) reflect his research in seventeenth-century France and England.

Victor Heitzman, Professor, Faculty of History, Moscow University, is a researcher at the Institute of Universal History, where he has specialized in twentieth-century Soviet history of international relations and foreign policy, notably *The USSR and the Problem of Disarmament between the World Wars* (1959, 1963), and *The USSR and the Problem of Disarmament, 1945–1959; The History of International Negotiations* (1970).

Valentina Isaeva, Ph.D., Faculty of History, Moscow University, was a researcher at the Institute of Universal History until her death in 1991. *Isocrates and the Problems of the Greek Polis in the Fourth Century Before Christ* [forthcoming] reflect her work in the social and political thought of classical Greece.

Jaroslav Shapov, a Professor and Corresponding Member of the Russian Academy of Sciences, is affiliated with the Institute of Universal History. Research in Medieval Russia resulted in his *Ancient Russian Princes' Statutes: XI–XV Centuries* (1976), *The Byzantine and South Slavonic Legal Heritage: XI–XV Centuries* (1978), and *State and Church in Russia in the XI–XV Centuries* (1989).

Tatiana Telyukova, Ph.D., Institute of International Relations, Moscow, is a researcher at the Institute of Universal History. She specializes in the historic peace movements in the Netherlands and Russia and has published articles on the Dutch peace movement of 1977–1985.

Consultants

John Whiteclay Chambers II, Professor of History at Rutgers University, is an authority on the U.S. peace movement of the early twentieth century, on conscription, and on militarism and society. **William Edgerton,**

Professor Emeritus of Slavic Languages and Literatures at Indiana University, has played a key role in the development of Slavic studies in the United States and is the authority on the worldwide influence of Tolstoy. **Udo Heyn,** Professor of History at California State University, Los Angeles, is an expert on medieval social thought, with particular emphasis on the evolution of law. **Karl Holl,** Professor of History at the University of Bremen, not only is a widely published authority on the history of internationalist and peace movements in Germany and on the life of Ludwig Quidde, but also has been the leader of the German Working Group on peace research in history. **Steven Huxley** is an independent researcher and historian in Helsinki, Finland, whose pioneering study explored the Finnish nonviolent resistance movement at the turn of the twentieth century. **Nicholas Ivanov** is a researcher at Institute of Universal History whose interests include twentieth-century reform movements. **Dorothy V. Jones,** a research associate at the Newberry Library, Chicago, and an associate of the History Department, Northwestern University, has written authoritatively on the ethical structure of internationalism. **Helen Nechaeva** is an historian affiliated with the Russian Archives of Modern History. **David S. Patterson,** chief, operations staff, Office of the Historian, U.S. Department of State, has authored studies on the U.S. peace movement, 1887–1914, and on diplomatic history.

PEACE/MIR

The idea of an international community belongs to those great institutions, to those "civilizing ideas" which, though slow in their action and subject to eclipses, are nevertheless positive forces that generate political and social change. The most intransigent realist cannot deny their reality or their strength, for it is observation itself that establishes the refusal of man's active nature to consider itself subject to ineluctable laws and the unwillingness of his oral nature to regard as invariably just what is effectively imposed in fact. All moral judgment involves elements that transcend the results of experience; all human activity postulates some ideal the pursuit of which is the sole alternative to passive contemplation.

Charles De Visscher

Theory and Reality in Public International Law
(Princeton, N.J.: Princeton Univ. Press, 1957), 99–100

Introduction

PEACE. This word, like the French *paix*, derives from the Latin *pax* and *pais*. The verb form *to pacify* derives from Latin *pacis* plus *facere* (to make). In English *peace* and *pacify* convey a wide range of meanings, from the inner tranquillity of the human spirit to order within and among societies, and from the existence of harmony to the absence of war.

MIR. Before the revolution of 1917 and the reform of spelling in the Russian language, there were two words with the same sound (meer). *MNPb* referred to the absence of quarreling, hostility, discord, and war, or conversely to accord, unanimity, friendliness, friendship, and benevolence. *MiPb* meant the universe, specifically the earth, or humanity and also communities of peasants and their meetings. In modern Russian, the same word *MNP (mir)* conveys, therefore, both "the absence of war" and "the world" or "the universe."

The fact that many levels of meaning are conveyed by *peace* and *mir* is of more than linquistic interest. In all their variety these words convey different dimensions of human experience with disorder, discord, fighting, and war, and also with their opposites. These words voice historic human needs, hopes, and aspirations. They are the sounds of humanity reflecting upon itself, on its dilemmas, and on its destiny. Most specifically and most commonly, they affirm that there are alternatives to war.

There is a Russian proverb: "peace stands until war, war until peace"[1] That is to say, peace will last only as long as war does not occur, and war until peace is concluded. Probably the saying dates from antiquity. In the twelfth century it was thought to exist "before our forefathers," but it was quoted as a matter of course in medieval Russia. Then, without any centralized state, peace could be interrupted abruptly by a ruler of any one of the Russian principalities or by conflict with

3

external foes. The political leader Vladimir Monomakh recalled that he had conducted eighty-three military campaigns and concluded nineteen peace treaties with a single enemy. It is little wonder that the people of that time had a fatalistic sense of the spontaneous, unpredictable cycle of war and peace.

The proverb as it appears in the Kiev Chronicle probably represented more than fatalism. It was quoted in connection with a proposal for an alliance of principalities that might ensure uninterrupted peace, and those who repeated the old formula added, "we are tired of war."[2] Nonetheless, the old cycle of peace and war in Europe continued for another eight hundred years.

Thus the first question raised by the selections in this volume is: *Do war and peace alternate spontaneously and unpredictably in an unending cycle, or are they real alternatives?* Increasingly in the modern era, people have asked governments to "give peace a chance."[3] Nevertheless, organized violence has continued, its scale and threat magnified in our global, interdependent, and nuclear age. Is it realistic to hope for uninterrupted peace and, if so, on what grounds?

That question has been answered differently in various eras. Although other periods are different from our own, they are nonetheless relevant to us because our foreign policies are based on institutions and assumptions that have accumulated over time. Therefore, it is useful for us to consider previous thinking about these issues. It is important to consider the historical context of earlier thinkers and activists in order to distinguish the specific problems they addressed from the ways in which they interpreted war and peace.

How should peace be understood? At most, it implies the ideal of harmony and tranquillity. Often this ideal has been sought in the life of the spirit—in the individual soul or in spiritual communities. Some of the selections in this volume document that search for inner or communal peace. Others project the ideal of peace onto society as a utopian vision. More often, especially in the modern age, achieving peace is linked to the problems of achieving social and political justice.

At the very least, peace implies the absence of organized violence, or warfare. It implies, therefore, a degree of order among the units of society. Understood in this way, the problem of achieving peace is the problem of social order. This raises a second question: *Is peace a set of relationships among sovereign states or a political condition imposed by the powerful?* Each of these alternatives has been attractive at different times.

There was a hope in Panhellenic Greece that incessant warfare among the sovereign city-states could give way to a stable relationship. A similar hope accompanied the rise of modern nation-states, and it has produced a large array of international agreements, procedures, and institutions. All of them were designed to develop conventions and laws by which the rights of sovereign states can be defined and their conflicts of interest can be negotiated without resorting to warfare. Many of the selections in this book, especially from the modern period, can be evaluated in terms of their effectiveness in dealing with specific obstacles to peace. To what extent do they also address basic causes of war? Are they parts of a comprehensive approach, or are they incidental, inconsistent, and even contradictory?

Order has also been sought by the imposition of superior force, whether unilaterally by a single power or multilaterally by a powerful coalition. There were those who hoped that the Alexandrian empire would bring order to the Hellenistic world, and later those who trusted Roman law backed by military force. In medieval Europe the role of imposing peace was assigned to both the Roman Catholic Church and the Holy Roman Empire, and then to the rising Russian empire and, in the West, to expanding national states. The idea of forcefully imposing peace was the core of some of the celebrated peace plans of the early modern period: it was part of the rationale for the wars of empire in the eighteenth century; it was the basis of the Versailles Treaty ending World War I; and it was embodied in the collective security provisions of the United Nations. In the modern period, indeed, it has been combined both with arrangements to guarantee an order of sovereign nations and with a supreme world government. Some of the selections in this volume assert the value of various forms of imposed peace. What was their merit in specific historical circumstances? Is an imposed peace compatible with the ideas and institutions of national sovereignty?

The idea of an order of sovereign states and the idea of an imposed order both assumed that peace is a condition of a stable status quo. On the other hand, peace has also been associated with purposeful changes in the human condition.

This idea has had great force in the nineteenth and twentieth centuries. On the one hand, it has been argued that procedures for attaining a just and equitable order are required even to obviate the resort to warfare. On the other hand, it has been held that peace implies more than the absence of war, that it involves social justice. There is, therefore, a third question to answer: *Is it sufficient to think of peace merely as the absence of war, or Is it necessary to create an alternative social order?*

Sometimes war has been justified as the prerequisite of peace. The

European wars of the French Revolution were rationalized by the idea that peace required a social revolution. The Allied campaigns in the First and Second World Wars were justified on the grounds that the old hierarchies of Wilhelmine and Nazi Germany, respectively, had to be swept away in order to make way for a new order of democracy. The Communist International rationalized class warfare in the interest of a new order of economic justice.

Peace also has been interpreted as part of the social process. Thus, provisions for the cessation of violence and the peaceful adjudication of conflict accompanied the medieval transformation from feudal to national societies. During the eighteenth-century Enlightenment, peace was sometimes understood as being necessary for orderly change, and this notion was developed by socialists and internationalists in the nineteenth century. After World War I peace advocates related peace to social transformation, arguing both that ending organized violence is the condition for achieving justice and that it requires significant changes in popular attitudes and values, such as nationalism. Advocates of peace in modern western history have identified warfare with the exclusive interests of the powerful, and they have sought peace by broadening popular influence. In all these respects, many of the selections in this volume imply that peace, even understood as the absence of warfare, proceeds from ideas about justice within and between nations, basic individual rights, the peaceful settlement of disputes, and fundamental principles of international life.

The variety of the ways in which war and peace have been treated suggests a fourth question: *What is the relationship of the way that peace is conceptualized to the conditions of race, religion, ethnicity, gender, social and political organization, and to historical context?* Put another way, the issue is whether there are universal principles of peace or only relative arrangements for order in particular societies and historical periods. How can perceptions that come from specific experience be related to universal ethical principles?

Of course, it is possible to conclude simply that all ideas about peace reflect only the interests of specific groups. But it may be suggested too that although various groups interpret the problem of war from their own points of view, they all contribute unique insights and perspectives to a common problem—a common human situation. In this regard, the selections in this volume can be studied for what they contribute from different contexts to our cumulative understanding.

Every systematic attempt to end warfare, or even to bring it under some kind of control, has envisioned some kind of social or ethical principle. Throughout western history, therefore, there has been a search for principles of peace in religious, moral, and political terms. These have been applied both to the consciences of individuals and to the rules that govern states. The variety of principles expressed in this volume, and the fact that non-Western cultures are not represented in it, raises the related problem of whether or not the ideas of peace in Western civilization are normative for the whole world. This second issue cannot be resolved merely by the study of Western ideas, of course; but it is important to keep in mind precisely because virtually all authors assume that their principles *are* universal and normative.

It may also be asked, in the fifth place: *What is the relationship between the principles of peace governing personal, group, national, and international levels? What is the relationship between the ideals and institutions of peace?* A special contribution of the Hebraic and Christian tradition was the idea that peace is a universal principle with a claim on individuals—or on groups of individuals in voluntary association. In one form or another, this idea became the basis for absolute pacifism—the total rejection of violence in human relations. For some individuals and groups (especially religious groups), this universal principle is understood as the fundamental meaning of peace: it is a form of loyalty to a divinely ordained and ultimate imperative or duty. Thus the rejection of military service has become widely accepted as a basic right of conscience.

The objection here is to violence itself. In the words of Alexander Solzhenitsyn, "The 'War-Peace' dichotomy contains a logical mistake. ... War is a mass display of unending, centuries-old world violence,— dense, high-flown, gaudy, but far from unique. The logically balanced and morally true dichotomy is 'Peace-Violence.' "[4] The idea of rejecting violence itself can be traced historically through some of the documents in this volume. Especially in the twentieth century it has been combined with a belief that individuals and groups can counter acts of violence with nonviolent action that is effective in practical terms.

The development of an absolute ethic of peace was paralleled by the evolution of a relative ethic that is known as the just war tradition. This remains the dominant form of peace ethics in the Western tradition, although it has been significantly modified in the era of total war. Its history, too, can be traced in some of the documents of this volume. In general, it assumes that warfare can be justified only under certain circumstances and for the purpose of restoring or achieving a peaceful order. The principles of the just war tradition form the ethical basis for most international law and agreements, as well as for institutions de-signed to limit the occasion and conduct of warfare. It must be asked to what extent just war principles really contribute to peace under modern conditions.

The just war tradition assumes that warfare can and should be at least limited. It does not assume that war can be ended. From the late medieval period through the eighteenth century, however, a belief grew that the cycle of war and peace can be broken by common action. In the nineteenth century, the force of this belief was greatly accelerated by the rise of citizen peace societies that introduced innovative peace proposals and brought pressure on governments to adopt them. This approach evolved into the peace movements of the twentieth century, and it was reflected in some of the diplomacy of governments.

The principles behind the innovations of the past century are political and social, and they can be discerned in numerous proposals for specific tactics and strategies to attain international peace. From the competition among many ideas and programs, therefore, a sixth question arises: *What is the relationship of principles to tactics and strategies for peace?* Indeed, what approaches are most appropriate to the conduct of modern warfare and the organization of modern society?

Despite the many innovative international procedures and institutions that were developed by the middle of the twentieth century, warfare continued to plague humankind on a horrendous scale. War is not only an event. It is a human institution with its own forms of organization, economics, values, and principles. The institution of war is called militarism, and its expansion in the twentieth century raises the question: *What is the force of militarism, as an ideology and as a form of political and economic interest, in relation to peace, when understood as social values and institutions?* Can militarism be mitigated and, if so, how?

This seventh question returns us to the first one—the question implied in the citation of the ancient Russian proverb in the Kiev Chronicle: *Are peace and war phases in a never-ending cycle, or are they real alternatives for humankind?*

1

Premodern Ideas of Peace
800 B.C.–A.D. 1815

What was peace or war in the lives of the ancients? We can but speculate. Aside from shards of their pottery and fragments of writing, their spears and their pruning hooks, we have only the collective memories preserved in their sacred myths. Such were the Homeric poems of the Greeks, probably composed by 800 B.C. for militant aristocrats whose exploits they glorified—stories about the virtues and foibles of mortals and of gods in combat. The early sagas of the Hebrews also described a people who, like their national god, often elevated wrath and violence to a positive virtue. The wars of mythic memory—indiscriminate, sometimes genocidal, and always sacred—were stages upon which the human drama was played. Trial by combat was the appointed means of settling disputes, and wars were instruments of divine purpose.

Even so, those myths contained an alternative vision. Although both of the Homeric poems were dominated by the war myth, the older *Iliad* was more crude and violent than the *Odyssey*, which reflected some respect for justice and moderation. A century later Hesiod of Greece depicted warfare with all the terrors related by Homer, but without glory. Instead, he voiced the distress of the victims of poverty and war, contrasting their condition with a Golden Age when people lived in prosperity and peace.

Thus the ancients bequeathed two versions of what is ideal and real. On the one hand, the mythic memory regarded warfare as an inevitable and divinely ordained test of virtue, and on the other, it saw war as a calamitous departure from the rules of virtue that yield peace and prosperity. For two millennia after Hesiod, people in the West struggled to

9

understand war and peace, exploring assumptions about the nature of community, conflict, and social justice.

When, in the nineteenth century, Western people developed industrial economies, broadly based political systems, and an world of commerce and empire, they inherited a rich legacy of ideas. That heritage is the subject of this chapter. Because it covers such a long duration of history, the chapter is organized in two major parts: "From Antiquity," for the period through the Roman empire, and "Toward Modernity," from the Roman empire through the eighteenth century.

From Antiquity: Harmony, Conflict, and Justice

From the eighth century B.C. to the fourth century A.D., warfare was extensively debated and discussed, both philosophically and practically. During this time several periods of crisis stimulated creative thought about war and peace. For the Hebrews the critical period was that of their exile (722 B.C. from the kingdom of Israel, and 586 from the kingdom of Judah until Persian rule in 538). For the Greeks it was the wars against Persia (about 546–478 B.C.), the Peloponnesian wars among the city-states (460–404 B.C), and the wars of the Macedonian Empire under Philip II and Alexander III, the Great (359–323 B.C.). The Romans inherited a good deal of Greek political thought and adapted it to their growing empire. But just when an imperial peace was secured under Emperor Augustus, from 27 B.C. to A.D. 14, the early Christians built on the Hebrew and Greek traditions to give the idea of peace a new dimension. If peace itself was rarely the subject of systematic discussion in antiquity, it nonetheless acquired several important although disparate attributes: (1) it was regarded as an expression of harmony in nature, (2) it was explored in terms of political and social conflict, and (3) it was identified with a moral order of social and personal ethics.

Harmony in the Natural Order

Early Greek poets and dramatists, and Roman ones later, contrasted the painful discord of war with the harmony of peace. Sometimes this theme was expressed as the myth of a Golden Age, a myth that was widespread in the ancient Middle East: humanity had fallen from an ideal state of peace to a worldly condition of interminable struggle. Greek philosophers also developed the notion of natural harmony into a vision of universal, peaceful civilization in the distant future.

The idea of peace as a *harmonious, prosperous natural* order was threaded through Graeco-Roman thought and ritual. In Greek mythology the goddess of peace was Eirene, one of several goddesses of order and equity (the Horae) identified with the weather and the seasons as well as with the fertility of the earth. Guardians of the natural order, they also cared for human life, social order, and prosperity. A statue of Eirene at Athens showed her holding the god of wealth; by the Romans she was depicted as a youthful maiden with a cornucopia in her left arm and an olive branch or Mercury's staff in her right. The lyric poet Pindar of Thebes appealed: "Kindly Goddess of Peace, daughter of Justice, that makest cities great; thou that holdest the master-keys of councils and of wars, receive from Aristomenes the honor due for a Pythian victory; for thou knowest with perfect fitness the secret of gentleness, both in giving, and in taking."[1] In this sense, peace was a favor from the gods, whom mortals must supplicate and satisfy (document 1.1).

The harmony of nature was explored by philosophers such as Pythagoras (sixth century B.C.), whose influence reached Italy and Sicily. Arguing for the essential unity of the universe and deducing natural harmony from mathematical regularities, Pythagoras extended his principles to oppose discord and violence. For him and some other pre-Socratic philosophers, reason was the true authority, and personal identity was not limited by the city state: "to a wise man, the whole world is open; for the native land of a good soul is the whole earth."[2]

Following the era of Socrates in the fifth century, philosophers of the Cynic school rejected most social institutions, including enforced authority, and idealized the individual as a citizen of the world. Later, Stoic philosophers such as Zeno of Citium based their thinking on a reasoned interpretation of nature, rejecting physical violence and all distinctions of race, caste, and sex in favor of universal human equality. Speculative and pantheistic, the Stoic vision of universal peace was a significant idea in an era of violent tribal and national loyalties.[3] This idea became influential in Hellenistic and Roman circles from the second century onwards. Seneca, an exponent of the Stoic tradition, was torn between his experience with the irrational violence of human beings and his stoic belief in rational, harmonious nature: "We are mad, not only individually, but nationally . . . ," he wrote. "Deeds that would be punished by loss of life when committed in secret, are praised by us because uniformed generals have carried them out. Man, *naturally* the gentlest class of being, is not ashamed to revel in the blood of others."[4] Seneca concluded that "there are two commonwealths—the one a vast and truly common state . . . in which we look neither to this corner of the earth nor to that, but measure the bounds of our citizenship by the path of the sun; the other, the one to which we have been assigned by the accident of birth." The highest wisdom is to withdraw from the state, he held, and to cultivate the kind of peace that is inner tranquillity.[5]

In the first century B.C., the Roman poets Tibullus and Virgil identified peace with nature, depicting war as the enemy of agricultural life and prosperity (documents 1.2, 1.3). This was a theme that stretched back through Aristophanes and Pindar to the farmer-poet Hesiod. Virgil's *Georgics,* a detailed treatise on agriculture in elegant poetic form with many allusions to mythology, was also a complex allegory contrasting the values that yield peace, life, and civilization to the values that sow combat, destruction, and disintegration. Virgil began work on the *Georgics* in 37 B.C., when Rome was convulsed by civil war, and at the end of book I he appealed to Octavian Caesar (Augustus) to put "right this world that our disastrous age has overturned."

Document 1.1

Aristophanes: Peace the Sole Support

From *The Peace,** fifth century B.C.

Chorus (singing)

Hail! hail! thou beloved divinity! thy return overwhelms us with joy. . . . From thee came all blessings. Oh! much desired Peace! thou art the sole support of those who spend their lives tilling the earth. Under thy rule we had a thousand delicious enjoyments at our beck; thou wert the husbandman's wheaten cake and his safeguard. So that our vineyards, our young fig-tree woods and all our plantations hail thee with delight and smile at thy coming.

---

* *The Peace* (421 B.C.) is the second of three plays in which Aristophanes appealed for an end to the Peloponnesian War, the others being *The Acharnians* (426 B.C.) and *Lysistrata* (411 B.C.). It is the story of a farmer who takes his case for peace directly to heaven, only to find it empty of all except the demon of war and the goddess Peace, who is held captive in a pit. People from various Greek states come to her rescue. As it becomes clear that some of them are impeding the work, the Chorus cries, "Come, friends, none but the husbandmen on the ropes" (thus suggesting that farmers are the true friends of peace). Peace is restored to earth, and the Chorus, praising the goddess, sends the farmers home.

Document 1.2

Tibullus: Let Peace Tend Our Fields

From "Against War," first century B.C.

Who was the first discoverer of the horrible sword? How savage was he and literally iron! Then slaughter and battles were born into the world of men: then to grisly death a shorter road was opened. . . .

What madness is it to call black Death to us by warfare! It is ever close upon us: it comes unseen on silent feet. Below there are neither cornlands nor well-kept vineyards; only wild Cerberus and the ill-favored mariner of the stream of Styx.* There wanders a sallow throng beside the dusky pools with eyeless sockets and fire-ravaged hair.

Nay, the hero is he whom, when his children are begotten, old age's torpor overtakes in his humble cottage. He follows his sheep, his son the lambs, while the good wife heats the water for his weary limbs. So let me live till the white hairs glisten on my head and I tell in old man's fashion of the days gone by. Let Peace in the meantime tend our fields. Bright Peace first led the oxen under curved yoke to plough. Peace made the vine plants grow and stored the grape juice that from the father's jars might pour wine for the son. In peace shine hoe and ploughshare; but the grisly arms of the rugged soldier rust preys on in the dark.

Document 1.3

Virgil: Who Masters Nature's Laws

From *Georgics*,† first century B.C.

So many wars, so many shapes of crime!
The plough dishonored, fields left lying waste
Now that their men are drafted; curving scythes
Are pounded into shape for ruthless swords.
War in Germany, and in the East:
Neighboring towns dissolve their legal bonds,

---

* Cerberus was the mythological three-headed dog guarding the gates of Hades (hell). The Styx was the river of Hades, across which the dead were transported by the aged Charon.

† The word "georgics," which Virgil adopted for his title, was a Greek term for "the facts of farming."

And march across each other's boundaries.
Unholy Mars bends all to his mad will:
The world is like a chariot run wild
That rounds the course unchecked and, gaining speed,
Sweeps the helpless driver on to his doom.
. . . .
Oh that farmers understood their blessings!
Their boundless joys! A land far off from war
Pours forth her fruit abundantly for them.
. . . .
Although his white wool is not stained with dye,
His oil not spoiled with perfumes from the East,
His rest is sound, his life devoid of guile.
. . . .
The farmer lives in peace, his children all
Learn how to work, respect frugality,
Venerate their fathers and the gods:
Surely, Justice, as she left the earth,
In parting left her final traces here.
. . . .
Blessed is he who masters nature's laws,
Tramples on fear and unrelenting fate,
. . . .
Not for him "the mandate of the people,"
The royal cloak of kings, not dissonance
Creating civil wars, the swift onslaught
From Balkan coalitions; not for him
The Roman State or Empire doomed to die.

Conflict in the Political Order

The Greek word for peace, the name of the goddess *Eirene,* probably originated in relation to the verb for "I conjugate, I confirm, I order," and it implied repose and concord. Certainly it meant the opposite of war. By the time of Hesiod, it implied harmony, prosperity, and equity. In the fifth and fourth centuries B.C., however, it became identified with practical relief from war, as in peace negotiations. *Eirene,* or peace, was not only an ideal but also a very practical matter of creating political and social order.[6]

The contrast between the lofty rhetoric of war and its human reality was dramatized by Greek playwrights, whose skepticism permeated the

Athenian political scene. Brought down to earth, war was interpreted *as a natural phenomenon*, and Plato and Aristotle, among others, related peace to practical politics within and among the city-states. In this context the Greeks faced the problem of competing sovereignties, which, despite diplomatic innovations, they were unable to solve. Under the *imposed authority* of the Macedonian empire of Philip II and Alexander III, and subsequently of Rome, the idea of peace became attached to the concept of a universal political order.

The Greek city-states engaged in war throughout the fifth and fourth centuries, first against the Persians, then against one another, and finally against Persia once more. They changed allies almost at whim, although they were almost all grouped into rival Athenian and Spartan alliances during the great Peloponnesian War of 431–404 B.C., which aggravated the struggle for political control in each state and often led to civil conflict. Even primitive weapons produced total warfare, and with it destruction, refugees, and plague. Wrote Herodotus, "no man is so foolish as to desire war more than peace: for in peace sons bury their fathers, but in war fathers bury their sons."[7] And Pindar of Thebes observed, "to the inexperienced war is pleasant, but he that has had experience of it, in his heart sorely fears its approach."[8] Those remarks suggest a skeptical realism about war.

Realism pervaded the great mythic tragedies of Sophocles, Euripides, and especially Aeschylus (document 1.4). There was some hope that tragedy might be redeemed: "Sing the song of woe, the song of woe, but may the good prevail!"[9] But for Aeschylus, at least, whatever justice may be in war can be on no human scale, for the sins of the father are visited on his children and a host of innocents besides: "affliction wanders impartially abroad and alights on all in turn."[10] Warfare is depicted as retribution: just or not, it does not solve the problems that occasion it. Realism about war was accompanied by skepticism about its merit.

Skepticism was characteristic of the age. It was voiced by pre-Socratic philosophers called Sophists, and by Aristophanes, whose comedies satirized Athens in the Peloponnesian War, its politics, and its politicians. Each of his plays ridiculed conventional wisdom on war. In the last one, *Lysistrata*, the women of the several warring cities conspire to withhold sex from the men until peace is made. The political acumen normally attributed to men and not women is inverted in the play: warfare—"men's business"—seems trivial compared with the women's work for peace. Skeptical about the wisdom and motives of those in authority, Aristophanes in *The Acharnians* concluded simply: "we have no common sense."

In this atmosphere war was widely criticized for its effects. It was shown to be destructive and costly. Xenophon, a military commander and historian, even proposed a "board of guardians of peace" as a part of his economic program (document 1.5). Like him, Lysias, Isocrates, and other public leaders also complained that imperialist wars had alienated Athens from her allies and left her vulnerable. Most important, war had undermined the stability and social values on which depended the internal peace of the state. Thus Thucydides, also a military commander and historian, linked war to revolution (document 1.6), and Isocrates attributed the decline of public morality and democracy in Athens to the policy of imperialism, concluding that "the soul of a state is nothing else than its polity."[11] It was not war itself to which these Greeks objected: rather, they opposed fighting in futile and counterproductive causes or in ways that demeaned their society.

This line of thought was pursued philosophically by Plato, following the method of rational inquiry pioneered by Socrates. Although Plato, like his teacher, interpreted civil law as the instrument of political good, he idealized the state more than Socrates did, seeing it as an embodiment of the community. He regarded warfare as a necessary function of government, but one which should be pursued with wisdom and moderation. Aristotle later made the same assumption, and he was clear that war should not be an end in itself (document 1.7). Peace in this sense was not an absolute state of harmony. Rather, it was the kind of order that was practical for a good society, where law and force must discipline passion.

Plato also made a crucial distinction between war and civil strife: the latter involves hostility to kindred, and those who should be friendly, whereas war is hostility to that which is alien and foreign (document 1.8).[12] Aristotle even more bluntly defended war against "those of mankind who [are] designed by nature for subjection."[13] This idea, widely accepted in the ancient world, became the basis for Greek proposals to secure peace by a PanHellenic offensive against Persia: peace was natural for Greeks, war for Asians. The Romans, too, assumed that subject peoples were naturally inferior, and, like the Greeks, they also accepted natural class differences.

The search for peace *within* Greek states took the form of experiments with constitutional government of various kinds. The goal was to reconcile conflicts of interest and even to change political control under some accepted principle of authority. The experiments were frustrated by civil war, as Thucydides and Isocrates among others noted.

The search for peace *among* Greek states was a different matter, because all of them claimed sovereign authority over their territories, client states, and colonies. In an effort to minimize warfare among sovereign states, the Greeks experimented with forms of diplomacy: they gave immunity to ambassadors and even resident consuls; they assumed some rules of war (which they often violated); they conducted peace negotiations and arbitration, developed bilateral and even multilateral treaties, and made several attempts to form regional confederations with decision-making power apportioned among their members.

Despite their inventiveness, the Greeks achieved only intermittent truces. In desperation, some of their leaders turned to the hegemonic power of Persia and then Macedon for guarantees of their peace treaties (document 1.9). Even that was not sufficient. Order was finally *imposed* on the Greek states by the Macedonian empires of Philip II and Alexander the Great, and later by Rome.

When he offered peace to Darius III of Persia, Alexander the Great wrote, "You shall have whatever you persuade me to give. And in the future, when you send, send to me as Supreme Lord of Asia, and do not direct what you require as on equal terms, but tell me, as lord of all your possessions, if you have need of aught."[14] Between 336 and 323 B.C., Alexander briefly imposed his empire from Greece and Thrace in the west to the Indus River in the east. Upon his death the division of territory led to a series of wars until Asia Minor was absorbed by the Romans about 190 B.C. Empires were clearly based on military force, but they were often interpreted as an attempt to establish peace in the sense of a universal political order. This was an old ambition. The Greek historian Xenophon attributed it to Cyrus, the founder of the Persian Empire, and Alexander claimed it as his own. Similarly, the first Roman emperor, Gaius Octavius Augustus, was celebrated for ending both civil and foreign wars. His empire was interpreted as "a peace or truce" imposed on the known world—the *pax romana* (document 1.10).

The Latin word for peace is *pax*. It is related to *pacisci:* to make a pact that defines a relationship. But the relationship with other states under the *pax romana* was quite different from that assumed by the Greeks or by modern international law, under which in theory each party has sovereign rights. For the Romans, an alliance signified submission to the authority of Rome. Thus, the treaty that ended war with Antiochus in the Near East began, "There shall be friendship between Antiochus and the Romans for all time if *he fulfills* the conditions of the treaty."[15] *Pax* also suggested security and tranquillity, because it could refer to a

sacred agreement for friendly relations in the absence of military pressure, but it still implied an order of accepted authority. Peace in this
sense was essentially an extension of power.

The Romans invested their power with a universal and altruistic
ideology, partly by adapting Greek stoic philosophy to their own sense
of world mission. Their client states understood this ideology. Some
of them used it to flatter their patron (document 1.11). Under the
pax romana order was enforced between diverse peoples subject to the
same authority and law, *jus gentium*. With the consolidation of empire
at the end of the first century B.C., there were hopes for a new Golden
Age of peace (document 1.12). But there was also cynicism (document 1.13): said a defeated Briton, "To plunder, butcher, steal, these
things they misname empire: they make a desolation and they call it
peace."[16]

Document 1.4

Aeschylus: Mad, Inspiring to Frenzy Is War

From the Chorus, in *The Seven Against Thebes*,
fifth century B.C.

For piteous it were thus to hurl to destruction a city of olden time,
made slave and booty of the spear, in dust and ashes laid by Heaven's
decree and ignominious ravage of Achaean men. Piteous, too, for her
captive daughters (ah me, ah me!), young and old, to be haled by their
hair, like horses, while their raiment is rent about them. A city made
desolate waileth as the captive spoil is borne off to its doom 'mid mingled
cries. Grievous in truth is the fate my fear forebodes.

. . . Aye, for many and wretched are the miseries (alas, alas!) when a
city is taken. Man drags off man, or slays, or carries fire: the whole city
is befouled with smoke. Mad, inspiring to frenzy, slaying the people,
defiling holiness is war.

Tumult reigns through the town, against it advances a towering net
of ruin. Man encounters man and is laid low by the spear. For the babes
at their breast resound the wailing cries of young mothers, all streaming
with blood. Kindred are the prey of scattering bands. Pillager encounters
pillager; the empty-handed hails the empty-handed, fain to have a part-
ner, all greedy neither for less nor equal share. Good reason is there to
surmise the issue of deeds like this.

Document 1.5

Xenophon: The Economics of Peace

From "Ways and Means," fourth century B.C.

. . . I presume that those states are reckoned the happiest that enjoy the longest period of unbroken peace . . . , for if the state is tranquil, what class of men will not need her? . . .

If, on the other hand, any one supposes that financially war is more profitable to the state than peace, I really do not know how the truth of this can be tested better than by considering once more what has been the experience of our state in the past. He will find that in the old days a very great amount of money was paid into the treasury in time of peace, and that the whole of it was spent in time of war; he will conclude on consideration that in our own time the effect of the late war on our revenues was that many of them ceased, while those that came in were exhausted by the multitude of expenses; whereas the cessation of war by sea has been followed by a rise in the revenues, and has allowed the citizens to devote them to any purpose they choose.

Document 1.6

Thucydides: The Peloponnesian War

From *History of the Peloponnesian War*, fifth century B.C.

To such excesses of savagery did the revolution go [Corsica, 427 B.C.]; and it seemed the more savage, because it was among the first that occurred; for afterwards practically the whole Hellenic world was convulsed, since in each state the leaders of the democratic factions were at variance with the oligarchs, the former seeking to bring in the Athenians, the latter the Lacedaemonians [that is, Spartans]. And while in time of peace they would have had no pretext for asking their intervention, nor any inclination to do so, yet now that these two states were at war, either faction in the various cities, if it desired a revolution, found it easy to bring in allies. . . .

And so the cities began to be disturbed by revolutions. . . . The ordinary [meaning of words] was changed as men thought fit. Reckless audacity came to be regarded as courageous loyalty to party, prudent hesitation as specious cowardice, moderation as a cloak for unmanly weakness, and to be clever in everything was to do naught in anything. Frantic impulsiveness was accounted a true man's part, but caution in deliberation a specious pretext for shirking. . . .

The cause of all these evils was the desire to rule which greed and ambition inspire, and also, springing from them that ardor which belongs to men who once have become in factious rivalry.

So it was that every form of depravity showed itself in Hellas in consequence of its revolutions, and . . . there was no assurance binding enough, no oath terrible enough, to reconcile men; but always, if they were stronger, since they accounted all security hopeless, they were rather disposed to take precautions against being wronged than able to trust others.

Document 1.7

Aristotle: War for Peace

From *The Nicomachean Ethics*, fourth century B.C.

. . . we do business in order that we may have leisure; and carry on war in order that we may have peace.* Now the practical virtues are exercised in politics or in warfare . . . for no one desires to be at war for the sake of being at war, nor deliberately takes steps to cause a war: a man would be thought an utterly bloodthirsty character if he declared war on a friendly state for the sake of causing battles and massacres.

Document 1.8

Plato: War and Civil Strife

From *The Republic*,† fifth century B.C.

It seems to me that we have two terms, war and civil strife, so there are two things, and the terms apply to differences in two fields, one of

---

* Aristotle specified that the proper objects of war include prevention from being enslaved, and sovereignty over subject people and "those who deserve to be slaves." The object of laws governing warfare is "peace." *Aristotle: Politics*, trans. H. Rackham (LCL, 1932), 611.

† In the *Republic* Plato explored the meaning of a good society by discussing the requirements of an ideal one.

one's own kindred, the other of outside strangers. Enmity with one's own is called civil strife, whereas enmity to strangers is called war.

. . . I say that the Greek race is related and akin, while the barbarians are outsiders and strangers.

We shall say then that Greeks fighting barbarians or barbarians fighting Greeks are at war, that they are natural enemies, and this enmity is to be called war; but when Greeks fight Greeks, they are by nature friends, and in those circumstances Greece is sick and in a state of civil strife. . . .

[The citizens of the ideal Republic] being Greeks, they will not ravage Greece, they will not burn the houses, nor will they maintain that all the inhabitants of each city are their foes, men, women and children, but only a few, those who caused the quarrel. For all these reasons, as the majority are their friends, they will not ravage the country or destroy the houses. They will carry their quarrel to the point of compelling those who caused it to be punished by those who were guiltless and the victims of it.

. . . this is how our citizens must behave toward their enemies, and toward barbarians they must behave as the Greeks now do toward each other.

Document 1.9

Isocrates: Universal Peace

From "On the Peace," fifth century B.C.

I maintain, then, that we should make peace, not only with the Chians, the Rhodians, the Byzantines and the Coans, but with all mankind, and that we should adopt [those treaties] which we have entered into with the king of Persia and with the Lacedaemonians, which ordain that the Hellenes be independent, that the alien garrisons be removed from the several states, and that each people retain its own territory.* For we shall not find terms of peace more just than these nor more expedient for our city.

---

* Writing ca. 355 B.C., Isocrates here reverses his earlier opposition to the "Peace of Antalcidas" (387 B.C.) in which Persia guaranteed the independence of the states in Greece at the price of absorbing those in Asia Minor. A few years later Isocrates vested his hope for peace in Philip II of Macedon and the old dream of a pan-Hellenic alliance against Persia.

Document 1.10

Florus: The Peace of Caesar Augustus

From *Epitome of Roman History,* second century A.D.

Now that all the races of the west and south were subjugated, and also the races of the north, those at least between the Rhine and the Danube, and of the east between the Cyrus and Euphrates, the other nations too, who were not under the rule of the empire, yet felt the greatness of Rome and revered its people as the conqueror of the world. . . . Thus everywhere throughout the inhabited world there was firmly-established an uninterrupted peace or truce, and Caesar Augustus ventured at last . . . to close the double doors of the temple of Janus, which had previously been shut on two occasions only, in the reign of Numa and after the first defeat of Carthage.* Next, devoting himself to securing tranquillity, by many strict and severe enactments he restrained an age which was prone to every vice and readily led into luxury. For all these great achievements he was named Perpetual Imperator and Father of his Country. It was also discussed in the senate whether he should not be called Romulus, because he had established the empire; but the name of Augustus was deemed more holy and venerable, in order that, while he still dwelt upon earth, he might be given a name and title which raised him to the rank of a deity.

Document 1.11

Polybius: The Special Mission of Rome

From *The Histories,* second century B.C.

. . . So it is in your power, ye men of Rome, to give a magnificent accretion of strength to your friends, and yet not diminish the splendor of your own role.† For the ends you propose to achieve are not the same as those of other people. Other men are impelled to armed action by the

---

* Janus, the porter of heaven, opened the year and was the guardian of gates. The gates of a passageway in Rome, commonly called a temple, were traditionally kept open in wartime and closed in peace—closed, if Florus was right, only in the reign of the legendary king Numa Pompilius (715–673 B.C.) and again ca. 241 B.C.

† Polybius here recounts the appeal of emissaries from Rhodes to the Roman Senate which was considering a general settlement in Asia Minor, 189–88 B.C.

prospect of getting into their power and annexing cities, stores, or ships. But the gods have made all these things superfluous for you, by subjecting the whole world to your dominion. What is it, then, that you really are in want of, and what should you most intently study to obtain? Obviously praise and glory among men, things difficult indeed to acquire and still more difficult to keep when you have them. . . . You went to war with Philip and made every sacrifice for the sake of the liberty of Greece. For such was your purpose and this alone—absolutely nothing else— was the prize you won by that war. But yet you gained more glory by that than by the tribute you imposed on Carthage. For money is a possession common to all men, but what is good, glorious, and praiseworthy belongs only to the gods and those men who are by nature nearest to them.

Document 1.12

Horace: *Pax Romana*

From *The Odes and Epodes,* first century B.C.

When I wished to sing of fights and cities won, Apollo checked me, striking loud his lyre, and forbade my spreading tiny sails upon the Tuscan Sea. Thy age, O Caesar, has restored to farms their plenteous crops and to our Jove the standards stript from the proud columns of the Parthians; has closed Quirinus' fane empty of war*; has put a check on license, passing righteous bounds; has banished crime and called back home the ancient ways whereby the Latin name and might of Italy waxed great, and the fame and majesty of our dominion were spread from the sun's western bed to his arising.

While Caesar guards the state, not civil rage, nor violence, nor wrath that forges swords, embroiling hapless towns, shall banish peace. Not they that drink the Danube deep shall break the Julian laws, nor Getae, Seres, faithless Parthians, nor they by Tanais born. On common and on sacred days, amid the gifts of merry Bacchus, with wife and child we first

---

* Quirinus was an early Roman god of war, "fane" a temple. Below, the *Getae* were a Thracian people driven north of the Danube; the *Seres* indicated Chinese in a general way; the *Parthians* had expanded from an area southeast of the Caspian Sea to create a formidable kingdom, but contenders for their throne appealed for Augustus's support, returning battle standards won from Roman troops; the *Tanais* is a great river from central Russia, the Don, regarded as the division between Europe and Asia. Anchises, mentioned in the last line, was the mythological father of Aeneas by Venus (Aphrodite).

will duly pray the gods; then after our fathers' wont, in measures joined
to strains of Lydian flutes, we will hymn the glories of the heroic dead,
Troy and Anchises and benign Venus' offspring.

Document 1.13

Queen Boudicca: A Briton's View of *Pax Romana*

Words attributed to the queen and priestess of the Iceni tribe*
by Dio in *Roman History*, first century A.D.

. . . although some among you may previously, through ignorance of
which was better, have been deceived by the alluring promises of the
Romans, yet now that you have tried both, you have learned how great
a mistake you made in preferring an imported despotism to your ances-
tral mode of life, and you have come to realize how much better is
poverty with no master than wealth with slavery. . . . Have we not been
robbed entirely of most of our possessions, and those the greatest, while
for those that remain we pay taxes? Besides pasturing and tilling for
them all our other possessions, do we not pay a yearly tribute for our
very bodies? How much better it would be to have been sold to masters
once for all than, possessing empty titles of freedom, to have to ransom
ourselves every year!

Peace and Justice in a Moral Order

From the earliest recorded time, ideas of peace implied a religious
cosmology and the search for some kind of moral order. Hesiod interpreted peace as a conditional gift from the gods. The Hebrews identified
their nation with the one god, Yahweh; and just before and during their
diaspora, or exile between 750 and 550 B.C., their prophets created a
vision of universal peace based on justice. The destiny of their people
was to be the instrument of this moral order. Jesus, called Christ, built
on that prophetic vision to develop an ethic of personal choice, in which
justice implied the recognition of the sacrosanct in everyone. As a minority within the Roman empire, his disciples had to interpret his ethic, and
from their moral struggle came the position of nonresistance—the refusal
to employ violence either for or against secular power. Thus in the an-

---

* Called Boudicca in this translation, and commonly known as Boadicea, she took
her life in A.D. 61 after the failure of her rebellion against Rome.

cient world peace was understood as an expression of divine will and human values.

Hesiod was a Greek farmer and poet who lived in Boeotia about 700 B.C. One of his poems, *Works and Days,* is largely a manual of agriculture, but it is prefaced by a long discussion of ethics (document 1.14).[17] This, in turn, is based on the account of Creation and the history of the gods in Hesiod's other surviving poem, *Theogony.*

Hesiod attributes divine qualities to physical and psychical attributes, and he explains events in nontemporal terms. His universe has a framework of moral laws that relate to the idea of peace in three ways. First, Hesiod describes struggle as both good and bad, given the human condition. Second, he explains that condition by assuming a Golden Age in which mortals lived without care or conflict, and from which humanity fell into toil and violence. The strife *(Eris)* with which humans are burdened is thus cosmic: it deifies the discord among the gods that Zeus has inflicted upon mortals. Third, Hesiod assumes that once Zeus has established order among the gods, he has further set Justice, Good Law, and Peace to "watch over the works of mortal men."[18] Human beings still are burdened with strife and toil, but they are also accountable to Zeus for such justice and peace as they can achieve.

Judaic[19] cosmology was monotheistic and historical. It assumed the existence of a creator god whose purpose is manifested in the temporal order of cause-and-effect relationships. From the time of the exodus out of Egypt with Moses, about 1290 B.C., the Israelites understood themselves to be the chosen people of the sovereign god, Yahweh.[20] As they became a settled people (through conquest which they explained as the will of Yahweh), they identified their nation and god not only with warfare but with Mosaic law. Divine laws and wars together provided a framework for social order under powerful kings like David and Solomon between 1000 and 922 B.C. Success in war depended on being faithful to Yahweh's design, so that "Israelite religion replaced the mythological wars of the gods with the historical struggle of man against the word of God."[21]

From the eighth to the sixth century B.C., the Israelites experienced a crisis of faith. The northern kingdom of Israel was absorbed by the Assyrian Empire (722–721), and the southern one, Judah, fell to the succeeding Babylonian Empire (597 B.C.). Jewish leadership was exiled until it was restored to Jerusalem in 538 by edict of Cyrus, whose Persian Empire succeeded Babylonia. Throughout this era prophets explained the suffering of their people as the result of ignoring Yahweh's word—especially worshipping other gods and failing to do justice. The prophets

called for repentance and obedience, warned of catastrophe, and promised that the Lord would favor the faithful. In the process, they extended
the idea of Yahweh's moral sovereignty to all peoples and redefined the
destiny of Israel: through its sacrifices, it would be the instrument of
God's universal justice and peace. In this way they linked "the redemption of Israel with that of the nations."[22] Along with other themes, and
despite episodes of militant resistance in the Hellenistic and Roman eras,
this view of peace was incorporated into Jewish religious culture (document 1.15).

The Hebrew word for peace, *shalom,* is layered with connotations
that reflect the complexity of the idea as it evolved in Jewish experience.
Its opposite is not war as much as it is deceit, adversity, extermination,
and injustice, so that it conveys a sense of friendship and loyalty, serenity,
prosperity, legal and social order. It can refer to an agreement not merely
for a cessation of hostilities but also for mutual good will. For the individual, it conveys health and well-being; for society, freedom from conflict; for both, wholeness and harmony with the will of God.

Included in the message of the Hebrew prophets were predictions of
a messiah, or savior, who would lead Israel, overthrow the order of
violence, and inaugurate a righteous peace. Jesus, called Christ, was
understood by his followers to be that messiah. He drew upon the prophetic idea of peace and justice, but he emphasized the ethical responsibility of individuals, and his message was universal—to people of all
nations and classes.

Jesus rejected violence, but the significance of his nonviolence is in
what he advocated (document 1.16). He spoke to and for the outcasts of
the world—the poor and powerless, in whom the dominant Graeco-
Roman tradition found no virtue. He preached virtuous conduct without
self-righteousness—unlike Seneca and the Stoics, for whom nonviolence
expressed moral superiority. He advocated love for the alien as well as
the kindred—in contrast to Plato's distinction between war and civil
strife. He insisted that the prophetic peace of God is achieved as people
choose to act toward one another in light of the sacredness of all people.
He taught, as Paul reported, that evil is altogether real and that people
are called to resist it, but not in ways that violate other people (document
1.17). In this sense, he understood the chosen people of God to be all
those who elect to live in peace.

The message of Jesus was essentially an understanding of God, or
ultimate reality. But it was also a standard of ethics, or right action,
that was addressed to individual believers in all nations. Christians, as
followers of Jesus became known, were enjoined to practice the new

standard of values even if it conflicted with custom or political authority. Indeed, there was a continuing tension within the early Christian community between accommodating to and separating from the Roman empire.

Despite isolated persecutions, such as those of Nero and Domitian in the first century A.D., the new religion spread through the lower and middle urban classes of the empire, at first in the hope of Christ's imminent second coming. Until A.D. 250, Christians were threatened mainly by local cults, ethnic conflict, and divisions over their own beliefs. In response, they developed organized churches and a canon of faith. Their strategy was to convert people to their belief, and so they had reason to value the empire because it imposed on the Mediterranean world a measure of order, toleration, and freedom of travel and communication. Increasingly, Christians interpreted the *pax romana* as an institution that facilitated their evangelical mission.

At the same time, they limited their allegiance to political authority. Specifically, they refused to take an oath to Roman gods or to the emperor as deity. To Christians it seemed that the oath would surrender their primary responsibility to the one God and, therefore, to moral independence. A related issue was military service. There were Christian soldiers by the third century, and their number became significant in the fourth. Until then the Roman army was voluntary and limited to citizens. Except on the edges of the empire, it had mostly civil functions such as enforcing law, collecting taxes, and maintaining public facilities. Nonetheless, some church leaders advised against military service on the grounds that a soldier had to take oaths and participate in cultic rituals, which would surrender his absolute loyalty to God, and that military life compromised morality. In a larger sense, the Christian strategy of conversion was counterpoised to the destructive force of arms (document 1.18). As the church drew increasingly close to the empire in the fourth century, antimilitarism set apart those Christians for whom killing was always wrong (document 1.19).

The early Christian idea of peace was thus activist in two respects: it affirmed the social power of converting people to a new standard of values, and it asserted limits to the authority of the state over individuals.

Document 1.14

Hesiod: Strife, Justice, and Peace

From *Works and Days*, ca. 700 B.C.

There was never one kind of Strife.* Indeed on this earth
two kinds exist. The one is praised by her friends,
the other found blameworthy. These two are not of one mind.
The one—so harsh—fosters evil war and the fray of battle.
No man loves this oppressive Strife, but compulsion
and divine will grant her a share of honor.
The other one is black Night's elder daughter;
and the son of Kronos,† who dwells on ethereal heights,
planted her in the roots of the earth and among men.
She is much better, and she stirs even the shiftless on to work.
A man will long for work when he sees a man of wealth
who rushes with zeal to plow and plant
and husband his homestead. One neighbor envies another
who rushes to his riches. This Strife is good for mortals.

. . . .

At first the immortals who dwell on Olympos
created a golden race of mortal men.
That was when Kronos was king of the sky,
and they lived like gods, carefree in their hearts,

. . . .

and lived in peace and abundance as lords of their lands,
rich in flocks and dear to the blessed gods.

. . . .

I wish I were not counted among the fifth race of men,
but rather had died before, or been born after it.
This is the race of iron. Neither day nor night
will give them rest as they waste away with toil
and pain. Growing cares will be given them by the gods,
and their lot will be a blend of good and bad.

---

* In Hesiod's *Theogony*, Strife's progeny include pains, oblivion, famine, battles, murders, quarrels, lies, argument, lawlessness, and ruin. Only in *Works and Days* does the poet attribute to Strife a constructive sister.

† Zeus overthrew his father, Kronos (or Cronos), to become the supreme god.

Justice* howls when she is dragged about by bribe-devouring men
whose verdicts are crooked when they sit in judgment.
Weeping and clothed in mist, she follows through the cities
and dwellings of men, and visits ruin on those
who twist her straight ways and drive her out.
But those who give straight verdicts and follow justice,
both when fellow citizens and strangers are on trial,
live in a city that blossoms, a city that prospers.
Then youth-nurturing peace comes over the land, and Zeus
who sees afar does not decree for them the pains of war.

Document 1.15

Amos and Isaiah: Prophetic Peace

From the books of Amos and Isaiah, eighth century B.C.,
in the Holy Bible

Amos†

For thus says the Lord to the house of Israel. . . . "I hate, I despise
your feats, and I take no delight in your solemn assemblies. Even though
you offer me your burnt offerings and cereal offerings, I will not accept
them, and the peace offerings of your fatted beasts I will not look upon.
Take away from me the noise of your songs; to the melody of your harps
I will not listen. But let justice roll down like waters, and righteousness
like an ever-flowing stream."

Isaiah§

"What to me is the multitude of your sacrifices?" says the Lord;
"I have had enough of burnt offerings of rams and the fat of fed

---

* Justice (Dike) was the daughter of Zeus by Themis (Established Custom). Her sisters
were Good Law (Eunomia) and Peace (Eirene).

† Amos came from Judah but was active in the northern kingdom of Israel on the eve
of the Assyrian conquest (ca. 750 B.C.). This passage addresses not only the northern
kingdom but all the Israelite people.

§ Isaiah was active in Judah when the Assyrians conquered and dispersed the kingdom
of Israel (722–721 B.C.) and then reduced Judah to vassalage. Chapters 40–66 of the book
of Isaiah were the work of a second author ("Second Isaiah") just before the Persian
conquest, which ended Jewish exile in Babylonia. Thus the whole book spans the prophetic
era.

beasts; I do not delight in the blood of bulls, or of lambs, or of he-goats. . . .

Wash yourselves; make yourselves clean; remove the evil of your doings from before my eyes; cease to do evil, learn to do good; seek justice, correct oppression; defend the fatherless, plead for the widow. . . . If you are willing and obedient, you shall eat the good of the land; but if you refuse and rebel, you shall be devoured by the sword; for the mouth of the Lord has spoken."

It shall come to pass in the latter days that the mountain of the house of the Lord shall be established as the highest of the mountains, and shall be raised above the hills; and all the nations shall flow to it, and many peoples shall come, and say: "Come, let us go up to the mountain of the Lord, to the house of the God of Jacob; that he may teach us his ways and that we may walk in his paths." For out of Zion shall go forth the law, and the word of the Lord from Jerusalem.* He shall judge between the nations, and shall decide for many peoples; and they shall beat their swords into plowshares, and their spears into pruning hooks; nation shall not lift up sword against nation, neither shall they learn war any more.

There shall come forth a shoot from the stump of Jesse, and a branch shall grow out of his roots.† And the Spirit of the Lord shall rest upon him, the spirit of wisdom and understanding, the spirit of counsel and might, the spirit of knowledge and the fear of the Lord. And his delight shall be in the fear of the Lord. He shall not judge by what his eyes see, or decide by what his ears hear; but with righteousness he shall judge the poor, and decide with equity for the meek of the earth. . . .

The wolf shall dwell with the lamb, and the leopard shall lie down with the kid, and the calf and the lion and the fatling together, and a little child shall lead them. . . . They shall not hurt or destroy in all my holy mountain; for the earth shall be full of the knowledge of the Lord, as the waters cover the sea.

And the effect of righteousness will be peace, and the result of righteousness, quietness and trust forever.

. . . Thus says God, the Lord, . . . "I am the Lord, I have called you in righteousness, I have taken you by the hand and kept you; I have given you as a covenant to the people, a light to the nations, to open the eyes

---

* Jerusalem was the site of Israel's temple to Yahweh.

† Jesse was the father of king David. Isaiah predicts the return of Israel under Davidic leadership after exile, and he prophesizes a reign of universal peace.

that are blind, to bring out the prisoners from the dungeon, from the prison those who sit in darkness."

Document 1.16

Jesus Christ: Blessings of the New Law

From the books of Matthew and Luke, first century A.D.,
in the Holy Bible

Blessed are the poor in spirit, for theirs is the kingdom of heaven.

Blessed are those who mourn, for they shall be comforted.

Blessed are the meek, for they shall inherit the earth.

Blessed are those who hunger and thirst for righteousness, for they shall be satisfied.

Blessed are the merciful, for they shall obtain mercy.

Blessed are the pure in heart, for they shall see God.

Blessed are the peacemakers, for they shall be called sons of God.

Blessed are those who are persecuted for righteousness' sake, for theirs is the kingdom of heaven.*

Blessed are you when men revile you and persecute you and utter all kinds of evil against you falsely on my account. Rejoice and be glad, for your reward is great in heaven, for so men persecuted the prophets who were before you.

. . . Love your enemies, do good to those who hate you, bless those who curse you, pray for those who abuse you. To him who strikes you on the cheek, offer the other also; and from him who takes away your cloak do not withhold your coat as well. Give to every one who begs from you; and of him who takes away your goods, do not ask them again. And as you wish that men would do to you, do so to them.

If you love those who love you, what credit is that to you? For even sinners love those who love them. And if you do good to those who do good to you, what credit is that to you? For even sinners do the same. And if you lend to those from whom you hope to receive, what credit is that to you? Even sinners lend to sinners, to receive as much again. But love your enemies, and do good, and lend, expecting nothing in return; and your reward will be great, and you will be sons of the Most High;

---

* The word *righteousness* is similar to *justice; eirenopoios,* the word for *peacemaker,* may be understood in the sense of "one having the virtues of moderation and fairness."

for he is kind to the ungrateful and the selfish. Be merciful, even as your Father is merciful.

Judge not, and you will not be judged; condemn not, and you will not be condemned; forgive, and you will be forgiven; give, and it will be given to you.

Document 1.17

Paul: Live Peaceably with All

From the book of Romans,* first century A.D., in the Holy Bible

Let love be genuine; hate what is evil, hold fast to what is good; love one another with brotherly affection; outdo one another in showing honor. . . . Rejoice in your hope, be patient in tribulation, be constant in prayer. Contribute to the needs of the saints, practice hospitality.

Bless those who persecute you; bless and do not curse them. . . . Live in harmony with one another; do not be haughty, but associate with the lowly; never be conceited. Repay no one evil for evil, but take thought for what is noble in the sight of all. If possible, so far as it depends upon you, live peaceably with all. Beloved, never avenge yourselves, but leave it to the wrath of God; for it is written, "Vengeance is mine, I will repay, says the Lord." No, "if your enemy is hungry, feed him; if he is thirsty, give him drink; for by so doing you will heap burning coals upon his head." Do not be overcome by evil, but overcome evil with good.

Document 1.18

Clement of Alexandria: The Arms of Peace

From *Miscellanies and Cohortatio ad gentes,*
second century A.D.†

. . . Justice is the peace of life and governs its stability and tranquillity.

---

* Paul, a converted Jew from Tarsus in Asia Minor, was a contemporary of Jesus. As a Roman citizen, he was tried for his faith in Rome and executed there under Nero, ca. A.D. 64.

† Clement headed a school at Alexandria that related Christianity to Hellenistic philosophy, notably Neoplatonism, and initiated scholarly study of the Judaic and Christian scriptures.

. . . The trumpet of Christ is his Gospel. He sounded his trumpet and we listened. Let us therefore learn to handle the arms of peace. Offering our breasts to justice, taking up the sword of faith and donning the helmet of salvation, let us take up as well the sword of the spirit, which is the word of God. These are our arms, and nowhere will they inflict wounds.

Document 1.19

Lactantius: Always Wrong to Kill

From *The Divine Institutes*,* fourth century A.D.

. . . For when God forbids killing, He not only prohibits us from free-booting [piracy], which is not permitted even by public laws, but He also advises that those things also, which are regarded as lawful among men, should not be done. So, neither will it be permitted a just man . . . to enter military service, nor can he accuse anyone of a capital crime, because there is no difference whether you kill a man with a sword or a word, since the killing itself is prohibited.

Therefore, in this command of God, no exception whatsoever must be made. It is always wrong to kill a man whom God has intended to be a sacrosanct creature.

Toward Modernity: Tranquillity, Imposed Order, Just War, and Eliminating War

The fourth century opened a new historical epoch. Emperor Diocletian, who had made himself the object of worship, launched a persecution of Christians in 303, which his successor, Galerius, intensified until his death eight years later. But in 313 religious toleration became imperial policy under the emperor Constantine, who converted to Christianity and in 325 called and presided over a churchwide council of bishops at Nicea.

---

* Lactantius, who had suffered under Diocletian's persecution of Christians in 303, in his old age became tutor to Constantine's son. His comprehensive survey of the Christian faith, written between 300 and 317, reflects his overall acceptance of the Roman state and society, with the important exception that he prohibits killing, and therefore warfare, for Christians.

As the church and empire became allied, citizenship came to be identified with Christianity. By 416 service in the army was limited to members of the faith, and eventually, except for a small number of Jews and Moslems, to be a European virtually meant to be a member of the church. Although there had been some accommodation between Christian leaders and Roman authority even before Constantine, the consolidation of church and state was historically abrupt and significant.

In the fifth century the Roman Empire, then nominally ruled from Constantinople, or Byzantium, was attacked by warrior tribes from northern Europe and Asia. The Eastern, or Byzantine, Empire retained its identity and even reconquered territories in the western Mediterranean during the sixth century, so that the church at Constantinople remained aligned with a centralized government that regularly intervened in its political, administrative, and theological disputes. The empire crumbled in the West, where various invading peoples settled and were assimilated. The Christian church penetrated the tribal ruling classes, made conversions, and extended its influence. The Western church, whose authority was totally centered in Rome, had to deal with decentralized political units and diverse peoples even after the Carolingian Empire of the ninth century. Thus the idea of peace evolved quite differently in the East and West until the modern era.

It is possible to identify four general approaches to peace between the fourth and eighteenth centuries: (1) the search for a spiritual peace beyond violence, which came to characterize some voluntary nonviolent communities; (2) the idea of civilized order imposed by a supreme authority, conceived either as the Roman Catholic church or as a secular empire; (3) the "just war" tradition, in which warfare, although regarded as necessary and legitimate, was brought within law; and (4) proposals to eliminate war.

The Peace of Inner Tranquillity

Several fourth-century theologians expounded an approach that thereafter characterized Orthodox religion in the East: they internalized and spiritualized the idea of peace. Their thinking drew upon the New Testament apostles and also on Neoplatonic philosophy as well as other, perhaps Asian, sources. Parallels existed in the medieval church of the West but there spirituality competed with other approaches to peace.

The Eastern church of the fourth century was not only tied to an imperial government, it was also racked by theological controversy and political conflicts. For Saint Basil the Great there was no alternative to the wars that determined the fate of the empire—and therefore the church—but unity and peace was possible for the Christian community. Such a peace was tranquillity, the serenity of the soul that is in communion with God. Saint Basil tried to imbue the church with a sense of spiritual consensus beyond rational dispute. He sought to take the faithful beyond violence, beyond even enmity. He preached that the promised peace of a future kingdom of God and a future life was immediately available to the believer. Such a peace could create a community of believers.

For Saint Gregory of Nazianzus, violence was a consequence of separation from God. The cosmos being by nature harmonious, humanity reaps the discord it sows. Specifically, the empire suffered from its own heresy: "The disintegration of the defeated fatherland, the many precious objects destroyed, the land drenched in blood and strewn with corpses, a foreign people overrunning and occupying the country . . . must be ascribed to our ill-will and to our repeated impiety with regard to the Trinity."[23] This religious explanation for war pervaded the medieval cosmology (document 1.20). Its corollary was that inner serenity is available to those who know and accept God's peace, and that external peace can be found only by a community of believers (document 1.21).

The most extreme search for tranquillity was conducted by thousands of ascetic hermits who renounced society for a life of contemplation, spreading in the fourth century from Egypt throughout the Hellenistic East. Asceticism was a reproach to the churches, enmeshed as they were in politics, land holding, and factionalism. In many cases it was a rejection of violence. As it grew, the ascetic movement became organized as monasticism. Over time it was accommodated by the church as a special vocation for communities of believers dedicated to a life of contemplation and manual labor, often accompanied by acts of mercy. Saint Basil himself founded and supervised monasteries, and his writings contributed to their liturgical life. The monastic movement carried Orthodox Christianity into Russia and Eastern Europe, where it taught the ideal of inner peace: the believer, like the monastery, could be an island of spiritual tranquillity in the midst of worldly violence.

Western monasticism was formalized in the sixth century along lines established by Saint Benedict. In a region fragmented by tribal invasions and feudal warfare, it was the bastion of Christian expansion and survival. It was the only voluntary, legally autonomous form of society until the rise of new cities. Generally it provided a model of nonviolence in a society ruled by force. The monasteries, relatively isolated, preserved

classical learning and canon law; as they became increasingly prosperous, they acquired an interest in social as well as spiritual peace. Thus,
in the ninth and tenth centuries, the abbots of the wealthy French monastic order of Cluny tried to restrain feudal warfare in their area. While
granting the legitimacy of force in society, they rejected the unbridled
violence of feudalism and thereby contributed to efforts to limit warfare.

Saint Francis of Assisi was converted while a soldier, renouncing war
and violence, along with wealth. A model of inner serenity, he also
preached and acted for social peace. Members of his Franciscan Order,
established early in the thirteenth century and formally incorporated in
1223, were largely townsmen rather than rural monks, who undertook
itinerant lives of poverty, charity, and peacemaking. Moreover, the
Order affiliated lay men and women who remained in their homes and
workplaces but took vows of poverty, spirituality, and nonviolence (document 1.22). A similar dispensation was given in 1201 to the lay order
of the Humiliati, a voluntary community in the Lombard region of Italy,
once it clearly accepted church discipline.

Some twelfth-century voluntary, or intentional, communities rejected not only violence but also the authority of the Roman church,
whose wrath they incurred. Such were the Cathars and Waldenses of
northern Italy and southern France—lay groups with their own spiritual
leaders. They turned to primitive Christianity, studying the Bible in their
own languages instead of the official Latin, refusing to bear arms or
take oaths, and rejecting those sacraments that they regarded as non-
scriptural. Subjected to severe persecution by Rome for over two hundred years, some of them finally accepted church discipline; but others
scattered across Europe and spread their idea of peace.

Perhaps influenced by the Waldenses, Petr Chelčický fathered the
Unity of Czech Brethren, a minority of the Czech-speaking people in
Moravia and Bohemia who broke away from the Roman Catholic
Church in the fifteenth-century. Chelčický taught that the community of
believers is answerable only to its own law of love, and that it must
separate from the system of force with which governments maintain
order. This approach may be called *nonresistance* because it did not
challenge the legitimacy of the secular state, even though it rejected violence and even military or government service. Rigorous nonresistance
faded among the Czech Brethren by the 1520s, when it reappeared
among the Anabaptist reformers of Switzerland and spread to Germany
and the Low Countries.

The Anabaptists' insistence on free churches—religious communities independent of the state—reinforced the position of nonresistance. Considering themselves disciples of the biblical Christ, radical Anabaptists made Christian love their absolute standard of ethics. Because they understood that such an ethic was not possible for the larger society, they withdrew into their own communities. As formulated in 1527, nonresistance was related to nonconformity: peace implied separation from the world.[24] The principle was not adopted by all Anabaptists, but it characterized some of them, notably the Mennonites of the sixteenth century and the German Brethren of the eighteenth (document 1.23). Threatened with military conscription, several of their communities eventually migrated to Russia and North America. Together with the Quakers, these religious groups became known as "peace churches."

The Society of Friends, called Quakers, was formed during the British civil wars of the seventeenth century. By 1661, Quakers identified themselves with the total rejection of war. They based their "Peace Testimony" on the biblical Sermon on the Mount and on their belief in the "inner light"—the idea that divine truth is revealed directly to everyone willing to receive it. This principle led Quakers to emphasize the equal worth of all persons, and therefore to reject the taking of anyone's life. It also contributed to their antiauthoritarianism, because some measure of truth is accessible to all (including non-Quakers, even non-Christians), and to their disposition to deal with conflict through collective reasoning, or consensus.

Ideas of humanism and rational progress modified the extent to which Quakers withdrew into their own communities. Despite many differences among them, Friends shared a central tradition by the end of the eighteenth century: they separated themselves from the custom of war and refused the demands of the state to participate in it, but they acknowledged their responsibility to contribute to peace in the larger society (document 1.24). In this respect, the Quaker peace testimony combined nonresistance and peace advocacy in an effort to go beyond violence—altogether in their own community and as much as possible in the world.

Document 1.20

The Russian Chronicle: War Is God's Punishment

From an eleventh-century sermon *

Intestine [domestic] strife is incited by the craft of the devil. For God wishes men not evil but good; while the devil takes his delight in cruel murder and bloodshed, and therefore incites quarrels, envy, domestic strife, and slander. When any nation has sinned, God punishes it by death or famine or barbarian incursion, by drought or a plague of caterpillars or by other chastisements, until we repent of our sins and live according to God's commandment. For he says unto us through the mouth of his Prophet, "Turn unto me with all your hearts in fasting and lamentation" (Joel, ii, 12). . . . Having heard these words, let us apply ourselves to good, seek justice, and free the oppressed. Let us do penance, not returning evil for evil nor slander for slander, but let us rather bind ourselves with love to the Lord our God. Let us wash away all our transgressions with fasting, with lamentation, and with tears, nor call ourselves Christians as long as we live like pagans.

Document 1.21

Gregory of Nyssa: The Peace in Our Life

From "On Perfection," fourth century

. . . Recognizing Christ as "peace," we shall exhibit the true title of Christian in ourselves through the peace in our life. For the One "has slain enmity," as the apostle says. Let us not, therefore, bring it to life in ourselves, but rather show through our life that it is dead. Let us not raise up against ourselves through anger and backbiting what has been rightly deadened for our salvation by God. This would destroy our souls and bring about an evil resurrection of what is rightly dead. . . . Therefore, let us also reconcile, not only those fighting against us on the out-

---

* The occasion for this sermon was a defeat of Russian princes in 1068. The defeat is ascribed to dissent among the princes. The author perceives that invasion, like other disasters, is beyond the power of medieval man but that the internecine conflicts are the fault of the princes themselves. The analogy to Israel is established by frequent citations of the prophets. On another level, this sermon reflects a common call for unity against the nomads.

side, but also the elements at variance within us, in order that no longer may the "flesh lust against the spirit and the spirit against the flesh." Subjecting the spirit of the flesh to divine law, let us live peacefully, having been dissolved into the new and peaceful man and having become one from two. For the definition of peace is the harmony of dissonant parts.

Document 1.22

The Franciscans: A Community of Peacemakers

From the Venice Rule, thirteenth century, and the Peace Prayer
of Saint Francis, twentieth-century formulation

First Rule* of the Third Order

They are to make a confession of their sins three times a year and to receive Communion at Christmas, Easter, and Pentacost. They are to be reconciled with their neighbors and [are] to restore what belongs to others. . . .

They are not to take up lethal weapons, or bear them about, against anybody.

All are to refrain from formal oaths unless where necessity compels, in the cases excepted by the Sovereign Pontiff in his indult [authority], that is, for peace, for the Faith, under calumny, and in bearing witness.

Prayer†

Lord,
Make me an instrument of your peace:
Where there is hatred, let me sow love;
Where there is discord, harmony;
Where there is injury, pardon;
Where there is error, truth;
Where there is doubt, faith;

---

* The Rule of 1221 (here the Venice version) established the basic principles of the Third Order of Penitents (lay Franciscans) concerning their spiritual life and duty to perform acts of mercy, care for the sick and poor, and reconcile enemies among themselves and others.

† The "Peace Prayer of St. Francis" is not of his own authorship, but has become identified with him by usage. This version includes petitions from Italian, Spanish, and French versions that often do not appear in English ones.

Where there is despair, hope;
Where there is darkness, light;
Where there is sadness, joy;

O Divine Master,
Grant that I may not so much seek:
To be consoled, as to console;
To be understood, as to understand;
To be loved, as to love.
For, it is in giving, that we receive;
It is in forgetting self, that we find ourselves;
It is in pardoning, that we are pardoned; and
It is in dying, that we are born to eternal life.

Document 1.23

The Mennonites: Nonresistance

From Menno Simons, *The Foundation of Christian Doctrine,*
sixteenth century, and Simeon Rues, *Present State of the
Mennonites,* eighteenth century

Menno Simons *

... Our weapons are not weapons with which cities and countries
may be destroyed, walls and gates broken down, and human blood shed
in torrents like water. But they are weapons with which the spiritual
kingdom of the devil is destroyed and the wicked principle in man's
soul is broken down. . . . Christ is our fortress; patience our weapon of
defense; the Word of God our sword; and our victory a courageous,
firm, unfeigned faith in Jesus Christ. And iron and metal spears and
swords we leave to those who, alas, regard human blood and swine's
alike.

Simeon Friderich Rues †

... They [Mennonites] believe that the government is ordained of
God, and therefore render willing obedience to its laws and commands.

---

* Menno Simons of Friesland had joined the Anabaptists by 1536, and such was his
leadership that his followers became known as Mennonites. His expression of nonresistance was essentially pastoral rather than theological or dogmatic, according to the historian Peter Brock.

    † Rues, a German Lutheran pastor, here reports his observation of Dutch Mennonites.

They teach that taxes and duties must be paid without murmuring and without asking for what purpose they are to be used. They are thankful to God for the blessing of being permitted to live a quiet and peaceable life under the protection of the government. They believe, however, that in the church of Christ there is no room for government as such, and if all people were true Christians . . . there would be no need for cruel governments. But since this has never been realized and it cannot be hoped that it will be realized, God has instituted the office of government. . . . They say . . . that the duties of a magistrate and of a Christian do not agree, for the worldly governments must exercise vengeance, force, and violence, but this is forbidden to the believer under the New Testament dispensation.

Document 1.24

The Quakers: The Peace Testimony

From "A Declaration,"* seventeenth century

Our principle is, and our practices have always been, to seek peace and ensue [pursue] it and to follow after righteousness and the knowledge of God, seeking the good and welfare and doing that which tends to the peace of all. We know that wars and fightings proceed from the lusts of men . . . , out of which lusts the Lord hath redeemed us, and so out of the occasion of war. . . . All bloody principles and practices, we, as to our own particulars, do utterly deny, with all outward wars and strife and fightings with outward weapons, for any end or under any pretense whatsoever. And this is our testimony to the whole world. . . .

. . . the spirit of Christ, by which we are guided, is not changeable, so as once to command us from a thing as evil and again to move unto it; and we do certainly know, and so testify to the world, that the spirit of Christ, which leads us into all Truth, will never move us to fight and war against any man with outward weapons, neither for the Kingdom of Christ, nor for the kingdoms of this world.

And as for the kingdoms of this world, we cannot covet them, much less can we fight for them, but we do earnestly desire and wait, that by the Word of God's power and its effectual operation in the hearts of men, the kingdoms of this world may become the kingdoms of the Lord, and of his Christ, that he may rule and reign in men by his spirit and

---

* This declaration was signed by George Fox and others in 1661 after Quakers had been accused of complicity in an attempt to overthrow the government.

truth, that thereby all people . . . may all come to witness the prophet's words who said, "Nation shall not lift up sword against nation, neither shall they learn war any more." . . .

So, we whom the Lord hath called into the obedience of his Truth have denied wars and fightings and cannot again any more learn it. . . .

The Imposed Order of Christian Empire

One idea of peace was, as we have seen, the spirit of tranquillity beyond violence. Other ideas of peace accepted the inevitability of violence, but tried to minimize it for the sake of social order. An early approach was to impose order through a supreme authority. When Constantine emerged as sole emperor in the fourth century, for example, the old notion of a *pax romana* was fused with Christian hope (document 1.25). Although his empire crumbled, the ideal of an imperial peace endured in various forms into the modern era.

The Byzantine Empire contracted after the fifth century, partly under pressure from Slavic peoples and, nearer to the Black Sea, the Rûs. Greek Christian ideas of morality permeated Russian leadership as it consolidated territories that became the loose Empire of Kiev of the ninth century. Thus, Vladimir Vsevolodovitch Monomakh, one of the most educated and talented Russian princes before the thirteenth-century Mongolian invasions, advised his sons that righteous rule was necessary for peace (document 1.26).

In 475 imperial rule in the East was separated from the West, where the church at Rome had acquired a position of authority. Having largely adopted the hierarchical organization of the empire, the Western church adapted to the feudal structure that evolved among various independent tribes. When the Frankish leader Charles the Great (who ruled 768–814) consolidated several of them, he allied his state with the papacy, both to protect it from threatening tribes such as the Lombards and to authenticate his own claims of independence from the Eastern empire at Constantinople. Charlemagne had himself crowned by the Roman pontiff in 800 to symbolize that his new Carolingian empire embodied the Constantinian ideal (document 1.27).

The idea of Christian empire rested on two basic distinctions. First, Europeans were distinguished from other people by the civilizing influence of their religion. This attitude, like the Greek view of non-Greeks, made it seem natural to seek peace within Europe while mounting wars against Turks, Moslems, or other people who threatened European civilization. In fact, Pope Urban II justified the crusade as an instrument of

European peace. "You murder and devour one another, you wage wars," he observed. "Let this mutual hatred stop; let these quarrels abate; let these wars cease. . . . Begin the journey to the Holy Sepulcher, conquer that land which the wicked have seized, the land which was given by God to the children of Israel and which, as the Scripture says, 'is all milk and honey.' "[25] For such a militant mission—and also for conversion by the spoken word—popes claimed imperial leadership.

Second, the order of the spirit was distinguished from that of society. Each realm was presumed to have its own authority: in spiritual matters, the Roman Catholic church with the pope at its head; in worldly affairs, the emperor. This ideal model was compromised, however, by the shifting distribution of power.

On the one hand, the Catholic church itself was a temporal power. It was the largest landholder in Italy, it claimed sovereign jurisdiction over central Italian territories, and its bishoprics and monasteries controlled land and political offices throughout Europe. As a result, while the church asserted its autonomy, emperors from Charlemagne to Frederick II in the thirteenth century and Charles V in the sixteenth claimed some jurisdiction over the church as part of their divine calling to protect its spiritual integrity.

On the other hand, the Holy Roman Empire was based on shifting alliances and marriages among feudal overlords and kingdoms, and not on truly centralized power. In their struggle for influence, emperors found themselves sometimes allied with the church and other times contending with it. The church and empire competed even to legitimate the Crusades. In fact, the ideal of imperial peace was a "phantom,"[26] an illusion that obscured a complex struggle for power and authority.

Dante Alighieri understood that struggle. He fought in the factional battles of Florence, was politically active when the city resisted papal interference, and fled into exile under a death sentence. And yet his political treatise, *De Monarchia* (ca. 1308), was an exercise in pure reason. Pointing out that the church would have greater moral and spiritual force if it were not compromised by worldly ambition, he argued that an emperor is "essential for the well-being of the world," that the Roman Empire had been divinely ordained, and that the emperor's authority comes from God, not from the church. Dante had in mind a world state that would secure peace and justice among its component kingdoms, and he believed that political legitimacy rested on wisdom and justice (document 1.28).

In the years after Dante, the idea of imperial peace was increasingly secularized, and later it was nationalized in the imperial ideologies of

Spain, France, Britain, and other powers. In the broadest sense, however, his vision of peace, justice, and freedom, secured through a single universal government in which no national state is absolutely sovereign anticipated modern world federalism.

Document 1.25

Eusebius: Empire of the Romans and of God

From *Ecclesiastical History,** fourth century

. . . Constantine, the greatest conqueror, excelling in every virtue that comes from godliness, with his son Crispus, an emperor most dear to God and in every way like his father, recovered their own East, and rendered as one united realm the Empire of the Romans, as of old, bringing under their peace all of it from the rising of the sun on both sides of the inhabited earth, north and south, even to the farthest limits of the declining day. Thus, then, men were relieved of all fear of those who formerly oppressed them, and they set about celebrating . . . , honoring first of all God, the universal King, for so they had been instructed, and then the devout emperor with his sons dear to God. . . . Thus, then, were put forth in every place from the hand of the victorious emperor decrees full of benevolence and laws that provided evidence of munificence and true piety.

Document 1.26

Monomakh: The Duty of the Ruler

From *The Russian Primary Chronicle,* twelfth century

. . . in my sorrow I took up the Psalter, and when I opened it, this passage struck my eye: "Why art thou cast down, my soul? Why doest thou disquiet me?" . . . I collected these precious words, and arranged them in order, and copied them:† . . . "Rival not with evildoers, nor

---

* Eusebius (ca. 260–339), a biblical scholar and bishop of Caesarea, was a contemporary and admirer of Constantine. His *History* ends when Constantine had become sole emperor in 323, three years before killing his eldest son, Crispus.

† Monomakh was prince of Chernigov, Pereysaslev, and after 1113 of Kiev. He passed legislation on behalf of the people, was a patron of the clergy, and encouraged literature. Addressed to his sons but designed for general use, his Testament opens with reflections from Psalms 43:5 and 37.

envy the doers of unrighteousness. For the evildoers shall be cut off, but those who wait upon the Lord shall inherit the earth. But yet a little while, and the sinner shall not be; he shall seek his place and shall not find it. The meek shall inherit the earth, and shall rejoice in the abundance of peace. . . . The wicked have drawn out the sword, they have bent their bow to cast down the poor and the needy, and to kill the just of heart. The sword shall enter into their own hearts, and their bows shall be broken. . . . I have been young and now am old, yet I have not seen the righteous forsaken nor his seed begging bread. The righteous man is ever merciful and lendeth, and his seed is blessed." . . .

As you read these words, my sons, praise God who has shown us his mercy and admonished you through the medium of my poor wit. Give heed to me. . . .

. . . Above all things, forget not the poor, but support them to the extent of your means. Give to the orphan, protect the widow, and permit the mighty to destroy no man. Take not the life of the just or the unjust, nor permit him to be killed. Destroy no Christian soul even though he be guilty of murder. . . .

Receive with affection the blessing of bishops, priests, and priors, and shun them not, but rather, according to your means, love and help them, that you may receive from them their intercession in the presence of God. Above all things, admit no pride in your hearts and minds, but say, "We are but mortal; today we live and tomorrow we shall be in the grave. All that thou has given us is not ours, but thine, and thou has but lent it to us for a few days." . . .

Be not lax in the discipline of your homes, but rather attend to all matters yourselves. Rely not upon your steward or your servant, lest they who visit you ridicule your house or your table. When you set out to war, be not inactive, depend not upon your captains. . . . When journeying anywhere by road through your domain, do not permit your followers or another's company to visit violence upon the villages or upon the dwellings, lest men revile you. . . .

Visit the sick, and accompany the dead, for we are all but mortal. Pass no man without a greeting; give him a kindly word. Love your wives, but grant them no power over you. This is the end of all things: to hold the fear of God above all else. If you forget all my admonition, read this counsel frequently. Then I shall be without disgrace, and you shall profit thereby.

Document 1.27

Charlemagne and Christian Empire

From letters of 796, Charlemagne to Pope Leo III, and 799,
Alcuin of York to Charlemagne

Charlemagne

. . . For it is our task, with the aid of divine goodness, to defend the
holy church of Christ everywhere from the attacks of pagans without
and to strengthen it within through the knowledge of the Catholic faith.
And it is your duty, O Holy Father, with your hands raised high to God,
after the manner of Moses, to aid our armies so that by your intercession
with God, our leader and benefactor, the Christian people may always
and everywhere be victorious over the enemies of His Holy Name, and
the name of Our Lord Jesus Christ be proclaimed throughout the world.

Alcuin of York *

. . . For there were three persons most high in this world. There is
the [papacy], the imperial dignity, the secular power of the second Rome,
[and] the royal dignity, in which the ordering of our Lord Jesus Christ
has placed you [Charlemagne], the ruler of Christian people, in power
more excellent than the other dignities mentioned, more clear in wisdom,
more sublime in the authority of government. For lo! in you rests the
entire safety of the churches of Christ. You are the avenger of evil, the
guide of those who wander, the consoler of the afflicted, and the exaltation of the good. . . .

Document 1.28

Dante: World Government

From *Il Convito* and *De Monarchia*, fourteenth century

. . . In order to prevent . . . wars and to remove the cause of them
through all the earth . . . there must of necessity be Monarchy, that is to

---

* Alcuin of York (735–804) was a member of Charlemagne's court who helped
formulate the ideology of Christian empire; but on occasion he challenged what he regarded as his ruler's excessive use of force. Here he refers to Leo III, who became pope in
796, to the emperor Constantine V in Constantinople, and to Charlemagne. He urges the
importance of extending Frankish protection to the church at Rome for the consolidation
of the West and for its independence from the East.

say one sole principality; and there must be one Prince, who, possessing all, and not being able to desire more, holds the kings content within the limits of the kingdoms, so that peace may be between them . . . which, being obtained, men can live happily, which is the end for which man was born.*

It is clear that a dispute may arise between two princes, neither of whom is subject to the other, and that this may be their fault or their subjects'; therefore a judgment between them is indispensable. However, since neither can take cognizance over the other . . . there needs to be a third person enjoying wider jurisdiction who by right rules over both of them. . . . [By extension, this leads to the need for] a first and supreme judge whose judgment will either directly or indirectly solve all disputes: he will be the Monarch, or Emperor.

. . . the Monarch has nothing to desire, since the ocean alone is the limit of his jurisdiction—unlike other princes . . . whose jurisdictions are limited by one another's frontiers. It follows that of all mortals the Monarch can be the purest incarnation of justice. . . . And since to live in peace . . . is the chief of human blessings, and since justice is the most powerful means towards it, . . . who but a person ignorant of the world's meaning would doubt that justice is most powerfully served by the Monarch? For if there is a Monarch then he cannot have any enemies.

. . . Monarchy is necessary for perfect world-order.

Of course, when we say "mankind can be governed by one supreme prince" we do not mean to say that minute decisions concerning every township can proceed directly from him. . . . For nations, kingdoms, and cities have different characteristics which demand different laws for their government, law being intended as a concrete rule of life. . . . But our meaning is that mankind should be ruled by a common law issuing from him and applied to those characteristics which are common to all men. . . .

. . . Monarchy is essential to the well-being of the world.

. . . two guides have been appointed for man . . . : there is the Supreme Pontiff who is to lead mankind to eternal life in accordance with revelation; and there is the Emperor who, in accordance with philosophi-

---

* By "Monarch" and "Monarchy" Dante means the sovereign emperor and empire, not a ruler of one sovereign nation or kingdom among others. The first paragraph of this excerpt, from *Il Convito* (*The Banquet*, ca. 1304–1308), succintly introduces the theme that is developed laboriously in *De Monarchia* (*Monarchy*, ca. 1308), from which the rest of the document is taken. At the time of the writing, Dante was in exile from Florence for his resistance to the papal party.

cal teaching, is to lead mankind to temporal happiness. None would reach this harbor . . . [unless humanity were freed from greed] so as to rest in the tranquillity of peace; and this is the task to which that protector of the world must devote his energies who is called the Roman Prince. His office is to provide freedom and peace for men as they pass through the testing-time of this world. . . . The temporal Monarch receives his authority directly, and without intermediary, from the Source of all authority [God].

The Just War Tradition of Limited War

The main approach to peace in western civilization is the just war tradition. The word *tradition* appropriately suggests a way of thinking about peace and war instead of a body of law or doctrine (although international law and theory are parts of the tradition). This tradition reflects a common understanding that was formed in the Middle Ages and has been refined and institutionalized in the modern era.

The word *just*, in "just war" can be misleading. In the tradition, no war is "just" in the sense that it is absolutely moral or wholly good, even if it is relatively justifiable, or merited. Only under certain conditions can warfare be regarded as just, therefore, and the point of the tradition is to establish the criteria that restrict warfare as an instrument of peace (in the sense of social order).

In the modern formulation, there are two sets of criteria for evaluating the merit of warfare: (1) the circumstances in which it is right to go to war *(jus ad bellum)*, and (2) the conditions on which the conduct of war may be ethical *(jus in bello)*. In the first case it is generally assumed that war may be undertaken only by a legitimate authority, for a reasonable cause, and with an ethical purpose. In the second, it is generally conceded that warfare should be conducted with immunity for designated noncombatants and with specific restrictions on the use of force (proportionality).

Thus, in the just war tradition, peace refers to those criteria that limit the occasion for war and the conduct of warfare.

The tradition has roots in Roman thought, notably Cicero, and in the writings of Augustine, bishop of Hippo, who integrated classical thinking with Christian theology. Augustine wrote when church authority depended on the power of the Roman empire, which itself was under attack (in 430, the year of his death, his own city was under siege by the Vandals). In his *De Civitate Dei,* he distinguished the earthly city of mankind, which is present in the institutions of both state and church, from the City of God, which is present to humanity only in divine grace, as mediated through the church. Because nothing that is mortal is good in itself, everything temporal is judged against the standard of the ideal. Because ideal peace is of God, it cannot be expected of worldly institutions. Therefore, organized force—including war—is required to maintain civilization, including the church, although it is justifiable only as the instrument of righteous peace.

Augustine's ideas about war did not become important until they were revived and developed in the twelfth and thirteenth centuries. About 1140 a Benedictine monk, Gratian, published the *Decretum,* an interpretive compilation of some 3,800 texts relating to church administration. This collection, which became the basis of canon (church) law, included definitions of just war by Isidore of Seville and Augustine. A century later Thomas Aquinas brought the just war idea into systematic theology, stressing especially the conditions under which war might be undertaken *(jus ad bellum):* it must be declared by legitimate authority, to redress an injustice committed, and with the intention to restore a peaceful order (document 1.29).

The later development of Canon law included elaborations of Aquinas' definition. And because the legitimate authority of princes and popes was itself disputed, the question of individual conscience was raised: What should an individual do if a ruler waged war that seemed unjust? The vows taken by Crusader knights, for example, prohibited killing Christians: Could a knight refuse to serve his lord in a war among . them? In general, it was held that a subject should obey the ruler, although a strong line of interpretation reserved the ultimate right of conscience for the individual.[27]

By this time, though, the just war tradition had also developed criteria for the conduct of war *(jus in bello).* In this respect it drew upon the code of chivalry and on a large body of law and custom related to the Peace and Truce of God. ⏤

In the feudal society of the Middle Ages, a warrior class combined political and military roles. Combat, for this class, was a form of trial— a way of settling disputes over issues or authority. Within the warrior class there emerged professional mounted soldiers, or "knights"—either independent mercenaries or dependent warriors holding land in return for their services—who fought more or less under a common code of behavior. The code eventually specified a set of duties and responsibilities, including rules that restrained knightly combat.

This code of chivalry was institutionalized by the orders of those created knights during the crusades: the protection of Christians became the corollary of war against Islam. On the assumption that war is part of God's order of nature, the code attempted to limit warfare to the professional class of knights and, in their interest, to control the terms of fighting. By the fourteenth century the chivalric code had been elaborated in detail (document 1.30); parts of it, including provisions for immunity from war of designated noncombatants, had been integrated into secular and canon law.

The difficulty was that the chivalric code was routinely violated both by armed men who preyed on civilians and also by powerful knights who drew the countryside into their personal feuds but resisted the expanding jurisdiction of towns and kingdoms. The victims of feudal violence, often led by local clerics, responded with the Peace and Truce of God.

About 990 a local bishop brought together clerics, knights, and peasants in his region and secured from the fighting men an oath neither to seize church lands nor to attack the clergy or poor (document 1.31). Within half a century, similar provisions for a *Pax Dei,* or Peace of God, covered most of France and parts of Italy, Spain, and Germany, popularized by common folk and clerics. The Peace of God was supplemented with the *Treuga Dei,* or Truce of God, which tried to prohibit fighting during specified days and seasons (document 1.32). Together the Peace and Truce were expanded to include immunity from attack for merchants and the defenseless, and even the prohibition of classes of weapons.

Evolving from sworn oaths enforced by the threat of excommunication to legal edicts backed by force, the Peace and Truce were merged and disseminated through church decrees, leagues like the Hanseatic cities, special courts, and laws promulgated by local princes, cities, and rulers who were consolidating their territories (document 1.33). Thus the concept of public peace became institutionalized just when the intense struggle between church and secular authorities resulted in the separate development of canon and secular law. The effectiveness of the Peace and Truce of God is debatable, but it is clear that they contributed to the just war tradition in several ways: they legitimated restrictions on the conduct of warfare, especially immunity for noncombatants; they subordinated personal violence to law; they broadened the base of authority; and they suggested that violence might be controlled, at least within territories under a centralized jurisdiction.

The measures that helped to control feudal warfare did not deal with two other forms of so-called just war: violence against non-Christians and warfare between sovereign states.

In the Crusades the church argued that fighting Moslems met the conditions of a just war. Some significant church leaders, however, opposed the armed Crusades and advocated instead the spiritual sword of conversion. The Franciscans, observing the military failures in the Middle East, placed special emphasis on spiritual conversion. When Spain conquered and colonized Central America in the sixteenth century, voices were raised against the atrocities of war and servitude imposed on American Indians. The converted colonialist, political activist, and church theologian Bartolomé de Las Casas carefully documented colonial abuses and insisted that "the Indians are free men and must be treated as such" (document 1.34). He won support for reform at court and influenced a papal pronouncement from Pope Paul III that Indians "are by no means to be deprived of their liberty or the possession of their property, even though they be outside the faith of Jesus Christ. . . . nor should they be in any way enslaved." [28] Heavy-handed Spanish colonialism continued of its own momentum in the Americas, but the just war tradition had been extended by an assertion of universal human rights.

The problem of war between sovereign states was partly addressed by the development of diplomacy. Even in the anarchy of feudal Europe, some popes employed arbitration and negotiation in efforts to settle secular disputes. Later the power and independence of the church enabled popes to supplement diplomacy with the threat of religious sanctions such as excommunication. Accordingly, they intervened in numerous conflicts between rising nation-states. When the church lost power to those states, it turned to forms of diplomacy based on persuasion.

By the fifteenth century secular rulers too had acquired diplomatic experience. They held summit conferences, and they supplemented warfare with negotiation, treaties, truces, and marriage alliances. There was pressure to do so, because military technology was making warfare ever more costly, and the continuing threat of external invasion made unity seem more important in the late medieval period.

Under these circumstances unity took the form of agreements for common defense, or what the twentieth century would call "collective security." An early and typical case was the Lyubech Assembly of 1097 (document 1.35), when Russian princes in the region of Kiev tried to overcome the divisions that weakened them in the face of Turks and other marauding peoples. Although they agreed on the principle that formalized the feudal system in Russia, the princes continued their own wars of expansion. None of the similar attempts for unity from the Urals to the Atlantic Ocean endured, but one was of particular importance. This was the 1518 pact among the rulers of the Holy Roman Empire,

England, France, and Spain, with the sanction of the Pope, who agreed to impose collective sanctions on aggressive action by any one of them or their allies. Although the pact only delayed war for a few years, it signified an important development in the just war tradition: a multinational treaty that defined aggression carefully and excluded it from justifiable wars.

The just war tradition was given its modern form in the sixteenth and seventeenth centuries, when war and international relations received systematic analysis, notably from Las Casas, Francisco de Vitoria, and Francisco Suarez in Spain; William Ames and John Locke in England; and Dutch-born Huig van Groot, or Hugo Grotius.[29] Creating the basis for a body of international law by building on previous theory and formalizing existing customs, they shifted the emphasis of the just war tradition.

These scholars grounded the tradition in natural law and reason as well as in theology (document 1.36). They also emphasized the criteria for the conduct of war *(jus in bello)* more than the authority for waging it *(jus ad bellum)*. As to the legitimacy of war, they placed a strong burden of proof on the ruler to evaluate conflict carefully and to assess war in relation to the welfare of the people: the ruler, in this view, is the servant of society, not the sword of God. Moreover, these writers enlarged upon the right and duty of conscientious objection to military service by individuals who are not convinced of the justness of a particular war.

With regard to the conduct of war, they based immunity for noncombatants on a concept of justice instead of class or vocation, as previously: those who are innocent of prosecuting warfare or of choosing it should be spared; those who are victims of the wars of others—the dependents of the vanquished, including future generations—should not be penalized. Grotius developed rules for the conduct of warfare in great detail, applying a principle of moderation, or reasonableness, that was roughly comparable to the penalties levied in civil law.

Beyond codifying the customs of nations, the early formulators of international law worked from concepts of social obligation and purpose. The just war tradition, as it emerged from this body of analysis, interpreted war "as a human enterprise, subject to human controls."[30]

Document 1.29

Thomas Aquinas: Justifiable War

From *Summa of Theology*, thirteenth century

Three conditions are necessary for a just war. First, that the ruler have the authority to declare war. A private individual may not declare war, for he can rely on his superior's judgment to protect his rights; nor has he any right to mobilize the people, which must be done in war. But since responsibility for public action is committed to the rulers, they are charged with the defense of the city, the kingdom, or the province subject to them. And just as in punishing criminals they are justly defending the state with civil arm against all internal disturbance . . . , so also they are responsible to defend the state against external foes with war weapons. . . .

Second, a just cause is required, so that those who are attacked for some fault merit such an attack. Hence Augustine says . . . : "Those wars are usually defined as just that avenge injuries, as when a nation or state should be punished for neglecting to amend some injury inflicted or to restore what was taken unjustly."

Third, a right intention on the belligerents' part is required—either to promote some good or to avoid some evil. Hence Augustine says . . . : "For the true worshipers of God even wars are peaceful, not waged out of greed or cruelty, but from the zeal for peace, to restrain evil or to assist the good." But it can happen that even if war is waged by legitimate authority with just cause, nevertheless the war may be made unjust through evil intention. For Augustine says . . . : "The desire to hurt, the cruelty of vendetta, the implacable and severe spirit, arrogance in winning, the thirst for power and such things—all these are rightly condemned in war." *

---

* In subsequent articles Aquinas proposes that it is unlawful for clerics to fight, although they may otherwise help with war, that it is lawful to ambush an enemy, and that it is lawful to fight on holy days.

Document 1.30

Honoré Bonet: The Code of Chivalry

From *The Tree of Battles,* fourteenth century

What is war? . . . war is nothing other than discord or conflict that has arisen on account of certain things displeasing to the human will, to the end that such conflict should be turned into agreement and reason. . . .

Where did war first exist and why? . . . it was in Heaven, when our Lord God drove out the angels. . . . Hence it is no great marvel if in this world there arise wars and battles, since they existed first in Heaven. So we must consider how wars and battles have happened in this world, and especially wars against the Christian Faith, and Holy Church. . . .

. . . We see that, by its nature, each thing created in this world assumes nature and condition to resist its contrary. . . . I ask then, since such rebellion and discord occur by nature among other creatures, if human nature, which is the noblest of all, must not also possess this condition, namely, that one person should oppose another . . . ? This must indeed be the case, and it is of common occurrence. . . .

You must know . . . that one of the chief foundations of battle is strength; but we must consider carefully what sort of strength we mean.

. . . I say that strength of soul is the chief foundation; for according to the Holy Scripture, the man who is not loved by God will never be strong in battle, and it is virtue of soul to be of good counsel, and to know how to command well those who are to fight the battle. . . .

Now we must consider how we may recognize whether a man has in him this virtue of strength. . . . As a first sign you will observe that he finds all his pleasure and all his delight in being in arms, and in just wars, and in defending all just causes, quarrels, and holy arguments. The second sign is that a man, seeing the great ill and peril incurred in making such a war . . . should yet not quit his purpose, nor for any labor or travail fear to expose his body to fair fight and strict justice.*

Now we must consider other people who, of right, have safe-conduct in time of war; for you have heard above how prelates, chaplains, dea-

---

* Having demonstrated the inevitability of warfare and the merit of virtue in fighting, Bonet prescribes the behavior of knights and other feudal classes in war and battle. Among some 130 specific cases discussed is the rule of safe conduct, with which this excerpt concludes. By Bonet's time, the chivalric code had been supplemented by the Peace and Truce of God, which helped to institute this principle.

cons, and also converts, hermits, pilgrims, and all the people of the Holy Church, should be in security, since even if they have no safe-conduct, it matters not, for they have it by law.

And I add that ox-herds, and all husbandmen, and ploughmen with their oxen, when they are carrying on their business, and equally when they are going to it or returning from it, are secure, according to written law. And in truth that this should be so is not without good reason, because it is expedient and convenient for all sorts of people, since those who cultivate the soil plough and work for all men and for everybody, and all manner of folk live of their labor. Therefore right reason does not permit that they should receive any ill or annoyance, seeing also that they have no concern with war or with harming anyone.

Document 1.31

The Archbishop of Bordeaux: A Peace of God

From a tenth-century document

Following the example of my predecessors, I, Gunbald, archbishop of Bordeaux, called together the bishops of my diocese in a synod at Charroux* . . . and we, assembled there in the name of God, made the following decrees:

1. Anathema against those who break into churches. If anyone breaks into or robs a church, he shall be anathema unless he makes satisfaction.

2. Anathema against those who rob the poor. If anyone robs a peasant or other poor person of a sheep, ox, ass, cow, goat, or pig, he shall be anathema unless he makes satisfaction.

3. Anathema against those who injure clergymen. If anyone attacks, seizes, or beats a priest, deacon, or any other clergyman, who is not bearing arms (shield, sword, coat of mail, or helmet), but is going along peacefully or staying in the house, the sacrilegious person shall be excommunicated and cut off from the church, unless he makes satisfaction, or unless the bishop discovers that the clergyman brought it upon himself by his own fault.

---

* Charroux was near Poitiers, Vienne, France. Anathema was a form of damnation by excommunication and separation from the church and its services, which were held to be essential for salvation. These provisions were extended elsewhere to prohibit the seizing or robbing of peasants, church lands, or merchants.

Document 1.32

The Archbishop of Arles: A Truce of God

From "Truce of God, Made for the Archbishopric of Arles, 1035–41"

This is the peace or truce of God which we have received from heaven through the inspiration of God . . . ; namely, that all Christians, friends and enemies, neighbors and strangers, should keep true and lasting peace one with another from vespers on Wednesday to sunrise on Monday, so that during these four days and five nights, all persons may have peace, and . . . may go about their business without fear of their enemies.*

All who keep the peace and truce of God shall be absolved of their sins by God. . . .

Those who have promised to observe the truce and have willfully violated it, shall be excommunicated . . . , accursed and despised here and in the future world. . . .

If anyone has killed another on the days of the truce of God, he shall be exiled and driven from the land. . . . If anyone has violated the truce of God in any other way, he shall suffer the penalty prescribed by the secular laws and shall do double the penance prescribed by the canons.

Document 1.33

Henry IV: A Peace of the Land

From "Peace of the Land Established by Henry IV," † twelfth century

In the year of the incarnation of our Lord 1103, the [Holy Roman] emperor Henry established this peace at Mainz, and he and the archbishops and bishops signed it with their own signatures. The son of the king and the nobles of the whole kingdom, dukes, margraves, counts, and

---

* This is a communication from Reginbald, archbishop of Arles, commending the Truce of God to the clergy of Italy. Attempts were made also to exempt holy seasons from war.

† This peace was declared after Henry had fought for over thirty years with German princes and Catholic popes over the extent of his imperial jurisdiction. Civil war resumed the following year, when even Henry's son conspired against him.

many others, swore to observe it. Duke Welf, duke Bertholf, and duke Frederick swore to keep the peace from that day to four years from the next Pentecost. They swore to keep peace with churches, clergy, monks, merchants, women, and Jews. This is the form of the oath which they swore:

No one shall attack the house of another or waste it with fire, or seize another for ransom, or strike, wound, or slay another. [There follows a list of penalties for offenses.]

Document 1.34

Bartolomé de Las Casas: Peace Is the Birthright of All Peoples

From "Declaration of the Rights of the Indians,"* sixteenth century

. . . All unbelievers, whatever their sect or religion and whatever their state of sin, by Natural and Divine Law and by the birthright of all peoples, properly possess and hold domain over the things they have acquired without detriment to others, and with equal right they are entitled to their principalities, realms, states, honors, jurisdictions, and dominions. War against unbelievers for the purpose of subjecting them to Christian control, and to compel them by this means to accept the Christian faith and religion, or to remove obstacles to the end that may exist, is reckless, unjust, perverse, and tyrannical. The sole and definitive reason of the Papacy for granting the supreme rule and imperial sovereignty of the Indies to the monarchs of Castile and Léon was to preach the Gospel, spread the Faith, and convert the inhabitants; it was not to make these monarchs richer princes or greater lords than they already were.

---

* Las Casas persuaded Charles V and the Supreme Council of the Indies to order reforms in the colonies to protect the rights of Indians (1542), and he launched a campaign for their enforcement in New Spain. This culminated in an assembly of bishops at Mexico City, June and July 1546, which endorsed the "Declaration." Surely the document was largely of his authorship, certainly it reflected his views.

Document 1.35

The Lyubech Congress: Collective Peace

From *The Russian Primary Chronicle,* eleventh century

Svyatopolk, Vladimire, David son of Igor, Vasil'ko son of Rostislav, David son of Svyatoslav, and Oleg his brother met at Lyubech to make peace, and said to one another, "Why do we ruin the land of Rus [Russia] by our continued strife against one another? The Polovcians harass our country in diverse fashions, and rejoice that war is waged among us. Let us rather hereafter be united in spirit and watch over the land of Rus, and let each of us guard his own domain: with Svyatopolk retaining Kiev, the heritage of Izyaslav, while Vladimir holds the domain of Vsevolod, and David, Oleg, and Yaroslav between them possess that of Svyatoslav. . . ." On this convention they took oath to the effect that, if any one of them should thereafter attack another, all the rest, with the aid of the Holy Cross, would be against the aggressor. Thus they all said, "May the Holy Cross and the entire land of Rus be against him," and having taken oath, returned each to his domain. Accompanied by David, Svyatopolk arrived in Kiev, and all the people rejoiced. There was only the devil to be distressed by this display of affection.*

Document 1.36

Hugo Grotius: The Law of War and Peace

From *The Law of War and Peace,* seventeenth century

Prolegomena

Now, being thus fully convinced . . . that there is some law common to all nations which applies both to the initiation of war and to the manner in which war should be carried on, . . . I observed everywhere in Christendom a lawlessness in warfare of which even barbarous nations would be ashamed. Nations would rush to arms on the slightest pretext or even without cause at all. And arms once taken up, there would be an end to all respect for law, whether human or divine, as though a fury had been let loose with general license for all manner of crime.

---

* The account continues, "Satan now incited certain men" to conspire against others, and the agreement broke down.

And the spectacle of this monstrous barbarity has led many men . . . to the opinion that all arms should be forbidden a Christian, whose rule of life is mainly the loving of all men. . . . A remedy must therefore be found for both schools of extremists—for those that believe that in war nothing is lawful and for those for whom all things are lawful in war.

Whether War Can Ever Be Just

But this question itself, as well as others which follow, must be first examined by reference to Natural Law. . . . It is man's first duty to preserve himself in the state of nature, his next being to retain what is in conformity with nature and reject all that is opposed to it. . . . There is nothing in the first principles of nature that is repugnant to war. On the contrary, everything rather favors it. For the object of war, which is the preservation of life and limb, and the retention or acquisition of things useful to life, is very agreeable to those first principles. . . . But right reason and the nature of society, which must be examined in the next and chief place, do not prohibit all force, but only that which is repugnant to society, namely, that which invades the right of another. . . .

What we have just said, that all war is not repugnant to Natural Law, may be further proved from sacred history . . . [and also] by the consent of all nations, and particularly of judicious men. . . .

Therefore, it is quite clear that by Natural Law, which may also be called the Law of Nations, all warfare is not to be condemned. And history and the laws and customs of all peoples teach us quite plainly that war is not condemned by the voluntary Law of Nations. . . .*

Of the Causes of War

. . . by causes I mean "just" causes; for there are other causes which are merely considerations of utility, and are therefore quite distinct from those in which the sense of right, or the "just," operates. . . .

Most writers assign three just causes of war—defense, recovery of property, and punishment. . . .

Of Unjust Causes of War

Mere dread of a neighboring Power is not, as we have already said, a sufficient cause. For a defensive war to be just, it ought to be necessary,

---

* By "voluntary law of Nations," Grotius referred to the particular laws and customs of various peoples, as distinct from universal principles of natural law that he believed to be the basis of justice.

which is not the case unless it is clear that our neighbor has not only the power, but the intention, to injure us, and unless the evidence of that intention is practically conclusive. . . .

Nor do the advantages which accrue to us from war create a right. . . .

And equally unjust is it, under pretext of discovery, to raid occupied territory, even though the occupants are godless and almost brainless savages. . . .

Another unjust cause of war is the desire for liberty, whether that of individuals or that—autonomy or self-government—of States. . . .

Nor is it less unjust to seek to subjugate, by force of arms, those we deem fit only to be slaves, . . . for we have no right to force a man even to what is to his advantage. . . .

A Warning Not to Engage in Warfare Rashly, Even for Just Cause

. . . right reason suggests . . . that life is of more value than liberty, for it is the foundation of all temporal good and the occasion for all eternal happiness, and this whether you consider it either in relation to an individual or to a whole people. . . . And what I have said of liberty I would have understood of other desirable things—they should be sacrificed if there otherwise would be a more, or even equally, justifiable fear of a greater mischief. For, as Aristides well says, to save a ship it is the custom to throw overboard the cargo, and not the passengers. . . .

Rare, then, is that cause of war which cannot, or ought not to be disregarded—that "cause which," as Florus says, "is more savage and unendurable than war itself." . . .

Moderation in Conquest

My last advice is this—that however complete and absolute be the power which the conquerors have obtained, the conquered should be treated with clemency, in order that the interests of each may become the interest of both. . . .

The Conclusion, with Admonitions to Good Faith and Peace

. . . I am anxious for good faith especially, lest all hope of peace be taken away, as well as for other reasons. For, according to Cicero, not only is each State held together by good faith, but even that greater society of nations. . . .

. . . peace having once been made, no matter upon what conditions, ought to be most strictly kept, because of the sanctity of that which we have called good faith. . . . For what Cicero has said about private friendships is no less fitly applicable to public—that as all friendships are to be preserved most religiously and faithfully, so especially should those which have resolved a state of war into a happy peace.

Eliminating War: Peace Advocacy

The just war tradition asserted that peace (in the sense of order) is realistic only as a set of criteria that limit warfare, which, it assumed, is a necessary condition of society. Virtually all attempts to restrict warfare were made by the dominant classes. In the midst of the widespread violence of the thirteenth and fourteenth centuries, however, there were spontaneous, popular movements for peace in the form of mass devotionals, processions, and demonstrations: perhaps 400,000 people converged on Verona one day in 1233, perhaps 200,000 on Rome in September 1399.[31] These crowds were not asking for a mere limitation of warfare; they were appealing for an end to it. Such movements were the precursors of peace advocacy.

By the sixteenth century, the feudal and Catholic structure of western Europe was being supplanted by the development of modern nation-states, along with capitalism and Protestant religions. The century was marked by a breathtaking surge of spiritual culture, art, and science, but it was also an epoch of bloody and almost incessant warfare that culminated in the devastating Thirty Years War (1618–1648), while the shadow of the Turkish empire posed a threat that preoccupied the rulers of the region. The way was open for modern peace advocacy.

The advocacy of peace was heralded by outcries against violence and by appeals for an end to destructiveness and irrationality. The preeminent voice was that of Desiderius Erasmus of Rotterdam. The recognized leader of European humanists, Erasmus condemned war most eloquently in his classic *Complaint of Peace* and in his shorter, more urbane reflections on adages, or proverbs (document 1.37). He insisted that human nature is ordained for peace and not war, and that a ruler's legitimacy comes not from power itself, but rather from the use of power for the general welfare. On rationalist and Christian-ethical grounds, he regarded warfare as both senseless and sinful. His thought was in sharp contrast to the ideas of his contemporary, Niccolò Machiavelli, who identified legitimacy with power itself and interpreted peace as a flexible instrument of state.

As monarchies were established and consolidated in the seventeenth and eighteenth centuries, there emerged a number of proposals for a peace of sovereign equals. These projects were based not only on the ideology of law and on the cultural humanism of the High Renaissance but also on practical considerations. The proposals, assuming that peace could be achieved by the rational organization of international society, variously recommended diplomatic negotiation, mediation, arbitration, an international court, disarmament, and—as a last resort—collective security. Neglecting complex political and economic structures at first, they concentrated on the relationships among rulers.

The general object was to secure international order by a loose confederation of states. This was suggested in 1623 by the French poet and philosopher Emeric Crucé, who called for political and religious tolerance, and recommended a permanent, worldwide organization of ambassadors that would conduct continuous diplomacy (document 1.38). If negotiations failed to settle a conflict, he thought, the member states should enforce a settlement with economic and even military sanctions.

Like Erasmus, Crucé appealed to the noblesse-oblige of princes to implement his plan. In contrast, Maximilien de Béthune, Duc de Sully, proposed to rely on power in order to achieve his "Grand Design" for European peace. Sully attributed his plan to Henry IV of France, under whom he had served until the king's assassination in 1610. Henry had attempted to form a series of European alliances that would reduce the power of the Hapsburgs, but Sully went further, envisioning a European federation. His ideas were familiar to the Quaker philanthropist William Penn. Appealing to economic benefits and to the religious ideal of social harmony, Penn interpreted peace as a practical instrument for social order. He proposed that a confederation of European states should be formed by treaty, rather than by force (document 1.39), and he even recommended that it should include an international tribunal and re-sponsibility for disarmament.

The concept of confederation was explored early in the eighteenth century by Charles François Irénée Castel de Saint-Pierre, an abbé and member of the French court, who invented numerous projects for social improvement. In several versions of his "Project for Perpetual Peace," Saint-Pierre elaborated on Sully's "Grand Design," relying on the en-lightened self-interest of monarchs to achieve his vision. In mid-century the French philosopher Jean Jacques Rousseau rewrote the abbé's project for publication.

In the process, Rousseau gave the idea of a European confederation its classic expression (document 1.40). As much as he admired Saint-Pierre's proposal, however, Rousseau dismissed it as a noble dream (other philosophers, such as Leibnitz and Voltaire, did not even give it that much dignity). For Rousseau the difficulty was that, like other authors of grand designs, the abbé had neglected the sources of war—economic and cultural interests and the arbitrary power of rulers. The "Project for Perpetual Peace" was itself reasonable, wrote Rousseau, but the contemporary structure of power was not: "One cannot conceive of the possibility of a federative union being established, except by a revolution. And, that granted, who among us would venture to say whether this European federation is to be desired or to be feared."[32]

The idea of enduring peace came to be taken seriously only when it was systematically related to the structure of power. This was accomplished by Immanuel Kant. For this German philosopher peace was an ideal that had the force of history: it was the logical culmination of the extension of civil society from the smallest to the largest units, and it was the condition for self-preservation. Peace was requisite for liberty and social order, and it must embrace all nations. The essential question that Kant addressed, therefore, was not whether there was merit in a federation of nations for peace. He assumed there was. Rather, the interesting problem was the conditions under which federation might be achieved.

Kant framed his essay (document 1.41) in the form of a proposed treaty. He identified two approaches. The first one, negative conditions for peace (in the "Preliminary Articles" of the treaty), reflected the familiar just war tradition of limiting the use of violence. The second approach, positive conditions (in the "Definitive Articles"), was more innovative. It related the mutual interests of nations to open commercial intercourse, and it proposed that they could be constrained from going to war if their governments were constitutional and representative, with a separation of executive and legislative power. Acutely aware of the American and French revolutions, Kant believed that the prospects for peace involved economic and political structures. Enduring peace is possible, he thought, only in a federation of free societies. By relating international peace to changes in the internal distribution of power, Kant anticipated nineteenth-century analyses.

By the time that he wrote his essay, the French Revolution had yielded another approach: peace through social revolution. Finding the causes of war to be the arbitrary power of monarchs and vested class interests, revolutionaries proclaimed that their movement, however violent, served the cause of peace. As revolutionary France became locked in war with other European powers, it was natural to argue that international order required the liberation of Europe (document 1.42). This idea of peace through revolution would return with force in the twentieth century.

Document 1.37

Desiderius Erasmus: Proverbs

From "Dulce Bellum Inexpertis," and "Spartum Nactus Es, Hanc Orna," sixteenth century

"Dulce Bellum Inexpertis"

Among the choicest proverbs, and widely used in literature, is the adage: . . . war is sweet to those who have not tried it. . . . If there is anything in mortal affairs which should be . . . avoided in every possible way, guarded against and shunned, that thing is war; there is nothing more wicked, more disastrous, more widely destructive, more deeply tenacious, more loathsome, in a word more unworthy of man, not to say of a Christian. Yet strange to say, everywhere at the present time war is being entered upon lightly, for any kind of reason, and waged with cruelty and barbarousness, not only by the heathen but by Christians, not only by lay people but by priests and bishops, not only by the young and inexperienced, but by the old who know it well; not so much by the common people and the naturally fickle mob, but rather by princes. . . . And the result of all this is, that war is now such an accepted thing that people are astonished to find anyone who does not like it; and such a respectable thing that it is wicked (I nearly said heretical) to disapprove of the thing of all things which is most criminal and most lamentable. How much more reasonable it would be to . . . [wonder] that a peaceful creature, whom nature made for peace and loving-kindness (the only one, indeed, whom she intended for the safety of all), should rush with such savage insanity, with such mad commotion, to mutual slaughter. . . .

First of all, if one considers the outward appearance of the human body, does it not become clear at once that nature, or rather God, created this being not for war, but for friendship . . . ? For she endowed every one of the other living creatures with its own weapons. . . . Only man was produced naked, weak, tender, unarmed, with very soft flesh and a smooth skin. Among his members nothing would seem to have been intended for fighting and violence; rather even I might say that the other creatures, almost as soon as they are born, are self-reliant and able to protect themselves, but only man makes his appearance in such a condition that he must depend for a long time on the help of others. . . . And so the appearance she gave him was . . . mild and gentle, bearing the signs of love and goodness. She gave him friendly eyes, revealing the soul. She gave him embracing arms. She gave him the significance of a kiss, a union by which soul meets with soul. On him alone she bestowed laughter, the sign of merriment; on him alone, tears, the mark of mercy and pity. A voice she gave him too, . . . friendly and caressing.

Not content with all this, nature gave to him alone the use of speech and reason, the thing above all which would serve to create and preserve goodwill, so that nothing should be managed by force among men.

Thus we have sketched, in outline, the portrait of man. Now if you like, we will put up on the other hand, for comparison, the picture of war. Imagine now that you see before you the barbarous cohorts whose very faces and shouts strike terror to the heart; the iron-clad troops drawn up in battle array, the terrifying clash and flash of arms, the hateful noise and bustle of a great multitude, the threatening looks, harsh bugles, startling peal of trumpets, thunder of the bombards . . . ; a mad uproar, the furious shock of battle, and then wholesale butchery, the cruel fate of the killers and the killed, the slaughtered lying in heaps, the fields running with gore, the rivers dyed with human blood. It sometimes happens that brother falls on brother, kinsman on kinsman, friend on friend, while the general madness rages, and plunges his sword into the vitals of one who never gave him cause for offense, even by a word. . . . Not to mention other evils, common and trivial in comparison: the trampled crops, the burnt-out farms, the villages set on fire, the cattle driven away, the girls raped, and the old men carried off captive, the churches sacked, robbery, pillage, violence and confusion everywhere. And I am leaving out the things which result from any war, however successful and right it might be: the grinding of the peasantry, the over-taxing of the landowners, . . . so many women widowed and children orphaned, so many homes made houses of mourning, . . . contempt of duty, indifference to law, readiness to dare any kind of crime. . . . And the most serious thing of all is that this deadly pestilence cannot be contained within its own limits, but once it has begun in one corner it floods like a contagious disease into the surrounding regions, and even sweeps the more distant ones with it into the general uproar and turmoil, either for reasons of trade or because of an alliance or a treaty. In fact war is born from war, and a make-believe war leads to a real one, and from a tiny war a huge one grows. . . .

To me it does not even seem recommendable that we should now be preparing war against the Turks.* The Christian religion is in a bad way, if its safety depends on this sort of defense. Nor is it consistent to make good Christians under these auspices. What is taken by the sword is lost by the sword. Are you anxious to win the Turks for Christ? Let us not display our wealth, our armies, our strength. Let them see in us not only the name, but the unmistakable marks of a Christian: a blameless life, the wish to do good even to our enemies, a tolerance which will withstand all injuries, contempt of money, heedlessness of glory, life held lightly. . . . I will say further, and I wish it were more daring than true, if you take away the name and sign of the Cross, we are just like Turks fighting Turks. . . .

"Spartam Nactus Es, Hanc Orna"

This proverb tells us that whatever province we happen to have made our own, we must fit ourselves to it, and suit our behavior to its dignity. . . .

. . . This saying should be engraved everywhere in the halls of princes, *You have obtained Sparta, adorn it;* you will hardly find one of them who really thinks out what it is to play the part of a prince, or who is satisfied with his own dominion and does not try to extend his frontiers. The duty of a prince is to make provision in every kind of way for the needs of the state, to preserve public liberty, to foster peace, to cut out crime with the least possible hurt to his own people, to take care that he has reverend and upright magistrates. So when he is completely unconcerned with these things, . . . then this proverb must be dinned into him: *You have obtained Sparta, adorn it.* Again, when he neglects the realm which is his own and spends his time abroad, coveting the dominions of others; when he drags his people into the most hazardous situations, completely exhausts them and risks himself and the well-being of all on the gamble of war, . . . then is the time to bring forward this adage, *You have obtained Sparta.*

---

* Erasmus added that he would not absolutely condemn a *defensive* war against the Turks, who threatened southeastern Europe, so long as it was conducted "with Christian minds and with Christ's own weapons."

Document 1.38

Emeric Crucé: A New World Order

From *The New Cyneas*, seventeenth century

. . . a city should be chosen where all sovereigns would always have ambassadors so that any differences that should rise would be settled by a decision of the whole assembly. The ambassadors of the parties involved would set forth their masters' complaints, and the other deputies would judge them dispassionately. To give more weight to this decision, advice would be sought from the great republics too, for these nations would also have their ministers in the same place. . . . If anyone should refuse to follow the decision of such an august body, he would incur the ill-will of all the other rulers who would certainly have the means to bring him back to the path of reason.

Now the most suitable place for such an assembly would be the territory of Venice, since it is neutral and not partial to any ruler. Another advantage is its location. It is situated near the most powerful monarchies on earth: the Pope, the two emperors, and the King of Spain. It is not far from France, Tartary, Muscovy, Poland, England, and Denmark. As for Persia, China, Ethiopia, and the East and West Indies, they are indeed far removed from the others, but navigation can overcome this difficulty. . . .

To give this assembly more authority, all the said princes would swear to consider as inviolable any law passed by the majority of votes cast and to take up arms against those who sought to oppose it. The council, then, . . . would try to keep everyone on good terms with one another. It would attempt to anticipate causes of discontent and smooth them over by peaceful means if possible, by force if necessary.

In short, . . . if [a prince] has some cause for complaint, let him present his arguments to the general assembly as the most competent judge imaginable. This is the principal means of establishing world peace, and the one on which all the others depend. This is where we must begin. For as long as sovereigns keep to themselves and have no communication with each other through their ambassadors, they will try to expand their kingdoms whatever the price, and will always find a sufficient pretext for encroaching upon one another. If, however, they are satisfied with their present fortune, if they pay the just claims of their people as they ought to do, if they unite within the framework of this assembly of which they will constitute the membership, there will be nothing that can delay or disrupt a just peace.

... We are no longer living in an age when one should be dreaming of trophies to be won. We must do away with these barbarous customs and show the people the road to humanity and true honor so that they will not continue to live so brutally. We must establish the reign of reason and justice, and not violence, which is fit only for beasts. In the past men have been most free with human life. We have seen a universal deluge of their blood capable of turning the land and sea red. Enough. It was a bloodletting necessary to purge the world of its vicious and super-fluous humors, and God wanted to use this means to establish monarch-ies. Now that they are firmly resting on the pilings at long possession, they must not be shaken, but rather reinforced by lasting peace. . . .

Preventing evil that might come from outside is not enough. Domes-tic difficulties can be more perilous. So, after all the princes have reached an agreement, each must oversee the affairs of his kingdom so that the behavior of his own subjects does not endanger the unity we are trying to establish. In so doing, he will not only benefit his people by contribut-ing toward the maintenance of a general peace, but his own state will become secure if he can prevent, through sound policies, the disturbances that result from a disruption of morals and unbridled license.

Document 1.39

William Penn: The Peace of Europe

From *The Present and Future Peace of Europe,*
seventeenth century

He must not be a man but a statue of brass or stone, whose bowels do not melt when he beholds the bloody tragedies of this war. . . .* What can we desire better than peace, but the grace to use it? . . .

Government then is the prevention or cure of disorder, and the means of justice, as that is the means of peace: for this reason there are sessions, terms, assizes, and parliaments, to overrule men's passions and resentments, so that they may not be judges in their own cause, nor

* Penn wrote during the War of the League of Augsburg (1688–1697), in which England and the Netherlands were allied against France, which threatened their commercial empires and the territory of the Holy Roman Empire. In England the war was mainly supported by mercantile interests and opposed by landowning classes. Penn appealed to practical economic and political considerations in his essay, although he was motivated by religious convictions. He had become a leading Quaker and had founded the Pennsylvania colony as an experiment in Quaker governance.

punishers of their own wrongs. . . . Not that men do not know what is right, their excesses, and wherein they are to blame—by no means: nothing is plainer to them. But so depraved is human nature, that without compulsion some way or other, too many would not readily be brought to do what they know is right and fit, or avoid what they know they should not do. . . .

In my first section, I showed the desirableness of peace; in my next, the truest means of it, to wit, justice and not war. And in my last, that this justice was the fruit of government, as government itself was the result of society which first came from a reasonable design in men of peace. Now if the sovereign princes of Europe . . . would delegate their representatives to meet in a general diet, estates, or parliament, and there establish rules of justice . . . and bring before this sovereign assembly all differences between one sovereign and another . . . , then if any of the sovereignties that constitute the diet should refuse to submit their claim or pretensions to the whole, or to abide by and fulfill its judgment thereof, should resort to arms or delay their compliance, in that case all the other sovereignties, united as one force, would compel the submission of the dispute and enforce a sentence so that peace would be obtained and continued in Europe. . . .

The composition and proportion of this sovereign body, or imperial state, does, at first glance, seem to carry with it no small difficulty as to how to distribute votes, given the inequality of the princes and states. But . . . if it is possible to have an estimate of the yearly value of the several sovereign countries whose delegates are to make up this august assembly, then the determination of the [proportionate] number of persons or votes in the states for every sovereignty will not be impracticable. . . .

To avoid quarrels over precedence, the [assembly] room may be round and have various doors at which to come in and go out. If the whole number [of delegates] were cast in tens, with each choosing one individual, those designated might preside by turns, being the one to whom all speeches should be addressed, and who should collect the sense of the debates, and state the question for a vote, which, in my opinion, should be by [secret] ballot after the prudent and commendable method of the Venetians. . . .*

I will conclude this my proposal for a European, sovereign, or imperial diet, parliament, or estates with the point which I have touched upon

* The bulk of Penn's long essay consists of practical suggestions of this kind and of answers to possible objections to the scheme of government.

before . . . , that by the same rules of justice and prudence by which parents and masters govern their families, and magistrates their cities, and estates their republics, and princes and kings their principalities and kingdoms, Europe may obtain and preserve peace among her sovereignties. For wars are the duels of princes; and as government in kingdoms and states prevents men from being judges and executioners for themselves, overrules private passions as to injuries or revenge, and subjects the great as well as the small to the rule of justice, so that power might not vanquish or oppress right, . . . it will not be hard to conceive or frame, nor even to implement the design I have here proposed.

Document 1.40

Jean-Jacques Rousseau: European Confederation

From *A Project of Perpetual Peace,* eighteenth century

Let us agree, then, that in relation to one another the European powers are properly speaking in a state of war, and that all the partial treaties between particular powers represent passing truces rather than true peace, either because these treaties have generally no other guarantee than that of the contracting parties, or because the rights of the two parties are never thoroughly settled. . . .

Once the sources of the evil are recognized, they indicate their own remedy, if any such exists. Everyone sees that all societies are molded by common interests; that all divisions spring from opposing interests; that a thousand accidental occurrences can change and modify both these factors, once society is called into being; therefore there must necessarily be some power with sanctions to regulate and organize the movements of its members, in order to give to common interests and mutual engagements that degree of solidity which they could not assume by themselves. . . .

Let us now see in what way this great work, begun by chance, can be brought to perfection by reason, and how the free and voluntary fellowship which unites the European States, by assuming the strength and stability of a true political body, can be changed into a real Confederation.

. . . it is necessary that the Confederation should be so general that no considerable Power would refuse to join it; that it should have a judicial tribunal with power to establish laws and regulations binding on all its members; that it should have an enforcing and coercive power to constrain each state to submit to the common counsels, whether for action or for abstention. Finally, that it should be firm and enduring, so that its members should be prevented from detaching themselves from it at will the moment they think they see their own particular interest running contrary to the general interest. . . .

From time to time here are held amongst us, under the name of congresses, general diets whither representatives of all the states of Europe solemnly go only to return as they went; where they assemble together to say nothing; where all public matters are handled pettily; where there are full debates on such questions as whether the table shall be round or square, whether the hall shall have more or fewer doors, whether such a plenipotentiary shall have his face or his back to the window, whether another shall walk two inches more or less in paying a call, and a thousand other questions of equal importance, which have been uselessly discussed for three centuries, and which are assuredly worthy to occupy the politicians of our own.

Possibly the members of one of the assemblies may some day be endowed with common sense; . . . they may receive orders from their respective sovereigns to sign the treaty of the general confederation, which I suppose to be summarily contained in the five following articles.

By the first, the contracting sovereigns shall establish amongst themselves a perpetual and irrevocable alliance, and name plenipotentiaries to hold in some fixed place a permanent Diet or Congress, where the differences of contracting parties would be regulated and settled by way of arbitration or judicial decisions.

By the second shall be specified the number of sovereigns whose plenipotentiaries are to have a voice in the assembly, those who are to be invited to agree to the treaty, the order, the time, and the manner in which the presidency shall pass from one to the other for equal terms, and finally the relative quota of the contributions to the common expenses and the manner of raising them.

By the third, the Confederation shall guarantee to its members the possession and government of all the states each of them controls at the moment, as well as the succession, elective or hereditary, according to whichever is established by the fundamental laws of each country; and in order to put an end once and for all to all the disputes which are constantly reviving, it shall be agreed to take present possession and the latest treaties as the basis of the mutual rights of the contracting Powers, . . . no member being permitted under any pretext whatsoever to take the law into his own hands, or take up arms against his fellow members.

By the fourth the cases shall be specified in which any Ally guilty of infringing the Treaty is to be put under the ban of Europe and proclaimed a common enemy—that is to say, if he refuse to carry out the decisions of the great Alliance, if he make preparations for war, if he negotiates treaties contrary to the terms of the Confederation, and if he take up arms to resist it or to attack any one of the Allies.

It shall be agreed also by the same article that the States shall arm and act together offensively . . . and at the common expense against any state under the ban of Europe, until it shall have laid down its arms, carried out the sentences and rulings of the Congress, repaired the wrongs, refunded the costs, and even given compensation for any warlike preparations it may have made contrary to the Treaty.

Lastly, by the fifth article, the plenipotentiaries of the European Federal Body shall always have the power, on the instructions of their Courts, to frame in the Diet by a majority of votes . . . the regulations which they shall judge to be important in order to secure all possible advantages to the European Republic and each one of its members; but it shall never be possible to change any of these five fundamental articles except with the unanimous consent of all the members of the Confederation. . . .

What are the questions that must be put to enable us to form a correct judgment upon this system ? . . .

The first question is whether the proposed Confederation would attain its end with certainty and be sufficient to give to Europe a solid and enduring peace; the second, whether it is to the interest of the rulers to establish this Confederation and to purchase a stable peace at this price. . . .

As to that, let us consider the motives which make princes take up arms. These motives are either to make conquests or to defend themselves against an invader, or to weaken a too powerful neighbor, or to maintain their own rights when assailed, or to end a quarrel which has not been settled amicably, or lastly to fulfill the engagements of a treaty. There is neither cause of nor pretext for war that you cannot place under one of these six heads. But it is evident that none of these six motives can exist in the new state of things that I contemplate.

First, conquests will have to be renounced from the impossibility of making them, considering that everyone is sure to be stopped on the way by greater forces than those he is able to marshal; thus, whilst risking the loss of everything, it is beyond his power to gain anything. . . .

The same reason which deprives each prince of any hope of conquests deprives him at the same time of any fear of being attacked; and not only are his estates (guaranteed to him by all Europe) assured to him just as are the private possessions of the citizens in a civilized country, but they are even more so than were he their own sole defender, in proportion as the whole of Europe is stronger than he is alone. . . .

As regards maintaining their rights, it must first be said that innumerable obscure quibbles and intricate claims will be completely swept away by the third article of the confederation, which settles definitely all the reciprocal rights of the Allied Sovereigns upon the basis of present possession. . . . The same thing can be said of the injuries, wrongs, and reparations, and of all the different unforeseen disputes which might arise between two sovereigns; the same power which has to defend their rights, has to redress their grievances. . . .

It is impossible therefore for the confederation once established to leave any seeds of war amongst its members, or for its object of Perpetual Peace not to be perfectly realized by the proposed scheme if it were carried out.

It remains for us now to examine the other question, which concerns the advantage of the contracting parties; for one feels how vain it would be to give the public interest precedence over the private. To prove that peace is generally preferable to war means nothing to whosoever thinks he has reasons for preferring war to peace, and to show him how to establish a lasting peace is only to incite him to oppose it.

In fact, they will say, you take away from Sovereigns the right of doing justice to themselves, that is to say the precious right of being unjust when they please. You take away from them the power of aggrandizing themselves at the expense of their neighbors. You make them renounce . . . this display of power and terror with which they like to frighten the world, and that pride of conquest from which they derive their renown; in a word, you force them to be just and peaceable. What will be the compensations for so many cruel deprivations?

I should not be so bold as to reply with the Abbé de Saint-Pierre that the true glory of princes consists in securing the public good and the happiness of their people; . . . let us confine ourselves to their interests. . . .

As to the dependence which each one will be under to the common tribunal, it is very clear that it will diminish none of the rights of sovereignty, but on the contrary will strengthen them, and will make them more assured by article three, which guarantees to each one not only his territory against all foreign invasion, but also his authority against all rebellion by his subjects. The princes accordingly will be none the less absolute, and their crowns will be all the more secure, so that in submitting their disputes to the judgment of the Diet as among equals, and renouncing the dangerous power of seizing the possessions of others they only make sure of their true rights and give up those which do not belong to them. . . .

Let us also recapitulate the advantages of European arbitration for the princes of the confederation.

(1) A complete assurance that their present and future quarrels will always be terminated without war. . . .

(2) Matters of dispute eliminated or reduced to a very small compass by the cancellation of all bygone claims which will compensate the nation for what they give up and confirm them in what they possess.

(3) Entire and perpetual security of the person of the prince and of his family and of his territories and of the order of succession fixed by the laws of each country, both against the presumption of unjust and ambitious pretenders and against the revolts of rebel subjects.

(4) Perfect certainty of the execution of all reciprocal engagements between prince and prince by the guarantee of the European Commonwealth.

(5) Perfect and perpetual liberty and security of trade, both between state and state and for each state in distant lands.

(6) Total and perpetual suppression of their extraordinary military expenditure by land and by sea in time of war, and considerable diminution of their ordinary expenditure in time of peace.

(7) A marked progress in agriculture and population, in the wealth of the state, and in the revenues of the prince.

(8) An opportunity for the promotion of all the institutions which can increase the glory and authority of the sovereign, the public resources, and the happiness of the people.

Certainly it does not follow that the sovereigns would adopt this project (who can answer for other people's intelligence?) but only that they would adopt it if they consulted their true interests; for the reader must observe that we have not supposed men to be such as they ought to be—good, generous, disinterested, and loving public good from motives of human sympathy—but such as they are, unjust, greedy, and preferring their own interests to everything else. The only thing we assume on their behalf is enough intelligence to see what is useful to themselves, and enough courage to achieve their own happiness. If, in spite of all this, this project is not carried into execution, it is not because it is chimerical, it is because men are crazy and because to be sane in the midst of madmen is a sort of folly.

Document 1.41

Immanuel Kant: Perpetual Peace

From *Perpetual Peace: A Philosophical Essay,*
eighteenth century

First Section

Containing the Preliminary Articles of Perpetual Peace Between States *

1. "No treaty of peace shall be regarded as valid, if made with the secret reservation of material for a future war."†

2. "No state having an independent existence—whether it be great or small—shall be acquired by another through inheritance, exchange, purchase or donation."

3. "Standing armies . . . shall be abolished in course of time."

4. "No national debts shall be contracted in connection with the external affairs of the state."

5. "No state shall violently interfere with the constitution and administration of another."

6. "No state at war with another shall countenance such modes of hostility as would make mutual confidence impossible in a subsequent state of peace; such are the employment of assassins . . . or of poisoners . . . , breaches of capitulation, the instigation and making use of treachery . . . in the hostile state."

Second Section
Containing the Definitive Articles
of a Perpetual Peace Between States

A state of peace among men who live side by side is not the natural state . . . , which is rather to be described as a state of war; that is to say, although there is not perhaps always actual open hostility, yet there is a constant threatening that an outbreak may occur. Thus the state of peace must be *established.* . . .

---

* Kant framed his essay as though its propositions were articles in a treaty. Much more than that, they are elements of an inquiry into the relationship of politics and morality, and their substance is developed in his commentary on them. The "preliminary articles" are the conditions for the peaceful coexistence of sovereign states, and the "definitive articles" are the conditions for international order.

† Kant distinguishes a general treaty of peace, which is a contract not to go to war, from a peace treaty settling a particular dispute, which is a form of truce.

1. "The civil constitution of each state shall be republican." *

. . . If, as must be so under this constitution, the consent of the subjects is required to determine whether there shall be war or not, nothing is more natural than that they should weigh the matter well, before undertaking such a bad business. . . .

2. "The law of nations shall be founded on a federation of free states." . . .

The method by which states prosecute their rights can never be by process of law—as it is where there is an external tribunal—but only by war. Through this means, however, and its favorable issue, victory, the question of right is never decided. . . . Hence there must be an alliance of a particular kind which we may call a covenant of peace *(foedus pacificum)*, which would differ from a treaty of peace *(pactum pacis)* in this respect, that the latter merely puts an end to one war, while the former would seek to put an end to war for ever. . . .

. . . For states, in their relation to one another, there can be, according to reason, no other way of advancing from that lawless condition which unceasing war implies, than by giving up their savage lawless freedom, just as individual men have done, and yielding to the coercion of public laws. . . . States, however, [reject this, so that] instead of the positive idea of a world-republic, if all is not to be lost, only the negative substitute for it, a federation averting war, maintaining its ground and ever extending over the world may stop the current of this tendency to war and shrinking from the control of law. . . .

3. "The rights of men, as citizens of the world, shall be limited to the conditions of universal hospitality." †

We are speaking here, as in the previous articles, not of philanthropy, but of right; and in this sphere hospitality signifies the claim of a stranger entering foreign territory to be treated by its owner without hostility. . . . These relations may at least come under the public control of law, and thus the human race may be brought nearer the realization of a cosmopolitan constitution.

. . . the inhospitable behavior of the civilized nations, especially the commercial states of our continent, . . . on visiting foreign lands and

---

* Kant distinguishes republican government, which is representative and in which executive and legislative functions are separated, from democratic government, in which sovereign authority belongs only to the people as a whole.

† Kant here adds to the law of nations a concept of world citizenship *(jus cosmopoliticum)* which he acknowledges is based on a minimal, and therefore universal, human right. This right of hospitality, which applies to both host and visitor, is the basis for Kant's philosophical condemnation of colonialism.

races—this being the equivalent in their eyes to conquest—is such as to fill us with horror.

Appendix 1
On the Disagreement between Morals and Politics with Reference to Perpetual Peace

Politics says, "Be wise as serpents"; morals adds the limiting condition, "and guileless as doves." If these precepts cannot stand together in one command, then there is a real quarrel between politics and morals.

The moral politician will always act upon the following principle: "If certain defects which could not have been avoided are found in the political constitution or foreign relations of a state, it is a duty for all, especially for the rulers of the state, to apply their whole energy to correcting them as soon as possible . . . ; and this they should do even at a sacrifice of their own interest." . . .

. . . in theory, there is no quarrel between morals and politics. But subjectively, in the self-seeking tendencies of men . . . this disagreement in principle exists and may always survive; for . . . the true courage of virtue in the present case lies not so much in facing the evils and self-sacrifices which must be met here as in firmly confronting the evil principle in our own nature and conquering its wiles. . . .

. . . the pure principles of right have objective reality—that is to say, [they] are capable of being practically realized—and consequently . . . politics in the real sense cannot take a step forward without first paying homage to the principles of morals. . . . We cannot devise a happy medium between right and expediency, a right pragmatically conditioned. But all politics must bend the knee to the principle of right, and may, in that way, hope to reach, although slowly perhaps, a level whence it may shine upon men for all time.

Document 1.42
Anarcharsis Cloots, Revolutionary Peace
From *The Universal Republic,** eighteenth century

We must insist on complete fusion, a confederation of individuals, or else corporate bodies will reappear with their divisive spirits. And

---

* Cloots was a German noble from West Prussia who between 1776 and 1784 was converted to Paris culture and, in 1789, to the French Revolution. In this treatise of 1793, why are corporate groupings dangerous? Because it is more difficult to contain them within legal parameters than for simple individuals. . . . Provincial and national bodies are the greatest affliction of the human species. . . . One body is not likely to war against itself, and humanity will live in peace when it will form one single body, one nation alone.

A dispute that [now] costs the lives of millions of men, that ravages towns and cities, that destroys monuments, that desolates the countryside and workshops, that demands the construction of prisons called fortresses and the support of murderers called soldiers—such a dispute would cost no more than two sheets of paper or two appearances before a justice of the peace, when all men are citizens of the same nation. Italians in Genoa war against Italians in Venice, but French in Nantes only go to court against French in Bordeaux. We would never have any bloody entanglements with London or The Hague if France [included those areas].

. . . Let us take advantage of our ascendancy over the spirit of divided peoples. Let us profit from our imposing size and our favorable geographic position in the center of Europe on the [Atlantic] Ocean and on the Mediterranean. Let us exploit the universality of our language. . . . One nation, one assembly, one prince.* How can this utopian plan, which uncomprehending thinkers compare to the dream of the Abbé de Saint-Pierre, be attained? . . . Saint-Pierre asked the incoherent powers of Europe to form a bizarre and ridiculous confederation, which would have called for war as much as peace; I am proposing an absolute leveling, a complete overthrow of all the barriers which check the interests of the human family. . . . That balance [of European power] will not be able to tilt [lean] towards liberty for a moment unless all the tyrants are struck by a lightening bolt.

. . . Ancient rivalries will disappear along with ancient names and demarcations. The economy will be immense, the taxes will be light and happiness will be unfettered. . . . Everything that does not negate social life shall have its fullest development. . . . Humanity will triumph over the partisans of slavery. . . . the universal establishment of the Rights of Man will replace universal tyranny.

I challenge anyone to show me a single article of our Declaration of

---

he argued that the Revolution had to be extended, even forcibly, to all humanity. He was executed during the Great Terror of March 1794.

* "Prince" should be understood as "executive authority."

Rights* which cannot be applied to all peoples, to all climates, ... to men of color, to Poles, to Genevese. .... It will be on the debris of all the thrones that we will build the edifice of the universal republic. We know now what free men can do, and the proud and measured capabilities of the French people since the King's flight let us envision the harmony of the earth after the fall of the oppressors. ....

The golden age will reappear when the people rule ... ; the revolution of France is the beginning of revolution in the world. As long as we have neighbors, armies, fortresses, our existence will be precarious and insecure; we will be tested by stormy violence. Generous and courageous children of free Nature: imagine that the aim of our association means simply the individual and group conservation of liberty, property, and security. . . ; give the single sovereign people its primary dignity and you will assure the happiness of France and of the Universe eternally.

---

* The Declaration of the Rights of Man and Citizen, 26 August 1789, by which the French Revolution replaced feudalism with the rule of law, citizenship, and collective sovereignty. Below, the "King's flight" refers to the fact that Louis XVI and Marie Antoinette fled to Varennes in June 1791. They were captured and returned to Paris, where they had to accept the constitution of 1791.

2

Citizen Initiatives and Official Agreements
1815–1914

Between the wars of the French Revolution and the outbreak of the Great War of 1914, the idea of peace advocacy was transformed into its modern forms of pacifism and liberal internationalism. From religious and philosophical foundations, peace thinking became a secular ideology that argued for a lawful international order and respect for the rights of peoples. Citizens organized for that cause. By the early twentieth century there were perhaps three hundred thousand European and North American peace activists from over a hundred peace societies that together formed a transnational movement and shared a common ideology they called "pacifism."[1] The rise of organized citizen peace initiatives, their varied approaches, and some tentative official agreements to limit warfare are the themes of this chapter.

The first part documents a major innovation in thinking about peace —the idea that citizen organization and initiative can make a difference in international relations. The wars of the French Revolutionary years focused attention on the massive human costs of violent conflict, and one result was the creation of the first private citizen peace societies. Self-styled "friends of peace" were initially drawn from dissenting Protestant churches whose active members were already engaged in anti-slavery campaigns. This white, male, middle-class membership sought to persuade contemporaries that war violated the teachings of Jesus Christ— that it was collective murder and not a legitimate means to a political end.

These peace societies differed from earlier "peace churches," for which peace was the special ethic of an already committed membership.

The new citizen peace groups reached out to legislatures, cabinets, executives, eminent leaders, and God-fearing Christians everywhere. Gradually their Gospel appeal was replaced by the newer languages of political economy, sociology, international law, history, and anthropology, and peace advocates developed a secular vocabulary. By mid-century, "friends of peace"(as they often called themselves) convened international congresses that attracted intellectual and political leaders from Europe and North America.

Public campaigns against warfare were affected by nineteenth-century trends that were reshaping western civilization, particularly industrialization, the penetration of hitherto inaccessible continents by global traders and colonizers, and the slow growth of constitutional and democratic practices in some areas of Europe. A major war could disrupt supplies of raw materials needed by European factories, with frightening social and economic consequences, and it would endanger the merchant shipping of even neutral nations. Seeking security in an armed peace, or deterrence, modern nations diverted resources and investment from their social and economic infrastructure to military buildup. Large standing armies and elite officer corps, typical of continental states, required public taxation that was increasingly challenged as wasteful and antidemocratic.

In response to these changes, and encouraged by new studies in political economy, a vocal segment of the middle classes emphasized the practical considerations of peace. Continental peace advocates modified the religious and ethical assertions characteristic of the early Anglo-American peace societies. In addition, they slowly incorporated new democratic ideals, especially human rights, into proposals for organized international peace. Before the American and French Revolutions, most peace theorists accepted the sovereign right of kings over their subjects. Afterwards such thinking became anachronistic, and peace proposals assumed that a just international order required the establishment of just domestic systems.

The promise of citizen peace activism was symbolized by the successful, widely publicized peace congress of 1849 in Paris, presided over by the eminent French author Victor Hugo. Any sense of progress was abruptly shattered, however, when from 1854 to 1871 the horrendous destructiveness of modern warfare was dramatized in the Crimean War, the American Civil War, and wars of national unification by Italy and Germany—conflicts which, except for the Crimean War, were legitimated by claims of liberation and national self-determination.

When the artillery was silenced in 1871, peace activists reappeared quickly and in many new areas. During the last thirty years of the century, their societies and publications spread throughout Europe and the United States, and women joined men in the cause. In 1889, French and British legislative leaders created the Interparliamentary Conference for International Arbitration, later renamed the Interparliamentary Union. That same year a European meeting began the Universal Peace Congresses, which two years later established a headquarters in Bern as the International Peace Bureau.[2] Both of these peace "internationals" sought to inform human relations with a new vision of peace. Bertha von Suttner, a major leader of the movement, captured that vision in her Nobel Peace Prize speech of 1906, when she observed that "two philosophies, two eras of civilization, are wrestling with one another and that a vigorous new spirit is supplanting the . . . old" (document 2.10). Thus the fledgling peace movement worked for an orderly, legal, international system that would replace the ancient order based on hierarchy, authority, militarism, and warfare.

The second part of this chapter documents several currents of citizen peace thinking, each with its distinctive programs, that evolved by the twentieth century: liberal internationalism, economic critiques of war; social justice, including socialism; objections to colonial exploitation; and the refusal to obey illegitimate authority, including both Christian nonresistance and pragmatic noncooperation.

Although all peace advocates promoted international order, it is helpful to distinguish some as *internationalists* because they emphasized an order that would be achieved through inter-nation relations. These activists were mostly middle-class, and their leaders included economic liberals who wanted to free commercial intercourse from governmental control. Some of them advocated a permanent congress of nations, an international court, or even European union. Most of them emphasized international law and agreements to use negotiation, mediation, and arbitration before declaring war. By the middle of the nineteenth century there was already an international campaign for arbitration treaties, and it expanded when Great Britain and the United States successfully arbitrated a dispute over Britain's violation of its neutrality during the American Civil War. By the twentieth century, some internationalists were advocating international organization.

For a wide array of peace activists, including most of those in the Interparliamentary Union, liberal internationalism was the only approach likely to gain any government support. Its most famous European exponent was Frédéric Passy, co-winner of the first Nobel Peace Prize (1901). In the United States it came to be associated with the Carnegie

Endowment for International Peace, and in Tsarist Russia with the circle around Pavel Milyukov. It was not a position that abjured war altogether, and some of its supporters even agreed that an international army or police would be needed to enforce peace.

Leading internationalists criticized war economically, both for its destructiveness and waste, and also on the grounds that the arms race diverted resources from more constructive investment (Xenophon had said as much). Dynamic economies require conditions of peaceful, open exchange, which, they maintained, could be strengthened by freeing trade and cutting off funds for munitions industries with a vested interest in warfare.

A more encompassing approach to peace than either inter-nation or economic arrangements was developed by nineteenth-century democratic-republicans and socialists. In some respects they followed Kant's assertion that republican governments are requisite for international order, but they also extended his argument from political participation to include social justice.

Democratic-republicans argued that no oppressed people could be expected to renounce its inalienable right to free itself, by force if necessary, without national self-determination, secular education, a disestablished church, universal suffrage, constitutional government, and guarantees of civil rights. Thus, for instance, a European pact to establish an arbitration tribunal would be illegitimate if the signatories remained silent on Russian control of Poland or British repression of Ireland. For some activists human rights included women's emancipation, and by the end of the century peace issues and suffrage campaigns were often joined.

For socialists, domestic justice required a redistribution of wealth and a change in the control of property. Most of them insisted that their program was so distinctive that they could not cooperate with democrats and republicans, despite the weakness of both groups relative to those in power. Still, socialist thinkers and organizations could not avoid the issue of peace, even though initially it was not their primary concern. The International Working Men's Association (the First International) was formed in 1864. Under the leadership of Karl Marx, it became a highly centralized party of individual members, but it was nonetheless racked by ideological controversy until it was formally disbanded in 1876. In those years socialists were forced by wars of national unification to develop positions on militarism, conscription, the conditions of a just war, and the issue of nationalism. The Second International Association of the Working Man (the Second International) was organized in 1889 as a loose federation of socialist parties. War-related issues increasingly intruded upon its meetings and divided socialists between the competing demands of international class solidarity, on the one hand, and of the workers' patriotic attachments, on the other.

Extending their concern for social justice to imperialism, some peace advocates challenged the creation of colonial empires by war. Although few of them doubted the inherent superiority of Europeans and Americans, or their ethical obligation to uplift other peoples, they argued that the West contradicted its own ideals when it forced its civilization on other cultures for the purpose of exploitation. In words that recalled those of Isocrates, David Starr Jordan warned his fellow Americans against imperialism: "The greatness of a nation lies not in its bigness but in its justice, in the wisdom and virtue of its people, and in the prosperity of their individual affairs."[3]

Another current of peace thought was noncooperation with illegitimate authority. Previously identified with religious communities, the idea of nonresistance was interpreted as the social responsibility of the individual in the writing of Henry David Thoreau. Moreover, the religious appeal of Anglo-American activists early in the century was amplified later by Leo Tolstoy in Russia, who demanded absolute noncompliance with the State, nonresistance to violence, and refusal to bear arms. Only when men refuse to do evil, he argued, will evil not be done. Meanwhile, pragmatic forms of noncooperation were developed in Hungary, especially under the leadership of Ferenc Deák, and in the Finnish campaign against Russification of 1898 to 1905. Those efforts to mobilize populations for nonviolent resistance to oppressive authority anticipated the nonviolent struggle that was conducted by the Indian leader Mohandas Gandhi in the twentieth century.

The third part of the chapter documents government negotiations to limit or avoid the horrific consequences of industrial weaponry. A series of conventions, beginning with the creation of the International Red Cross (1864) and concluding with two conferences at The Hague (1899 and 1907), produced a new element in peace thinking: the regulation and containment of warfare by international agreement. There were short-lived treaties outlawing specific weapons, longer-lasting agreements on the treatment of innocents, the wounded, and prisoners, and even tentative steps toward the pacific settlement of disputes. They provided a basis for the more complex international arrangements of the twentieth century.

In August 1914 none of the official pledges signed by the Powers nor any of the citizen initiatives—bourgeois or socialist—were sufficient to prevent the explosion that thinking people had feared. Peace activists of the nineteenth century, while calling for a peaceful international order, had overwhelmingly emphasized their national loyalty. Suddenly those two values were polarized. The result was that the First World War profoundly altered peace activism: liberal internationalists divided, the majority supporting the war in the hope of building a more peaceful postwar order, a minority of them rejecting warfare and forming new societies; socialists also divided over support or opposition to the war, thus contributing to the destruction of the Second International; women's peace groups became more assertive and activist; and nonresistant pacifists became conscientious objectors to military service.

The warnings of nineteenth-century peace prophets about the pyramids of dead in modern warfare came true. In place of the quick victory promised by the generals, four years of raging conflict produced massive death and disease, economic collapse, the decline of European primacy, political revolution in Russia, and the emergence of the United States as a major world power. Although the idea of peace as international order was still associated with the military power of sovereign nations, the nineteenth century had nonetheless set precedents for the twentieth: the rise of citizen peace organizations, varied approaches to peace and internationalism, and a few tentative steps toward intergovernmental negotiations to constrain war.

Initiatives and Organizations

In 1815, as European diplomats gathered in Vienna to liquidate the legacy of the French Revolution and Napoleon, small groups of private citizens in the United States and in England held their own meetings to organize societies opposed to war. Thus began a century of citizen action against war and in favor of a rule of law to solve conflicts among civilized states. By 1914, when World War I broke out, there were peace activists from the Urals to the Rocky Mountains, and in Japan and Australia. What arguments did they develop, and what kinds of societies did they form?

Initially they were religious. Angered at the waste of blood and treasure in twenty-five years of war and revolution in Europe and, to a lesser extent, in the United States, private citizens and religious leaders organized peace societies in New York, Massachusetts, and Ohio in 1815, and in London the next year. Their object was to persuade the public and government leaders that among Christian nations war was not viable, moral, or acceptable. That was the point of the widely distributed essay *A Solemn Review of the Custom of War Showing that War is the Effect of a Popular Delusion and Proposing a Remedy* (document 2.1). In it Noah Worcester, a Unitarian minister and the founder of the Massachusetts Peace Society, blended religious and utilitarian arguments. As the century progressed and peace societies spread from the Atlantic borderlands across the European continent, the early religious rhetoric was muted in favor of secular, practical arguments for a rule of law among civilized nations.

The change from appeals based on the teachings of Jesus Christ to rational, pragmatic, and legalistic arguments is illustrated in a pamphlet by Angelo Umiltà (document 2.2) that summarized the work of the Ligue Internationale de la Paix et de la Liberté (1867–1936). Founded at a stormy congress in Geneva, presided over by the Italian revolutionary and patriot Giuseppe Garibaldi, the league represented the "democratic" or "radical" wing of the continental peace movement. It promoted "civil education" by unofficial citizen groups, and it related international peace to civic and political rights. Efforts were made from 1864 to 1869 to collaborate with the First International, but they failed because radical democrats and socialists disagreed on the essentials of democracy.

Women's involvement in peace activism became ever more common during the nineteenth century. In Germany, whose culture was then hostile to advocates of both feminism and peace, the labors of Margarethe Leonore Selenka led to an explosion of support from women's associations for the Hague Peace Conference of 1899. Selenka coordinated an international women's campaign that collected several million signatures on petitions and held demonstrations in Europe, North America, and Japan. Afterward, she summarized women's strategy to encourage diplomats to take the Hague Conference agenda seriously (document 2.3). Her observation that pacifism was a natural issue for women became a widely shared view among middle-class peace advocates before World War I.

The argument that peace could be achieved through education also became increasingly familiar as public education expanded. In the United States early in the twentieth century, Lucia Ames Mead added peace education to the women's and social issues about which she was active. Believing in the gradual transformation of public opinion, she urged a new curriculum to train teachers and their students in the principles of the rule of law. In particular, she offered a new definition of patriotism and a vision of history that emphasized common human achievements in place of martial and political chronologies (document 2.4). Mead's initiatives were similar to those undertaken by women teachers active in the peace movements of Great Britain, France, Italy, Belgium, and to a lesser extent, Germany.

In Tsarist Russia, where political activity was severely restricted, peace societies were created in major urban centers such as St. Petersburg, Moscow, Kiev, Odessa, Riga, and Tallinin in the decade before World War I. The Moscow society, chartered in June 1909 (document 2.5), was founded by members of the State Duma, professors of international law, and members of the "People's Freedom" political party. Among the most fervent supporters of international peace in Tsarist Russia was Pavel Nikolaevich Milyukov, a professor of history and leader of the Constitutional Democratic Party (and briefly minister of foreign affairs in the Provisional Government of 1917). Milyukov argued that the arbitrary force of war had become "no less utopian" than the idea of nonresistant peace, and that the interdependence of the modern world requires "peaceful coexistence" (document 2.6).

Document 2.1

Noah Worcester: The Custom of War

From A Solemn Review of the Custom of War, 1815

War has been so long fashionable among all nations, that its enormity is but little regarded; . . . it is usually considered as an evil necessary and unavoidable. Perhaps it is really so in the present state of society, and the present views of mankind. But the question to be considered is this: cannot the state of society and the views of civilized men be so changed as to abolish a barbarous custom . . . ?

Some may be ready to exclaim, none but God can produce such an effect as the abolition of war; and we must wait for the millennial day, . . . but God works by human agency and human means. . . . If ever there shall be a millennium in which the sword will cease to devour, it will probably be effected by the blessing of God on the benevolent exertions of enlightened men. . . .

A war between two nations is generally produced by the influence of a small number of ambitious and unprincipled individuals; while the greater part of the nation has no hand in the business until war is proclaimed.

A vast majority of every civilized nation have an aversion to war, such an aversion that it requires much effort and management to work up their passions. . . . [Where peoples are civilized and Christians] more powerful exertions are necessary to excite what is called the *war spirit*. . . . If then, as great exertions should be made to excite a just abhorrence of war as have often been made to excite a war spirit, . . . we may be very certain that rulers would find little encouragement to engage in any war, which is not strictly defensive. And as soon as offensive wars shall cease, defensive wars will of course be unknown.

. . . Every soldier ought to be impressed with the idea that offensive war is murderous, and that no government on earth has any right to compel him to shed blood in a wanton and aggressive war. . . .

. . . if the eyes of people could be opened in regard to the evils and delusions of war, would it not be easy to form a confederacy of nations, and organize a high court of equity, to decide national controversies? Why might not such a court be composed of some of the most eminent characters from each nation, and a compliance with the decision of the court be made a point of national honor. . . ?

Let every Christian seriously consider the malignant nature of that spirit which war makers evidently wish to excite, and compare it with the temper of Jesus, and where is the Christian who would not shudder at the thought of dying in the exercise of the common war spirit. . . .

Is it not possible to form powerful peace societies, in every nation in Christendom, whose object shall be to support government and to secure the nation from war? . . . Let printing presses be established . . . to fill every land with news papers, tracts and periodical works. . . . [Let education for peace have a place in] families, common schools, academies and universities. . . . Let lawyers, politicians and divines, and men of every class who can write or speak, consecrate their talents to the diffusion of light, and love, and peace, . . . that "the sword shall *not* devour forever."

Document 2.2

Angelo Umiltà: The International League

From "A Lecture to the Friends of Peace," 1891

Founded in Geneva in September 1867 under the patronage of Victor Hugo and the honorary presidency of Garibaldi, the International League for Peace and Freedom is an association of free and committed people, of any nationality, who, supporting the ideas of . . . Immanuel Kant, maintain that policy must be the application of morality, that human life is inviolable. Based on the principle of the autonomy of the human person, the League insists that respect for the inviolability and independence of peoples is an unchallengeable premise. From the principle of liberty follows that of equality, which . . . leads to the solidarity of interests and human and national fraternity among truly civilized peoples.

The nation, large or small, is . . . created by nature, by language, tradition, history and the will of those who make it up. To attack the liberty, the independence, the territorial integrity of a civilized nation . . . is like invading a neighbor's home, running him out and expropriating his property. . . .

Thus, war among civilized peoples is a *crime:* the so-called right to make war does not exist—it is confused with the right to self-defense, a sacred right, . . . an absolute duty for all men who cherish their families, nations and freedom.

The historical development of humanity has reached the stage where *law* governs the relationship among citizens. . . . Thus, what is possible, useful and necessary for the security and happiness of citizens in each state must be possible, useful and necessary . . . for the security and prosperity of different states. . . .

. . . League activists have never stopped proclaiming that *men* and civilized *peoples* have the *same needs,* the *same interests,* the same *rights,* and the *same duties.* . . .

From 1867, the League defined its terrain. Its principal aim is the *elimination of war* . . . by federation, neutralization and arbitration; it . . . believes as a maxim that the *social question,* inseparable from political questions, must be . . . solved peacefully by the application of the same fundamental ideals—the autonomy of the individual person, . . . liberty, justice, solidarity, intellectual and professional education which is free and obligatory; by the systems of insurance, savings, mutual aid societies, gradually spread through all social classes.

The transformation, reduction and abolition of permanent armies, a scourge for Europe and the principal reason for the current financial collapse and the conditions of inferiority in comparison to the American competitor—there is the object which many [peace] societies are struggling to achieve. The League is a school of civic education; . . . its program that of European democracy. . . . The League realizes the need for Europe to renounce its militaristic regime . . . and create a federation or face degeneration. It wants war to cease being the *ultima ratio* of the powers. . . .

In its journal, *Les Etats-Unis d'Europe,* whose title is also a program, the League developed the principles on which it founded its system of peace keeping: *neutralization, federation, arbitration.*

Document 2.3

Margarethe Leonore Selenka: Women for Peace

From *Women's International Demonstration
for the Peace Conference*, 1899

This publication is addressed . . . to all those women who took part in the Demonstration of the fifteenth of May 1899 on the occasion of the Peace Conference of the Hague* . . . , a lasting remembrance of their co-operation in the memorable act where . . . women of the whole civilized world stood by one another in a firmly-knit bond of unity. . . .

[It] is also intended to arouse within those wider feminine circles . . . , hitherto aloof from the Peace Movement and the Woman's Movement, sympathy and courage to give their help . . . to the solution of important humanitarian questions to which both movements devote their energy. . . . Women have shown by this international action, in which several millions of them participated, that their voice can be emphatically uplifted in the name of a great question. . . . This voice should not again be hushed.

On that day when the Tsar's Manifesto first came to my knowledge, it seemed to me [that] the women of the whole universe, must bear witness. . . . The movement was . . . started on an extensive international scale by means of [a] circular [that was sent to] representatives of the Women's movement in every country where it already had a footing. . . . The result was marvelous: [18 out of 23 countries] joined enthusiastically in the movement. [A public meeting was even organized in Japan.] This success is the more to be admired as in Japan such public demonstrations are naturally something quite new. Not content, the Japanese women have founded a Society . . . which numbers over eight thousand members . . . and which, besides representing the Peace Movement, undertakes the task of elevating the social position of Japanese women. . . .

Of the European countries, Russia especially became engaged . . . under the leadership of Madame Anna de Schabanoff, head physician of the St. Petersburg Children's Hospital. . . . It is true that the Russian women had . . . little prospect of success, as public meetings in general, especially those of a political character, are not allowed in Russia; all the more meritorious therefore was the energy of these enthusiastic leaders

---

* Regarding the 1899 Hague Conference, and the Tsar's invitation, see the commentary in third part of this chapter, and "Official International Agreements," documents 2.33, 2.34, and 2.35.

who [overcame] this obstacle. On the 15th May, fifty public meetings took place [perhaps the first public women's meetings in that country]. . . .

In Spain, also, it was . . . that the first public meetings of women sprang into being. . . .

The entire demonstration so accurately running its course and in which the women of three divisions of the world, in 565 almost simultaneous public assemblies, stood forth, united, bears ample witness to women's activity and their capability of being nobly inspired [in the service] of an important question of humanity and the higher culture; . . . it also shows their power of organizing on a large scale.

The occurrence of the Hague Conference [revealed that] the passive part women had hitherto played in all questions of international politics [was] incompatible with the responsibility concurrent to their new social elevation. . . . The Hague Conference . . . struck the ear and the conscience of a generation of women who . . . in their struggle for new rights, claim . . . the privilege of new duties.

Are not the Peace Question and the Women's Question akin in the origin of their being? Both of them . . . contain a strong ethical element, firmly bound up with the most pressing social and economic needs.

Document 2.4

Lucia Ames Mead: Patriotism and Peace

From *Patriotism and Peace:
How to Teach Them in Schools,* 1910

A college professor with no comprehension of what the new peace movement means, has recently cited the words of certain extremists who, he avers, would remove all reference to wars from history . . . [and] who would make 'mollycoddles' of American boys by disparaging militarism. Possibly there may be persons who would like to falsify history by eliminating all reference to war, but they are not in the new School Peace League, and have no standing in the peace movement. There is no public question so little understood to-day by persons with diplomas and degree and who are intelligent on general subjects as the movement [for peace]. So far from being a movement toward what is negative, invirile, and sentimental, it is intensely practical and aggressive, and demands the highest courage and bravery. It touches current problems of stupendous financial and ethical importance, and it does not concern itself with the millennium.

The league is not composed of "faddists," nor will it seek to add new burdens to the already overcrowded curriculum. Beyond the hour or two of special instruction on Peace Day—May 18—no further claim will be laid on the time schedule. What the league aims to do rather is to lead to a change of emphasis in instruction and of point of view on the part of the teacher; to broaden the relationship between the school and the nation and family of nations; to lessen race prejudice and Chauvinism; and to remove certain current fallacies which are costing the nations yearly vastly more than their whole budgets for education.

The object . . . is to prepare teachers who have not yet studied the movement to realize its scope and their own responsibility in developing that wide sympathy and sense of justice which will make increased invention a blessing and not a menace. Today the physicist and inventor get their largest returns from creating engines of destruction.

The first thing to be emphasized is that justice and peace between nations will be achieved an indefinite time before justice and peace within nations. This is the reverse of the popular notion. No Hague tribunals or international agreements will prevent civil war, or lynchings, or murder. Universal peace, in the sense of justice and good will over all the earth, can be achieved only in an indefinite future . . . when all men are brothers. But the business necessities of the world will stop war between nations a thousand years before humanity masters licentiousness, intemperance, and the evils . . . in our social fabric. . . . [The peace movement] aims to substitute world organization for disorganization, . . . to bring nations to court just as we bring individuals, cities and states to court. The coercive powers will be three—a small international police force, public opinion, and the economic boycott or non-intercourse, as the final penalty.

One fallacy that has misled the layman is that the military expert knows the nation's military needs better than other men do. . . . It is impossible [for men] who have spent forty years in the study of war games . . . to appreciate the new science of world organization and a settlement of international difficulties by world court.

. . . The following facts every teacher should know by heart: In all our three foreign wars since we became a republic less than 15,000 men were slain by foreign bullets; but every year more than ten times as many of our citizens are slain by preventable tuberculosis! In four recent years 60,000 more citizens have been killed by accident than were killed by bullets or died of wounds in four years of Civil War! We destroy annually six or seven times as much by fire as does all Europe. We have criminally wasted our forests, our water power, our free land and the deposits in our mines. Our only enemies are within. Yet we are spending two-thirds of our national revenue on past war and future war . . . to defend us from suppositious foreign foes [rather] than from the real foes that attack our lives and property. . . .

Document 2.5

The Charter of the Moscow Peace Society

From *Peace Society in Moscow*, 1913

The goals of the Society [are]:

(a) research into and popularization of information about international law; educating the public about international peace, arbitration tribunals and international peace conferences;

(b) through publications and lectures, the Society will disseminate information about the increasing interdependence of peoples that are the result of scientific, economic, cultural and philanthropic developments;

(c) The Society will advocate respect for the humanitarian needs of prisoners, war wounded, women and children in wartime and the importance of respecting religious and cultural monuments during wartime;

(d) The Society will serve as a center for information on international peace, introduce people interested in these issues to each other, collect a library of relevant published materials and create an archive for peace writings.

Document 2.6

Pavel N. Milyukov: Arms Limitation

From *The Armed Peace and the Limitations of Arms*, 1911

The idea of peace is as old as the reality of war. . . . in its development it has passed several stages which [have] gradually brought it nearer to [the current] final stage.

The first [was an appeal] to the conscience of man in the name of . . . religion [which declared that] murder is sin; war is murder, . . . based on the direct teachings of the founder of Christianity. . . . [When the

Church established itself] outside the state, . . . war was sanctioned by church authorities; . . . but there were always . . . sects which strove to revive the spirit and teachings of the first Christians . . . : "nonresistance to evil." [This position inspired, however,] a very wide-spread view that the defendants of peace [were] utopians. . . .

If it is impossible to base peace on conscience, is it possible to base [peace] on the diametric opposite—force? . . . Conquerors [often] proclaimed that the idea of general peace [was] the final goal and justification of their conquests. [Their] idea of universal power is . . . the rule of one nation over all others . . . , the idea of a chosen people. [This] might flatter the self-respect of a people, . . . their conceit and self-confidence . . . , but this idea is not appropriate to our times. . . . The universal control by one people over others is no less utopian than the idea of peace . . . based on voluntary decency. . . . The contemporary world [will not tolerate] superiority but demands peaceful coexistence of peoples based on . . . the recognition of their mutual independence . . . and equality.

. . . The creation of centralized states in Europe when governments [became subject] to law [made] possible the legal . . . relations of nations. . . . Agreements could be concluded in the name of the people, not the rulers. International peace could be established as a legal superstructure over the state . . . through the organization of civilized nations.

Programs for International Peace

Liberal Internationalism

To persuade governments and peoples that alternatives to warfare could effectively defend a nation, that civilized states had little reason to wage armed struggle with each other, and that the rule of law could replace the use of war—these were the programs of citizen peace societies. Always a small minority, peace activists challenged widely held assumptions: that war was a political reality, a divine retribution, or an unavoidable necessity. They were challenged, in turn, to produce "practical" alternatives to war that would preserve national interest and sovereignty.

Even before the rise of peace societies, Vasily Fedorovich Malinovsky, a diplomat and then director of the progressive lyceum at which Pushkin studied, had attempted to meet that challenge with his proposal for a common European alliance and council (document 2.7). Malinovsky, who advocated democracy and the equality of all peoples and nations, devised one of the first plans for the abolition of slavery. His peace proposal provides continuity between the paper plans of the seventeenth and eighteenth centuries and the organized liberal internationalism of the nineteenth.

British and North American peace advocates realized that their domestic campaigns against militaristic, expansionist foreign policies required parallel activities in other nations. The London Peace Society (1816, later the British Peace Society) began sending agents and lecturers to the Continent in the 1830s. British activists organized the first international congress of peace campaigners in 1843. A second peace congress met in Brussels five years later, as a result of an initiative coordinated by Auguste Visschers, a Belgian political economist, Richard Cobden, a British legislator and free trade peace campaigner; and Elihu Burritt, a self-educated American blacksmith. In the mid-nineteenth century, peace groups launched an international movement that developed the ideas of liberal internationalism.

Burritt believed that the peace message had to be directed to the broadest mass of people, not merely the powerful elites, and he devoted his life to that work. The League of Universal Brotherhood, which he organized in England and the United States, claimed thousands of supporters among farmers and working people. In an address to the 1848 international peace congress in Brussels (document 2.8), Burritt suggested that modern nations could establish a congress of nations and apply existing international law, in a manner similar to that of the Congress and Supreme Court of the United States. As a future model, he introduced the vision of a "Congress of Nations" developed by his compatriot, William Ladd, who had founded the American Peace Society in 1828.[4]

Victor Hugo went further than either Malinovsky or Burritt, arguing that the logical future of Europe was a United States of Europe, a society that would parallel the formation of the French nation from once disparate, warring provinces. Best known as a novelist and poet, but also an active politician, Hugo agreed to chair the 1849 Peace Congress in Paris. He knew that his vision would not be achieved in the near future, but his speech (document 2.9) reflected the optimism of revolutionary Europe before the resurgence of counterrevolutionary and antirepublican forces.

In the second half of the nineteenth century, the idea of an organized community of nations subject to a rule of law attracted increasing numbers of supporters. At the same time, however, the international system was being shaped by the arms race, the rival alliances of Great Powers in

Europe, the multiplication of protectionist tariff policies, and overseas expansion in which the United States participated. The international peace movement, formally organized in the Universal Peace Congress and the Interparliamentary Conference (later the Interparliamentary Union), wrestled with aggressive nationalism and continual international crises. In this context, Ivan Novikoff (better known in the West as Jacques Novicow), a Russian author of seventeen books on sociology and peace, urged pacifists to shift from legalistic arguments to a broader, innovative vision (document 2.10). He warned liberal internationalists that issues of poverty and social justice could not be severed from international peace.

Although prominent peace advocates were attracted to Novicow's argument, the eminent Austrian writer and peace campaigner Bertha von Suttner had frequently warned other leaders that they might alienate central European and religious delegates by attaching social agendas to peace issues. Bertha von Suttner had become a famous peace activist with the amazing success of her novel, *Die Waffen Nieder* (*Lay Down Your Arms!*, 1889), which was translated into 16 languages and 40 editions by 1914 and became known as the *Uncle Tom's Cabin* of the peace movement.[5] After the Russo-Japanese War and the Russian Revolution of 1905, von Suttner edged towards Novicow's view of peace activism, although she never abandoned her belief in arbitration as the centerpiece of propaganda. When she accepted the Nobel Peace Prize of 1905, the first woman to win it, von Suttner interpreted the future in broad terms—as two distinct visions of political power wrestling for global control (document 2.11).

Alfred Fried, editor of *Die Friedenswarte* from 1899 to 1921 and a leading German peace activist before World War I, became persuaded that Novicow's criticism of the movement required a total rethinking of its strategies: peace propaganda had to be based on a more scientific analysis of international relations and eliminate appeals to human decency. Fried advocated what he called "revolutionary pacifism." (document 2.12). Peace advocates must identify those arenas where both governments and private professional societies could strengthen international dependencies and commitments.

Like Fried, the American philosopher William James urged peace activists to address militarism at its point of greatest appeal, and not merely to decry its destructiveness. In "The Moral Equivalent of War" (document 2.13), James urged peace advocates to develop a psychological and moral substitute for war, a practical alternative to its passion and excitement and a substitute for the teaching of discipline. To this end

James proposed that the youth of all classes be required to do routine, unattractive labor in a kind of work corps. Such social service might help to bridge the vast gulf between classes, which itself fed militarism. James, Fried, von Suttner, and Novicow all reflected a growing interest early in the twentieth century in relating the internationalist idea of peace to practical issues of security and social justice.

Document 2.7

Vasily Malinovsky: A Common European Alliance

From "Deliberations on Peace and War," 1803

Europe is ripe for peace. Laws, customs, sciences and trade unite Europeans, thus forming Europe into some kind of incipient community. Even languages distinguishing one nation from another do not constitute a significant hindrance in inter-communications, for in the majority of cases they are very much alike, and some of them can serve as common European languages.

Many European nations have a common origin, they are all mixed. It would be a shame for them to see each other as enemies. They all possess numerous virtues calling for respect and following. A "European:" this should be the name for all the citizens of the most enlightened country in the world, and then it will arouse respect and appreciation in every corner of the globe.

We may hope that the blessed time will come when Europe is a common home for all of its citizens and will not be tortured by wars any longer. Why delay this bliss? Why not put an end to war's fatalities—or haven't we suffered enough? . . .

Common Alliance and the Council

Any alliance is concluded in pursuit of individual interests of the two or several countries. But a Common European Alliance can more than compensate for the advantage of those minor alliances. This challenge calls not for treatises, but for laws fixing a country's independence and territoriality and regulating relationships between the peoples.

To get these laws observed, a general council should be set up, consisting of plenipotentiaries of the allied countries. This council should monitor public security and property ownership, prevent any disruptions in tranquillity, and settle emerging disagreements between the peoples in the established order. Its decisions should be always unanimously effected by all the allies; and to rule out any bias, no special arrangements between separate countries can be made. . . . In case a power refuses to observe the General Council's decisions, it should be stripped of all common benefits and excluded from communication. In case of further obstinacy, a joint force should be used to induce compliance. No lawless action of one country against another should go unpunished, and even conciliation of the aggrieved party cannot give the offender impunity, as no one is entitled to violate the sacred rule of law once it is enacted to secure peace and stability.

In fact, armaments and troop deployment precede war; and that is the reason that in order to prevent war, armaments should be legally limited to the amount required in emergency or imminent danger of attack. The habit of accompanying negotiations with armaments reveals the impotence of international laws and the urgency of such reliable regulations as will always resolve who is right and who is wrong, just as in a civil court. . . .

When so many nations, diverging in their interests, reconcile their aspirations they cannot connive at illegalities. Those who agree with one another face those who oppose them or are indifferent. But after concluding a general alliance, European powers will deem their interests inseparable and will never allow one of them to harm another in violation of common principles.

Document 2.8

Elihu Burritt: A Congress of Nations

From a speech to the Peace Congress at Brussels, 1848

The first great object . . . to be obtained by a Congress of Nations is a *well-defined Code of International Law*. This has been acknowledged by eminent jurists, and proved by centuries of painful experience, to be a prime necessity. . . .

In asking for the creation of [a] tribunal and fixed code of International Law, we do not necessarily ask for any serious innovation upon the established usages and acknowledged principles of nations. [We ask that an International Assembly be called] to revise and reconstruct the present code of International Law and present it to the National Legislatures which they represent. . . .

. . . Let us suppose that . . . every million of inhabitants [elect a representative to the Congress of Nations]; then we have an Assembly [350 members] . . . about as large as the British House of Commons. . . . The first work of this august Senate . . . is the appointment of a Committee on International Law. . . . They [study] all the legal wisdom of the world. . . . These statutes are discussed, amended and adopted, and then transmitted for discussion and adoption to the National Legislatures. . . . [After six months there is] a fixed, well-digested code . . . , the common law of the people. . . .

. . . The illustrious Senate now enters upon the second department of its labors and provides for the erection of a Grand International Tribunal or permanent High Court of Nations which shall decide all serious questions of controversy between the nations represented, according to the code thus adopted. . . . Two jurists from each nation [are appointed] to compose the Bench of Judges [which] shall immediately replace the Congress that created it.

The opening of this High Court of Nations, . . . must open a new era in the condition and prospects of mankind. A seat for life . . . is the highest appointment within the capacity of any nation. . . . Wherever a question arose . . . , the thought of war would not occur. . . . Each party would say to its government, "There is the law; there is the Court; there sit the Judges! refer the case to their arbitrament and we will abide by their decision." Instead of the earth . . . shaken with the thunder of conflicting armies and deluged with blood, to settle a question of right or honor, we should see reported . . . the case of England *versus* France, Prussia *versus* Denmark, or Mexico *versus* the United States. . . . The Supreme Court of the United States is frequently occupied with a lawsuit between two states, . . . New York *versus* Virginia, or Ohio *versus* Pennsylvania, will often be found on the list of cases. . . . A resort to arms never occurs to the inhabitants of either of the litigant states.

The community of nations is slowly approximating . . . the condition of the family circle. Now is the time to organize . . . these social tendencies and national affinities into a fixed system. . . .

Document 2.9

Victor Hugo: A United States of Europe

From an address to the International Peace Congress, 1849

Gentlemen, this sacred idea, universal peace, all nations bound together in a common bond, the Gospel for their supreme law, mediation substituted for war . . . : I ask you, is it practicable? . . . Yes! . . . I do not merely say it is [possible] , but I add that it is inevitable.

. . . if four centuries ago at the period when war was made by one district against the other, between cities, and between provinces, . . . someone had dared to predict to Lorraine, to Picardy, to Normandy, to Burgundy:—"A day will come when you will no longer make wars—a day shall come when you will no longer arm men one against the other; . . . you will still have many disputes to settle; . . . but do you know what you will substitute [for] armed men, cavalry, infantry, cannon, falconets, lances, pikes and swords:—you will select . . . a ballot-box from which shall issue—what?—an assembly, which shall be . . . the soul of all, . . . which shall make the sword fall from every hand, . . . which shall say . . . , Live in peace! And on that day . . . you will no longer be hostile tribes, you will be a people: you will no longer be Burgundy, Normandy, Brittany or Provence—you will be France!" If, at the period I speak of, some one had uttered these words, . . . all the great politicians . . . would have cried out "What a dreamer! . . . What ridiculous folly!" . . . Well. I say with you, we who are assembled here, tell France, England, Prussia, Austria, Spain, Italy, Russia . . . , "A day will come when . . . the arms you [carry] will fall, . . . when war will appear as absurd and . . . impossible between Paris and London, between St. Petersburg and Berlin, between Vienna and Turin, as it would be now between Rouen and Amiens, between Boston and Philadelphia. A day will come when you, France,—you, Russia—you, Italy— you, England—you, Germany—all of you, nations of the Continent, will, without losing your distinctive qualities . . . , be blended into a superior unity, and constitute a European fraternity. . . . A day will come when the only battlefield will be the market open to commerce and the mind . . . , when bullets and bombshells will be replaced by ballots, by the universal suffrage of nations, by the venerable arbitration of a great Sovereign Senate, which will be to Europe what the Parliament is to England, . . . the Diet is to Germany, . . . the Legislative Assembly is to France, . . . when cannon will be in public museums just as an instrument of torture is now, and people will be astonished how such a thing could have been. A day will come when those two immense groups, the United States of America and the United States of Europe, . . . shall extend the hand of friendship across the ocean, exchanging their produce, their commerce, their industry, their arts, their genius, clearing the earth, peopling the deserts, improving creation under the eye of the Creator. . . ." Nor is it necessary that four hundred years should pass away for that day to come. . . .

. . . See what discoveries issue daily from human genius, . . . how distances become less and less. . . . Before long, men will traverse the earth . . . [and] the electric wire of concord shall encircle the globe and embrace the world. Yet, gentlemen, when I reflect on all that Providence has done in favor and human policy against, a sad and bitter thought comes to mind . . . : the nations of Europe expend each year for the maintenance of armies a sum amounting to two thousand millions of francs, and which, by adding the expense of maintaining establishments of war, amounts to three thousand millions. Add to this the lost . . . days of work of more than 2,000,000 men . . . and you will [see] that the standing armies of Europe cost annually more than four thousand millions.

. . . If for the last thirty-two years, this enormous sum had been expended [on labor, education, industry, commerce, navigation, agriculture, science, art], do you know what would have happened? The face of the world would have been changed. . . . Misery would no longer be found and what do you think would disappear? Revolutions.

Document 2.10

Jacques Novicow: What Pacifists Must Do

From "A Sense of Direction for the Peace Movement," 1901

The 19th century has seen the achievement of one of the greatest revolutions known to history—the democratization of civilized societies. . . . Governments now exist for the popular masses and not [vice versa].

Since the interests of the masses have become the central issue, the question of poverty becomes compelling and formidable. While once only the comforts of the great and powerful received any consideration, no one can ignore the millions of the miserable who inhabit the bottom rungs of society any longer.

. . . the socialist solution [argues] that we are poor because the fruits created by workers are not equitably distributed. The worker does not obtain the entire remuneration for his labor. The owner takes a part far greater than what is legitimately his. . . . But, having recognized that the socialists are perfectly correct up to a point, . . . their solution to the problem of poverty is insufficient. . . .

. . . There are two ways to obtain needed goods. One can work the soil and fashion its products (labor, production and exchange) or one can expropriate things fashioned by others (theft, brigandage, conquest).

... Our contemporary social institutions arose from the idea that theft is profitable.

Instead of devoting time to developing the planet ... men have [organized] armies and navies to invade neighboring territory. ...

How should we become wealthy? ... By scrupulously respecting the rights of neighbors ... , [which] means:

1. that no society is obliged to submit by force to arrangements contrary to its interests. ... International differences ... must be submitted to tribunals ... ;

2. that no nationality must be forced to submit to political controls contrary to its desire. ... The national boundaries of a people will be established by free will of citizens expressed in plebiscites.

[Only pacifists] summon the nations to ... regulate international differences ... , but their outlook is too constrained. Seeing how difficult it is to attain international arrangements, even those as harmless as voluntary arbitration, pacifists draw back from the challenge of the task. They fear alienating governments by [demanding] the federal union of civilized states. Pacifists are very wrong to show themselves so timorous. ... The popular masses will not be attracted except by a striking, shining light.

The pacifist party ought have no fear of frightening governments ... ; it must have a very advanced program because it has a special function to fulfill in societies—that of opening new horizons, of showing the path ... to peoples and governments.

... Peoples must be promised something to awaken their interest—for example, an average income of 10,000 francs per family, an existence worthy of man, and a chicken in their pots, not only on Sundays as Henry IV wanted, but everyday. In a word, peoples must be made to understand that the sordid poverty which entraps them can be changed. ... Precisely because pacifists, as federalists, alone can solve the problem of poverty, they will be proudly and justly called the true tribunes of the peoples and the future redeemers of humanity.

Document 2.11

Bertha von Suttner: Internationalism and Unification

From "The Evolution of the Peace Movement," 1906

Let us look around us in the world of today and see whether we are really justified in claiming for pacifism progressive development and positive results. A terrible war, unprecedented in the world's history, recently raged in the Far East [the Russo-Japanese War, 1904–1905]. This was followed by a revolution . . . which shook the giant Russian empire. . . . [In] Central and Western Europe . . . we have distrust, threats, saber rattling, press baiting, feverish naval buildup, and rearming everywhere. Fortresses are being erected, submarines built, whole areas mined, airships tested for use in war; and all this with such zeal—as if to attack one's neighbor were the most inevitable and important function of a state. Even the printed program of the second Hague Conference . . . proclaims it as virtually a council of war. Now in the face of all this, can people still maintain that the peace movement is making progress?

. . . We must understand that two philosophies, two eras of civilization, are wrestling with one another and that a vigorous new spirit is supplanting the blatant and threatening old. No longer weak and formless, this promising new life is already widely established and determined to survive. Quite apart from the peace movement, . . . there is taking place in the world a process of internationalization and unification. Factors contributing to the development of this process are technical inventions, improved communications, economic interdependence, and closer international relations. The instinct of self-preservation in human society, acting almost subconsciously, as do all drives in the human mind, is rebelling against the constantly refined methods of annihilation and against the destruction of humanity.

. . . The adherents of the old order have a powerful ally in the natural law of inertia inherent in humanity . . . against change. Thus pacifism faces no easy struggle. This question of whether violence or law shall prevail between states is the most vital of the problems of our eventful era. . . . The advocates of pacifism are well aware how meager are their resources of personal influence and power. . . . On the solution of this problem depends whether our Europe will become a showpiece of ruins and failure [or] a civilization of unimagined glory. . . .

Document 2.12

Alfred Fried: Reformist and Revolutionary Pacifism

From *The Basis of Pacifism*, 1909

. . . [Both] reformist and revolutionary pacifisms exist. . . . *Reformist pacifism* attacks superficial manifestations of war . . . without examining causes. The causes of war reside in the anarchy of international relations which requires violence to settle differences. Reformist pacifism does not direct its efforts against the international anarchy. . . .

Most peace keeping activity in contemporary politics is little more than reformist pacifism; this is what heads of state, ministers, parliamentarians or diplomats [mean by] 'maintaining' peace . . . or 'avoiding' war. All their effort is directed towards prolonging the truce. . . . The same is true for reformist pacifism [which agitates] to end war by merely reducing armaments or by the simple creation of international jurisdictions.

Revolutionary pacifism, on the other hand, turns its energies against the causes of war. By eliminating causes, that is, instilling order instead of anarchy in the relations among peoples, it [aims for a new definition of] "peace" in the current world system.

. . . Global organization is far more advanced than most contemporaries realize; . . . what is missing is *the conscious awareness by mankind*. . . . Pacifism, basically, is no more than a task of intellectual awakening.

. . . We pacifists are not merely the means of . . . improving the insight of our contemporaries. . . . We are the living witnesses of this development. . . .

. . . War is a State action which, before becoming a fact, was initially wanted by an isolated individual or by a group which agreed with him. . . . A small group seeks to influence . . . the masses. All the arguments about patriotism, national honor, heroism, etc. are part of this preparation . . . ; lying about the true nature of relationships, . . . exaggerating facts, inflaming dangers . . . , all to alarm the mass. . . . Asserting that war is . . . decided by . . . peoples themselves constitutes the grossest travesty. . . . We speak of "England" which presumably is fighting against "German" competition; of "France" which demands revenge; of "Italy" which wants to control the Adriatic; of "Russia" which aspires to dominate Constantinople, etc. when in reality it is a small circle of men who cultivate these aspirations. . . . We must create institutions to restrain easily unleashed popular hatreds.

Having thus identified the causes of war inside states, . . . [we must work to immunize the masses]. All we can hope to do is to make them increasingly unwilling to listen to the persuasion of those wanting war. [This is a] fundamental difference which separates reformist and revolutionary pacifism. . . .

The forces inherent in the anarchy are too powerful, the mental preparation of the masses is too deeply shaped to expect "immunization" to work rapidly enough. . . . a second line of defense must be developed . . . to contain popular passions. . . .

We find these institutions in specific international arrangements whose aim is to prevent the masses from taking leave of their senses. . . . The first Hague Conference succeeded in creating . . . international commissions of inquiry . . . to be invoked when sudden crises arise. . . .

. . . The second part of our program, the positive encouragement of the natural processes of organization [requires] the development of technology. . . . Technology multiplies relations and relations are the agents of organization. . . .

. . . International collaboration and conscious centralization of diverse interests are the signs of the development of global organization . . . : societies, unions, syndicates, trusts, offices, secretariats and international assemblies. . . . These international unions must become aware of their pacific power. . . .

Law follows relationships. . . . At the moment when relationships develop among men, certain norms are born which control these rapports. . . . Pacifist effort [must accelerate] the evolution of justice in law. . . .

Document 2.13

William James: The Moral Equivalent of War

From "The Moral Equivalent of War," 1910

The war against war is going to be no holiday excursion or camping party. The military feelings are too deeply grounded to abdicate their place among our ideals until better substitutes are offered than the glory and shame that come to nations, as well as to individuals. . . .

Modern war is so expensive that we feel trade to be a better avenue to plunder; but modern man inherits all the innate pugnacity and all the love of glory of his ancestors. To show war's irrationality and horror is of no effect on him. The horrors make the fascination. War is the *strong* life. . . .

At the present day, civilized opinion is a curious mental mixture. The military instincts and ideals are as strong as ever, but are confronted by . . . criticisms which sorely curb their ancient freedom. Innumerable writers are showing up the bestial side of military service. Pure loot and mastery seem no longer morally avowable motives, and pretexts must be found for attributing them solely to the enemy. . . .

All reflective apologists for war at the present day take it religiously. It is to them a sort of sacrament . . . , a permanent human *obligation*. . . .

Pacificists ought to [consider] the aesthetical and ethical point of view of their opponents. . . . So long as antimilitarists propose no substitute for war's disciplinary function, no *moral equivalent* of war, analogous, as one might say, to the mechanical equivalent of heat, so long they fail to realize the full inwardness of their situation. And as a rule they do fail. The duties, penalties, and sanctions pictured in the utopias they paint are all too weak and tame to touch the military-minded. Tolstoy's pacifism is the only exception to this rule, for it is profoundly pessimistic as regards all this world's values, and makes the fear of the Lord furnish the moral spur provided elsewhere by the fear of the enemy. . . .

. . . All the qualities of a man acquire dignity when he knows that the service of the collectivity that owns him needs them. If proud of the collectivity, his own pride rises in proportion. No collectivity is like an army for nourishing such pride; but it has to be confessed that the only sentiment which the image of pacific cosmopolitan industrialism is capable of arousing in countless worthy breasts is shame at the idea of belonging to *such* a collectivity. . . . Where is the savage "yes" and "no," the unconditional duty?

. . . Where is anything that one feels honored by belonging to?

Having said thus much in preparation, I will now confess my own utopia. I devoutly believe in the reign of peace and in the gradual advent of some sort of socialistic equilibrium. The fatalistic view of the war-function is to me nonsense. . . . And when whole nations are the armies, . . . war becomes absurd and impossible from its own monstrosity. . . .

. . . But I do not believe that peace either ought to be or will be permanent on this globe, unless the states pacifically organized preserve some of the old elements of army discipline. A permanently successful peace-economy cannot be a simple pleasure-economy. In the more or less socialistic future towards which mankind seems drifting we must still [discipline ourselves to the requirements of] this only partly hospitable globe. . . . Martial virtues must be the enduring cement: intrepidity, contempt of softness, surrender of private interest, obedience to command, must still remain the rock upon which states are built. . . .

Let me illustrate my idea more concretely. . . . If now—and this is my idea—there were, instead of military conscription, a conscription of the whole youthful population to form for a certain number of years a part of the army enlisted against *Nature*,* . . . injustice would tend to be evened out. . . . The military ideals of hardihood and discipline would be wrought into the growing fibre of the people; no one would remain blind as the luxurious classes now are blind, to man's relations to the globe he lives on, and to the permanently sour and hard foundations of his higher life. To coal and iron mines, to freight trains, to fishing fleets in December, to dishwashing, clothes-washing, and window-washing, to road-building and tunnel-making, to foundries and stokeholes, and to the frames of skyscrapers, would our gilded youths be drafted off, according to their choice, to get the childishness knocked out of them, and to come back into society with healthier sympathies and soberer ideas. They would have paid their blood-tax, done their own part in the immemorial human warfare against nature; they would tread the earth more proudly, . . . they would be better fathers and teachers of the following generation.

. . . I spoke of the "moral equivalent" of war. So far, war has been the only force that can discipline a whole community, and until an equivalent discipline is organized, I believe that war must have its way. But I have no serious doubt that [such a moral equivalent can be organized]. . . .

The martial type of character can be bred without war. . . . The only thing needed henceforth is to inflame the civic temper as past history has inflamed the military temper.

Economic Critiques of War and Militarism

Throughout the nineteenth century, liberal political economists argued that prosperity required peace: economic development depended on international trade and finance, which were undermined by war and the arms race. In Great Britain, the Manchester School of Economics pioneered the "free trade and peace" position associated with Richard Cobden, a member of the House of Commons who was widely admired among progressive political economists in Europe. At the 1849 Universal Peace Congress in Paris, Cobden urged peace activists to address the relationship between wealth and warfare by campaigning against all war loans, whether from banks or from private individuals (document 2.14). Cutting the supply of money or credit—"the sinews of war"—would be

---

* An army enlisted "against *Nature*" implied, in the context of that time, the challenge of mastering natural forces and making them productive; it was not James' intent to destroy natural resources.

a major step against organized slaughter, he held. Monies saved could be invested in a wide range of useful projects.

Cobden's analysis was expanded by the self-made Polish millionaire, financier, and railway entrepreneur Ivan Bliokh (known in the West as Jean de Bloch), who published a scholarly six-volume study of the technical, economic, and political impact of modern war (document 2.15). Invited to discuss his ideas with Tsar Nicholas II, de Bloch was credited with influencing the decision to convene the first Hague Peace Conference in 1899.[6] His exhaustive study of the impact of modern war on the economies of Europe concluded that the social order and civilization itself would be destroyed if the Great Powers sent their weaponry and standing armies into the field.

In addition to the misuse of investment capital and undermining of European economies, the arms race was attacked for the hypocrisy with which it cloaked its greed. This was the point made by an English journalist and activist, George Herbert Perris, to the 1913 Universal Peace Congress at The Hague, the last such meeting before World War I. In his report on "war industrialists and militarism" (document 2.16), Perris summarized research on the interlocking directorates of the arms industries, which demonstrated that for weapons manufacturers the only real "enemy" was the loss of profit. By that time, war and the arms race were attacked by both capitalist and socialist critics for depressing and distorting economic development.

Document 2.14

Richard Cobden: The Sinews of War

From a speech at the Second General Peace Congress,
Paris, 1849

Resolved: The Congress condemns all loans and taxes intended for the prosecution of wars of ambition and conquest.

I have the honor to submit . . . a motion condemnatory of loans for warlike purposes. My object is to promote peace by withholding the sinews of war. I propose that this Congress shall make an appeal to the consciences of all those who have money to lend. I do not allude to a few bankers who appear before the world as loan contractors. In reality they are the agents only for collecting funds from smaller capitalists. It is from the savings and accumulations of the merchants, manufacturers, traders, agriculturists, and annuitants of civilized Europe, that warlike govern-

ments can alone supply their necessities, and to them we would appeal
. . . not to lend their support to a barbarous system which obstructs
commerce, uproots industry, annihilates capital and labor, and revels
amidst the tears and blood of their fellow-creatures. . . . War has become
an expensive luxury. It is no longer a question of bows and arrows,
swords and shields. Battles are now decided by artillery, and every discharge of a cannon costs from twelve to fifteen francs; I wish with all my
heart it were ten times as much. The consequence is that when countries
behind the rest of Europe in civilization enter upon hostilities, they are
obliged immediately to draw upon the resources of more civilized states
—in other words, to raise a loan; and how is the money thus borrowed
from the savings of honest industry expended? What is war in our day?
Has it learned any of the charities of peace. Let us see. I hold in my hand
an extract from a proclamation issued at Pesth, dated 19th July, and
signed "Haynau."* Paying forgiveness for your outraged feelings, I will
read it:

> Any individual who shall, either by word or action or by wearing any
> revolutionary signs or emblems, dare to support the cause of the rebels;
> any individual who shall insult one of my soldiers, or those of our brave
> allies, either by words or blows; any individual who shall enter into
> criminal relations with the enemies of the crown, or who shall seek to
> kindle the flame of rebellion by reports spread for a sinister purpose, or
> who shall be rash enough to conceal arms, or not deliver them up
> within the day fixed by my proclamation, shall be put to death without
> the shortest possible delay, and on the spot where the crime shall be
> committed, without distinction of condition or sex.

. . . . I ask you, has war borrowed any of the charities of Christianity? Have modern warriors repudiated the practice of the barbarians of
antiquity? For my part, I can see no difference between Attila and Haynau, between the Goth of the fifth and the Goth of the nineteenth century. But we address ourselves to those who, by their loans, really hire
and pay men who commit these atrocities, and we say, 'It is you who
give strength to the arm which murders innocent women and helpless
old age; it is you who supply the torch which reduces to ashes peaceful
and inoffensive villages and on your souls will rest the burden of these

---

* General Haynau's forces, serving the Hapsburg monarchy, repressed the revolutions
in northern Italy and Hungary in 1849.

crimes against humanity.' I shall be told that it is useless to make an appeal to the sensibilities of men who, with money lying unproductive at the bottom of their pockets, are thinking of nothing but five per cent. I will undertake to prove . . . that peace will offer a far better field for the employment of the savings of agriculture than the field of battle, and that she will afford a much more profitable investment for the accumulations of industry than in partnership with Haynau and Co.

Document 2.15

Jean de Bloch: The Future of War

From *The Future of War*, 1898 and 1902

In recent times war has become even more terrible than before in consequence of perfected weapons of destruction and systems of equipment and training utterly unknown in the past. What is graver still, the immensity of armies and the training of soldiers in entrenchment [will create hitherto unimagined] difficulties. . . . There can be no doubt that with modern firearms the impression which battle makes on armies will be incomparably greater than before. . . . Infantry and artillery fire will have unprecedented force while aid to the wounded will be made more difficult by the great range both of small-arms and of artillery. Smoke will no longer conceal from the survivors the terrible consequences of the battle and every advance will be made with full appreciation of the probabilities of extermination. From this, and from the fact that the mass of soldiers will have but recently been called from the field, the factory, and the workshop, it will appear that even the psychical conditions of war have changed. Thus in the armies of Western states the agitation against war may extend even so far as the materialization of socialist theories subverting the bases of monarchies.

. . . the present conditions cannot continue to exist for ever. The peoples groan under the burdens of militarism. . . . We see in France and Germany preparation of new artillery to [best employ] the new smokeless powder. Millions are expended on the construction of new battleships and cruisers. . . . Can the present incessant demands for money from Parliament for armaments continue forever without social outbreaks? . . . Still graver are the economic and social convulsions which war will call forth in consequence of the summons . . . of almost the whole male population, the interruption of maritime communications, the stagnation in industry and trade, the increase in the price of the necessaries of life, and the destruction of credit. Will . . . governments [not] find it impossible . . . [to maintain] their armies, satisfy the requirements of budgets . . . , [and] feed the destitute remainder of the civil population?

In a future war, . . . instead of professional soldiers, will appear whole peoples with all their peculiar virtues and failings. . . . The elements contending in a future war will be all the moral and intellectual resources of nations, all the forces of modern civilization, all technical improvements . . . : the combined fruit of the culture of the civilized world.

. . . European states [must ask themselves the question]—what will result [from] these armaments and this exhaustion, what will be the nature of a future war, . . . is it possible to conceive the settlement of . . . questions by means of the cataclysm which . . . a war between five Great Powers with ten millions of soldiers would cause? . . . For twenty, forty years, millions have been wasted on fruitless armaments which cannot be employed and by means of which the decision of international disputes is inconceivable. . . .

That war will finally become impracticable is apparent. The question is . . . , when will the recognition of this inevitable truth be spread among European governments and peoples?

Document 2.16

George H. Perris: The Business of War

From an address to the Universal Peace Congress, 1913

We have this year, for the first time, I think, in the history of the Peace Movement, an analysis, something like a scientific analysis, of the methods by which war material is supplied to three of the greatest countries in the world. In the case of the German Empire, Dr. Liebknecht has placed before the Reichstag the results of his inquiries. In the case of France, M. Delaisi has embodied the results of his inquiry in a little pamphlet. . . . I have myself made a similar inquiry so far as concerns the great manufacturers of armaments for the British Empire. . . . Liebknecht's revelations in Germany have attracted peculiar attention;* but

---

* Francis Delaisi's "little pamphlet" was an extensively researched exposé of the interrelated French and German arms industry; Karl Liebknecht, son of Wilhelm Liebknecht and leader of the Social Democratic party, was imprisoned in 1907–08 for his published views on militarism.

what the investigations that have been made in England and France prove is, that this disease is substantially the same in all the great countries of the world.

. . . I suppose that it is natural for people who do not know the international peace movement, and who say that pacifists are sentimentalists, to . . . believe that the great names of Krupp and Schneider and Armstrong and others are properly honored, . . . that the armaments are necessary for the peace of the world, and that the makers are excellent citizens . . . under the control of the respective Governments giving them orders.

The students of this nefarious trade . . . know that the reality behind the appearance is somewhat different. [First there is] the immense wealth of the trade in armaments. Seven of the many companies in Great Britain . . . have a total capital of £30 million . . . : these firms, instead of being competitive business, are [international monopolies]. The plea that one company competes with another and makes honest sales to its Governments is pure pretense. . . .

You may remember the case of the Deutsche Munitions und Waffen-Fabrik . . . [which holds a] considerable share in French companies and [exerts] a provocative influence in the Parisian press [to sustain] competition and jealousy [for] orders for armaments. . . . In England, we have a combination of the British and German Nobel companies—an Anglo-German dynamite alliance! . . . There is no difficulty whatever, when profits are at the end of the road for a Frenchman and a German to walk together . . . , no more difficulty than for a Frenchman and an Englishman to walk together. They are patriots both. . . .

I will take the case of Messrs. Armstrong, Whitworth and Coy. [Co.] as a sample of the patriotism of these traders. . . . The chairman is one Sir Andrew Noble, and I beg you to note the impartiality of his patriotism. He is a Baronet and a Knight Commander of the Bath of Great Britain; a member of the Order of Jesus Christ of Portugal; and a Knight of the Order of Charles the Third of Spain. He is also a First Class of the Sacred Treasure of Japan, a Grand Cross of the Crown of Italy, and is decorated with Turkish and Chilian and Brazilian honors. His patriotism is truly the larger patriotism but unlike our patriotism, it has a strict cash basis. Messrs. Armstrong will build warships for any country in the world. . . . They are constantly sending armor-plate to all parts of the world. . . . If they sell a battleship to a foreign country it becomes an argument for increasing the British fleet in turn, and that means a new increase of orders for Armstrong . . . ! Some of you have no doubt looked down . . . upon the chimneys of the Pozzuoli-Armstrong Company which pollute the Bay of Naples. Here Great Britain helps to maintain the fighting force of Germany's ally. There is also the Ansaldo-Armstrong Company of Genoa. These companies not only build for Italy but also for Turkey. . . . You also remember the curious triangular puzzle lying over the destinies of the Far East in the relations of Russia, Japan and China. The Armstrong Company has its own ordnance and armor-plate works in Japan. It is always seeking orders for armaments in China. At the same time in conjunction with two other British firms, Maxims and John Brown and Coy., and also in connection with Blohm and Voss of Hamburg and Messrs. Schneider, this triple alliance is building up a new fleet for Russia—at the cost of the famine-stricken peasantry. . . . Another British syndicate is building a new fleet for Portugal which is always trembling on the brink of bankruptcy. . . . The Armstrong, Vickers and Brown firms are now building up great ordnance shipbuilding works in Canada for the exploitation of the innocent patriotism of the people of that colony. What country is the enemy of Canada? . . .

. . . there is carried on an industry which has no frontiers whatever to its greed, no limits to its . . . pitiless exploitation of the weakness and folly of human nature. . . . The sole interest of these firms consists in embroiling one nation with another. These preach nationalism . . . of a chameleon character which changes its color with every order. . . . Some of you must wonder . . . where the hill tribesmen of India, where the slave traders of the Persian Gulf, where the Somalis, where the revolutionists of the South American States . . . get their rifles and munitions of war. The fact is, there is no conscience whatever in the trade of death. . . . These great companies will sell their deadly weapons to anyone. . . .

. . . The business of the International Peace Congress and the international peace movement is a rescue business, . . . to rescue Governments from what is put upon them by this corrupt and debasing trade, . . . to rescue some of our fellow-men from grinding toil and disease, brought upon them by the burdens they have to carry. . . . I hope you will help me . . . not only to break the false reputation for national honor of these firms, but break the superstition . . . that the weapons of the soldier are defenses of national honor and influence. If we do that, it will be impossible for Armstrongs to build up a fleet in Italy, to beat a fleet they have set up in Spain, impossible for Japan to defeat Russia with both fleets built by the same firm. Superstition is the great enemy of the peace movement. When we have destroyed this superstition, we shall see men can stand up, for the first time free and equal, able to share, in peace, the fruits of their industry.

Social Justice, Socialism, and Peace

The links among international peace, social justice, and economic equality were forged in the nineteenth century, notably with the growth of Marxist socialism, which asserted that war was an inevitable product of class antagonism and that, accordingly, the abolition of private property must precede the end of warfare. Other social theorists were less adamant about property but insisted that democratic states were required for a pacific order.

That point was made early in the century by Robert Owen, an industrialist and reformer who established a model community for impoverished workers at New Lanark, Scotland. Owen insisted that the new industrial system developing in Great Britain did not have to produce great gaps between rich and poor or warfare among nations. At a 1834 meeting of trades unionists, he presented a *Charter of the Rights of Humanity*, which connected the redistribution of wealth to the abolition of war. Owen explicitly included peace as a human right, and he urged that differences among nations could be settled in an annual congress of nations.

The French social critic Victor Considérant became convinced that peace would only follow one last struggle to abolish monarchy and aristocracy. In 1849, alarmed by the impending triumph of counterrevolutionary forces over embryonic republics in the Italies, the Germanies, Hungary, Austria, and France, he appealed to bourgeois and radical forces to collaborate in creating a democratic continent, preferably in a war of ideas, not cannon (document 2.17).

By that time Karl Marx and Friedrich Engels had developed the idea of "scientific socialism," which altered the debate on the relationship of war and peace to social justice. In their 1848 essay, *The Communist Manifesto* (document 2.18), Marx and Engels linked class struggle, the control of the means of production, and the idea that a "nation" was essentially a political unit that served ruling-class interests. By arguing that the working class in every country was defined by its relationship to capital, and not by its membership in a nation, they created an idea of internationalism quite different from the liberal and nationalist positions. In later editions of the *Manifesto,* Engels recognized that, because history "progresses" and conditions change, some of the arguments of the original *Manifesto* (along with some of the political parties that it mentioned) had lost their significance. Neither he nor Marx had ever believed that their analyses ought to be frozen in time. "In view of the gigantic strides of modern industry" since 1848 "and of the accompanying improved and extended party organization of the working class," Engels wrote in 1872, ". . . this program has in some details become antiquated."[7]

In the last quarter of the century, the arms race exploded on an unprecedented scale, portending disaster for the classes of people who would suffer most from economic ruin or whose lives would be sacrificed as soldiers in a general war. Engels proposed in 1893 that standing armies should be reduced to short-term militias by international treaty.[8] He hoped to reduce both military establishments and the influence of the military elites with huge bodies of men at their command. The suggestion was not pursued, and socialists were left with the question of what the working classes ought to do in the event of war.

The issue was raised at meetings of the First International, and it troubled the Second International. Socialists condemned standing armies as a threat to democratic rights and called for defensive militias, but they worried that conscripted soldiers would shoot their working-class "brothers" in a general strike for peace. Socialist leaders from the potentially belligerent nations, France and Germany, opposed resolutions by international congresses that called for an unenforceable general strike in the event of war. Few supported that strategy when the Dutch anarchist-socialist Domela Nieuwenhuis urged it upon the Second International in Zurich (1893). Instead, the majority endorsed a resolution presented by Wilhelm Liebknecht, a leading German socialist who had earned credibility on the issue by refusing to endorse war against France in 1870. Liebknecht's resolution called on workers to struggle against the outbreak of war but avoided recommending specific tactics, because only the overthrow of capitalism would bring peace (document 2.19).

After the Zurich meeting, the eminent Russian Marxist theoretician Georgy Plekhanov (1856–1918), refined the Social-Democratic position in "Power and Violence" (document 2.20). Plekhanov proposed a flexible and pragmatic approach, urging the use of violence only when it had a chance of success and no other method worked. The central objective of the movement was to attain power, he observed calmly, not to flout muscular strength against the technologically lethal armory of the state.

The continued threat of war in Europe and actual warfare overseas came repeatedly onto the agenda of socialist national and international congresses. The extreme left, represented by the antimilitarist, antipatriotic Gustave Hervé of France, continued to advocate absolute refusal to serve, sabotage, general strike, and direct action against conscription. Centrists like Jean Jaurès of France and August Bebel of Germany argued that the object of socialism was to make the nation more hospitable for proletarian interests, so that workers could influence a pacific foreign policy. Thus, they said, the proletariat had to defend a besieged nation and to prevent unjust wars. Jaurès, a highly respected scholar and popular socialist politician, offered a practical system to restructure the military in his *The Army of a Democracy* (document 2.21). He would reduce arms expenses, curb the arms race, and undercut the social tensions occasioned by a conscripted army under an elite officer corps. At its 1907 Stuttgart meeting, the International again faced this complex issue. Attempting to bridge conflicting positions, it passed its most famous resolution on war (document 2.22).

Jaurès' assassination by an extremist nationalist in August 1914, as World War I began, symbolized the politics of violence that overwhelmed socialists and others for whom social justice was the condition for peace. About the same time a feminist, socialist exile from Russia, Alexandra Kollontai, observed in dismay as the German Social Democratic Party, the largest in the Second International, voted to support war credits and thus helped to bury the movement. Her recollection of that moment (document 2.23) is an epitaph for pre-1914 socialist antiwar positions.

Document 2.17

Victor Considérant: The Last War

From The Last War and the Permanent Peace, 1850

The next war, which will be the last war, will be fought like all wars with cannon, but in this war cannon will only be of secondary importance. Principles, sentiments and ideas will be the decisive artillery of this supreme struggle.

Preparations for it are monumental. Never has Europe contained such a number of soldiers. From the Rhine to the Volga, the armies of despotism cover the earth like morning mists.

So that these armies can be quickly changed into forces of liberty, . . . one thing must happen: Democracy must not betray itself; it must remain faithful to . . . association and liberty.

Today . . . a banner shines in the sky of Europe . . . on which five words are written: ALL PEOPLES ARE BROTHERS.

This is the principle of social Democracy, its most important idea . . . is fraternity, the brotherhood of nations and races. . . .

In 1831 Poland wanted to break the Moscovite stranglehold. Despite

prodigious heroism, she had to silence her fire. That was just. That
. . . aristocratic revolution disdained the people. The Polish aristocracy
[rejected] the emancipation of the serfs. Instead of having to struggle
against a people, the Tsar only had an army to defeat. The defenders of
slavery fell back into slavery. That was justice. . . .

Finally the official representatives of the French Revolution of 1848,
. . . this revolution . . . which inspired other peoples, which promised to
help them; these official republicans . . . have betrayed the promises of
the Revolution. . . .

All these egotisms have been met with punishment and each punishment is a useful lesson. . . . Do not say that God abandoned you: you
have very well abandoned yourselves.

The privileged ones, the aristocrats, the emperors and kings understand their solidarity. . . . They behave like a single person in Europe and
everywhere, they have won.

The formula for Democracy is Association, the sacred word of the
new order. . . . Association means LIBERTÉ for all and FRATERNITÉ towards all. As long as you do not respect the liberty of others as your own
. . . you are . . . not worthy of Liberty . . . The immediate objective . . .
will be the harmonic organization of Europe, . . . the free association of
all liberated nationalities . . . and thus, the inauguration of PERPETUAL
PEACE.

Men of the bourgeoisie, remove your support from the cause of the
feudal families . . . and cease making war on the peoples. . . . Withdraw
your support and their power will fall.

What Does Social Democracy Want

Democrats do not want disorder . . . ; they want real, true, natural,
free and stable order.

The peoples, independently and freely united, will multiply fruitful
relations and create the great peaceful confederation of European civilization, a prelude to the collective unity of the globe. Fortresses and
ramparts will be razed, frontiers opened, armies dismissed or converted
into industrial armies. . . . War, conquest, barbarism will be buried. . . .

The last war will be the war for European independence. It will
fatally weaken despotism and kill war. . . . To arms, then, to arms for
the last war! ALL PEOPLES ARE BROTHERS.

Document 2.18

Karl Marx and Friedrich Engels: Classes and National Wars

From *The Manifesto of the Communist Party*, 1848

The Communists are distinguished from the other working-class parties by this only: 1. In the national struggles of the proletarians of the different countries, they point out and bring to the front the common interests of the entire proletariat, independently of all nationality. 2. In the various stages of development which the struggle of the working class against the bourgeoisie has to pass through, they always and everywhere represent the movement as a whole.

The Communists are . . . reproached with desiring to abolish countries and nationality.

The workingmen have no country. We cannot take from them what they have not got. Since the proletariat must first of all acquire political supremacy, must rise to be the leading class in the nation, must constitute itself *the* nation, it is, so far, itself national, though not in the bourgeois sense of the word.

National differences and antagonisms between peoples are vanishing gradually from day to day, owing to the development of the bourgeoisie, to freedom of commerce, to the world market, to uniformity in the mode of production and in the conditions of life corresponding thereto.

The supremacy of the proletariat will cause them to vanish still faster. United action, of the leading civilized countries at least, is one of the first conditions for the emancipation of the proletariat.

In proportion as the exploitation of one individual by another is put an end to, the exploitation of one nation by another will also be put an end to. In proportion as the antagonism between classes within the nation vanishes, the hostility of one nation to another will come to an end.

Document 2.19

The Second International: War and the General Strike

From resolutions of the Zurich Congress, the Second International, 1893

Domela Nieuwenhuis proposed (for the Dutch delegation):
The Congress resolves [that] at the moment a government issues a

declaration of war, the international workers' party be prepared to call a general workers' strike everywhere where workers can exercise influence . . . and in the . . . nations declaring war, [to refuse] to perform military service. [Resolution defeated]

Wilhelm Liebknecht proposed (for the German delegation):

The position of the workers on war is clearly expressed in the resolution of the Brussels Congress [1891] on militarism. In every country, the international revolutionary Social Democratic movement has opposed . . . the chauvinist impulses [lusts] of the ruling class; has tightened ever more closely the bonds of solidarity connecting workers from all lands and incessantly worked towards the abolition of capitalism by which humanity is divided into two enemy camps and peoples are set against each other. With the abolition of class domination, war will also disappear. The overthrow of capitalism will bring world peace. [Resolution adopted]

Document 2.20

George Plekhanov: Force and Violence

From "Power and Violence," 1893

Utopian socialists, rejecting violent means as a principle, become dogmatists. Social-Democrats reject neither violence nor peaceful means of agitation, and realize that violent means are inevitable in certain circumstances. Moreover they know . . . that there is a deep gulf between power and violence. It is *power* and only power that Social Democrats strive to attain. Violence can only be used under certain circumstances. Given the current conditions in civilized nations, it is in the interests of the proletariat not to be carried away by violent action. [We] advocate peaceful and legal agitation. However, even when we reject a violent form of action, we are not impeding the development of the revolutionary force of the proletariat. . . .

Class struggle is [often] compared to warfare. Naturally, the latter is characterized by many violent acts but no halfway intelligent drill-master does not know the huge difference between the power of an army and just any random violence committed by that army; or, . . . that violent action at the wrong time will only hurt those who do it.

. . . there are . . . completely reasonable people . . . who confuse power with violence and who are naive enough to be surprised that socialists consider the local conditions and reject gambling with the future of their party for the immediate cheap satisfaction of breaking a few police restrictions. . . .

Document 2.21

Jean Jaurès: Democracy and Military Service

From *Democracy and Military Service*, 1911

It is imperative, both for Socialism and for the Nation, to define what the military institutions and the external policy of Republican France should be. . . . [In] a new order in which labor shall be . . . supreme, France needs . . . peace and security, [to avoid] the sinister diversion of foreign adventures. . . .

To ensure peace by a plain policy of wisdom, moderation and rectitude, by the definitive repudiation of all aggressive enterprises, by the loyal acceptance and practice of the new methods of international law . . . ; on the other hand, to ensure peace, courageously, by the establishment of a defensive organization so formidable that every thought of aggression is put out of the mind of even the most insolent and rapacious: these are the highest aims of the Socialist Party. . . . How can the Socialist Party speak with authority [for] that form of national defense which seems most efficacious if there is a doubt . . . as to whether we have a real interest in national defense itself?

Socialism . . . must not content itself with vague formulas [but must advocate] military education, gymnastic societies, Rifle Clubs, field exercises. . . . [Socialists] *demand, as they are entitled and obliged to demand, that the Nation shall organize its Military Forces without any regard for class or caste, with a single eye to national defense itself.*

. . . The organization of national defense and the organization of international peace are but two different aspects of the same great task. For whatever adds to the defensive strength of France increases the hope of peace, and whatever success France attains in organizing peace on the basis of law and founding it upon arbitration and right will add to its own defensive strength. . . .

. . . The radical fault of our Military System is that . . . it does not really represent the armed nation. [The] system is based on the supposed inferiority of the reserves as compared with the Active Army. . . . I am convinced that long service in barracks is the outcome of erroneous ideas [and] seriously undermines the defensive power of France. . . .

An examination of the Swiss system shows that the Two Years' Service is not based on . . . technical needs. . . . The Swiss period of service is founded on the conditions necessary to produce efficient soldiers and, if three or four months are sufficient to give the Swiss soldier his Military Education, it is clear that two years cannot be necessary to make a French soldier.

. . . The success of the Swiss system is largely due to the thorough preparatory training of the youth of the Nation, [where] all officers rise from the ranks, . . . promoted step by step from the humblest positions. . . . What especially strikes a Frenchman [is] the liberty of thought and action which these Swiss officers enjoy. They are formed into associations, which meet freely and publicly. . . . They address public and collective petitions. They call upon the authorities to consider . . . questions or reforms; and when a bill is brought forward, they discuss it in a spirit free alike from revolt and from servility.

. . . The people knows well that war must only be the last resource. Let the people be ever on the watch to stamp out the first sparks of war. . . . Let the people . . . prepare a code of international law against the . . . violent enterprises of capitalist imperialism. . . . Let it widen every attempt at arbitration. Let it not yield to the . . . temptation of laughing at the Hague Tribunal, but rather strive to strengthen it. . . . European democracy is gradually accustoming itself to the grandeur of international thought.

Document 2.22

The Second International: The Working Class and War

From a resolution of the Seventh International
Socialist Congress, 1907

The Congress . . . declares once more that the struggle against militarism cannot be separated from the Socialist class struggle. . . .

The Congress, therefore, considers it as the duty of the working class and particularly of its representatives in the parliaments to combat the naval and military armaments with all their might, . . . and to refuse the means for these armaments, . . . [and] to work for the education of working-class youth.

The Congress sees in the democratic organization of the army, in the substitution of the militia for the standing army, an essential guarantee that offensive wars will be rendered impossible. . . .

The International is not able to determine in rigid forms the anti-militarist actions of the working class, which are naturally different in different countries and for different circumstances of time and place. But it is its duty to co-ordinate and increase to the utmost the efforts of the working class against war. . . .

The Congress is convinced that . . . by a serious use of arbitration . . . , the benefit of disarmament can be secured to all nations, making it possible to employ for cultural purposes the enormous expenditure of money and energy which are swallowed up by military armaments and war.

If a war threatens to break out, it is the duty of the working classes and their parliamentary representatives in the countries involved, supported by . . . the International Socialist Bureau, to exert every effort in order to prevent the outbreak of war. . . .

In case war should break out anyway, it is their duty to intervene in favor of its speedy termination, and with all their powers to utilize the economic and political crisis created by the war to rouse the masses and thereby to hasten the downfall of capitalist class rule.

Document 2.23

Alexandra Kollontai: An Epitaph for Hope

From *The Autobiography of a Sexually Emancipated Communist Woman*, 1926

The outbreak of the World War found me in Germany. . . . I was . . . no enemy of Germany and still less a Russian patriot. To me the war was an abomination, a madness, a crime, and from the first moment onwards—more out of impulse than reflection—I inwardly rejected it and could never reconcile myself with it up to this very moment. The intoxication of patriotic feelings has always been something alien to me. . . . I felt an aversion for everything that smacked of super-patriotism. . . . Strange to say, I was present in the Reichstag on August 4, the day the war budget was being voted on. The collapse of the German Socialist Party struck me as a calamity without parallel. I felt utterly alone. . . .*

---

* Exiled in 1914, Kollontai later became the first woman minister in the first Bolshevik government in 1917. Her career in government was as stormy as her pre-1914 life as a professional revolutionary and organizer.

Objections to Colonial Exploitation

Aggressive, often murderous, policies accompanied the colonial expansion of the industrial powers, which often was justified as bringing civilization to savages—in Rudyard Kipling's famous phrase, "the white man's burden." Most peace activists shared the view that western civilization and Christianity were superior to other cultures and religions, and that Europeans were obligated to free "lesser" peoples from oppressive superstitions (non-Christian religions) or social practices such as slavery, infanticide, child marriage, polygamy, and suicide by widows. Not all peace advocates believed that non-European peoples were culturally "backward," as the selection from Frédéric Passy indicates (document 2.25), but they unanimously denounced colonial violence, brutality, and extermination.

Objections to colonizing wars began early in the century. The French campaign in Algeria, July 1830, was denounced, for example, by Jean Jacques, Comte de Sellon, founder of the Société de la Paix de Genève, the first avowed peace society on the continent. Sellon objected both on behalf of the French soldiers placed in harm's way and for the natives, attacked in their own homes by so-called Christians. Warfare was never justified, he wrote (document 2.24), for the sake of bringing a higher civilization to inferior peoples.

In the last third of the century, the frenzied growth of European imperialism coincided with the expanding peace movement. The recognized dean of European peace activists prior to World War I was Frédéric Passy, co-winner of the first Nobel Peace Prize in 1901. An independent in the French Chamber of Deputies during the 1880s, he opposed expansion into Tonkin China (Vietnam), and criticized his compatriots for their hypocritical willingness to view Vietnamese peoples differently from Alsatians and Lorrainians who had been absorbed into Germany in 1871 (document 2.25).

In 1898 and 1899 peace advocates were astounded when governments usually admired as models of international restraint, the United States and Great Britain, went to war against far weaker adversaries, Spain and the South African Boers. The U.S. victory over Spain in Cuba and the Pacific led to the forcible occupation of the Philippines and other former Spanish possessions, which incited organized anti-imperialist agitation throughout the United States. The campaign enlisted David Starr Jordan, a naturalist and president of Stanford University, who urged immediate withdrawal from the Philippines, arguing that its people had earned their independence by challenging Spanish rule—just as the American colonists had done by challenging the British (document 2.26). About the same time, a British journalist and social crusader, William T. Stead, demanded that the Universal Peace Congress at Glasgow in 1901 denounce British policy in South Africa. Britain had played a significant role in shaping an arbitration convention for the 1899 international conference at The Hague, just before it rejected South African overtures for arbitration. In his speech (document 2.27), Stead condemned the British government for violating the very principle of international law that it had urged upon other nations.

Organized international pacifism finally condemned colonialism at the 1910 Universal Peace Congress in Stockholm, in a "Code de la Paix" that included more than a dozen protocols articulating the rights of native peoples. On the eve of World War I, the movement proposed that The Hague machinery be expanded to hear cases for independence and self-government brought by native groups against European colonizers. Peace advocates were seeking a nonviolent alternative to bloody revolutionary upheavals against European colonial domination.

Document 2.24

Jean Jacques, comte de Sellon: War and Colonization

From "Letter on the War," 1830

Monsieur,

You have doubtless heard that the French entered Algiers . . . and thus achieved the main object of the campaign. . . . If the French army had failed in this mission, I would have not taken up my pen because nothing is more eloquent than a defeat to preach against war; but, instead [it] was blessed by the elements and by everything that skill adds to bravery. Thus, this is the moment to say to those who are called by Providence to watch over the happiness of peoples, that whatever be the material advantages of a military expedition, they are always bought at, too high a price. . . .

Let us agree, that the conquest of Algiers is the first milestone planted on the highway of African civilization; let us agree that all the results of this event [apparently prove optimistic] predictions . . . ; let us agree that the seizure of Algiers will end piracy: can we examine the real cost of such advantages?

Why does anyone want to civilize Africa? It is to introduce Christianity—and especially, its spiritual side. Well, is there anything in the world more foreign, more contrary to this spirit than war, which permits the legal practice of all kinds of violence? Why should we want to civilize Africa? To establish trade between it and Europe. Well, we begin by massacring those with whom we claim we want to create new relationships . . . ! In 1829, I expressed the hope that the European powers would mutually agree to create a new grand plan to open caravan routes into the African interior. Frequent and numerous contacts between these powers and the pasha of Egypt offer much promise to attain positive aims without bloodshed. . . . in the nineteenth century, Christian missionaries are more appropriate than the soldiers which our wild animals have sent out. . . .

Document 2.25

Frédéric Passy: The French Conquest of Vietnam

From a speech in the French Chamber of Deputies, 1885

. . . How can this be! Here are peoples whom, recently, you . . . agreed [were not] inferior races . . . but now, you label them as "late comers" to civilization [who need tutelage]. . . . [Your] gifts of labor and peace—you give with an iron fist; they are imposed! You demonstrate your superiority by fire and bloodshed! And, at the same time, as devoted Frenchmen and Alsatians, you loftily denounce the crimes and outrages of conquest in Europe; at the same time, you refuse to admit the right of any European power to make off with a scrap of another's territory. . . . You claim not only to have the right but the *duty* to dominate, enslave and exploit other peoples who are, perhaps, less developed than we are in terms of civilization but who have, nonetheless, their own personality, their nationality and are no less attached to their independence and native soil than we are.

"They are poor, they are weak," you say. These are savage areas, miserable, ignorant, where men still live hidden in lairs like half-animals (or like the peasants, our fathers of the good old days . . .); nonetheless, as barbaric and savage as they might be, they love their country as much as we; where, like us, perhaps more than us . . . —they are attached to freedom.

Gentlemen, in your eyes there are rulers and morsels of territory which are nothing because they have no material value in your markets.

. . . These lands are life itself, blood and body, for these poor people; for them it is Alsace, it is Lorraine. . . .

. . . We remember the way in which the Spanish . . . were lost by America and ruined by their colonies; . . . the way those men were impoverished by the gold found in the mines of the New World which prevented them from developing the land; how they abandoned both manufacturing and agricultural skills in Spain to go on distant expeditions for blood-soaked treasures which then ran through their hands; . . . that, in a dozen years after Columbus, the Indian population was reduced by six-sevenths (and that in 25 years, from one million to 12 or 15,000). . . .

[We feel] amazement at the catastrophes for which these talents are responsible. . . .

I dare to envision a different ideal for France.

Document 2.26

David Starr Jordan: The U.S. Conquest of the Philippines

From "The Question of the Philippines," 1899

I wish to maintain a single proposition. We should withdraw from the Philippine Islands as soon as . . . we can. It is bad statesmanship to make these alien people our partners; it is a crime to make them our slaves. . . .

Why do we want the Philippines? What can we do with them? What will they do to us?

. . . By the fortunes of war the capital of the Philippine Islands fell, last May, into the hands of our navy. . . . Our final treaty of peace has assigned to us the four hundred or fourteen hundred islands. . . . To these we have as yet no real title. We can get none till the actual owners have been consulted. We have a legal title of course, but no moral title. . . . For the right to finish the conquest of the Philippines and to close out the insurrection which has gone on for almost a century we have agreed on our part to pay $20,000,000 in cash, for the people . . . and the land which they have cultivated. . . .* The price is too high . . . when we

---

* Jordan refers to the fact that the United States defeated the Spanish colonial force in the Philippines during the Spanish-American War of 1898, and that in the peace settlement Spain relinquished its claims there, as well as in Puerto Rico and Guam, for $20 million. There was at the time a Filipino independence movement led by Emilio Aguinaldo, as Jordan notes.

observe that the failure of Spain placed the Islands not in our hands but in the hands of their own people, a third party, whose interest we . . . have as yet failed to consider. Emilio Aguinaldo, the liberator of the Filipinos, the "Washington of the Orient," is the *de facto* ruler of most of the territory. In our hands is the city of Manila, alone, and we cannot extend our power except by bribery or by force. . . .

"Who are these Americans?" Aguinaldo is reported to ask, "these people who talk so much of freedom and justice and the rights of man, . . . and who stand as the Spaniards did between us and our liberties?" . . .

We know nothing of Philippine matters, save through cablegrams passed through government censorship. . . . The Filipinos are not rebels against law and order but against alien control. . . . We may easily destroy the organized army of the Filipinos but that does not bring peace. In the cliffs and jungles, they will defy us for a century as they have defied Spain. . . .

I can not see one valid reason why we should want them, nor any why they should want us. . . . Our philanthropy is less than skin deep. . . . I am sure that their possession can in no wise help us, not even financially or commercially. . . .

The idea that every little nation must be subject to some great one is one of the most contemptible products of military commercialism. . . . If we behave honorably towards the people we have freed, we shall set a fashion which the powers will never dare to violate.

Document 2.27

William T. Stead: The British in South Africa

From "On the British Refusal to Use Arbitration
in South Africa," 1901

Mr. W. T. Stead (London) rose to read a resolution at the Universal Peace Congress in Glasgow, 1901.

I wish to recall this Congress . . . to practical questions of the immediate moment. I have drawn up a resolution which I want to submit. . . . The Hague Conference led the nations to the stream of arbitration. It depends upon us whether they shall be induced to drink. All the general resolutions addressed to Governments are of practically no use at all. What we have to do is appeal to the peoples. . . . It is necessary that when nations go against the sentiment of the civilized world, there should be an explosion of pacific sentiment. (Hear, hear) I see precious little explosion here: and if a Peace Congress will not explode, how do you think the general public will do so? (Laughter) I propose to add some explosive matter to the resolutions by moving the following address:

> The Hague Conference having recommended four different methods of avoiding war— . . . mediation, international commissions of inquiry, . . . special commissions, and . . . arbitration pure and simple—the Congress declares that any State by refusing to adopt any one of them when proffered by its opponent loses its right to be regarded as a civilized Power. In such a country, excommunicate of humanity, the Congress is of opinion that while the war lasts no public religious service . . . be held that is not opened by a confession of blood-guiltiness on the part of that nation, and closed by a solemn appeal on the part of the congregation to the Government to stop the war by the application of The Hague methods. (Cheers)

. . . This amendment is based on the very simple and fundamental principle that no person with his hands dripping with his neighbor's blood unjustly shed should go before his God and ask a blessing. (Applause) . . . The main facts are plain and clear— . . . we are at war . . . as a direct consequence of the fact that we returned haughty and repeated refusals to repeated applications to refer the questions in dispute to arbitration. . . . Even if we were absolutely right and President Kruger was absolutely wrong, when he implored that the question should be submitted to arbitration, we indignantly refused . . . ; I say that upon our heads lies the curse of civilization and humanity . . . and the responsibility for the blood of those . . . who have died in South Africa. Perhaps tomorrow we shall read another telegram from Lord Kitchener announcing another "good bag" . . . and yet we call ourselves a Christian nation! [The South Africans] are defending the principles we are met to defend. . . . What is the good of the resolutions passed at The Hague when not one of us has the heart of a mouse to say 'Damn! Damn! Damn!' on all people who carry on war. . . . England at the present moment is engaged in a war that make us [the] excommunicate of humanity.

The Refusal to Obey Illegitimate Authority

Direct action against war and militarism, such as the refusal to fight or to pay taxes, was developed outside socialist circles. As articulated by Henry David Thoreau and Leo Tolstoy, it was an essentially moral form of action, whereas in Hungary and Finland, it was practical and political.

The ideas of Henry David Thoreau, a New England writer who sometimes supported his independent way of life by working as a laborer, became especially significant in the twentieth century. His essay "Resistance to Civil Government" (document 2.28) clarifies the citizen's obligation to oppose illegitimate authority by individual action: one should refuse to pay taxes or support the routine business of a government which itself violates human rights. Thoreau's night in jail for refusing to pay a poll tax in Massachusetts that indirectly supported both slavery and the United States war with Mexico (1846) has inspired subsequent nonviolent protesters in human rights and peace action.

At the end of the century, Leo Tolstoy went further, demanding a commitment that was totally hostile to the refined arguments of liberal internationalists and socialists. Internationally acclaimed as the author of *Anna Karenina* and *War and Peace,* Tolstoy insisted that Christian words become living deeds in absolute pacifism. In essays published in British journals between 1894 and 1899 (document 2.29), he urged young men to refuse military service when drafted, and to accept prison or even execution rather than to kill or even train to kill another human being. His passionate attack on the organized peace movement reflected his impatience with the legalistic arguments that justified defensive war. He rejected peace projects that compromised with state power, and his denunciation of the Hague Conference (1899) typified his insistence that "armies will only be . . . abolished when people cease to trust governments."

Tolstoy's influence extended to European and American peace advocates and to Mohandas Gandhi of India, and his writings played a major role in Bulgarian cultural life from the beginning of the century to 1949. His international fame protected him from government reprisal in Russia. There his following grew, thousands of persons participating in Tolstoyan agricultural colonies, and endured up to the end of the 1930s.[9]

Although writers such as Thoreau and Tolstoy promoted the idea of nonviolent resistance to illegitimate authority as a moral duty, it also grew as a practical form of political action. Throughout the 1850s, Hungarians used passive noncooperation against the Hapsburg monarchy. Resistance, which continued until the compromise of 1867, included demonstrations, boycotts, nonpayment of taxes, and symbolic actions. The basis of nonviolent strategy was articulated by Ferenc Deák (1803–76), who warned that violence would undermine not only unjust authority but law itself. The Finnish people, a semiautonomous Grand Duchy of Russia in the nineteenth century, drew upon Hungarian precedents when they were threatened by systematic Russification at the end of the century. They effectively applied various forms of noncooperation in a campaign thoroughly grounded in secular nonviolent theory, most succinctly articulated by Viktor Theodor Homén (document 2.30).

Document 2.28

Henry David Thoreau: Resistance to Civil Government

From "Resistance to Civil Government," 1849

How does it become a man to behave toward this American government today? I answer, that he cannot without disgrace be associated with it. I cannot for an instant recognize that political organization as *my* government which is the *slave's* government also.

All men recognize the right of revolution; that is, the right to refuse allegiance to, and to resist, the government, when its tyranny or its inefficiency are great and unendurable. . . . When a sixth of the population of a nation which has undertaken to be the refuge of liberty are slaves, and a whole country is unjustly overrun and conquered by a foreign army, and subjected to military law, I think that it is not too soon for honest men to rebel. . . . What makes this duty the more urgent is the fact that the country so overrun is not our own, but ours is the invading army.

. . . This people must cease to hold slaves, and to make war on Mexico, though it cost them their existence as a people. . . .

[If the injustice caused by a government machine] is of such a nature that it requires you to be the agent of injustice to another, then, I say, break the law. Let your life be a counter friction to stop the machine.

. . . Those who call themselves Abolitionists should at once effectually withdraw their support, both in person and property, from the government of Massachusetts, and not wait till they constitute a majority of one, before they . . . prevail through law. . . . any man more right than his neighbors constitutes a majority of one already.

Under a government which imprisons any unjustly, the true place for a just man is also a prison. The proper place to-day, the only place which Massachusetts has provided for her freer and less desponding spirits, is in her prisons. . . . If the alternative is to keep all just men in prison, or give up war and slavery, the state will not hesitate which to choose. If a thousand men were not to pay their tax-bills this year, that would not be a violent and bloody measure, as it would be to pay them, and enable the State to commit violence and shed innocent blood. This is, in fact, the definition of a peaceable revolution, if any such is possible.

. . . [In refusing to pay taxes] I simply wish to refuse allegiance to the State, to withdraw and stand aloof from it effectually. . . . I quietly declare war [on] the State. . . .

Document 2.29

Leo Tolstoy: Civil Disobedience and Nonviolence

From "Patriotism," 1896, and
"On the Peace Conference at the Hague," 1899

"Patriotism"

Open the newspapers on any day you like and you will always see, every moment, some black spot, a possible cause for war. Now it is Korea, again the Pamirs, Africa, Abyssinia, Armenia, Turkey, Venezuela, or the Transvaal. The work of robbery ceases not for an instant; now here, now there, some small war is going on incessantly, . . . and a great real war may, must, begin at some moment.

Obviously, to avoid war, it is necessary . . . to destroy the root of war. And that is the exclusive desire for the well-being of one's own people; it is patriotism. . . . Therefore to destroy war, destroy patriotism. . . .

It will be said, "Patriotism has welded mankind into states, and maintains the unity of states." But men are now united in states; that work is done; why now maintain exclusive devotion to one's own state, when this produces terrible evils for all states and nations? . . .

A Russian should rejoice if Poland, the Baltic Provinces, Finland, Armenia, should be separated, freed from Russia; so with an Englishman in regard to Ireland, India, and other possessions; and each should help to this because, the greater the state, the more wrong and cruel is its patriotism. . . . Therefore, if we really wish to be what we profess to be, we must not only cease our present desire for the growth of our state, but we must desire its decrease, its weakening. . . . As long as we praise patriotism, and cultivate it in the young, so long will there be armaments to destroy the physical and spiritual life of nations; and wars, vast, awful wars, such as we are preparing. . . .

"On the Peace Conference at the Hague"

... The aim of the (Hague) Conference will be, not to establish peace, but to hide from men the sole means of escape from the miseries of war, which lies in the refusal by private individuals of all participation in the murders of war.

With those who refuse military service on conscientious grounds, governments will always behave as the Russian government behaved with the Dukhobors.* At the very time when it was professing to the whole world . . . its peaceful intentions, it was . . . torturing and ruining and banishing the most peaceable people in Russia, merely because they were peaceable, not in words only, but in deeds, and therefore refused to be soldiers. All the European governments have met, and still meet refusals of military service in the same way, though less brutally. That is how the governments of Austria, Germany, France, Sweden, Switzerland and Holland have acted. . . .

Liberals entangled in their much talking, socialists, and other so-called advanced people may think that their speeches in Parliament and at meetings, their unions, strikes, and pamphlets, are of great importance; while the refusals of military service . . . are unimportant. . . . The governments, however, know very well what is important to them and what is not. And the governments readily allow all sorts of liberal and radical speeches in Reichstags, as well as workmen's associations and socialist demonstrations, . . . in diverting people's attention from the great and only means of emancipation. . . . But governments never openly tolerate refusals of military service, or refusals of war taxes . . . because they know that such refusals expose the fraud of governments and strike at the root of their power. . . .

. . . With amazing effrontery, all governments [declare] that all the preparations for war, and even the very wars themselves . . . are necessary to preserve peace. In this sphere of hypocrisy and deception a fresh step is being made . . . : that the very governments for whose support the armies and the wars are essential pretend that they are concerned to discover means to diminish the armies and to abolish war. The governments wish to persuade the peoples that there is no need for private individuals to trouble about freeing themselves from wars; the governments themselves, at their conferences, will arrange first to reduce and . . . abolish armies. But this is—untrue.

---

* The Dukhobors were Christian nonresistant sects who migrated to Russia from western Europe partly in an attempt to escape conscription.

Armies will only be . . . abolished when people cease to trust governments and themselves seek salvation . . . in the simple fulfillment of that
law, . . . not to do to others what you wish them not to do to you—
above all, not to slay your neighbors. . . .

. . . The Conference can only divert people's eyes from the sole path
leading to safety and liberty.

Document 2.30

Victor Theodor Homén: Nonviolent Resistance in Finland

From "Passive Resistance," 1900

. . . True, the Finnish nation is neither great nor mighty, but up until
now its courageousness has always been acknowledged, and it does not
wish to die.

Our battle, however, is being carried out in a different way, a way
that requires as much persevering strength, manliness, and love as armed
struggle. Everyone agrees that our best defense is resolute passive resistance.

But what does this defensive means of the weak against the strong
called passive resistance consist of? One thing is sure, it cannot be
equated with the performance of either mild or radical protests which
end in compliance with the oppressor's demands. It is not that at all,
quite the contrary it is:

1. consistent refusal to cooperate with any illegal or violent act committed by a stronger party;

2. that these violent commands not be obeyed, followed or promoted to any degree. On the contrary, the realization of the schemes
against which passive resistance is aimed must be hindered through all
legitimate means;

3. that the enforced system of violence never be recognized. To sum
it up: noncooperation, disobedience, and nonrecognition.

To a certain extent, point 3. (nonrecognition) is the easiest to carry
out, and the only action it requires is the fulfillment of point 1., i.e., that
those involved do not further the legitimization of violent measures.
Nevertheless, if one is truly set to absolutely refuse to recognize the
validity of violent measures, then consistency requires that they not be
obeyed in practice; in other words, point 2. (disobedience) must be fulfilled.

We are thus led to the most difficult and extensive of the three points.

Most difficult, because it is a matter of action, and not just the action of some of our higher officials, but of the whole nation. . . .

If we survey the current predicament from a broad perspective, seeing our position in relation to general cultural development, then it is easy to recognize that we now have a greater chance than ever to emerge into world history. Now, right now, the principle of rights must finally begin to vanquish the principle of violence. Reform of this magnitude cannot be realized without great suffering and sacrifice on the part of those who are willing to fight for it. . . . Will we fail? No, we won't.

Everyone must participate. A kind of method is needed which will deprive the attacks which have been carried out against our nationality and our separate existence as a nation of their destructive power.

Concretely speaking, the three most recent illegally enacted Russian decrees must not be recognized as valid. But if the oppressor seeks to forcefully implement them . . . the greatest difficulties will not be on our side. The Russian Language Act does not directly pertain to the public at large, but only to officialdom. The offensive act restricting the freedom of assembly, however, affects us all. It can either simply be ignored or, in order to avoid confrontation, people may restrict themselves to private gatherings. In this way the implementation of this new decree will prove impossible. . . .

The immediate response to the act extending the rights of Russian salesmen must be for not a single Finnish man or woman to trade any longer with any Russian in this country. . . .

These examples suffice to show what attitude should be taken by the people as a whole toward the violent decrees and Russification measures, i.e., not even in the most insignificant matters should the will of violence be obeyed. When violence seeks to have its way, it must be forced at every step and every moment to display itself as violence. This is because in the course of time nothing exhausts the ravaging of violence more than when it is incessantly forced to show itself in its true form, in the shape of law-defiling violence. If nobody paves its way, then it will finally give rise to such resistance against it that it will be incapable of penetrating further. . . .

Because our opponent has nothing to fear from us physically, then our only defense is the respect which a people gives rise to when it fights for its rights not only in words but also in deeds. And it is effective defense, since history shows that in the long term it is stronger than any armies.

If our people adhere to right and truth then God will give it strength to endure until the dawn of a new morning.

Official International Agreements

At the 1815 Congress of Vienna, following the wars of the French
Revolution and Napoleonic conquests, the victors remade the map of
Europe. Most sovereigns agreed to a Holy Alliance, proposed by the
Russian Tsar, Alexander I, pledging to observe peace among themselves.
More concretely, Britain, Russia, Austria, and Prussia formed an alliance
to enforce the peace settlement (France was admitted in 1818). The
alliance held a series of consultations on common problems, the so-called
Congress System, or Concert of Europe. The alliance was weakened
by diverging English interests, sundered by revolutions (1847–49), and
destroyed with the Crimean War (1854–56), although it formed the
precedent for Great Power consultations in later crises. For most observers the Concert system enshrined the political status quo against territorial change and domestic revolutions. For some peace advocates, it
implied a new approach to international law and peacekeeping.

When a Swiss businessman, Henry Dunant,[10] accidentally wandered
onto the battlefield at Solferino during the war for Italian unification
(Piedmont-Savoy and France against the Austrians, 1859), he found
masses of wounded, abandoned by retreating troops. Dunant mobilized
local townspeople to help them. He then sought to persuade heads of
state that medical help for wounded men would not alter the outcome
of the battlefield. From Dunant's initiative there came a series of
agreements (1864–1899) on the treatment of the wounded, prisoners of
war, and civilian victims. None of those conventions impinged on national sovereignty or military priorities, but they were the forerunners of
twentieth-century arms limitations agreements.

The first of them was the 1864 Geneva "Convention on the Amelioration of the Wounded in Armies of the Field" (document 2.31), which
facilitated the work of the nongovernmental International Red Cross. It
also included protection for victims of maritime warfare. The Geneva
Convention was followed by the 1868 Declaration of St. Petersburg
(document 2.32) of the International Military Commission, which
sought to limit forms of weapons. Peace activists disdained these
agreements as futile attempts to humanize warfare, but they admitted
that government willingness to sign *any* commitment had potential for
the future. Citizen groups therefore continued to press their governments
to adopt permanent institutions and procedures for the peaceful resolution of conflict.

Meanwhile, in an effort to give international law a more scientific
foundation, European and American legal experts organized the Institute

of International Law and the International Law Association, both formed in 1873. Building on the example of Grotius, the specialists assumed that the law of nations is essentially the customary behavior of sovereign states. Accordingly, they made systematic efforts to codify the common standards by which nations related to one another, rules of conduct that were to be found in treaties, conventions, and diplomatic practices. Early in the twentieth century a journalist named Raymond L. Bridgman compiled a record of international conventions in communication, transportation, sanitation, and arbitration that he thought were evidence of a transnational society, which in turn heralded a coming world government.[11] In fact, when his book was published, there was in Brussels a coordinating center for nongovernmental international associations, which numbered over six hundred by 1914. The prevailing view of governments and most legal experts treated international law as the agreements of sovereign nations, their independence stronger than ever before, and the standards to which they might consent.

An initiative for broader international agreements came unexpectedly from the Russian Tsar. Nicholas II was motivated by a number of factors, which probably included the analyses of Jean de Bloch predicting that a general war would lead to a European bloodbath and bring down empires. In August 1898, Nicholas invited governments to meet and discuss ways to contain the arms race and avoid war (document 2.33). The Tsar's invitation was initially greeted with skepticism and derision from diplomats, but it generated an unexpectedly enthusiastic response from the public. Following a revision of the original rescript, or official document, the conference opened in May 1899 at The Hague.

Although the 1899 Hague Conference continued earlier attempts to limit warfare by concluding a series of conventions that prohibited specific weapons (document 2.34), it also broke new ground by considering alternative approaches to international conflict and by promising future conferences to develop them. A second Hague conference was held in 1907.

By the time of the Tsar's rescript, governments had experimented with pacific means of resolving disputes. One of the most promising of these was to submit differences to third party panels of arbitration. The disputes that were arbitrated during the nineteenth century were mainly issues such as boundaries or fishing rights, but there were a few cases of greater political significance. Such was the *Alabama* case between the United States and Great Britain, which was settled in 1872 by an international panel in Geneva. The panel upheld the American claim that the British government had not respected the laws of neutrality during the

U. S. Civil War.[12] The *Alabama* case not only became a model for the pacific resolution of differences, but also stimulated a renewed campaign for arbitration provisions, which increasingly were written into treaties. That campaign formed the political context of the tentative steps taken at the first and second Hague Conferences toward the resolution of disputes through arbitration, mediation, good offices, and neutral intervention (documents 2.35 and 2.36).

After the meeting of 1899, British plenipotentiary Sir Julian Paunce-fote evaluated the convention on the pacific resolution of disputes as follows: "That work, if it stood alone, would proclaim the success of the Conference. . . . It constitutes a complete code on the subject of good offices, mediation and arbitration. Its most striking and novel feature is the establishment of a Permanent Court of International Arbitration which has so long been the dream of advocates of peace, destined apparently, until now, never to be realized.[13] The limited conventions signed by governments in 1899 and 1907 provided a basis for the creation of the World Court at The Hague, but only in 1921 after the sobering impact of world war.

Document 2.31

The Geneva Convention of 1864: On the Wounded

From Convention for the Amelioration of the Wounded, 1864

ARTICLE 1: Ambulances and military hospitals shall be acknowledged to be neutral, and, as such, shall be protected and respected by belligerents so long as any sick or wounded may be therein. Such neutrality shall cease if the ambulances or hospitals should be held by a military force.

ARTICLE 2: Persons employed in hospitals and ambulances, comprising the staff for superintendence, medical service, administration, transport of wounded, as well as chaplains, shall participate in the benefit of neutrality. . . .

ARTICLE 5: Inhabitants of the country who may bring help to the wounded shall be respected, and shall remain free. The generals of the belligerent Powers shall make it their care to inform the inhabitants of the appeal addressed to their humanity, and of the neutrality which will be the consequence of it.

Any wounded man entertained and taken care of in a house shall be considered as a protection thereto. Any inhabitant who shall have entertained wounded men in his house shall be exempted from the quartering of troops, as well as from a part of the contributions of war which may be imposed.*

Document 2.32

The St. Petersburg Convention of 1868: On Weapons

From the Declaration of St. Petersburg

. . . Considering that the progress of civilization should have the effect of alleviating, as much as possible, the calamities of war;

That the only legitimate object that States should endeavor to accomplish during war is to weaken the military force of the enemy;

That for this purpose it is sufficient to disable the greatest possible number of men;

That this object would be exceeded by the employment of arms which uselessly aggravate the sufferings of disabled men, or render their death inevitable;

That the employment of such arms would, therefore, be contrary to the laws of humanity;

The contracting Parties engage, mutually, to renounce, in case of war among themselves, the employment, by their military or naval forces, of any projectile of less weight than four hundred grams, which is explosive, or is charged with fulminating or inflammable substances.

They agree to invite all the States which have not taken part in the deliberations of the International Military Commission, assembled at St. Petersburg . . . to accede to the present engagement. . . .

The contracting or acceding Parties reserve to themselves the right to come to an understanding, hereafter, whenever a precise proposition shall be drawn up, in view of future improvements which may be effected in the armament of troops, in order to maintain the principles which they have established, and to reconcile the necessities of war with the laws of humanity.†

* This Geneva Convention of 22 August 1864 was subsequently adapted to maritime warfare. The convention was first signed for Baden, Belgium, Denmark, France, Hesse, Italy, the Netherlands, Portugal, Prussia, Spain, Switzerland, and Württemburg. Nearly all nations subsequently adhered to it.

† The declaration was signed for Austria, Babaria, Belgium, Denmark, France, Great Britain, Greece, Italy, the Netherlands, Persia, Portugal, Prussia and the North German Confederation, Russia, Sweden and Norway, Switzerland, Turkey, and Württemburg.

Document 2.33

Nicholas II: The Call for the First Hague Conference

From the Rescript of the Russian Emperor and the Russian
Circular, 1898–1899

The Tsar's Rescript of 24 August 1898

The maintenance of general peace and a possible reduction of the excessive armaments which weigh upon all nations present themselves, in the existing condition of the whole world, as the ideal towards which the endeavors of all Governments should be directed.

The humanitarian and magnanimous ideas of His Majesty . . . have been won over to this view. In the conviction that this lofty aim is in conformity with the most essential interests and legitimate views of all Powers, the Imperial Government thinks that the present moment would be very favorable for seeking, by means of international discussion, the most effectual means of insuring to all peoples the benefits of a real and durable peace, and, above all, of putting an end to the progressive development of the present armaments. . . .

The economic crises, due in great part to the system of armaments, . . . are transforming the armed peace of our days into a crushing burden, which the peoples have more and more difficulty in bearing. It appears evident, then, that if this state of things were prolonged, it would inevitably lead to the very cataclysm which it is desired to avert, and the horrors of which make every thinking man shudder in advance.

To put an end to these incessant armaments and to see the means of warding off the calamities which are threatening the whole world—such is the supreme duty which is today imposed on all States.

Filled with this idea, His Majesty has been pleased to order me to propose to all the Governments whose representatives are accredited to the Imperial Court, the meeting of a conference which would have to occupy itself with this grave problem.

Count Mouravieff's Note of 11 January 1899

. . . The subjects to be submitted for international discussion at the Conference could, in general terms, be summarized as follows:

1. An understanding not to increase for a fixed period the present effective [size] of the armed military and naval forces, and at the same time not to increase the Budgets pertaining thereto; and a preliminary

examination of the means by which a reduction might even be effected in [the] future in the forces and Budgets above mentioned.

2. To prohibit the use in the armies and fleets of any new kind of firearms whatever, and of new explosives, or any powders more powerful than those now in use, either for rifles or cannon.

3. To restrict the use in military warfare of the formidable explosives already existing, and to prohibit the throwing of projectiles or explosives of any kind from balloons or by similar means.

4. To prohibit the use, in naval warfare, of submarine torpedo boats or plungers, or other similar engines of destruction; to give an undertaking not to construct, in the future vessels with rams.

5. To apply to naval warfare the stipulations of the Geneva Convention of 1864, on the basis of the additional articles of 1868.

6. To neutralize ships and boats employed in saving those overboard during or after an engagement.

7. To revise the Declaration concerning the laws and customs of war elaborated in 1874 by the Conference of Brussels, which has remained unratified to the present day.

8. To accept in principle the employment of good offices, of mediation and facultative arbitration in cases lending themselves thereto, with the object of preventing armed conflicts between nations; . . . and to establish a uniform practice in using them.

It is well understood that all questions concerning the political relations of States, and the order of things established by Treaties, as in general all questions which do not directly fall within the program adopted by the Cabinets, must be absolutely excluded from the deliberations of the Conference.

Document 2.34

The Hague Conference of 1899: The Rules and Customs of War

From the Final Act and The Laws and Customs of War on Land

Final Act

In a series of meetings, between May 18 and July 29, . . . the Conference has agreed, for submission for signature by the Plenipotentiaries, on the text of the Conventions and Declarations enumerated below and annexed to the present Act:

I. Convention for the peaceful adjustment of international differences.
II. Convention regarding the laws and customs of war by land.
III. Convention for the adaptation to maritime warfare of the principles of the Geneva Convention of the 22nd August, 1864.
IV. Three Declarations:
   1. To prohibit the launching of projectiles and explosives from balloons or by other similar new methods.
   2. To prohibit the use of projectiles, the only object of which is the diffusion of asphyxiating or deleterious gases.
   3. To prohibit the use of bullets which expand or flatten easily in the human body . . . .

The Conference is of opinion that the restriction of military charges, which are at present a heavy burden on the world, is extremely desirable for the increase of the material and moral welfare of mankind.

. . . The Conference expresses the wish that the Governments, taking into consideration the proposals made at the Conference, may examine the possibility of an agreement as to the limitation of armed forces by land and sea, and of war budgets.

Convention with Respect to the Laws and Customs of War on Land

Considering that, while seeking means to preserve peace and prevent armed conflicts among nations, it is likewise necessary to have regard to cases where an appeal to arms may be caused by events which [they could not prevent]; . . .

[The signatory governments have] adopted a great number of provisions, the object of which is to define and govern the usages of war on land.

. . . these provisions, the wording of which has been inspired by the desire to diminish the evils of war so far as military requirements permit, are destined to serve as general rules of conduct for belligerents in their relations with each other and with populations. . . .

On the Qualifications of Belligerents

ARTICLE 3. The armed forces of the belligerent parties may consist of combatants and non-combatants. In case of capture by the enemy, both have a right to be treated as prisoners of war.

On Prisoners of War

ARTICLE 4. Prisoners of war are in the power of the hostile Government, but not in that of the individuals or corps who captured them. They must be humanely treated. All their personal belongings, except arms, horses, and military papers, remain their property. . . .

ARTICLE 7. The Government into whose hands prisoners of war have fallen is bound to maintain them. Failing a special agreement between the belligerents, prisoners of war shall be treated as regards food, quarters, and clothing, on the same footing as the troops of the Government which has captured them. . . .

On the Sick and Wounded

ARTICLE 21. The obligations of belligerents with regard to the sick and wounded are governed by the Geneva Convention of the 22nd August, 1864, subject to any modifications which may be introduced into it.

On Means of Injuring the Enemy, Sieges, and Bombardments

ARTICLE 22. The right of belligerents to adopt means of injuring the enemy is not unlimited.

ARTICLE 23. Besides the prohibitions provided by special Conventions, it is especially prohibited: (a) to employ poison or poisoned arms; (b) to kill or wound treacherously individuals belonging to the hostile nation or army; (c) to kill or wound an enemy who, having laid down his arms, or having no longer means of defense, has surrendered at discretion; (d) to declare that no quarter will be given; (e) to employ arms, projectiles, or material calculated to cause superfluous injury. . . .

ARTICLE 25. The attack or bombardment of towns, villages, habitations, or buildings which are not defended is prohibited. . . .

ARTICLE 28. The pillage of a town or place, even when taken by assault, is prohibited. . . .

On Military Authority over Hostile Territory

ARTICLE 44. Any compulsion of the population of occupied territory to take part in military operations against its own country is prohibited. . . .

ARTICLE 46. Family honor and rights, the lives of persons, and private property, as well as religious convictions and practice, must be respected. Private property can not be confiscated. . . .

ARTICLE 56. The property of the communes, that of religious, charitable, and educational institutions, and those of arts and science, even when State property, shall be treated as private property. All seizure of, and destruction, or intentional damage done to such institutions, to historic monuments, works of art or science, is prohibited, and should be made the subject of proceedings.

Document 2.35

The Hague Conference of 1899: The Pacific Settlement of Disputes

From the Convention for the Pacific Settlement of International Disputes, 1899

ARTICLE 1. With a view to obviating, as far as possible, recourse to force in the relations between States, the Signatory Powers agree to use their best efforts to ensure the pacific settlement of international differences.

ARTICLE 2. In case of serious disagreement or conflict, before an appeal to arms, the Signatory Powers agree to have recourse, as far as circumstances allow, to the good offices or mediation of one or more friendly Powers.

ARTICLE 3. Independently of this recourse, the Signatory Powers recommend that one or more Powers, strangers to the dispute, should, on their own initiative, and as far as circumstances may allow, offer their good offices or mediation to the states at variance. . . .

ARTICLE 8. The Signatory Powers are agreed in recommending the application, when circumstances allow, of special mediation in the following form:

> In case of a serious difference endangering the peace, the States at variance choose respectively a Power, to which they entrust the mission of entering into direct communication with the Power chosen on the other side, with the object of preventing the rupture of pacific relations. . . .

ARTICLE 9. In disputes of an international nature involving neither honor nor essential interests, and arising from a difference of opinion on points of fact, the Signatory Powers recommend that the parties who have not been able to come to an agreement by means of diplomacy, should, as far as circumstances allow, institute an International Commission of Inquiry, to facilitate a solution of these disputes by elucidating the facts by means of an impartial and conscientious investigation.

ARTICLE 10. The International Commissions of Inquiry are constituted by special agreement between the parties in conflict.

The Convention for an inquiry defines the facts to be examined and the extent of the Commissioners' powers. [It determines procedure and must hear both sides of a dispute.]

ARTICLE 18. The Arbitration Convention implies an engagement to submit in good faith to the arbitral award.

On the Permanent Court of Arbitration

ARTICLE 20. With the object of facilitating an immediate recourse to arbitration for international differences which it has not been possible to settle by diplomacy, the Signatory Powers undertake to organize a Permanent Court of Arbitration, accessible at all times and operating, unless otherwise stipulated by the parties, in accordance with the Rules of Procedure inserted in the present Convention. . . .

ARTICLE 22. An International Bureau, established at The Hague, serves as a record office for the Court. . . .

ARTICLE 23. Within the three months following its ratification . . . each Signatory Power shall select four persons at the most, of known competency in questions of international law, of the highest moral reputation, and disposed to accept the duties of Arbitrators. . . .

ARTICLE 24. When the Signatory Powers wish to have recourse to the Permanent Court for the settlement of a difference that has arisen between them, the Arbitrators called upon to form the competent Tribunal to decide this difference must be chosen from the general list of Members of the Court. . . .

ARTICLE 26. . . . The jurisdiction of the Permanent Court may, within the conditions laid down in the Regulations, be extended to disputes between non-Signatory Powers, or between Signatory Powers and non-Signatory Powers if the parties are agreed to have recourse to this tribunal. . . .

Document 2.36

The Hague Conference of 1907: Peace in Principle

From "The Final Act and Conventions of the Second
International Peace Conference"

. . . The Conference, actuated by the spirit of mutual agreement and concession characterizing its deliberations,* has agreed upon the following declaration, which, while reserving to each of the Powers represented full liberty of action as regards voting, enables them to affirm the principles which they regard as unanimously admitted.

It is unanimous:

1. In admitting the principle of obligatory arbitration.

2. In declaring that certain disputes, in particular those relating to the interpretation and application of the provisions of international agreements, may be submitted to compulsory arbitration without any restriction.

Finally, it is unanimous in proclaiming that, although it has not yet been found feasible to conclude a Convention in this sense, nevertheless the divergences of opinion which have come to light have not exceeded the bounds of judicial controversy, and that, by working together here during the past four months, the collected Powers not only have learned to understand one another and to draw closer together, but have succeeded in the course of this long collaboration in evolving a very lofty conception of the common welfare of humanity. . . .

The Second Peace Conference confirms the resolution adopted by the Conference of 1899 in regard to the limitation of military expenditure; and inasmuch as military expenditure has considerably increased in almost every country since that time, the Conference declares that it is eminently desirable that the Governments* should resume the serious examination of this question.

It has besides expressed the following opinions:

1. The Conference calls the attention of the Signatory Powers to the advisability of adopting the annexed draft Convention for the creation

---

* The conference, in meetings from 15 June to 18 October 1907, drew up a series of conventions for the pacific settlement of international disputes, the limitation of the use of force to recover debts, opening hostilities, the laws and customs of land war, the rights and duties of neutrals in land war, the status of enemy merchant ships, the conversion of merchant ships into warships, submarine mines, naval bombardment, the laws and customs of naval war and the right of capture, the creation of an International Prize Court, the rights and duties of neutrals in a naval war, and the throwing of projectiles from the air.

of a Judicial Arbitration Court, and of bringing it into force as soon as an agreement has been reached respecting the selection of the judges and the constitution of the Court.

2. The Conference expresses the opinion that, in case of war, the responsible authorities, civil as well as military, should make it their special duty to ensure and safeguard the maintenance of pacific relations, more especially of the commercial and industrial relations between the inhabitants of the belligerent States and neutral countries.

3. The Conference expresses the opinion that the Powers may regulate, by special treaties, the position, as regards military charges, of foreigners residing within their territories.

4. The Conference expresses the opinion that the preparation of regulations relative to the laws and customs of naval war may figure in the program of the next Conference, and that in any case the Powers may apply, as far as possible, to war by sea the principles of the Convention relative to the laws and customs of war on land.

Finally, the conference recommends to the Powers the assembly of a Third Peace Conference. . . .*

* This meeting was to be held in 1915, but the Great War was occurring instead.

3

World War I and Peace
1914–1919

As Europe plunged into war in 1914, most statesmen and generals calculated that a short conflict would achieve their dreams of glory. Instead, the conflict turned into a stalemate of deadly trench warfare in the west and shifting, inconclusive slaughter in the east. It was a long, terrible nightmare, an incalculable disaster for all the European nations involved. For four years the continent absorbed the blood of at least 10,000,000 of its most vigorous population as well as thousands brought from overseas colonies. Finally the Central Powers became exhausted and collapsed. By the time it ended, the war had provoked revolution in Russia, embroiled the United States, and unleashed worldwide currents of social unrest and nationalism. It set the agenda for the twentieth century. It changed the agenda of peace.

When the war began, crowds had cheered in the major capitals of Europe as their forces marched off in splendor—from Vienna and Berlin, Moscow, Paris, and London. Fear for national survival was mixed with self-righteous idealism in every belligerent nation. Each people interpreted itself as the defender of a territory and a political order that its governing and intellectual class identified with its particular view of civilization. As deadlock ensued and the scale of purposeless killing became widely known, revulsion replaced enthusiasm, and rational minds sought to end not only this great war but, indeed, war itself.

The documents in this chapter illustrate five currents of thought to which writers on peace were drawn: an appeal to reason and conciliation, a rejection of militarism, a socialist revolution, a just society, and an international order. Each of these ideas had its origins long before

World War I, and each was developed more fully afterwards, but in the crisis of 1914–18 they were all sharpened and in some measure institutionalized.

In the early months of the carnage there were poignant appeals to reason and humanity in the interest of peace. Throughout the war there was even some outright opposition to it. The existence of even limited antiwar activity suggested the intensity with which some citizens felt obligated to dissent, at the risk of being charged with treason, whether on religious grounds or from political and pragmatic considerations. Moral challenges were expressed in conscientious objection to military service or to violations of civil rights and public trust.

In Europe political challenges came especially from socialists. Most Social Democrats in belligerent countries initially supported national war policies, but they became ever more critical as reality replaced the illusion of glorious victory. They advocated a negotiated peace and greater power for the working class. For revolutionary socialists, however, a lasting peace could come only with the annihilation of capitalist power. Thus Vladimir Ilyich Lenin hoped to turn the war of alliances into a war of classes. His view was institutionalized late in 1917, when the Bolshevik regime took power in Russia amid wartime extremity.

Progressives expected to advance social reforms through the war, and they overwhelmingly identified peace with military victory. On the other hand, a minority of them interpreted war as the epitome of social injustice. That view, inherited from the nineteenth-century by socialists, was also expressed by reformers, notably feminists, who distinguished between the interests of the governing elite and those of the broader society. Peace, they believed, required social justice across national boundaries.

The dominant formula for preserving peace was an organized international order. Especially in the last years of fighting, it was widely held that the sacrifice could be justified only by the prevention of a future war, which required institutionalizing principles of international conduct. Those principles, formulated through public debate and governmental negotiation, were in large measure a nineteenth-century heritage, but they were vested in a distinctly twentieth-century invention, the League of Nations. Despite its limitations, the League was imbued with a vision of international cooperation and collective security that for the most part had been limited to peace activists before the Great War.

Appeals for Conciliation

In 1914–15 most leaders from the prewar peace movement became convinced that enemy nations threatened the humane and cosmopolitan order which they valued. Nonetheless a few peace advocates maintained that war itself was the obstacle to an international order of reason and law.

Henri La Fontaine made that point early in the war. A lawyer, professor, and leading socialist politician in Belgium, La Fontaine had been active in the International Arbitration and Peace Association and in the Interparliamentary Union, and was president of the International Peace Bureau at Bern. The central committee of the Bureau became hopelessly deadlocked about responsibility for the war, and finally it took a neutral position. La Fontaine himself became convinced that the defeat of the Central Powers was necessary for enduring peace, and he was glad when the United States entered the war in 1917, but he continued to advocate the approach he had outlined in September 1914 (document 3.1). Although his ideas reflected a century of peace effort, they were forged by the Great War into a comprehensive program for postwar internationalism.

A few months after he made that appeal, La Fontaine joined Henri Golay, the Swiss secretary-general of the International Peace Bureau, in urging intellectuals everywhere to look beyond the "hatred and bitterness of war" to the "interdependence of nations."[1] Bertrand Russell challenged the Great War itself. A distinguished English mathematician and philosopher, Russell insisted that self-delusion and uncritical nationalism were precisely the qualities through which the masses of people had been mobilized for war (document 3.2). Intellectuals should resist those irrational impulses, Russell insisted: peace requires the courage of reason, elevated by the "great human purpose" of justice and ventured especially in wartime. Whatever the merits of Russell's assessment of the conflict, his critique foreshadowed postwar attempts to think skeptically and realistically about nationalism and international conflict. In the meantime, with a few exceptions, intellectuals identified peace with victory.

Socialist and labor parties in the belligerent countries, also with few exceptions, rallied to the national cause. Early in 1915 socialists from the neutral Nordic countries reminded their militant comrades of the peace principles of the Second International (document 3.3). The Scandinavians appealed for an early resolution of the war, which they identified with international capitalist interests.

The most dramatic appeal for an early peace came from women. On 28 April 1915 nearly twelve hundred of them gathered at The Hague. Coming from a dozen countries, some of them at war, the women formed the core of what would become the Women's International League for Peace and Freedom.[2] They met openly in wartime, insisted that the fighting stop, and called for a peace that would include not only justice among nations but also women's participation in international policymaking (document 3.4). Their congress sent delegations to neutral and belligerent capitals in order to promote a peace settlement through mediation by neutral nations. That effort failed, but the congress of 1915 signaled the rise of a new thrust in peace advocacy, one that was radically transnational and activist.

Although those women defended the principle of nationality, they rejected exclusive or aggressive nationalism. Peace had to reflect universal values, they insisted, and the true basis for international reconciliation was the "common ideals" of even those people who believed themselves to be fighting in self-defense. The women's resolutions complemented the religious appeal of Benedict XV, the Roman Catholic pope, six months earlier (document 3.5): together they contrasted a peaceful vision of mutual values to warfare, in which "all take as their supreme law their own self-interest."

Document 3.1

Henri La Fontaine: Pacifists and the War

From "What Pacifists Ought to Say," November 1914

For more than three months past diabolical and bloody war has been raging! . . .

. . . the frightful conflict has gone on, involving more than 18,000,000 combatants, paralyzing the entire economic and intellectual life of the world, imperiling the whole of civilization, preparing for the future a race physically and morally lowered, wasting a total sum of £8,000,000 a day of resources which would have assured the almost illimitable development of the nations.

Instead of the brightness and happiness that would have been associated with a glorious summer and a brilliant autumn, the earth has been filled with hatred, anguish and tears, and a river of blood floods the desolated fields.

Women, children and old people have seen their much-loved homes burned to the ground, and have been submitted to the most horrible outrages, and even to death, without being able to defend themselves. Never for twenty centuries of Christianity has a war been carried on with such an accumulation of horrors, and such a disregard of every law, human or divine.

We might boast because of all these disasters and all this vileness. For we have never tired of foretelling these necessary consequences of the policy of alliances, of the foolish development of armaments, of the want of foresight of the diplomats, of the international suspicion maintained, with the silent complicity of the highest authorities, by the worst devotees of a diseased or selfish nationalism.

We were not listened to, our prophecies were derided, our advice was laughed to scorn, while the time for conciliation, explanations and negotiations was still open. . . .

And now the calamity has happened, terrible, vast, crushing and cruel; and from all sides voices are raised which unite in one desire. They say: this must be the last war! They appeal to us, the pacifists, and anxiously ask whether the hour for reconciliation is really about to strike, and how a stable and lasting peace can be given to the world. . . .

1. We have constantly affirmed . . . that a juridical status, such as exists between individuals within States, ought to be substituted for the anarchy which since the beginning of time has controlled their international relations. This juridical status must be accepted by all States as it has for long been accepted by all individuals within States. The majority of States must also be able to insist on its observance by a recalcitrant State.

No lasting peace can be established, if any one State is at liberty to withdraw from the international jurisdiction freely established by all the States, any dispute which may arise between it and another State. If in order to enforce its claim it were permissible to it to resort to arms, all the States would have to arm against it and the world would continue to be faced with the terrible dilemma which was the cause of the present war. . . .

2. We think that all the States should take part in the conclusion of the next peace and in the preparation of the instrument which will sanction it. This general intervention of States is justified by the magnitude of the conflict going on before our eyes. It is not only the interests of the belligerents that are at stake. All the countries of the world are suffering, directly or indirectly, from the frightful European War. . . .

Their collective intervention is further necessitated by the universal character of the principles which the next treaty of peace will have as one of its principal objects to consecrate. At the same time if, from this point of view, the participation of the mediating States ought to be full and complete, their mission will be one entirely of conciliation and of advice so far as concerns the conditions which the victors will have the right of imposing on the vanquished. . . .

3. The problem which will logically come before the representatives of the States, after they have agreed to the establishment of an international jurisdiction, will be that of a conventional disarmament. . . .

Material disarmament should be accompanied by moral disarmament. With this object severe punishments should be enacted by the penal laws of the various countries against any who . . . stir up mutual hatred among the peoples. . . .

4. The right of the peoples freely to decide on their own destiny should be solemnly recognized. Respect for nationalities should be accepted as a principle, and there should consequently be granted to all peoples, whatever their degree of importance, the right to express their desire to be constituted as autonomous States or to be attached to some existing State. This right of free choice should be guaranteed by the general body of States. . . .

5. Diplomatic negotiations between States should no longer be carried on in secret and without the knowledge of the representatives of the peoples. . . .

6. The States would renounce forever the concluding of warlike alliances for offense or defense.

No convention, including that which will put an end to the present war, should bind the contracting States unless it has been submitted for the approval of the parliaments of those States. . . .

7. In order to put an end to economic rivalries, the preponderating causes of international conflicts, the States should agree to adopt free trade in all their commercial relations between their respective mother countries and their colonies. . . .

8. The less developed peoples should be placed under the collective protection of the States. . . .

9. The measures of execution, necessary for ensuring the prompt application of the principles which should form the basis of the treaty for putting an end to the war, should be entrusted to the third Peace Conference which should meet immediately after the definitive conclusion of peace. In addition to the objects mentioned above it will have to occupy itself with its own constitution into a permanent organ with regular and automatic sessions. . . .

Such is, in our opinion, on its principal lines, the policy of international pacifism. It aims at substituting for the resort to force the resort to law, for mutual defiance confidence and honesty, for brutal and murderous competition the widest co-operation, for the struggle for life the *entente* for life.

Document 3.2

Bertrand Russell: Intellectuals and the War

From "An Appeal to the Intellectuals of Europe," April 1915

I cannot but think that the men of learning, by allowing partiality to color their thoughts and words, have missed the opportunity of performing a service to mankind for which their training should have specially fitted them. The truth, whatever it may be, is the same in England, France, and Germany, in Russia and in Austria. It will not adapt itself to national needs: it is in its essence neutral. It stands outside the clash of passions and hatreds, revealing, to those who seek it, the tragic irony of strife with its attendant world of illusions. Men of learning, who should be accustomed to the pursuit of truth in their daily work, might have attempted, at this time, to make themselves the mouthpiece of truth, to see what was false on their own side, what was valid on the side of their enemies. They might have used their reputation and their freedom from political entanglements to mitigate the abhorrence with which the nations have come to regard each other, to help towards mutual understanding, to make the peace, when it comes, not a mere cessation due to weariness, but a fraternal reconciliation, springing from the realization that the strife has been a folly of blindness. They have chosen to do nothing of all this. Allegiance to country has swept away allegiance to truth. Thought has become the slave of instinct, not its master. The guardians of the temple of Truth have betrayed it to idolaters, and have been the first to promote the idolatrous worship. . . .

Men of learning, who are acquainted with the part played by collective error in the history of religion, ought to have been on their guard against assaults upon their credulity. They ought to have realized, from the obvious falsehood of the correlative opposite beliefs in many countries, that the myth-making impulse was unusually active, and could only be repelled by an unusual intellectual vigor. But I do not find that they were appreciably less credulous than the multitude. . . .

The fundamental irrational belief, on which all the others rest, is the belief that the victory of one's own side is of enormous and indubitable importance, and even of such importance as to outweigh all the evils involved in prolonging the war. It is possible, in view of the uncertainty of all human affairs, that the victory of one side or the other might bring great good to humanity. But even if this be the case, the beliefs of the combatants are not the less irrational, since there is no evidence such as would convince an impartial outsider. The Allies are convinced that their victory is for the good of mankind, and the Germans and Austrians are no less convinced in the opposite sense. . . . Meanwhile the evils produced by the war increase from day to day, and they, at least, must be admitted by both sides equally. . . .

Under the distorting influence of war, the doubtful and microscopic differences between different European nations have been exaggerated when it has become treason to question their overwhelming importance. Every educated man knew and acknowledged before the war began, and every educated man now knows without acknowledging, that the likenesses among European nations are immeasurably greater than their differences. Congresses, conferences, and international bodies of many kinds testified to the diffused consciousness of a common purpose, a common task in the life of a civilization. Suddenly, between one day and the next, all this is forgotten. . . . In a moment, all the great co-operative work for which academic bodies exist is set aside for the pleasure of indulging in bitter and trivial hatred.

This war is trivial, for all its vastness. No great principle is at stake, no great human purpose is involved on either side. The supposed ideal ends for which it is being fought are merely part of the myth. Every nation is fighting in self-defense, every nation is fighting to destroy the tyranny of armaments, every nation is fighting to show that unprovoked aggression cannot be practiced with impunity. Every nation pays homage to peace by maintaining that its enemies began the war. The fact these assertions carry equal conviction on both sides shows that they are not based on reason, but are merely inspired by prejudice. . . .

This war is not being fought for any rational end: it is being fought because, at first, the nations wished to fight, and now they are angry and determined to win victory. Everything else is idle talk, artificial rationalizing of instinctive actions and passions. . . .

Knowledge with elevation of mind is the chief instrument of human progress; knowledge without elevation of mind easily becomes devilish, and increases the wounds which man inflicts on man. . . .

Document 3.3

The Copenhagen Conference: An Appeal to Socialists

From "Appeal to Democratic Workingmen," 1915

In this moment, when the world is struck with terror at the horrible devastation this war has caused, the Conference desires to give expression to the firm and strong will to peace, existing within the nations represented at the Conference.

The delegates are of [the] opinion that the chief aim of the conference is to be the strengthening and uniting of that public will which, undoubtedly, in all countries, demands the end of the war in such a way that a permanent peace may be secured. To realize this aim, the conference addresses itself to the democratic workmen, particularly to those of the belligerent countries, pointing at the same time to those principles of international solidarity and proletarian conception of justice which have been sanctioned at all our international congresses. These principles were expressed by the Congress of Copenhagen, 1910, in the following way:

1. International compulsory arbitration.

2. Restriction of the preparations for war ending in final disarmament.

3. Abolition of secret diplomacy with full parliamentary responsibility as to foreign politics.

4. Recognition of the right of self-determination of nations, of resistance to oppression and war-intrigues.

The Conference considers it the duty of all socialistic parties to be active in order to render possible an early conclusion of the peace, and to work energetically in favor of such conditions of peace as may form a basis of international disarmament and of the democratization of foreign politics.

The Conference protests against the infringement of international right in the case of Belgium and expresses a hope that the Social Democracy in all belligerent countries will in the strongest way possible oppose every violent annexation. . . .

The Conference . . . hence summons the Socialists to work with the greatest energy in order to conquer the political power, so that Imperialism may be ruined, and that the International Social Democracy may fulfill its great mission of emancipating the people.

Document 3.4

The International Congress of Women: Appeal for Conciliation

From resolutions of the Women's International Peace Congress, April 1915

We women, in International Congress assembled, protest against the madness and horror of war, involving as it does a reckless sacrifice of human life and the destruction of so much that humanity has labored through centuries to build up.

This International Congress of Women opposes the assumption that women can be protected under the conditions of modern warfare. It protests vehemently against the odious wrongs of which women are the victims in time of war, and especially against the horrible violation of women which attends all war.

This International Congress of Women of different nations, classes, creeds, and parties is united in expressing sympathy with the suffering of all, whatever their nationality, who are fighting for their country or laboring under the burden of war.

Since the mass of people in each of the countries now at war believe themselves to be fighting, not as aggressors but in self-defense and for their national existence, there can be no irreconcilable difference between them, and their common ideals afford a basis upon which a magnanimous and honorable peace might be established. The congress therefore urges the governments of the world to put an end to this bloodshed and to begin peace negotiations. It demands that the peace which follows shall be permanent, and therefore based on principles of justice. . . .

This International Congress of Women resolves to ask the neutral countries to take immediate steps to create a conference of neutral nations which shall without delay offer continuous mediation. The congress shall invite suggestions for settlement from each of the belligerent nations, and in any case shall submit to all of them, simultaneously, reasonable proposals as a basis of peace. . . .

In order to urge the governments of the world to put an end to this bloodshed and to establish a just and lasting peace, this International Congress of Women delegates envoys to carry the message expressed in the congress resolutions to the rulers of the belligerent and neutral nations of Europe and to the President of the United States.

Document 3.5

Benedict XV: Appeal for Peace

From "To the Belligerent Peoples and to Their Leaders,"
July 1915

In the holy name of God, and in the name of our heavenly Father and Lord, by the Blessed Blood of Jesus, Price of man's redemption, We conjure you, whom Divine Providence has placed over the nations at war, to put an end at last to this horrible slaughter, which for a whole year has dishonored Europe. It is the blood of brothers that is being poured out on land and sea. The most beautiful regions of Europe, this garden of the world, are sown with corpses and with ruin: there, where but a short time ago flourished the industry of manufactures and the fruitful labor of the fields, now thunders fearfully the cannon, and in its destructive fury it spares neither village nor city, but spreads everywhere havoc and death. You bear before God and man the tremendous responsibility of peace and war; give ear to Our prayer, to the fatherly voice of the Vicar of the Eternal and Supreme Judge, to Whom you must render an account as well of your public undertakings, as of your own individual deeds.

The abounding wealth, with which God, the Creator, has enriched the lands that are subject to you, allow you to go on with the struggle; but at what cost? Let the thousands of young lives quenched every day on the fields of battle make answer: answer, the ruins of so many towns and villages, of so many monuments raised by the piety and genius of your ancestors. And the bitter tears shed in the secrecy of home, or at the foot of altars where suppliants beseech—do not these also repeat that the price of the long-drawn-out struggle is great—too great? . . .

. . . Blessed be he who will first raise the olive-branch, and hold out his right hand to the enemy with an offer of reasonable terms of peace. The equilibrium of the world, and the prosperity and assured tranquillity of nations, rest upon mutual benevolence and respect for the rights and dignity of others, much more than upon hosts of armed men and the ring of formidable fortresses. . . .

Rejection of the War

Conscientious Objection

The war required total mobilization and loyalty in every belligerent nation. Individuals who challenged the war were repudiated and ostracized. As peace became identified with victory, the word "pacifist" was applied narrowly and derisively to people who rejected all warfare— even the Great War. Because they valued the human community and often worked for social justice, pacifists felt especially vulnerable when they were isolated from their fellow citizens. In order to maintain some bonds of fellowship, they formed small societies, notably the Fellowship of Reconciliation in Britain and the United States. These societies, although Christian in inspiration (document 3.6), were not limited to churches with a heritage of nonresistance. They reflected the ethical individualism of Tolstoy and, like him, they identified with Jesus and the early Christian church.

Armies were raised by levies—that is, by conscription—but there were individuals in all the belligerent nations who refused military service on the grounds of principle, or conscientious objection. As chapter 1 indicated, the view that individuals must determine for themselves when warfare is justifiable had developed within the just war tradition as well as in nonresistant communities. During World War I, this principle was institutionalized in two ways, especially in Britain and the United States: conscientious objectors to military service were given official exemption from fighting, although often they were harassed, and societies were organized to support them.[3] In American law exemption was limited to members of recognized churches whose doctrine repudiated all war, but this was inadequate because some twentieth-century objectors were motivated by other religious traditions or by secular philosophies. Some of them objected to conscription itself, as did Evan Thomas (document 3.7), on the ground that an individual should resist not only warfare but also the militaristic and authoritarian social system of which it was part.

Document 3.6

The Fellowship of Reconciliation:
War Is Forbidden to Christians

From "The Basis" of the Fellowship of Reconciliation, 1914

[We believe:]

1. That Love, as revealed and interpreted in the life and death of Jesus Christ, involves more than we have yet seen, that it is the only power by which evil can be overcome, and the only sufficient basis of human society.

2. That, in order to establish a world-order based on Love, it is incumbent upon those who believe in this principle to accept it fully, both for themselves and in their relation to others, and to take the risks involved in doing so in a world which does not as yet accept it.

3. That, therefore, as Christians, we are forbidden wage war, and that our loyalty to our country, to humanity, to the Church Universal, and to Jesus Christ, our Lord and Master, calls us instead to a life service for the enthronement of Love in personal, social, commercial and national life.

4. That the Power, Wisdom and Love of God stretch far beyond the limits of our present experience, and that He is ever waiting to break forth into human life in new and larger ways. . . .

Document 3.7

Evan Thomas: Individual Responsibility for Peace

From a private letter to Norman Thomas,* April 1917

The whole problem [of the merit of the war] comes to be a question of relative values—which of the two is worse or better—and every such problem in the last analysis must be one of individual opinion. . . . Like

---

* In 1917 Evan Welling Thomas returned from England, where he was serving an Anglican church, in order to refuse conscription. He later became a professor of medicine and was chair of the War Resisters League during World War II. His brother, Norman Thomas, then a pastor in a poor district of New York City and secretary of the Fellowship of Reconciliation, was the leader of the American Socialist party from the 1920s into the 1940s.

all other relative judgments it admits of no absolute statement one way or the other, and so is of little value in determining the great eternal truths back of the universe.

To me the war is the inevitable result of the essentially false systems under which we live—a system founded on the principle of exclusive possession, where all values are relative and where force is the only possible ultimate arbiter—a system, all the gods of which are necessarily idols, whether they be portrayed in wood and stone or only in man's imagination. The result is a possession-mad civilization. . . . Such a social order necessarily accords first honors to those who possess most in their own exclusive right, thus creating for man values that are essentially selfish, with the result that wars may well be not only natural but even beneficial purges. . . .

But the point I am really desirous of showing here is that Germany is the inevitable result of this social order, exactly as are the landed interests in Britain, or the great promoters of American finance. . . . Hatred, under all circumstances, is both absurd and positively harmful. . . . The real blame must fall on the system . . . where the weak envy the strong, and the strong, not unnaturally, despise the weak; where suspicions and mutual distrust are the order of the day; and where the final arbiter must be force and might. . . . Our task, therefore, is to change the system. . . .

Taking the system as it is, the Allies seem to me to have more right on their side than the Central Powers; and, with the bulk of Americans feeling as they do, it may be far better that America should come into this war than stay out. But that does not make her entrance any the more ideal. At best it is only choosing the lesser of two evils because the majority of the people can't see a higher way.

What then is this higher way? In brief it is the abandonment of the use of force altogether, the way popularly known as "non-resistance," but which is actually the most thoroughgoing and powerful protest against our present false system that can possibly be made. It is the only way man can possibly gain the victory over this world or show his independence of the bondage to exclusive possession. It is the way of the only true freedom, and therefore the way of love, for freedom and love can never exist apart from each other in the heart of man. As it is the only conceivable way of freedom from external authority, so it is the only possible proof of a real belief in God, or in spiritual truths which are absolute and eternal. It is the way of example as opposed to compulsion. It is the way of belief as opposed to disbelief. It is the way of toleration as opposed to intolerance. Finally, it is the way that frankly accepts the fact of individual responsibility.

There is only one kind of preaching that matters and that is the life and example of the individual.

Political Opposition to War

What did peace mean in time of war, if not victory? In a few dramatic cases early in World War I opposition took the form of political action, mainly by socialists. In the Russian Duma, for example, the two small groups of socialists, the Mensheviks and Bolsheviks, jointly condemned the war and abstained from the vote of 4 August 1914 on military credits (document 3.8). At that time they were out-of-step with Russian workers, who had abandoned organized protest in the spirit of national solidarity, but the socialists' position became a basis for revolutionary leadership when the government became mired in wartime reversals. In the German Reichstag, the socialist leader Karl Liebknecht accepted party discipline and supported the first war loan of 4 August, despite his personal opposition to it. He broke ranks in December, however, and voted against the second war credits bill (document 3.9).[4] Opposition to the war grew among Social Democrats in Germany, and in 1917 it finally split the party.

British workers demonstrated against war up to the moment of decision, when, like their Russian, German, Austrian, and French comrades, they mostly accepted it. Still, Ramsay MacDonald and a few other leaders of the Independent Labour party broke with the dominant party position and refused to vote war credits, declaring: "International Socialism which cannot prevent Socialists from murdering each other and inflicting death . . . is not international Socialism at all."[5] During the war years, British peace activists concentrated on the issues of conscription, civil liberties, and the peace settlement.

In France an exceptional group of women risked censure and prison to challenge the official justification of the war and the general suspension of political differences. These women put peace ahead of victory in their pamphlets, newspapers, and public meetings, and they incurred the wrath of national law. On trial in March 1918 for distributing an illegal pamphlet, a teacher named Hélène Brion observed that although she was being treated as a traitor for her antiwar activity, as a woman she had never been allowed to influence *any* governmental decision (document 3.10). Her statement, which epitomized the emerging feminist critique of militarism, resembled the complaint of Russian socialists in the Duma that the people had not been consulted about the war to which they were being sacrificed. It was both a conscientious and a political affirmation of peace.

Italy was neutral until May 1915, when it entered the war against Austria and Germany. The drift toward intervention was challenged by the Vatican, bourgeois peace advocates, and the Italian Socialist party. Only the socialists organized significant political actions, which included parliamentary opposition, mass demonstrations, riots, and general strikes. Meanwhile, some Italian and Swiss socialists arranged a secret conference, 5–8 September 1915, in the village of Zimmerwald, Switzerland, where a few dissident socialists from neutral and belligerent nations urged the Second International to stand above the conflict and facilitate peace negotiations.[6] The International refused to jeopardize its wartime standing with socialists who were loyal to their nations, while in Italy the political opposition that continued after intervention was put down by the government and by the wave of patriotism that followed the Italian defeat at Caporetto in the fall of 1917.

By that time the United States had joined the war after two years of political controversy and organized opposition to armament and intervention. The day after the Congress declared for intervention, 6 April 1917, the Socialist Party of America held an emergency convention at St. Louis, where a large majority voted against the war. The majority report (document 3.11) was supported in a referendum of the membership. The party lost a significant minority of leaders, and, although it did not directly obstruct the war effort, it was persecuted as being unpatriotic because of its explicit opposition and its defense of conscientious objectors.

Document 3.8

Russian Socialists: War Is Against the People's Will

From a statement for the Bolsheviks in the
Fourth States Duma, 1915

A terrible and unprecedented calamity has broken upon the people of the entire world. Millions of workers have been torn away from their labor, ruined, and swept away by a bloody torrent. Millions of families have been delivered over to famine.

War has already begun. While the governments of Europe were preparing for it, the proletariat of the entire world, with the German workers at the head, unanimously protested.

Some circumstances (violation of the workers' press and workers' organizations) prevented the workers of Russia from protesting openly against the war. But at the time of great demonstrations of European workers against the war the hearts of the Russian workers were throbbing. And we, the representatives of the workers' class of Russia,* consider it as our duty to state that this war, provoked by the policy of seizures and violations practiced by all the capitalist states, is the responsibility of the ruling classes of all belligerent countries, that this war contradicts the feeling and mood of the conscientious members of the Russian proletariat, like that of the proletariat of the whole world.

Contrary to that false patriotism under the cover of which the ruling classes now lead their rapacious policy, the proletariat, the permanent protector of the freedom and interests of people, will do its duty and defend the people's culture against encroachments from within or from outside. But, stating that the people of Russia, like all peoples, are involved in the war against their will through the fault of the ruling classes, we regard it as necessary to emphasize all the hypocrisy and groundlessness of the calls for unity of the people with the government.

There can be no national unity when the authorities do not carry out the conscious will of the people, when the people are oppressed, when the masses carrying the burden of the war have no rights, when the workers' and peasants' press is stifled, when the workers' organizations are routed, when the prisons are full of those struggling for the freedom and happiness of the people, and when we have just come from the shooting of Petersburg workers by troops and police. There can be no unity with the authorities by all those nationalities of Russia who are exposed to persecution and live in the atmosphere of exploitation and oppression.

The conscious proletariat of the belligerent countries has not been sufficiently powerful to prevent this war and the resulting return of barbarism.

But we are convinced that the working class will find in the international solidarity of the workers the means to force the conclusion of peace at an early date. The terms of that peace will be dictated by the

---

* The Social-Democratic faction consisted of 13 deputies: 7 Mensheviks and 6 Bolsheviks. Among the most prominent was V. I. Khaustov, who read this statement. The States Duma was the legislative representative institution of the Russian Empire. The fourth Duma existed from 15 November 1912 to 6(19) October 1917.

people themselves and not by the diplomats of the rapacious governments.

We are convinced that this war will finally open the eyes of the great
masses of Europe, and show them the real cause of all the oppression
and violence that they endure, that therefore this new terrible explosion
of barbarism will be the last.

Document 3.9

Karl Liebknecht: Opposition to the Second War Loan

From the statement in the Reichstag, 2 December 1914

This war, which none of the peoples interested wanted, was not
declared in the interests of the Germans or of any other people. It is an
imperialist war for capitalization and domination of the world markets,
for political domination of important quarters of globe, and for the
benefit of bankers and manufacturers. From the viewpoint of the race of
armaments, it is a preventive war provoked conjointly by the war parties
of Germany and Austria in the obscurity of semi-absolutism and secret
diplomacy. It is also a Bonaparte-like enterprise tending to demoralize
and destroy the growing labor movement. That much is clear despite the
cynical stage management designed to mislead the people. This is not a
defensive war. We cannot believe the government when it declares it is
for the defense of the fatherland. It demands money. What we must
demand is an early peace, humiliating no one, peace without consequent
rancor. All efforts directed to this end ought to be supported. . . . The
only durable peace will be peace based on the solidarity of the working
masses and liberty. The Socialists of all countries must work for such a
peace even during the war. I protest against the violation of Belgium and
Luxemburg, against the annexation schemes, against military dictatorship, against the complete forgetfulness of social and political duties as
shown by the government ruling classes.

Document 3.10

Hélène Brion: Laws Neither Wanted Nor Discussed

From her closing statement at her trial, 29 March 1918

I appear here charged with a political crime but I am entirely deprived of political rights.

Because I am a woman, I am classed . . . by the laws . . . as inferior to all men in France and its colonies. Despite . . . all the degrees and certificates which I attained long ago, before the law I am not as equal as a black man in Guadaloupe or the Ivory Coast. *He* can participate by the ballot in the control of business in our common nation and *I* can not. I am outside the law! . . .

I protest against the application of laws . . . which I have neither wanted nor participated in making.

. . . It is because of feminism that I am an enemy of war.

The charge states that because of feminism, I struggle for pacifism. It distorts my propaganda [position] to serve its own ends. The opposite is the real truth. . . . for many years before the war, I argued militant feminism; since the war, I simply continued and I have never made a comment on our current evils without pointing out that if women had a say . . . in [public] questions, things would have turned out differently. . . .

I am an enemy of war because I am a feminist; war is the victory of brutal force; feminism can only triumph by moral force and intellectual superiority. There is an absolute antipathy between the two.

You men who alone rule the world . . . want to protect our children from the horrors of a future war, an admirable sentiment! . . . [We have had] 44 months of a fantastic, horrendous war not of two nations but of more than 20. . . . Have you considered the repercussions that the real privations have had on the well being that you imagine you will insure by continuing to fight . . . ?

From the beginning of the war, I always said and wrote everywhere: if you do not include women . . . , the new world that you pretend to fashion will be as unjust and as chaotic as the prewar world.

My argument has always been an appeal to reason: never have I called for violence. . . . Violence repels me. I have never practiced or recommended it.

Document 3.11

The Socialist Party of America: Against the War

From the majority report of the
St. Louis Convention, April 1917

The Socialist Party of the United States in the present grave crisis, solemnly reaffirms its allegiance to the principle of internationalism and working class solidarity the world over, and proclaims its unalterable opposition to the war just declared by the government of the United States. . . .

The Socialist Party of the United States is unalterably opposed to the system of exploitation and class rule which is upheld and strengthened by military power and sham national patriotism. We, therefore, call upon the workers of all countries to refuse support to their governments in their wars. The wars of contending national groups of capitalists are not the concern of the workers. The only struggle which would justify the workers in taking up arms is the great struggle of the working class of the world to free itself from economic exploitation and political oppression, and we particularly warn the workers against the snare and delusion of so-called defensive warfare. . . .

The mad orgy of death and destruction which is now convulsing unfortunate Europe was caused by the conflict of capital interests in the European countries . . .*

The war of the United States against Germany cannot be justified even on the plea that it is a war in defense of American rights or American "honor." Ruthless as the unrestricted submarine war policy of the German government was and is, it is not an invasion of the rights of the American people, as such, but only an interference with the opportunity of certain groups of American capitalists to coin cold profits out of the blood and sufferings of our fellow men in the warring countries of Europe.

It is not a war against the militarist regime of the Central Powers. Militarism can never be abolished by militarism.

It is not a war to advance the cause of democracy in Europe. Democracy can never be imposed upon any country by a foreign power by force of arms. . . .

Our entrance into the European conflict will serve only to multiply the horrors of the war. . . . It will give the powers of reaction in this country the pretext for an attempt to throttle our rights and to crush our democratic institutions, and to fasten upon this country a permanent militarism. . . .

. . . we recommend to the workers and pledge ourselves to the following course of action:

1. Continuous, active, and public opposition to the war through demonstrations, mass petitions, and all other means within our power.

---

* This thesis is developed in several paragraphs linking capital interests, imperialism, the arms race, and militarism.

2. Unyielding opposition to all proposed legislation for military or industrial conscription. . . .

3. Vigorous resistance to all reactionary measures, such as censorship of the press and mails, restriction of the rights of free speech, assemblage, and . . . limitation of the right to strike.

4. Consistent propaganda against military training and militaristic teaching in the public schools. . . .

5. Extension of the campaign of education among workers . . . to enable them by concerted and harmonious mass action to shorten this war and to establish lasting peace.*

Revolutionary Socialism

Revolution swept the Russian Tsar from power in the spring of 1917. At first the new representative soviets strengthened the Allied war effort because they were interpreted as a democratic front against monarchist Germany and Austria-Hungary. When the Bolsheviks took power in the autumn, however, their determination to obtain peace threatened the western alliance.

Meanwhile, the drama in Russia sharpened differences about the idea of peace. Whereas western leaders argued that military victory was required to achieve peace through a new international order, and numerous socialists and liberals held that international peace was the prerequisite of justice, a small minority of radical socialists insisted that world revolution and the victory of workers over the bourgeoisie were necessary to achieve a peaceful social order. That minority view of peace as a result of social revolution was held for the most part by the Bolsheviks (later communists) and it was institutionalized when they came to power in Russia.

The core of this idea was stated eloquently in December 1915 by a leader of the international socialist movement, Rosa Luxemburg, while she was in a German prison (document 3.12). Polish born, she participated in the Russian Revolution of 1905 and then became a leader in the Social Democratic party, where she advocated the mass strike as the weapon of the workers. She broke with the party leadership on the issue

---

* The war program of the party also included propaganda on the relation between capitalism and war, and protection of the American people from anticipated food shortages. Severely repressed during and immediately after the war, the party largely disintegrated.

of the nationalist war. For resisting it she was imprisoned from 1915 to 1918, and the following year she was murdered during the Spartacus revolt. At the 1915 Zimmerwald Conference in Switzerland, other dissident socialists called on workers to place "the irreconcilable working-class struggle . . . for the sacred aims of Socialism" above nationalism, and it also urged them to force a peace settlement on their governments (document 3.13).

About the same time V. I. Lenin was explicitly urging dissident socialists in Europe to "convert the imperialist war into a civil war" (document 3.14). Two years later, as fighting was continued by the Provisional Government of Russia, which replaced the Tsar, Lenin called on soldiers of all the belligerent countries to transform the national war into a class one (document 3.14). The Bolsheviks took power on 24–25 October (7–8 November on the European calendar), and they immediately appealed for a negotiated settlement in the belief that continued warfare would destroy their revolutionary achievements.[7] Four months later, with no prospect of international negotiations, Lenin accepted the harsh Treaty of Brest Litovsk.[8] Although he conceded that international civil war had to be deferred, he remained convinced that permanent peace required a sweeping social revolution.

The success of the Bolshevik revolution meant that Lenin's idea of peace as a result of social revolution was institutionalized in Russia along with his idea of revolution directed by a *disciplined* communist party (a dictatorship of the proletariat). That development contributed to the division of nations and peace groups in the interwar period.

Document 3.12

Rosa Luxemburg: Peace Is Socialist Will

From the Junius Theses,* December 1915

1. The world war has annihilated the work of forty years of European socialism: by destroying the revolutionary proletariat as a political

---

* Following discussion at the meeting of the group "International" on 1 January 1916, these theses, with a few changes suggested by Karl Liebknecht, were accepted in principle. After editorial modification, they were distributed as "Theses on the Tasks of International Social Democracy" in the *Political Letters*, no. 14 (3 Feb. 1916), and as an appendix to Luxemburg's "Juniuspamphlet" (later published as *Die Krise der Sozialdemokratie*, Bern, 1919).

force; by destroying the moral prestige of socialism; by scattering the workers' International; by setting its sections one against the other in fratricidal massacre; and by tying the aspirations and hopes of the masses of the people of the main countries in which capitalism has developed to the destinies of imperialism.

2. By their vote for war credits and by their proclamation of national unity, the official leaderships of the socialist parties in Germany, France and England (with the exception of the Independent Labour Party) have . . . induced the masses of the people to suffer patiently the misery and horrors of the war, contributed to the unleashing, without restraint, of imperialist frenzy, . . . and assumed their share in the responsibility for the war itself and for its consequences.

3. This tactic of the official leaderships of the parties in the belligerent countries, and in the first place in Germany . . . constitutes a betrayal of the elementary principles of international socialism, of the vital interests of the working class, and of all the democratic interests of the peoples. . . .

4. By this alone official social democracy in the principal countries has repudiated the class struggle in wartime and adjourned it until after the war; it has guaranteed to the ruling classes of all countries a delay in which to strengthen . . . their economic, political and moral positions.

5. The world war serves neither the national defense nor the economic or political interests of the masses of the people whatever they may be. It is but the product of the imperialist rivalries between the capitalist classes of the different countries. . . .

6. The policy of the imperialist states and the imperialist war cannot give to a single oppressed nation its liberty and its independence. The small nations . . . constitute only the pawns on the imperialist chessboard of the great powers. . . .

7. The present world war signifies, under these conditions, either in the case of "defeat" or of "victory," a defeat for socialism and democracy. It increases, whatever the outcome—excepting the revolutionary intervention of the international proletariat—and strengthens militarism, national antagonisms, and economic rivalries. . . . The present world war carries within itself the seeds of new conflicts.

8. World peace cannot be assured by projects . . . such as tribunals of arbitration by capitalist diplomats, . . . "disarmament" conventions, "the freedom of the seas," . . . "the United States of Europe," a "customs union for central Europe," buffer states, and other illusions. . . . The sole means of successful resistance, and the only guarantee of the peace of

the world, is the capacity for action and the revolutionary will of the international proletariat to hurl its full weight into the balance.

9. Imperialism, as the last phase in the life, and the highest point in the expansion of the world hegemony of capital, is the mortal enemy of the proletariat of all countries. . . . The final goal of socialism will be realized by the international proletariat only if it opposes imperialism all along the line, and if it makes the issue "war against war" the guiding line of its practical policy. . . .

10. In this framework, socialism's principal mission today is to re-group the proletariat of all countries into a living revolutionary force; to make it, through a powerful international organization which has only one conception of its tasks and interests, and only one universal tactic appropriate to political action in peace and war alike, the decisive factor in political life: so that it may fulfill its historic mission.*

11. The war has smashed the Second International. . . .

12. In view of the betrayal, by the official representatives of the socialist parties in the principal countries, of the aims and interests of the working class . . . it is vitally necessary for socialism to build a new workers' International. . . .

Document 3.13

The Zimmerwald Manifesto: Struggle for Peace

From the declaration proposed
by French and German socialists, 1915

WORKERS OF EUROPE!

The war has lasted for more than a year. Millions of corpses lie upon the battlefields; millions of men have been crippled for life. Europe has become a gigantic human slaughter-house. All science, the work of many generations, is devoted to destruction. The most savage barbarity is cele-brating its triumph over everything that was previously the pride of mankind.

Whatever may be the truth about the immediate responsibility for the outbreak of the war, one thing is certain: the war that has occasioned this chaos is the outcome of Imperialism, of the endeavors of the Capital-

---

* Although Luxemburg agreed with Lenin on the importance of a worker's revolution for lasting peace, she had in mind a movement that would be broadly democratic, rather than one directed by a disciplined leadership.

ist classes of every nation to satisfy their greed for profit by the exploitation of human labor and the treasures of Nature. . . .

. . . In every country the Capitalists who forge the gold of war profits from the blood of the people are declaring that the war is for national defense, democracy, and the liberation of oppressed nationalities. THEY LIE!

In reality they are actually burying on the fields of devastation the liberties of their own peoples, together with the independence of other nations. . . .

Intellectual and moral desolation, economic disaster, political reaction—such are the blessings of this horrible struggle between the nations. . . .

Workers!

Exploited, deprived of your rights, despised—you were recognized as brothers and comrades at the outbreak of the war before you were summoned to march to the shambles, to death. And now, when militarism has crippled, lacerated, degraded, and destroyed you, the rulers are demanding from you the abandonment of your interests, of your aims, of your ideals—in a word, slavish submission to the "national truce." . . .

We cannot, we dare not, any longer remain inactive in the presence of a state of things that is menacing the whole future of Europe and of mankind. For many decades the Socialist working class has carried on the struggle against militarism. . . .

But we Socialist Parties and working-class organizations which had taken part in determining this path have since the outbreak of war disregarded the obligations that followed therefrom. Their representatives have invited the workers to suspend the working-class struggle, the only possible and effective means of working-class emancipation. . . . And just as Socialist Parties failed separately, so did the most responsible representative of the Socialists of all countries fail: the International Socialist Bureau. . . .

In this intolerable situation we have met together, we representatives of Socialist parties, of Trade Unions, or of minorities of them, we Germans, French, Italians, Russians, Poles, Letts, Roumanians, Bulgarians, Swedes, Norwegians, Dutch, and Swiss, we who are standing on the ground, not of national solidarity with the exploiting class, but of the international solidarity of the workers and the working-class struggle. We have met together in order to join anew the broken ties of international relations and to summon the working class to reorganize and begin the struggle for peace.

. . . The task is to take up this fight for peace—for a peace without annexations or war indemnities. Such a peace is only possible when every thought of violating the rights and liberties of the nations is condemned. There must be no enforced incorporation either of wholly or partly occupied countries. . . . The right of nations to select their own government must be the immovable fundamental principle of international relations.

Organized Workers!

Since the outbreak of the war you have put your energies, your courage, your steadfastness at the service of the ruling classes. Now the task is to enter the lists for your own cause, for the sacred aims of Socialism, for the salvation of the oppressed nations and the enslaved classes, by means of the irreconcilable working-class struggle. . . .

Never in the history of the world has there been a more urgent, a more noble, a more sublime task, the fulfillment of which must be our common work. No sacrifice is too great, no burden too heavy, to attain this end: the establishment of peace between the nations.

Working men and women! Mothers and fathers! Widows and orphans! Wounded and crippled! To all who are suffering from the war or in consequence of the war, we cry out, over the frontiers, over the smoking battlefields, over the devastated cities and hamlets.

"Workers of all countries unite!"

Document 3.14

Vladimir Ilyich Lenin: From World War to Civil War

From *Socialism and the War,* 1915,
and "Appeal to the Soldiers," 1917

Socialism and War *

Socialists have always condemned wars between nations as barbarous and brutal. Our attitude towards war, however, is fundamentally different from that of the bourgeois pacifists (supporters and advocates of peace) and of the anarchists. We differ from the former in that we understand the inevitable connection between wars and the class struggle within a country; we understand that wars cannot be abolished unless classes are abolished and socialism is created; we also differ in that we regard civil wars, i.e. wars waged by an oppressed class against the

---

 * This is from a pamphlet written in the summer of 1915, just before the Zimmerwald Conference, and printed in German, French, Russian, and Norwegian.

oppressor class, by slaves against slaveholders, by serfs against landowners, and by wage-workers against the bourgeoisie, as fully legitimate, progressive and necessary. We Marxists differ from both pacifists and anarchists in that we deem it necessary to study each war historically (from the standpoint of Marx's dialectical materialism) and separately. There have been in the past numerous wars which, despite all the horrors, atrocities, distress and suffering that inevitably accompany all wars, were progressive, i.e., benefited the development of mankind by helping to destroy most harmful and reactionary institutions. . . .*

The war has undoubtedly created a most acute crisis and has immeasurably increased the distress of the masses. The reactionary nature of this war, and the unblushing lies told by the bourgeoisie of *all* countries to conceal their predatory aims with "national" ideology are . . . inevitably creating revolutionary moods among the masses. It is our duty to help the masses become conscious of these moods, deepen them and give them shape. This task finds correct expression only in the slogan: convert the imperialist war into a civil war; *all* consistently waged class struggles in wartime and all seriously conducted "mass-action" tactics inevitably lead to this. It is impossible to foretell whether a powerful revolutionary movement will flare up in connection with, during or after the first or the second imperialist war of the Great Powers; in any case it is our bounden duty to work systematically and unswervingly in this direction.

The Basle Manifesto [1912] makes direct reference to the example set by the Paris Commune, i.e., the conversion of a war between the governments into a civil war. Half a century ago, the proletariat was too weak; the objective conditions for socialism had not yet matured, there could be no co-ordination and co-operation between the revolutionary movements in all the belligerent countries . . . , [but] today it is unpardonable for a socialist to resign himself to a renunciation of activities in the spirit of the Paris Communards.

Appeal to the Soldiers

Brothers, soldiers!

We are all worn out by this frightful war, which has cost millions of lives, crippled millions of people and caused untold misery, ruin, and starvation.

---

* Lenin interprets World War I, by contrast, as a reactionary war, and he condemns socialists who either succumbed to nationalist loyalty or abandoned revolutionary struggle for parliamentary politics and internationalism. In this connection, he is particularly critical of Karl Kautsky (whose views are suggested in document 3.15).

And more and more people are beginning to ask themselves: What started this war, what is it being waged for?

Every day it is becoming clearer to us, the workers and peasants, who bear the brunt of the war, that it was started and is being waged by the capitalists of all countries for the sake of the capitalists' interests. . . .

Are we going to continue submissively to bear our yoke, to put up with the war between the capitalist classes? Are we going to let this war drag on by taking the side of our own national governments, our own national bourgeois, our own national capitalists, and thereby destroying the international unity of the workers of all countries, of the whole world?

No, brother soldiers, it is time we opened our eyes, it is time we took our fate into our own hands. . . . The revolution in Russia is only the first step of the first revolution; it should be followed and will be followed by others.

The new government in Russia . . . is a government of the capitalists. It is waging just as predatory and imperialist a war as the capitalists of Germany, Britain, and other countries. . . .

But in addition to the capitalist government, the Russian revolution has given rise to spontaneous revolutionary organizations representing the vast majority of the workers and peasants. . . .

Only if state power in . . . both Russia and Germany passes wholly and exclusively into the hands of the revolutionary Soviets of Workers' and Soldiers' Deputies . . . will the workers of both the belligerent countries acquire confidence in each other and be able to put a speedy end to the war on the basis of a really democratic peace that will really liberate *all* the nations and nationalities of the world.

Brothers, soldiers!

Let us do everything we can to hasten this, to achieve this aim. Let us not fear any sacrifices—and sacrifice for the workers' revolution will be less painful than the sacrifices of war. Every victorious step of the revolution will save hundreds of thousands and millions of people from death, ruin, and starvation.

Peace to the hovels, war on the palaces! Peace to the workers of all countries! Long live the fraternal unity of the revolutionary workers of all countries! Long live socialism.

Social Reformism

Great pressures for social reform and political participation preceded the outbreak of war, and they were aggravated by wartime stress. Many reformers attempted to advance their programs through the war itself. In the Atlantic democracies they attempted to harness the vast expansion of governmental power in order to improve social welfare, housing, public services, and the status of women and workers. In Germany, socialists and other dissidents opposed territorial annexation early in the war, and throughout it they resisted wartime centralization and repression, eventually taking power from the military government. For the most part, socialists and other reformers regarded the war as a prelude to an era of peace that would provide fertile ground for social justice. For them, as for Karl Kautsky of Germany, only peace could reinstate "an epoch of normal social development" toward equity within a national framework (document 3.16).[9]

For the small minority of reformers who were also wartime critics, peace not only contributes to reform, it *is* a social reform: war and social injustice alike are based on imposed, arbitrary authority, peace and justice require social accountability and political participation. In this sense, these dissidents probed and extended the idea of a connection between peace and republican forms of government, which had been made by Kant and, long before him, the Greeks.

Jane Addams, an American social worker held in public esteem long before she received the Nobel Peace Prize in 1931, insisted that it was both realistic and patriotic to advocate peace during wartime (document 3.17) It was realistic, she said, because warfare could not solve international conflicts. It was patriotic, she added, because it extended national ideals to universal principles such as government by consent and minority rights. Peace advocacy was changing, and in her restrained way Addams identified two characteristics of the movement that would emerge in the interwar period. First, it would include *political activism* by a wide range of peace advocates—from internationalists to absolute nonresistants. Second, it would include an emphasis on *transnationalism*—the idea that peace required social changes across boundaries, and not only the accommodation of conflicting national interests. Addams found both of those orientations in the Women's International League for Peace and Freedom, which she served as international president from 1915 to 1929.

A similar shift in emphasis could be seen in the women's movement of Britain. There the campaign for women's suffrage had escalated just before the war, winning support from the Labour Party and forging close relationships within the International Women's Suffrage Alliance. The international organization and several of its national branches were divided when some women tried to stand above the conflict while most others in belligerent nations rallied to the colors. As antiwar feminists sought ways to express themselves, a few of them explicitly connected warfare to male domination through the culture of imposed power, or violence: "this it is which, more than all other influences, has prevented the voice of woman being heard in public affairs until almost yesterday." [10] Maude Royden, feminist and vice-chair of the British committee of the 1915 Women's International Congress, concluded that injustice of class and gender is the result of societies in which war is the final arbiter: the corollary of social justice is peace (document 3.18).[11]

This idea was generalized and sharpened by the American writer and literary critic Randolph Bourne. Echoing Kautsky's declaration that war is "primarily a struggle of governments," Bourne distinguished the interests of the state from those of the larger society (document 3.19). "War is the health of the state," he argued, and it is waged at the expense of the people. Like Kautsky, Addams, Royden, and other precursors of postwar, reform-oriented pacifism, Bourne contrasted peace, when understood as justice, with war and social control. Like them, he assumed that order among nations, although important, was only part of the struggle for peace and justice within all nations. This perspective was institutionalized in the constitution of the International Labor Organization (document 4.4), which was formed as part of the Treaty of Versailles: "peace can be established only if it is based upon social justice."

Document 3.15

Karl Kautsky: The Possibility of Peaceful Society

From *Internationalism and War*, 1915

War is not a class struggle but first and foremost a conflict between governments. [This is true] even in democratic states and in those states where the majority of the people enthusiastically supports the war. War is declared by governments against governments and is conducted by governments. Of course, governments are only the legal representatives or instruments of certain classes, but even when states possessing the same economic structures come into conflict, the same class will conduct the war from both sides and that class will never be the proletariat. Nevertheless, the proletariat has an interest in the outcome of the war.

To be sure, the proletariat does not seem to have any immediate interest at risk in the outcome, but the victory of one government might promote its development and its struggle indirectly, while the victory of the other might retard its progress. Therefore, even though it may condemn war itself, the proletariat must take a stand for one side or the other when there is war. The especially thorny problem for us as socialists in times of war is to determine which side to support. . . .

Small states that are a party to the war, and, to no less a degree, the larger nations are fighting for their very existence. The situation for the great, stable nations is, however, different. Their independence is not threatened, nor is it likely that their integrity is. Democracy and the participation of the people in politics are so well developed in these that the loss of territory and its forcible annexation by a foreign nation would most likely become a source of weakness and disorder for the victor. Furthermore, the demand that a nation cede part of itself would provoke outraged resistance that would prolong the war substantially, . . . all for a purpose that is likely to bring the victor more harm than good.

Therefore, we would hardly expect that the vanquished state would find its sovereignty or integrity violated, but it must nevertheless consider the possibility that its economic base and material resources will have been considerably diminished.

Under some circumstances, this could become a positive impetus to move toward new, higher forms of production, but the devastation of the war and the distress of the vanquished will be so immense that even the most bold socialist reformer will find it difficult to build a new society upon such desolate ruins. . . .

Insofar as socialism is the intellectual heir of the idealism of revolutionary bourgeois democracy and of the international pacifist tendencies of free-trade industrialism—a legacy that it, of course, will not adopt wholesale and without change—it has been striving since its beginnings to achieve international partnership in the face of the international solidarity of reaction and the politics of sealed borders promoted by trade protectionists. . . .

The International is strongest in times of peace, weakest in times of war. Though certainly regrettable, this does not detract in the least from its significance in times of peace, i.e., in a period of normal social development.

The International is, however, not simply most effective in times of peace but is the most effective means of preserving peace. . . .

In any case, of all factors that work to maintain peace, the proletariat is the strongest. Its power has been increased enormously by the International, which comprised all the proletarian movements of the individual nations and gave the unified goal of a politics that would have preserved the peace, had it become dominant. The International has proclaimed that a world politics guaranteeing each nation economic development without violation of it is possible. That the proponents of this internationalist politics did not intend to betray national interest has been amply demonstrated by the socialist parties of the countries that are now a party to the war.

There is absolutely no foundation to the belief that the policies of the International were nothing more than a pretty phantasy dashed by the harsh realities of the war. On the contrary, these policies are deeply rooted in the life and circumstances of the proletariat. As soon as the possibility for peace activism appears, these policies will be rekindled with a new life and sense of purpose.

Document 3.16

Jane Addams: Pacifism and Patriotism in Wartime

From "Pacifism and Patriotism in War Time," 1917

The position of the pacifist in time of war is most difficult, and necessarily he must abandon the perfectly legitimate propaganda he maintained before war was declared. When he, with his fellow countrymen, is caught up by a wave of tremendous enthusiasm and is carried out into a high sea of patriotic feeling, he realizes that the virtues which he extols are brought into unhappy contrast to those which war, with its keen sense of a separate national existence, places in the foreground. . . .

In one position, however, we are all agreed, and to this as to an abstract proposition we must hold at all times, even after war has been declared: that war, although exhibiting some of the noblest qualities of the human spirit, yet affords no solution for vexed international problems; and that moreover after war has been resorted to, its very existence . . . tends to obscure and confuse those faculties which might otherwise find a solution.

In the stir of the heroic moment when a nation enters war, men's minds are driven back to the earliest obligations of patriotism, and almost without volition the emotions move along the worn grooves of blind admiration for the soldier and of unspeakable contempt for him who, in the hour of danger, declares that fighting is unnecessary. We pacifists are not surprised, therefore, . . . that we should not only be considered incapable of facing reality, but that we should be called traitors and cowards. It makes it all the more incumbent upon us, however, to demonstrate, if we can, that in our former advocacy we urged a reasonable and vital alternative to war, and that our position now does not necessarily imply lack of patriotism or cowardice. . . .

Pacifists and "Passivism"

First: The similarity of sound between the words "passive" and "pacifism" is often misleading, for most pacifists . . . , so far from passively wishing nothing to be done, contend on the contrary that this world crisis should be utilized for the creation of an international government able to make the necessary political and economic changes when they are due; we feel that it is unspeakably stupid that the nations should have failed to create an international organization through which each one, without danger to itself, might recognize and even encourage the impulse toward growth in other nations.

Pacifists believe that in the Europe of 1914 certain tendencies were steadily pushing towards large changes which in the end made war, because the system of peace had no way of effecting those changes without war, no adequate international organization which could cope with the situation. The conception of peace founded upon the balance of power or the undisturbed *status quo,* was so negative that frustrated national impulses and suppressed vital forces led to war, because no method of orderly expression had been derived.

We are not advocating the mid-Victorian idea that good men from every country meet together at The Hague or elsewhere, where they shall pass a resolution, that "wars hereby cease" and that "the world hereby be federated." What we insist upon is that the world can be organized politically by its statesmen as it has been already organized into an international fiscal system by its bankers or into an international scientific association by its scientists. . . .

Military Coercion or Social Control?

It has long been the aim of this government of ours and of similar types of government the world over to replace coercion by the full consent of the governed, to educate and strengthen the free will of the people through the use of democratic institutions, and to safeguard even the rights of minorities. This age-long process of obtaining the inner consent of the citizen to the outward acts of his government is of necessity violently interrupted and thrown back in war time; but we all realize that some day it must be resumed and carried forward again, perhaps on an international basis. Let us strive to keep our minds clear regarding it.

Some of us once dreamed that the cosmopolitan inhabitants of this great nation might at last become united in a vast common endeavor for social ends. We hoped that this fusing might be accomplished without the sense of opposition to a common enemy which is an old method of welding people together, better fitted for military than for social use. If this for the moment is impossible, let us at least place the spirit of cooperation above that of bitterness and remember the wide distinction between social control and military coercion. . . .

Peace and Justice

With visions of international justice filling our minds, pacifists are always a little startled when those who insist that justice can only be established by war, accuse us of caring for peace irrespective of justice. Many of the pacifists . . . have long striven for social and political justice with a fervor perhaps equal to that employed by the advocates of force, and we realize that a sense of justice has become the keynote to the best political and social activity in this generation. Although this ruling passion for juster relations between man and man, group and group, or between nation and nation, is not without its sterner aspects, among those who dream of a wider social justice throughout the world there had developed a conviction that justice between men or between nations can be achieved only through understanding and fellowship, and that a finely tempered sense of justice, which alone is of any service in modern civilization, cannot be secured in the storm and stress of war. This is not only because war inevitably arouses the more primitive antagonisms, but because the spirit of fighting burns away all of those impulses, certainly towards the enemy, which foster the will to justice. . . .

With such a creed, can the pacifists of today be accused of selfishness when they urge upon the United States not isolation, not indifference to moral issues and to the fate of liberty and democracy, but a strenuous endeavor to lead all nations of the earth into an organized international life worthy of civilized men?

Document 3.17

Maude Royden: War and the Women's Movement

From "War and the Woman's Movement," 1915

The Woman's Movement in all its aspects, but especially, of course, in its political one, is an assertion of moral force as the supreme governing force in the world. If its adherents are wrong, and it is physical force which is "the ultimate appeal," then the militarist is right, and the physically weaker sex, like the little and weak nation, has no claim that may not be set aside. The weak have no rights in a world governed by brute force; they have only privileges, which may be granted, revoked, or withheld. It has been the fundamental principle of the Woman's Movement that it claims rights and duties, but never privileges. . . . [Women] have rightly based their demand on the great principle that government rests upon consent, and that the use of physical force is not "the ultimate appeal," but a confession of failure. . . .

It is true that although the principles of militarism and feminism are fundamentally opposed many people do not know it. . . . There are militarists who believe themselves feminist, and feminists who are undoubtedly militarist. And, after all, since we are most of us perfectly aware that "logic is not a science but a dodge," we must beware of dismissing a paradox merely because it involves an *apparent* contradiction. When, however, the contradiction is real—when the opposition between two principles is fundamental—the human mind cannot for ever hold them both. One must drive out and destroy the other. Those feminists who had most closely thought out their position had already grasped the issue. When war broke out, and ordinary political activities were necessarily suspended, it seemed to them as inevitable that they should take up the task of combating the real enemy of women (and of civilization)—militarism—as it was that they should take their share in the relief of the physical miseries and material burdens of war. There was no question of opposition to the war itself within the great suffrage organizations, since the vast majority of their members believed that war had been forced upon us and was, on our part, a battle against a militarist ideal.* But there was a deep consciousness that the spirit of militarism is very hardly separated from the fact of war. . . . Women can do

* This is to say that most English women believed that in fighting Germany they were fighting a militaristic ideal then epitomized in the word *Prussianism*.

no greater service to the world than to increase the healthy skepticism of violence as a method of imposing ideals. . . .

War may claim for itself the power to destroy and to clear the ground. It can never construct or create. It is not the means by which ideals are imposed. There is ultimately no way of combating a wrong idea but the setting forth of a right one. Whether they are right who believe that moral force is "the ultimate appeal" against which coercion is vain and violence merely a counsel of despair, or they who see in physical force the real basis of government, let time show. One thing at least is certain—that as the Woman's Movement embodies the one creed and "militarism" the other, so these two must be in eternal opposition. The victory of one is the defeat of the other. . . . But if moral power be the true basis of human relationship, then the Woman's Movement is on a sure foundation and moves to its inevitable triumph. Its victory will be an element in the making of permanent peace, not because women are less liable to "war fever" than men, or more reluctant to pay the great price of war, but because their claim and its fulfillment involves the assertion of that which war perpetually denies.

Document 3.18

Randolph Bourne: War and the State

From "The State," 1919

To most of the Americans of the classes which consider themselves significant the war brought a sense of the sanctity of the State, which, if they had time to think about it, would have seemed a sudden and surprising alteration in their habits of thought. In times of peace, we usually ignore the State in favor of partisan political controversies, or personal struggles for office, or the pursuit of party policies. It is the Government rather than the State with which the politically minded are concerned. The State is reduced to a shadowy emblem which comes to consciousness only on occasions of patriotic holiday.

With the shock of war, however, the State comes into its own again. The Government, with no mandate from the people, without consultation of the people, conducts all the negotiations . . . which slowly bring it into collision with some other Government, and gently and irresistibly slides the country into war. For the benefit of proud and haughty citizens, it is fortified with a list of the intolerable insults which have been hurled towards us by the other nations; for the benefit of the liberal and beneficent, it has a convincing set of moral purposes which our going to war will achieve; for the ambitious and aggressive classes, it can gently whisper of a bigger role in the destiny of the world. The result is that, even in those countries where the business of declaring war is theoretically in the hands of representatives of the people, no legislature has ever been known to decline the request of an Executive, which has conducted all foreign affairs in utter privacy and irresponsibility, that it order the nation into battle. . . .

The moment war is declared, however, the mass of the people, through some spiritual alchemy, become convinced that they have willed and executed the deed themselves. They then with the exception of a few malcontents, proceed to allow themselves to be regimented, coerced, deranged in all the environments of their lives, and turned into a solid manufactory of destruction toward whatever other people may have, in the appointed scheme of things, come within the range of the Government's disapprobation. . . .

The patriot loses all sense of the distinction between State, nation and government. In our quieter moments, the Nation or Country forms the basic idea of society. We think vaguely of a loose population spreading over a certain geographical portion of the earth's surface. Our idea of Country concerns itself with the non-political aspects of a people, its ways of living, its personal traits, its literature and art, its characteristic attitudes toward life. . . . The Country, as an inescapable group into which we are born, and which makes us its particular kind of a citizen of the world, seems to be a fundamental fact of our consciousness, an irreducible minimum of social feeling.

Now this feeling for country is essentially noncompetitive . . . , a concept of peace, of tolerance, of living and letting live. But State is essentially a concept of power, of competition; it signifies a group in its aggressive aspects. . . .

The State is the country acting as a political unit, it is the group acting as a repository of force, determiner of law, arbiter of justice. International politics is a "power politics" because it is a relation of States and that is what States infallibly and calamitously are, huge aggregations of human and industrial force that may be hurled against each other in war. When a country acts as a whole in relation to another country, or in imposing laws on its own inhabitants, or in coercing or punishing individuals or minorities, it is acting as a State. . . .

Government, on the other hand, . . . is a framework of the administration of laws, and the carrying out of public force. Government is the idea of the State put into practical operation in the hands of definite, concrete, fallible men. . . . Government is the only form in which we can envisage the State, but it is by no means identical with it. That the State is a mystical conception is something that must never be forgotten. Its glamor and its significance linger behind the framework of Government and direct its activities.

Wartime brings the ideal of the State out into very clear relief, and reveals attitudes and tendencies that were hidden. . . . For war is essentially the health of the State. The ideal of the State is that within its territory its power and influence should be universal. . . . War sends the current of purpose and activity flowing down to the lowest level of the herd,* and to its most remote branches, . . . and the State becomes what in peacetimes it has vainly struggled to become—the inexorable arbiter and determinant of men's business and attitudes and opinions. . . .

. . . [Modern, mass war] cannot exist without a military establishment, and a military establishment cannot exist without a State organization. . . . For it meets the demands of no other institution, it follows the desires of no religious, industrial, political group. If the demand for military organization and a military establishment seems to come not from the officers of the State but from the public, it is only that it comes from the State-obsessed portion of the public, those groups which feel most keenly the State ideal. . . .

All of which goes to show that the State represents all the autocratic, arbitrary, coercive, belligerent forces within a social group, it is a sort of complex of everything most distasteful to the modern free creative spirit, the feeling for life, liberty and the pursuit of happiness. War is the health of the State. Only when the State is at war does the modern society function with that unity of sentiment, simple uncritical patriotic devotion, cooperation of services, which have always been the ideal of the State lover. . . .

International Organization

By early 1917 the fighting in Europe seemed interminable. War aims —the term for peace with victory—expanded in rough proportion to the enormity of losses on all sides. At the same time, however, the goal of peace as the prevention of war also grew strong: this horror should never be repeated. With the collapse of the Central Powers in 1918, the

---

* Bourne uses "herd" to convey the basic collectivity of human society, a collectivity that preceded the development of individuals and specialized groupings.

negotiation of a settlement straddled both versions of peace—to conclude the Great War on terms advantageous for the victors, and to preclude any future war. In some respects, each idea of peace compromised the other.

The idea of peace based on international order drew on proposals that had been made in the nineteenth century. It also drew on existing international law and on established procedures such as arbitration. In the early years of World War I, it was given a fresh and comprehensive formulation by citizen peace advocates—in La Fontaine's 1914 exposition of peace, for example, and in the resolutions of the women's congress at The Hague a few months later. Beyond appealing for an end to the carnage, the women devoted a great deal of attention to the principles that should govern an enduring peace (document 3.20). Various groups in Germany and the neutral countries also formulated peace proposals, but the most important ones came from the Fabian Society in England and the League to Enforce Peace in the United States (document 3.21). All of these programs anticipated features that later were embodied in the Covenant of the League of Nations. Most important, all of them assumed the creation of just such a league.

In May 1916 the League to Enforce Peace sponsored a large public meeting in Washington at which President Woodrow Wilson endorsed the idea of an association to enforce peace and justice among nations. That version of peace, which became the official war aim of the United States when it entered the war a year later, was defined in Wilson's "Fourteen Points" speech to the Congress of 8 January 1918 (document 3.22). Thus, the meaning of a peace to end war, and especially the form of a postwar association of nations, passed from public discussion into governmental purview.

The planning that led to the League of Nations involved all of the Great Powers arrayed against Germany, but it was primarily an Anglo-American endeavor, although Léon Bourgeois brought to it not only French presence but also, having represented France at both Hague conferences and being a member of the Permanent Court of Arbitration, the legacy of the prewar peace movement. Lord Robert Cecil shaped the British draft of the League Covenant, helped write the final version at Paris, and then made the League his career. Wilson was central to the process because for him, and unlike other heads of state, it was a central war aim.[12] Moreover, within his own government Wilson largely kept the drafting in his own hands or closely coordinated the work of others. That included draft proposals from the British, who envisioned an international alliance with occasional meetings to deal with disputes, and a

French draft for a permanent agency that could employ sanctions against aggressors. Wilson was especially influenced, however, by a proposal from General Jan C. Smuts, defense minister of South Africa, former member of the British War Cabinet, and a delegate to the Paris peace conference.

Looking beyond a peace treaty or even military security, Smuts was seeking international order in the midst of worldwide political and social transformation (document 3.23). He rejected the notion of a super-state, and with it the "theories of sovereignty" that implied "centralization, absorption, and denationalization of the weaker national constituents of the population." Rather, he insisted, states should be "controlled not by compulsion from above but by consent from below. Government by consent of the governed is our formula."[13] Smuts proposed a permanent, organic institution that would be "real, practical, effective as a system of world-government: . . . to the peoples the guarantee of peace, to the workers of all races the great international, and to all the embodiment and living expression of the moral and spiritual unity of the human race."[14]

There being no precedent for world government, it was necessary to negotiate compromises among various proposals. That task was complicated by the need to reconcile abstract principles (such as the self-determination of peoples) with realities such as existing empires and ethnic distributions and with conflicts of national interest and ambition. The final version was worked out in the peace settlement of Versailles, which included the Covenant of a League of Nations (document 3.24).

The League was organized as a permanent organization with a secretariat and headquarters in Geneva, Switzerland. Its governing body was an Assembly of all member nations that was to meet at stated intervals. Executive responsibility was delegated to a Council, composed of the major powers allied against Germany plus four other states to be elected on occasion. The League was expected to develop a plan for general disarmament. It was empowered to supervise the administration of former colonies by the major powers, as provided in separate peace treaties. It was authorized to enforce a procedure that would prevent aggressive wars and would include a Permanent Court of International Justice. It was expected in principle to secure humane conditions of labor and just treatment of colonial peoples, to supervise arms trade, to maintain commercial freedom, and to promote the international control of disease.

In all these respects the new League of Nations institutionalized ideals that had been formulated during the nineteenth century. It was designed to promote international cooperation. However much the

League might modify the state system as it carried out its assigned roles, its raison d'être was to guarantee the security of nations. Indeed, the principle of absolute sovereignty was preserved by the requirement that all decisions had to be unanimous.

The ideal of cooperation was tempered by a respect for power in international relations, so that the Covenant sanctioned limited use of force to enforce order among states. Force was authorized only to require that disputes be submitted to arbitration or adjudication, and warfare as a last resort was recognized as a legitimate national right. The new forms of international cooperation modified sovereignty, therefore, but they did not subject it to world government based on consent. It was widely understood that, as Wilson himself recognized, the League was only a starting point, and that a truly secure international order required stronger institutions built on a clearer consensus about peace than the ideas prevailing at the end of World War I.

Document 3.19

The International Congress of Women: Principles of Peace

From resolutions of the International Congress of Women, 1915

Respect for Nationality

This International Congress of Women, recognizing the right of the people to self-government, affirms that there should be no transference of territory without the consent of the men and women residing therein, and urges that autonomy and a democratic parliament should not be refused to any people.

Arbitration and Conciliation

This International Congress of Women, believing that war is the negation of progress and civilization, urges the governments of all nations to come to an agreement to refer future international disputes to arbitration and conciliation.

International Pressure

This International Congress of Women urges the governments of all nations to come to an agreement to unite in bringing social, moral and economic pressure to bear upon any country which resorts to arms instead of referring its case to arbitration or conciliation.

Democratic Control of Foreign Policy

Since war is commonly brought about not by the mass of the people, who do not desire it, but by groups representing particular interests, this International Congress of Women urges that foreign politics shall be subject to democratic control, and declares that it can only recognize as democratic a system which includes the equal representation of men and women.

The Enfranchisement of Women

Since the combined influence of the women of all countries is one of the strongest forces for the prevention of war, and since women can only have full responsibility and effective influence when they have equal political rights with men, this International Congress of Women demands their political enfranchisement.

Third Hague Conference
This International Congress of Women urges that a third Hague Conference be convened immediately after the war.

International Organization

This International Women's Congress urges that the organization of the Society of Nations should be further developed on the basis of a constructive peace, and that it should include:

(a) As a development of The Hague Court of Arbitration, a permanent International Court of Justice to settle questions or differences of a justiciable character. . . .

(b) As a development of the constructive work of The Hague Conference, a permanent international conference holding regular meetings, in which women should take part, to deal . . . with practical proposals for further international cooperation among the States. This conference should be so constituted that it could formulate and enforce those principles of justice, equality and good-will. . . .

The International Conference shall appoint: A permanent council of conciliation and investigation for the settlement of international disputes. . . .

General Disarmament

This International Congress of Women, advocating universal disarmament . . . by international agreement, urges as a step to this end that all countries should . . . take over the manufacture of arms . . . and should control all international traffic in the same. . . .

Commerce and Investments

The Congress urges that in all countries there shall be liberty of commerce, that the seas shall be free and the trade routes open on equal terms to . . . all nations. . . .

National Foreign Policy

This International Congress of Women demands that all secret treaties shall be void, [and] that national commissions be created and international conferences convened for the scientific study and elaboration of the principles and condition of permanent peace which might contribute to the development of an international federation. . . .

Women in National and International Politics

This International Congress of Women declares it to be essential, both nationally and internationally, to put into practice the principle that women should share all civil and political rights and responsibilities on the same terms as men.

Document 3.20

The League to Enforce Peace: A League of Nations

From resolutions of the League to Enforce Peace, 1917

We believe it to be desirable for the United States to join a league of nations binding the signatories to the following:

First: All justiciable questions arising between the signatory Powers, not settled by negotiation shall, subject to the limitations of treaties, be submitted to a judicial tribunal for bearing and judgment, both upon the merits and upon any issue as to its jurisdiction of the question.

Second: All other questions arising between the signatories and not settled by negotiation, shall be submitted to a Council of Conciliation for hearing, consideration, and recommendation.

Third: The signatory Powers shall jointly use forthwith both their economic and military forces against any one of their number that goes to war, or commits acts of hostility, against another of the signatories before any question arising shall be submitted as provided in the forego-ing.

Fourth: Conferences between the signatory Powers shall be held from time to time to formulate and codify rules of international law, which, unless some signatory shall signify its dissent within a stated period, shall thereafter govern in the decisions of the Juridical Tribunal mentioned in Article One.

Document 3.21

Woodrow Wilson: Peace Aims

From the Fourteen Points speech to the Congress, January 1918

We entered this war because violations of right had occurred which touched us to the quick and made the life of our own people impossible unless they were corrected and the world secured once for all against their recurrence. What we demand in this war . . . is that the world be made fit and safe to live in. . . . The program of the world's peace, there-fore, is our program; and that program, the only possible program, as we see it, is this:

1. Open covenants of peace, openly arrived at, after which there shall be no private international understandings of any kind but diplo-macy shall proceed always frankly and in the public view.

2. Absolute freedom of navigation upon the seas, outside territo-rial waters, alike in peace and in war, except as the seas may be closed in whole or in part by international action for the enforcement of interna-tional covenants.

3. The removal, so far as possible, of all economic barriers and the establishment of an equality of trade conditions among all the nations consenting to the peace and associating themselves for its maintenance.

4. Adequate guarantees given and taken that national armaments will be reduced to the lowest point consistent with domestic safety.

5. A free, open-minded, and absolutely impartial adjustment of all colonial claims, based upon a strict observance of the principle that in determining all such questions of sovereignty the interests of the popula-tions concerned must have equal weight with the equitable claims of the Government whose title is to be determined.

6. The evacuation of all Russian territory and such a settlement of all questions affecting Russia as will secure the best and freest cooperation of the other nations of the world in obtaining for her an unhampered and unembarrassed opportunity for the independent determination of her own political development and national policy and assure her of a sincere welcome into the society of free nations under institutions of her own choosing; and, more than a welcome, assistance also of every kind that she may need and may herself desire. . . .

7. Belgium, the whole world will agree, must be evacuated and restored, without any attempt to limit the sovereignty which she enjoys in common with all other free nations. . . . Without this healing act the whole structure and validity of international law is forever impaired.

8. All French territory should be freed and the invaded portions restored, and the wrong done to France by Prussia in 1871 in the matter of Alsace-Lorraine, which has unsettled the peace of the world for nearly fifty years, should be righted, in order that peace may once more be made secure in the interest of all.

9. A readjustment of the frontiers of Italy should be effected along clearly recognizable lines of nationality.

10. The peoples of Austria-Hungary, whose place among the nations we wish to see safeguarded and assured, should be accorded the freest opportunity of autonomous development.

11. Rumania, Serbia, and Montenegro should be evacuated; occupied territories restored; Serbia accorded free and secure access to the sea; and the relations of the several Balkan states to one another determined by friendly counsel along historically established lines of allegiance and nationality; and international guarantees of the political and economic independence and territorial integrity of the several Balkan states should be entered into.

12. The Turkish portions of the present Ottoman Empire should be assured a secure sovereignty, but the other nationalities which are now under Turkish rule should be assured an undoubted security of life and an absolutely unmolested opportunity of autonomous development, and the Dardanelles should be permanently opened as a free passage. . . .

13. An independent Polish state should be erected which should include the territories inhabited by indisputably Polish populations, which should be assured a free and secure access to the sea, and whose political and economic independence and territorial integrity should be guaranteed by international covenant.

14. A general association of nations must be formed under specific

covenants for the purpose of affording mutual guarantees of political independence and territorial integrity to great and small states alike.

Document 3.22

Jan Christiaan Smuts: A Real Organ of Government

From "The League of Nations: A Practical Suggestion,"
December 1918

... It is not sufficient for the league merely to be a sort of *deus ex machina,* called in very grave emergencies when the specter of war appears; if it is to last, it must be much more. It must become part and parcel of the common international life of states, it must be an ever visible, living, working organ of the polity of civilization. It must function so strongly in the ordinary peaceful intercourse of states that it becomes irresistible in their disputes; its peace activity must be the foundation and guarantee of its war power. How would it be possible to build the league so closely into the fabric of our international system?
... The process of civilization has always been towards the league of nations. ... Nations in their march to power tend to pass the purely national bounds; hence arise the empires which embrace various nations. ... In a rudimentary way all such composite empires of the past were leagues of nations, keeping the peace among the constituent nations, but unfortunately doing so not on the basis of freedom but of repression. ...
The attempt to form empires or leagues of nations on the basis of inequality and the bondage and oppression of the smaller national units has failed, and the work has to be done all over again on a new basis and an enormous scale. The vast elemental forces liberated by this war, even more than the war itself, have been responsible for this great change. In the place of the great empires we find the map of Europe now dotted with small nations, embryo states, derelict territories. Europe has been reduced to its original atoms. ...
What are those fundamental principles which must guide the league in its territorial policy as the general heir or successor of the defunct empires? They have been summed up for the last two years in the general formula of "No annexations, and the self-determination of nations.". . .*

---

* For Smuts these principles implied: (1) self-determination of territories formerly belonging to Russia, Austria, and Turkey; (2) supervision, by the league of nations, of those former territories not ready for self-government, with (3) administration by a state

The Constitution of the League

. . . Let us remember that we are only asked to make a beginning . . . and that our constitution should avoid all rigidity, should be elastic and capable of growth, expansion and adaptation to the needs which the new organ of government will have to meet in the process of the years. Above all it must be practical and be so devised as to be a real working organ of government.

And from this point of view let us proceed at once to discard the idea of a super-state which is in the minds of some people. No new super-sovereign is wanted in the new world now arising. States will here be controlled not by compulsion from above but by consent from below. Government by consent of the governed is our formula. The old empires were ruined by their theories of sovereignty, which meant centralization, absorption, and denationalization of the weaker national constituents of the population. . . .

But while we avoid the super-sovereign at the one end, we must be equally careful to avoid the mere ineffective debating society at the other end. . . . We want a league which will be real, practical, effective as a system of world-government.

The constitution of the league will be that of a permanent conference between the Governments of the constituent states for the purpose of joint international action in certain defined respects, and will not derogate from the independence of those states. It will consist of a general conference, a council, and courts of arbitration and conciliation.

The general conference, in which all constituent states will have equal voting power, will meet periodically to discuss matters submitted to it by the council. These matters will be general measures of international law or arrangements or general proposals for limitation of armaments for securing world peace, or any other general resolutions, the discussion of which by the conference is desired by the council before they are forwarded for the approval of the constituent Governments. . . .

The council will be the executive committee of the league, and will consist of the . . . authoritative representatives of the Great Powers, together with the representatives drawn in rotation from two panels of the middle Powers and minor states respectively, in such a way that the

---

mandated as an agent of the league, (4) provision for appeal from the local population for redress of abuse of the mandatory trust, and (5) essential disarmament in states and territories arising from old empires.

Great Powers have a bare majority. A minority of three or more can veto any action or resolution of the council. . . .

Its functions will be:

(a) To take executive action or control in regard to [mandates] or under any international arrangements or conventions;

(b) To administer and control any property of an international character, such as international waterways, rivers, straits, railways, fortifications, air stations, etc.;

(c) To formulate for the approval of the Governments general measures of international law, or arrangements for limitations of armaments or promotion of world peace.

The League and World Peace

Now it seems to me that some people expect too much from the new machinery of international arbitration and conciliation which emerges as the chief proposal for preventing future wars. War is a symptom of deep-seated evils; it is a disease or growth out of social and political conditions. While these conditions remain unaltered, it is vain to expect any good from new institutions superimposed on those conditions. Hence it is that I have argued all through this discussion for an inner transformation of international conditions and institutions. . . . The new institution of peace must not be something additional, something external, superimposed on the pre-existing structure. It must be an organic change; it must be woven into the very texture of our political organization, and must, so to speak, flow from the nature of things political. . . .*

As long as members of the league submit their disputes for inquiry and report or recommendation or decision by some outside authority, their obligation to the league will be satisfied, and thereafter they will be free to take any action they like, and even to go to war.

This may appear a weak position to take up; and yet . . . the utmost that it seems possible to achieve in the present conditions of international opinion and practice is to provide for a breathing space before the disputants are free to go to war; to create a binding moratorium or period of delay, during which the parties to the dispute agree not to proceed to extremes but to await the results of the inquiry or hearing to which their case has been referred. . . .

* In particular, Smuts recommended: (1) abolishing conscription and defining by league of militia size, (2) limiting armaments by league action, and (3) nationalizing the manufacture of weapons of war subject to inspection by the league council.

What are the penalties incurred by any party which breaks this covenant to observe the moratorium? This is the most important question of all in regard to the preservation of world peace. Without an effective sanction for the keeping of the moratorium the league will remain a pious aspiration of a dead letter. . . .

. . . The peace treaty shall provide that if any member of the league breaks its covenant [not to go to war until there is an arbitration award or a report by the council, and then not against a member which complies with the award or report] it shall *ipso facto* become at war with all the other members of the league, which shall subject it to complete economic and financial boycott. . . .

. . . If the future peace of the world is to be maintained, it will not be sufficient merely to erect an institution for the purpose of settling international disputes after they have arisen, it will be necessary to devise an instrument of government which will deal with the causes and sources of disputes. . . . For not only are men's minds prepared for the new peaceful order, but the sweeping away of the imperial systems of Europe leaves the space vacant which the new institution must occupy. The need, political and psychological, is imperative; the opportunity is unique; and only the blindness of statesmen could not prevent the coming of the new institution, which will, more than anything else, reconcile the peoples to the sufferings they have endured in this war. . . .

For there is no doubt that mankind is once more on the move. The very foundations have been shaken and loosened, and things are again fluid. The tents have been struck, and the great caravan of humanity is once more on the march. Vast social and industrial chances are coming —perhaps upheavals which may, in their magnitude and effects, be comparable to war itself. A steadying, controlling, regulating influence will be required to give stability to progress, and to remove that wasteful friction which has dissipated so much social force in the past, and in this war more than ever before. These great functions could only be adequately fulfilled by the league of nations. Responding to such vital needs and coming at such a unique opportunity in history, it may well be destined to mark a new era in the government of man, and become to the peoples the guarantee of peace, to the workers of all races the great international, and to all the embodiment and living expression of the moral and spiritual unity of the human race.

Document 3.23

The Covenant of the League of Nations

From "The Covenant of the League of Nations," 1919[*]

The High Contracting Parties
In order to promote international co-operation and to achieve international peace and security
by the acceptance of obligations not to resort to war,
by the prescription of open, just and honorable relations between nations,
by the firm establishment of the understandings of international law as the actual rule of conduct among Governments, and
by the maintenance of justice and a scrupulous respect for all treaty obligations in the dealings of organized peoples with one another,
Agree to this Covenant of the League of Nations.

ARTICLE 1
Membership

The original Members of the League of Nations shall be those of the Signatories which are named in the Annex to this Covenant and also such of those other States named . . . as shall accede without reservation to this Covenant. . . .

Any fully self-governing State, Dominion or Colony not named in the Annex may become a Member of the League if its admission is agreed to by two-thirds of the Assembly, provided that it shall give effective guarantees of its sincere intention to observe its international obligations, and shall accept such regulations as may be prescribed by the League in regard to its military, naval and air forces and armaments.

Any Member of the League may, after two years' notice of its intention to do so, withdraw from the League. . . .

ARTICLE 2
Executive Organs

The action of the League under this Covenant shall be effected through the instrumentality of an Assembly and a Council, with a permanent Secretariat.

[*] This edition includes amendments to 1927.

ARTICLE 3
Assembly

The Assembly shall consist of Representatives of the Members of the League.

The Assembly shall meet at stated intervals and from time to time as occasion may require at the Seat of the League or at such other place as may be decided upon.

The Assembly may deal at its meetings with any matter within the sphere of action of the League or affecting the peace of the world.

At meetings of the Assembly, each Member of the League shall have one vote, and may not have more than three Representatives.

ARTICLE 4
Council

The Council shall consist of Representatives of the Principal Allied and Associated Powers, together with Representatives of four other Members of the League . . . selected by the Assembly from time to time in its discretion. . . .*

The Council may deal at its meetings with any matter within the sphere of action of the League or affecting the peace of the world.

Any member of the League not represented on the Council shall be invited to . . . sit as a member at any meeting of the Council during the consideration of matters specially affecting the interests of that Member of the League. . . .

ARTICLE 5
Voting and Procedure

Except where otherwise expressly provided . . . decisions at any meeting of the Assembly or of the Council shall require the agreement of all the Members of the League represented at the meeting.†

---

* The principal Allied powers were the British Empire, France, Italy, and Japan; the United States was an Associated Power, and it did not join the League. The four other initial powers were Belgium, Brazil, Spain, and Greece. The number of seats designated by the Assembly was raised from four to six in 1922, and to nine in 1926 when Germany was allotted a permanent seat. The Council was obliged to meet at least once a year. Each of its members had one vote and one representative.

† Matters of procedure were to be decided by a majority. The first meetings of the Assembly and Council were to be summoned by the President of the United States.

ARTICLE 6
Secretariat

The permanent Secretariat shall be established at the Seat of the League. The Secretariat shall comprise a Secretary-General and such secretaries and staff as may be required.*

ARTICLE 8
Reduction of Armaments

The Members of the League recognize that the maintenance of peace requires the reduction of national armaments to the lowest point consistent with national safety and the enforcement by common action of international obligations.

The Council . . . shall formulate plans for such reduction for the consideration and action of the several Governments. . . .

The Members of the League agree that the manufacture by private enterprise of munitions and implements of war is open to grave objections. . . .†

ARTICLE 10
Guarantees Against Aggression

The Members of the League undertake to respect and preserve as against external aggression the territorial integrity and existing political independence of all Members of the League. In case of any such aggression or in case of any threat or danger of such aggression, the Council shall advise upon the means by which this obligation shall be fulfilled.

ARTICLE 11
Action in Case of War or Threat of War

Any war or threat of war, whether immediately affecting any of the Members of the League or not, is hereby declared a matter of concern to the whole League, and the League shall take any action that may be deemed wise and effectual to safeguard the peace of nations. In case any such emergency should arise, the Secretary-General shall, on the request

---

* Article 7 fixed the Seat of the League at Geneva, provided that all positions would be open equally to men and women, and guaranteed diplomatic immunity.

† The Council was to recommend measure for the control of arms and munitions. Article 9 established a permanent commission to advise the Council on military issues.

of any member of the League, forthwith summon a meeting of the Council.

ARTICLE 12
Disputes to Be Submitted for Settlement

The Members of the League agree that if there should arise between them any dispute likely to lead to a rupture they will submit the matter either to arbitration or judicial settlement or to inquiry by the Council, and they agree in no case to resort to war until three months after the award by the arbitrators or the judicial decision or the report by the Council.*

ARTICLE 13
Arbitration or Judicial Settlement

The Members of the League agree that whenever any dispute shall arise between them which they recognize to be suitable for submission to arbitration or judicial settlement, and which cannot be satisfactorily settled by diplomacy, they will submit the whole subject-matter to arbitration or judicial settlement.†

For the consideration of any such dispute, the court to which the case is referred shall be the Permanent court of International Justice . . . or any tribunal agreed on by the parties to the dispute. . . .

The Members of the League agree that they will carry out in full good faith any award or decision that may be rendered, and that they will not resort to war against a Member of the League which complies therewith. . . .

ARTICLE 14
Permanent Court of International Justice

The Council shall formulate and submit to the Members of the League for adoption plans for the establishment of a Permanent Court of International Justice. . . .

---

* An award was required within six months after the submission of the dispute.

† Such cases were specified as the interpretation of treaties, international law, the fact of a breach of an international obligation, or the amount of reparation for such a breach.

ARTICLE 15
Disputes Not Submitted to Arbitration or Judicial Settlement

If there should arise between Members of the League any dispute
likely to lead to a rupture, which is not submitted to arbitration or
judicial settlement . . . , the Members of the League agree that they will
submit the matter to the Council. . . .*

ARTICLE 16
Sanctions of Pacific Settlement

Should any Member of the League resort to war in disregard of its
covenants under Articles 12, 13, or 15, it shall, *ipso facto,* be deemed to
have committed an act of war against all other Members of the League,
which hereby undertake immediately to subject it to the severance of all
trade or financial relations, the prohibition of all intercourse between
their nationals and the nationals of the Covenant-breaking State, and the
prevention of all financial, commercial or personal intercourse between
the nationals of the Covenant-breaking State and the nationals of any
other State, whether a Member of the League or not.

It shall be the duty of the Council in such case to recommend to the
several Governments concerned what effective military, naval or air force
the Members of the League shall severally contribute to the armed forces
to be used to protect the covenants of the League.

The Members of the League agree, further, that they will mutually
support one another in the financial and economic measures which are
taken under this article, in order to minimize the loss and inconvenience
resulting from the above measures. . . .

Any member of the League which has violated any covenant of the
League may be declared to be no longer a Member of the League by a
vote of the Council concurred in by the Representatives of all the other
Members of the League represented thereon.†

ARTICLE 18
Registration and Publication of Treaties

Every treaty or international engagement entered into hereafter by
any Member of the League shall be forthwith registered with the Secre-

---

* Article 15 specified the procedure for handling a dispute and provided that the
Council could refer it to the Assembly.
† Article 17 invited non-member States that were parties to disputes to accept mem-
bership for the purpose of settling them under Articles 12 through 16.

tariat and shall, as soon as possible, be published by it. No such treaty or international engagement shall be binding until so registered.

ARTICLE 19
Review of Treaties

The Assembly may from time to time advise the reconsideration by Members of the League of treaties which have become inapplicable and the consideration of international conditions whose continuance might endanger the peace of the world.*

ARTICLE 22
Mandatory System

To those colonies and territories which as a consequence of the late war have ceased to be under the sovereignty of the States which formerly governed them and which are inhabited by peoples not yet able to stand by themselves . . . there should be applied the principle that the well-being and development of such peoples form a sacred trust of civilization. . . .

The best method of giving practical effect to this principle is that the tutelage of such peoples should be entrusted to advanced nations who . . . can best undertake this responsibility . . . as Mandatories on behalf of the League.†

ARTICLE 23
Social and Other Activities

Subject to and in accordance with the provisions of international Conventions . . . the Members of the League:

(a) will endeavor to secure and maintain fair and humane conditions of labor for men, women and children, both in their own countries and in all countries to which their commercial and industrial relations extend, and for that purpose will establish and maintain the necessary international organizations;

(b) undertake to secure just treatment of the native inhabitants of territories under their control;

---

* Articles 20 and 21 provided that the Covenant abrogated all obligations *inconsistent* with it but affirmed the validity of arbitration treaties and regional peacekeeping understandings, specifically the Monroe Doctrine.

† The article specified conditions for specific territories, noted general procedure, and authorized a permanent Commission to supervise the mandates.

(c) will entrust the League with the general supervision over the execution of agreements with regard to the traffic in women and children, and the traffic in opium and other dangerous drugs;

(d) will entrust the League with the general supervision of the trade in arms and ammunition with the countries in which the control of this traffic is necessary in the common interest;

(e) will make provision to secure and maintain freedom of communications and of transit and equitable treatment for the commerce of all Members. . . .

(f) will endeavor to take steps in matters of international concern for the prevention and control of disease.

ARTICLE 24
International Bureaus

There shall be placed under the direction of the League all international bureaus already established by general treaties if the parties to such treaties consent. All such international bureaus and all commissions for the regulation of matters of international interest hereafter constituted shall be placed under the direction of the League.*

---

* Article 25 specifically pledged support to Red Cross organizations. Article 26 provided for amendments to the Covenant.

4

Alternatives to War
1919–1939

The twenty years between 1919 and 1939 can be interpreted as an era between two separate wars or as a long truce within a single, massive, and complex conflict. In either case, each decade faced a distinct challenge: in the 1920s, on the ruins of the "Great War," to build international cooperation for stability and conflict resolution; and in the 1930s, in the midst of economic crisis and mounting aggression, to forestall a second and more ruinous world war.

"To promote international cooperation" was the first goal in the preamble to the League of Nations Covenant. For that purpose, the League generated programs to settle international disputes; care for displaced persons; stabilize economic relations; set standards in labor relations; administer former colonies of the defeated powers; protect minorities, women and children; further world health; and foster intellectual cooperation. Outside the League there was a significant movement for a union of European states. These initiatives, undertaken through governments, international agencies, and nongovernmental organizations, are illustrated in the first part of this chapter.

A second approach to peace was to eliminate or control weapons of war, which was implied by the second goal in the Covenant, "to achieve international peace and security." Disarmament, in the broadest sense of the word, involved a major effort by the League and nations in extensive negotiations and generated an international citizens campaign.

Beyond the emphases of international organization and disarmament, there were attempts to influence public opinion, attitudes, and values, which is the third theme of the chapter. The insights of social psychology and religion suggested that there were deep levels of violence beneath the surface of individual personalities and national cultures. In turn, this raised disturbing questions about the prospects for peace based on idealism or reason.

For many people, World War I had reinforced the view that war is a crime against mankind. That belief also was embodied in the League. Along with the pragmatic view that warfare is counterproductive to legitimate social values, it contributed to a fourth theme, of organized nonviolence. Traditional nonresistance continued, especially in Christian sects that emphasized inner tranquillity and obedience to moral law, but nonviolence also became associated with activism and efforts to influence foreign policy. And it led to two innovations: organized war resistance, in which people refused to support warfare in advance of a crisis, and nonviolent resistance, in which people mobilized for direct action against aggression or injustice.

Thus ideas of peace as order, security, justice, equity, and tranquillity commingled in the 1920s. Like their governments, peace activists and the general public reflected the shifting and diverse political and ideological currents of the decade.

Perhaps the most dramatic conflicts were those reflected in the fifth section of the chapter, the bitter struggles within the socialist and communist parties of Europe that spilled over into the labor and trade union movement and into the cultural avant-garde, where they dominated arguments over peace. Socialists who were called 'realist pacifists' favored peaceful change, including social reform, arbitration, and disarmament. Revolutionary socialists and communists, on the other hand, proclaimed that peace could come only with a victorious socialist revolution, a position that was all the more divisive because it was associated with Russia's foreign policy and its leadership in the Communist International.

The Bolshevik Revolution of 1917 had created an ideological, political, and economic gulf between the Soviet Union and the rest of Europe. In addition, the 1919 war settlement had divided the nations into winners, losers, and neutrals: victor states sought peace through strict enforcement of treaties, while the vanquished worked to revise them. As the world economy collapsed and revisionist states challenged the World War I settlement early in the 1930s, governments and citizen peace advocates became ever more polarized over ideology, national aims, and alternative approaches to peace. Liberals, socialists, and communists debated whether the peace treaty should be upheld or amended, whether the revisionist powers should be checked by coordinated action or appeased.

They divided over whether to apply economic and military sanctions at the risk of another, more terrible war, or to respond to aggression with moral pressure alone.

Collective security was a major initiative of the interwar period. This keystone of the League of Nations, which had alienated the United States, pledged each of its member states to support all the others against aggression or threats of aggression. Throughout the 1920s, and despite significant efforts, the League was unable to define or implement that obligation; and in the 1930s governments moved away from collective security, towards neutralism and appeasement. This development is documented in the sixth section of the chapter.

The extreme polarization that characterized the interwar period undoubtedly thwarted thoughtful and practical efforts to halt aggression. The spirit of confrontation was reinforced by the pervasive image of "the other," an unrelenting class, racial, national, or ideological enemy that bound groups and nations together in the face of fear and privation. Despite significant innovations in the ideas and institutions of peace, attempts to achieve international cooperation and security were frustrated by intractable differences. A second world conflagration followed, and reflection on its causes contributed to the next debate over alternatives to war.

International Cooperation

Institutions for international cooperation grew between the two world wars, even though the system of competing sovereign states predominated and eventually overwhelmed them. The fragile international organizations of this period were significant, however, for their very existence.

At the center of efforts to create a peaceful international order was the League of Nations, even though it had neither independent authority nor universal membership.[1] The provisions in its charter for collective action were ambiguous, and their implementation required sovereign nations to act together. Frequent failures to act in the common interest frustrated both the international civil service and the small powers that vested their security with the League. At the end of its first decade, Salvador de Madariaga, a Spaniard who headed the League's disarmament section for six years, outlined his vision for a more comprehensive peace organization (document 4.1). At the end of its second decade, the League was widely regarded as a failure.

An assessment of its significance should begin in 1919, however, and not with 1939.[2] At the outset, "its founders approved the basic principles of the traditional multistate system," as Inis Claude observed: "they accepted the independent sovereign state as the basic entity, the great powers as the predominant participants, and Europe as the central core of the world political system. . . . The task to which they set themselves was that of creating safety devices to obviate the repetition of such an unfortunate breakdown as had occurred in 1914. The League was the manifestation of a reform movement, an effort to improve the procedures and assist the operation of the world political system."[3] The 1919 reform introduced permanent inter-state institutions, and it implied a new standard of international morality.

The League's headquarters was in Geneva, Switzerland, the home of a growing international civil service devoted to economic, social, and humanitarian work. In that work the League was able to involve Germany and the Soviet Union, which originally were excluded from membership, as well as the United States, which rejected formal participation. Many League officials tried to shed their purely national identities in order to serve the larger cause of international reconciliation.

The new international civil service was epitomized by the League's first High Commissioner for Refugees, Fridtjof Nansen, the Norwegian scientist, explorer, and Nobel Peace Prize winner. Nansen directed the repatriation of a half million refugees and prisoners of war, mainly Russians, Germans, and Austrians.[4] He also mobilized relief for a terrible famine in Russia. Most of his refugee and relief work was achieved through voluntary, nongovernmental organizations. With the exceptions of Norway and the United States, governments were not generous in their support. Nansen complained of a "barren self-sufficiency, [and an] absence of any wish to understand other points of view, which is Europe's greatest danger," and he urged an alternative, transnational perspective.[5]

That view modified the interpretation of international law. Older approaches continued, including projects for codification and efforts to define the rights of nations; but several analysts questioned traditional assumptions about sovereign independence. James Brierly, the Chicele Professor of International Law and Diplomacy at Oxford and editor of the *British Yearbook of International Law,* accepted the idea that international law is based on the customary behavior of states, but he also insisted that it reflects collective social purpose and is evidence of a growing society of interdependent nations. Indeed, Brierly found the beginnings of constitutional law in the growth of international organizations that, rather than superseding national governments, facilitated cooperation among them (document 4.2).[6]

Such were the Permanent Court of International Justice, or the World Court, and the International Labor Organization, or ILO, which were affiliated with the League of Nations but had autonomous administrations. Unlike the earlier Court of Arbitration (a list of jurists available for service), the World Court judges met regularly at The Hague with a prescribed jurisdiction (document 4.3). They could hear only cases brought by governments, and only with the agreement of both parties to a dispute, but nonetheless by 1939 they had dealt with 79 cases, and the court had been recognized in about 600 international agreements. It was an instrument by which nations could delegate *jurisdiction* in specific cases without surrendering *sovereignty*.

The same principle applied to the International Labor Organization, which had a secretariat in Geneva. Its membership represented governments, business management, and organized labor from most nations. Ably directed from 1920 to 1932 by Albert Thomas, a moderate French socialist, the ILO conducted studies and conferences on standards for labor protection, furnished technical assistance, and gave labor a voice in League forums. Although it did not effect dramatic gains for the working class, it did increase the acceptance of key principles: that "labor is not a commodity," that the poverty of any group endangers the prosperity of others, and that freedom and economic security are universal human rights (document 4.4).

The League secretariat itself included several departments. One of them administered innovative treaties designed to protect racial and religious minorities in eastern Europe and Turkey and to prevent intervention on their behalf from neighboring countries (document 4.5). Negotiated between the Great Powers and the new, enlarged, or defeated states of eastern Europe, the treaties were guaranteed by the League, which established a delicate enforcement procedure to balance the claims of justice and state sovereignty. The system worked moderately well in the 1920s but disintegrated in the following decade.

The League also inherited the Mandate system.[7] In the treaties ending World War I, the British Empire and France acquired jurisdiction over vast territories in the Middle East, Africa, and Asia, but they were obligated to promote the welfare of those regions and facilitate their transition to self-government under League supervision. Annual reports were made to the Mandates Commission, which became one of the League's most durable and successful agencies. The complexities of mandated power are perhaps best known in relation to Britain's administration of Palestine (document 4.6), but other areas had difficult minority and border problems. Although it was not applied to existing colonies, the mandates system reinforced the idea that self-determination was a universal principle.

There were other areas of functional, problem-solving cooperation. The League's economic and financial section made information on economic conditions widely available; its communication and trade section developed conventions to regulate international ports and railroads; its committee on opium was in the forefront of drug reform; and other committees initiated reforms on child welfare and the traffic in women. Most successful of all, its health section compiled public health records, distributed medical information, standardized procedures, and launched effective campaigns against epidemics.

The League's Committee on Intellectual Cooperation specifically included peace in its agenda. Founded in 1922 and initially presided over by French philosopher Henri Bergson, the committee sought to improve the material condition and interaction of intellectual workers, and to mobilize them for peace. Indeed, one of its subgroups became the victim of belligerent nationalism when it tried to revise German and French history textbooks, and the physicist Albert Einstein was vilified in Germany when he joined the committee in 1922. Nevertheless, the committee stimulated the formation of international conferences and institutes, and it federated about forty national committees.

The League of Nations was supported by numerous national societies federated through a bureau in Brussels. Most of them were small, although the British one enlisted a half million persons. Those societies were, Francis Walters observed, "the true heirs of the peace movements of the nineteenth century."[8] In fact, each of the League's departments cooperated with public organizations in its field, thus creating a series of international *regimes,* or areas of nonexclusive jurisdiction, more or less under the League's aegis.

The international organization was complemented by a regional movement for a united Europe that had been anticipated by nineteenth-century peace advocates such as Count Henri de Saint-Simon and Victor Hugo. By 1923 the idea of federation claimed distinguished advocates among the intellectuals and industrial leaders of Europe. Within another year it acquired a substantial organizational base and popular recognition.[9] Soon it attracted political support, notably from the French: Edouard Herriot, the premier, and Aristide Briand, the foreign minister. The idea was endorsed in principle when Briand formally put it before the European governments in 1929 and 1930 (document 4.7); but in fact

Europe was disintegrating, and the project was relegated to a League of Nations commission of inquiry. There it languished, "one of the most, if not the most, creative and constructive movements in Europe between the two world wars."[10]

From that movement evolved the European Community of the 1990s. From other precedents in the interwar period there came the comprehensive international institutions of the second half of the century: the Nansen commission was succeeded by the United Nations Relief and Rehabilitation Agency; the World Court continued virtually unchanged, while the International Labor Organization became the first U.N. specialized agency; the rights of minorities were included in the Universal Declaration of Human Rights; the Mandates Commission became the U.N. Trusteeship Council; the Economic and Financial Organization developed into the International Monetary Fund and related agencies; the Health Organization was succeeded by the World Health Organization; and the Committee on Intellectual Cooperation broadened into the United Nations Educational, Scientific, and Cultural Organization.[11]

All of these agencies, initiated in some measure in the interwar period, shared a common goal of achieving peace through practical cooperation. Collectively, they embodied the concept of functionalism in international relations: conflict would be neutralized by scientific analysis and cooperative action. In various ways, they applied the principle stated in the constitution of the International Labor Organization: "universal peace . . . can be established only if it is based on social justice."

Document 4.1

Salvador de Madariaga: International Organization

From *Disarmament*, 1929

To begin with, disarmament is not an isolated problem; armaments are one of the features of our present international life. It is therefore hopeless to try to solve the problem of armaments in isolation from the remaining problems of the world. Indeed this idea seems to me to occupy the very basis of the question. As long as it has not been grasped, and as long as it does not impose itself on governments and peoples alike we shall be wasting our time in vain endeavors. We are in the presence of two facts, national armaments and wars, which are but two manifestations of international life in its present stage of development: just as individual armaments and duels are manifestations of national life in a certain stage of its development. . . . But while dueling and the disarming of individuals had to wait until the national state was strong enough to organize the political and judiciary life of the country, we hear everywhere of great schemes for disarming straight away and for outlawing war by incantation.

Let us now summarize our conclusions:

(1) Disarmament is a world problem. It can only be solved by the world as the world organized in a community.

(2) This World-Community must possess a Court with compulsory jurisdiction on all questions of a judicial character.

(3) This World-Community must possess a political organization with powers:

    (a) to seek the solution of disputes of a non-judicial character by all possible means,

    (b) to deal with the threat of war . . . ,

    (c) if necessary to lead the world in any action, moral or even physical, against law-breaking nations.

(4) The World-Community must possess a technical organization which will gradually bring under the world control the study and solution of a growing number of problems which are taking on a world-wide scope.

We consider an active Council of the League as an indispensable element in the creation and fostering of security. The world must feel that its business is well in hand. Such a transformation of the life of the Council would make the convention on arbitration and security here advocated a living thing instead of yet another solemn paper. The Council having thus proved a new spirit would have assumed sufficient authority for attempting the next task in the true preparation for disarmament.

Document 4.2

James L. Brierly: The International Law of Peace

From *The Law of Nations*, 1938

The theory of sovereignty was invented and developed by political theorists who were not interested in, and paid practically no regard to, the relations of states with one another; and it is not only inconsistent with the subjection of states to any kind of law, but it is in fact an impossible theory for a world which contains more states than one. . . .

There need be no mystery about the source of the obligation to obey international law. The same problem arises in any system of law and it can never be solved by merely *juridical* explanation. The answer must be sought outside the law, and it is for legal philosophy to provide it. The notion that the validity of international law raises some peculiar problem arises from the confusion which the doctrine of sovereignty has introduced into international legal theory. We have accepted a false idea of the state as a personality with a life and a will of its own, still living in a "state of nature," which is contrasted with the "political" state in which individual men have come to live. This assumed condition of states is the very negation of law, and no ingenuity can explain the coexistence of the two. But it is a notion as false analytically as it admittedly is historically. The truth is that states are not persons, however convenient it may often be to personify them; they are merely *institutions*, that is to say, organizations which men establish among themselves for securing certain objects, of which the most fundamental is a system of order within which the activities of their common life can be carried on. They have no wills except the wills of the individual human beings who direct their affairs; and they exist not in a political vacuum but in continuous political relations with one another. . . .

International law is in fact just a system of customary law,* upon which has been erected, almost entirely within the last two generations, a superstructure of "conventional" or treaty-made law, and some of its chief defects are precisely those which the history of law teaches us to expect in any system of customary law. Among these it is a common mistake to suppose that frequency of violation is one. Violations of the law are extremely rare in any customary system, and they are so in international law. The common impression to the contrary arises partly from the unfortunate concentration of popular interest on the laws of war which certainly are often broken, and partly from the fact that when a breach does occur it is often of a sensational character. But the laws of peace, which are far the most valuable part of the system, are on the whole regularly and unobtrusively observed in the daily intercourse of states; . . . it is not the existence of a police force that makes a system of

---

* By "customary law" Brierly means "something more than mere habit or usage; it is a usage felt by those who follow it to be an obligatory one" with or without the force of specific sanctions or punishments (p. 49).

law strong and respected, but the strength of the law that causes a police force to be organized.

The weakness of international law . . . manifests itself in three ways, all of which are characteristic of customary law in general: in the smallness of its range, in the uncertainty of many of its rules, and in the slowness of its development. . . .

Until very modern times government has been regarded as a purely national function, and intercourse between states has taken place through national officials. . . .

But diplomacy of this kind is only an instrument for conducting the business of one state with another, and not for conducting the *general* international business in which a number of states have an interest. This latter kind of business increased enormously in importance and amount during the nineteenth century, and it has led to the development of institutions which, while they cannot yet be regarded as giving a "constitution" to the international society, may not unfairly be described as a beginning of its constitutional law.

These institutions operate by organizing cooperation between the national governments and not by superseding or dictating to them, and they are, therefore, probably not so much the beginnings of an international "government," though the term is often convenient, as a substitute for one.

Document 4.3

The Permanent Court for International Justice

From the Statute of the Court, 1920

ARTICLE 1. A Permanent Court of International Justice is hereby established [16 December 1920], in accordance with Article 14, of the Covenant of the League of Nations. This Court shall be in addition to the Court of Arbitration organized by the Conventions of The Hague of 1899 and 1907, and to the special Tribunals of Arbitration to which States are always at liberty to submit their disputes for settlement.

Chapter I. Organization of the Court

ARTICLE 2. The Permanent Court of International Justice shall be composed of a body of independent judges, elected regardless of their nationality from among persons of high moral character, who possess the qualifications required in their respective countries for appointment to the highest judicial offices, or are jurisconsultants of recognized competence in international law.*

Chapter II. Competence of the Court

ARTICLE 36. The jurisdiction of the Court comprises all cases which the parties refer to it and all matters specially provided for in treaties and conventions in force.

The Members of the League of Nations and the States mentioned in the Annex to the Covenant may . . . declare that they recognize as compulsory, *ipso facto* and without special agreement, in relation to any other Member or State accepting the same obligation, the jurisdiction of the Court in all or any of the classes of legal disputes concerning:

(a) The interpretation of a treaty;

(b) Any question of international law;

(c) The existence of any fact which, if established, would constitute a breach of an international obligation;

(d) The nature or extent of the reparation to be made for the breach of an international obligation.

The declaration referred to above may be made unconditionally or on condition of reciprocity on the part of several or certain Members or States, or for a certain time.

In the event of a dispute as to whether the Court has jurisdiction, the matter shall be settled by the decision of the Court.

ARTICLE 37. When a treaty or convention in force provides for the reference of a matter to a tribunal to be instituted by the League of Nations, the Court will be such tribunal.

ARTICLE 38. The Court shall apply:

1. International conventions, whether general or particular, establishing rules expressly recognized by the contesting States;

2. International custom, as evidence of a general practice accepted as law;

3. The general principles of law recognized by civilized nations;

4. Subject to the provisions of Article 59, judicial decisions and the teachings of the most highly qualified publicists of the various nations, as subsidiary means for the determination of rules of law. . . .

---

* Located at The Hague, the Court was to consist of fifteen judges elected by the Assembly from the nominees of national groups in the Court of Arbitration. Chapter II, Articles 34–35, specified the conditions of membership in and access to the Court.

Document 4.4

The International Labor Organization

From the Constitution of the International Labor
Organization, 1919

Whereas the League of Nations has for its object the establishment of universal peace, and such a peace can be established only if it is based upon social justice;

And whereas conditions of labor exist involving such injustice, hardship and privation to large numbers of people as to produce unrest so great that the peace and harmony of the world are imperiled; and an improvement of those conditions is urgently required: as, for example, by the regulation of the hours of work, including the establishment of a maximum working day and week, the regulation of the labor supply, the prevention of unemployment, the provision of an adequate living wage, the protection of the worker against sickness, disease and injury arising out of his employment, the protection of children, young persons and women, provision for old age and injury, protection of the interests of workers when employed in countries other than their own, recognition of the principle of freedom of association, the organization of vocational and technical education and other measures;

Whereas also the failure of any nation to adopt humane conditions of labor is an obstacle in the way of other nations which desire to improve the conditions in their own countries;

The High Contracting Parties, moved by sentiments of justice and humanity as well as by the desire to secure the permanent peace of the world, agree to the following:

ARTICLE 387 [of the Versailles Treaty]. A permanent organization is hereby established for the promotion of the objects set forth in the Preamble.

The original Members of the League of Nations shall be the original Members of this organization, and hereafter membership of the League of Nations shall carry with it membership of the said organization.

ARTICLE 388. The permanent organization shall consist of:

(1) a General Conference of Representatives of the Members and,

(2) an International Labor Office. . . .*

---

* The membership of the General Conference and the governing body of the Labor Office was divided equally between member governments and their employers and working people.

ARTICLE 396. The functions of the International Labor Office shall include the collection and distribution of information on all subjects relating to the international adjustment of conditions of industrial life and labor, and particularly the examination of subjects which it is proposed to bring before the Conference with a view to the conclusion of international conventions, and the conduct of such special investigations as may be ordered by the Conference. . . .

ARTICLE 405. When the Conference has decided on the adoption of proposals with regard to an item in the agenda, it will rest with the Conference to determine whether those proposals should take the form: (a) of a recommendation to be submitted to the Members for consideration with a view to effect being given to it by national legislation or otherwise, or (b) of a draft international convention for ratification by the Members. . . .

Each of the Members undertakes that it will, within the period of one year at most from the closing of the session of the Conference, or . . . in no case later than eighteen months from the closing of the session of the Conference, bring the recommendation or draft convention before the authority or authorities within whose competence the matter lies, for the enactment of legislation or other action.

ARTICLE 427. The High Contracting Parties . . . recognize that differences of climate, habits, and customs, of economic opportunity and industrial tradition, make strict uniformity in the conditions of labor difficult of immediate attainment. But, holding as they do, that labor should not be regarded merely as an article of commerce, they think that there are methods and principles for regulating labor conditions which all industrial communities should endeavor to apply, so far as their special circumstances will permit.

Among these methods and principles, the following seem to the High Contracting Parties to be of special and urgent importance:

First.—The guiding principle above enunciated that labor should not be regarded merely as a commodity or article of commerce.

Second.—The right of association for all lawful purposes by the employed as well as by the employers.*

---

* In addition to these two general principles, specific standards were noted that included wages for "a reasonable standard of life," an eight-hour day and forty-hour week, a day of rest, abolition of child labor and provision for education, equal pay for men and women, equal treatment of all residents, and a system of inspection.

Document 4.5

The League of Nations: Minorities Treaties

From *The League of Nations and Minorities,* 1923

At the time of the Peace Conference in Paris, a commission was set up on May 1, 1919, called the Commission on New States . . . [which] was entrusted . . . with the work of drawing up draft treaties for the protection of minorities in the States of Eastern Europe.*

The first of these treaties, that with Poland, was signed on June 28, 1919, simultaneously with the Treaty of Versailles. . . . It had for a long time been the established procedure of the public law of Europe that, when a new State was created or when an existing State absorbed any considerable amount of territory, for the formal recognition of the situation by the Great Powers . . . , that it should undertake to apply certain definite principles of government, in the form of an agreement possessing an international character.† The new minorities treaties, however, differ in form from previous conventions relating to similar questions. This change of form is a necessary consequence and an essential part of the new system of international relations inaugurated by the establishment of the League of Nations. Formerly, the guarantee for provisions of this nature was vested in the Great Powers. Experience has shown that this arrangement was ineffective in practice, and it was also open to the criticism that it might give to the Great Powers, either individually or in combination, a right to interfere in the internal constitution of the States affected which could be used for purely political purposes. Under the new system the guarantee is entrusted to the League of Nations.§

The procedure to be followed . . . is as follows:

When the Secretariat of the League receives a petition concerning a

---

* Represented on the commission were France, the United States, Great Britain, Italy, and Japan.

† Early examples of such agreements include the Pact of Warsaw (1573), the Peace of Augsburg (1555), the Treaty of Westphalia (1648), and the Peace of Paris (1763). At the Congress of Vienna (1814–15), Paris (1856), and Berlin (1878), the Great Powers made specific demands for freedom of religion and other rights in ceded territories and new states, but these were rarely abided by or enforced.

§ Minorities treaties were signed between the Great Powers and the new and enlarged states of Poland, Czechoslovakia, Yugoslavia, Roumania (all 1919), and Greece (1920), and with the defeated powers of Austria, Bulgaria, Hungary (all 1919), and Turkey (1924). Agreements were made with Latvia, Lithuania, and Estonia upon their admission to the League.

minority question, the petition is examined by the Secretariat in order to ascertain whether it fulfills the five conditions necessary to make it admissible. If it does, the petition is communicated to the State concerned. If this State for any reasons raises objections to the admissibility of the petition, the Secretary-General submits the question to the President of the Council, who may invite two other members of the Council to assist him. If the State concerned so requests, this question of procedure may be put on the agenda of the Council. If the petition is declared admissible, the State concerned must announce within three weeks of being informed of this fact whether it wishes to make any remarks or not. If it does, it must present its remarks within two months. This period of time may be prolonged on the authority of the President of the Council. . . . The petition, together with the remarks of the government concerned, is then communicated to the members of the Council for purposes of information. Any State member of the League may, by request, obtain copies of these documents.

The President of the Council asks two other members of the Council to examine documents with him. If one of these three members or any other member of the Council considers it necessary, the question may be brought before the Council. The latter . . . may proceed in any manner and give any instructions that appear to it appropriate and effective in the circumstances. In case of a difference of opinion as to questions of law or fact between the State concerned and any State member of the Council, this difference will be considered as of international concern according to the terms of Article 14 of the Covenant, and the question may be referred to the Permanent Court of International Justice, whose decision will be final.

Document 4.6

The League of Nations: Palestine Mandate

From the League of Nations Mandate for Palestine, 1922

ARTICLE 1. The Mandatory shall have full powers of legislation and of administration save as they may be limited by the terms of this mandate.

ARTICLE 11. The Mandatory shall be responsible for placing the country under such political, administrative and economic conditions as will secure the establishment of the Jewish national home, as laid down in the preamble, and the development of self-governing institutions, and also for safeguarding the civil and religious rights of all the inhabitants of Palestine, irrespective of race and religion.

ARTICLE 22. English, Arabic, and Hebrew shall the official languages of Palestine. . . .

ARTICLE 24. The Mandatory shall make to the Council of the League of Nations an annual report to the satisfaction of the Council as to the measures taken during the year to carry out the provisions of the mandate. Copies of all laws and regulations promulgated during the year shall be communicated with the report.

ARTICLE 26. The Mandatory agrees that if any dispute whatever should arise between the Mandatory and another member of the League of Nations relating to the interpretation or the application of the provisions of the mandate, such dispute, if it cannot be settled by negotiation, shall be submitted to the Permanent Court of International Justice provided for by Article 14 of the Covenant of the League of Nations.

Document 4.7

Aristide Briand: European Union

From a speech of 11 September 1930

I am here today to tell you, on behalf of the twenty-seven European nations which assembled here three days ago, that, having given the matter their careful consideration, they have agreed that close co-operation in all international activities is of capital importance for the maintenance of peace.

Having discussed the question during the past year, and viewed the problem from every angle with the serious attention that Governments give to this kind of work, that is the conclusion we bring you—a conclusion which embodies a principle, a conclusion which is somewhat idealistic, perhaps, but still a conclusion.

And what next?

Ah! that is another matter. When it comes to the question of concrete achievement, of establishing a bond of union, a federal bond between Powers which still have so many individual preoccupations, we must proceed with caution and not do anything that might react adversely on the very object we have in view. . . .

The idea of a union of European nations was welcomed by all the most eminent intellectuals: it was welcomed by philosophers and by sociologists; it was, alas, welcomed also by the poets—to its very great detriment. It was looked on as one of those ideas that are immured in museums before they have ever been allowed to circulate in human society. It was placed in a glass case, and, when it was exhibited, people said: "This poet welcomed it, that philosopher advocated it." Perhaps they may even say: "One statesman who had cast prudence to the winds shared the ideas of those lofty minds." I trust something better awaits me than a corner in a museum.

An idea like this should, I feel, be given a chance to develop with some hope of being translated into a fact.

In any case, it was submitted to the Governments for consideration. . . .

. . . I have to thank the governments for the care with which they have studied it, and I congratulate them on the thoroughness of their deliberations. Every Government replied. . . .

At the meeting which we have just held here, in the orbit of the League, after I had read my report . . . , I was gratified to observe that this principle was still unanimously held, and that the European States, as their replies already indicated, considered a union between themselves of capital importance for the maintenance of peace. That is the conclusion which I have been asked to put before you. . . .

No one has anything to gain from . . . the circumstance of an old civilization being torn with dissension. . . . It is to everyone's interest that the European nations should draw near to one another, should unite, should seek a joint solution of their various problems, should regulate their economic activities and thereby be in a position to increase their capacity to absorb non-European products. That is the feeling today of all business men worthy of the name who approach the problems of economic life in a really broad and liberal spirit. . . .

. . . I would ask you to bear in mind the fact that twenty-seven of the nations represented here, all of them wholeheartedly devoted to the cause of the League, have studied the problem in all its aspects, have given it their fullest consideration, and have arrived at this conclusion: "We believe a bond of union linking together the peoples of Europe to be of capital importance for peace." Before we take our task in hand, we have need of you all; we need your moral support and your encouragement; we must feel that you are being quite frank with us, and that you have no part in that criticism which represents us as trying to compete, as it were, with the League. We want you to know that, running through our whole scheme, is a strain of filial affection which unites us to you, and,

before we take another step, we want the League to say, as it has already
said before in very similar circumstances: "Go forward, you are on the
right road; you are marching towards peace."

Disarmament and Arms Limitation

The League of Nations was charged "to reduce national armaments"
and control the munitions industry. The effort to do so was the League's
greatest effort; it was the subject of several governmental treaties and
was the basis for an international campaign by citizen groups. From
1920 to 1933 the idea of disarmament dominated the League's agenda
and the world's imagination.

E. D. Morel, a leading Labour member of the British Parliament who
was an expert on Africa, put the issue in a global context as part of
his broad attack on colonialism. Morel urged the European powers to
neutralize Africa by treaty in order to spare their weakest colonies from
an arms race among themselves. He warned: "If civilization is incapable
of rising to the height of a self-denying ordinance affecting the most
helpless section of the human race, the hopes centered in a League of
Nations are mere illusions."[12] The idea of a military-free zone gave way,
however, to the hope that an arms race might be contained.

In a general sense, disarmament meant reducing the capability for
waging war. This notion quickly fragmented into a confusing array of
problems and proposals. Two broad distinctions help to put the subject
into perspective. First, disarmament in the strict sense of reducing or
eliminating weapons of war may be contrasted with arms control, or
limiting weapons development and deployment. Second, attempts to
achieve arms reduction independently may be contrasted with efforts to
relate it to issues of security and other national interests.

One approach to disarmament was to prohibit certain types of weapons, as in the League-sponsored ban on chemical and biological weapons, the Geneva Protocol of 1925 (document 4.8). More ambitious were
proposals to abolish or severely reduce all weapons. Thus, at the 1922
Genoa Conference, the Soviet Commisar for Foreign Affairs, Georgi V.
Chicherin, endorsed the principle of general disarmament; and, in 1927,
Maxim Litvinov presented to the League a proposal for complete and
immediate disarmament (document 4.9).[13] The following year Litvinov
offered a plan to reduce specifically offensive weapons. Although both of
his proposals were rejected, his distinction between defensive and offensive weapons was revived in 1932 by U.S. President Herbert Hoover

(document 4.10). That year petitions for general disarmament were signed by millions of people and submitted to the League and national governments in connection with the Geneva Conference on disarmament (document 4.11).

In contrast with plans for disarmament were proposals for arms limitation, or arms control. An example of this approach was the 1921–22 Washington Conference on Arms Limitation, where the U.S. secretary of state, Charles Evans Hughes, obtained a naval treaty limiting the United States, Britain, Japan, France, and Italy to a fixed ratio of tonnage for capital ships (document 4.13). Coverage was extended to other categories of vessels by the London Treaty of 1930.[14] These treaties provided a ratio of power within which signatory nations could modernize their navies. Similar attempts to define fixed ratios for European land forces, complicated by the asymmetry of modern weapons systems and by differences in geopolitical strategies, were unsuccessful in the 1920s and were abandoned early in the next decade. In any case, the assumption of arms control—that war could be prevented by credible threats tempered by periodic negotiation—contradicted an essential point of disarmament, which was to minimize threat itself.

A second and related consideration was the relationship of disarmament (or arms control) to national security and other policy aims. President Wilson, in the fourth of his Fourteen Points, had advocated arms reduction to the "lowest point consistent with domestic safety," and article 8 of the League of Nations Convenant called for "the reduction of national armaments to the lowest point consistent with national safety and the enforcement by common action . . . to enforce international obligations." The Five Power Treaty of 1922 on naval limitation was accompanied by two agreements on political and economic issues in Asia and the Pacific.[15] The naval treaty could not have been signed in the absence of those additional treaties. Later that year a proposal to cut European land and air forces by a fixed ratio was rejected because it ignored the crucial link between armed forces and political issues. Fundamental disagreements within and among nations about national security and international obligations thwarted efforts to restrain or reduce military establishments.

The League nevertheless persisted in its quest for general disarmament. After the failure of extensive negotiations in 1923 and 1924, it established an international commission whose thorough research into technical issues only dramatized intractable political ones.[16] After exhaustive effort, in December 1930 the commission presented a draft convention to the Conference for the Reduction and Limitation of Armaments, which opened in Geneva on 2 February 1932. The Geneva Conference was held amidst a massive, worldwide clamor for disarmament that expressed both hope and fear. International conditions were rapidly deteriorating: depression gripped the world economy; bombs were falling in Asia; and militant nationalism was rising in Germany and elsewhere. By June 1932 negotiations were stalled.

President Herbert Hoover of the United States tried to revive the negotiations with a dramatic proposal to separate "police" from "defensive" forces and to reduce land armies by one-third (document 4.10). Essentially, he attempted to separate disarmament from security concerns (and specified no international security role for the United States). Welcomed by the League, the small powers, Soviet Russia, Italy, and Germany, Hoover's proposal was opposed by Britain, France, and Japan, and the conference reverted to fruitless discussions over technicalities. In October 1933, Germany withdrew from the conference and the League, and Adolf Hitler subsequently re-established the German air force, increased the navy, and introduced universal conscription. Faced with the prospect of a renewed arms race, the Geneva Conference adjourned on 11 June, unable to relate arms reduction to collective security.

Document 4.8

The Protocol on Chemical and Biological Weapons

From the Protocol Prohibiting Bacteriological Warfare, 1925

The undersigned plenipotentiaries, in the name of their respective Governments:

Whereas the use in war of asphyxiating, poisonous or other gases, and of all analogous liquids, materials or devices, has been justly condemned by the general opinion of the civilized world; and

Whereas the prohibition of such use has been declared in Treaties to which the majority of Powers of the world are Parties; and

To the end that this prohibition shall be universally accepted as a part of International Law, binding alike the conscience and the practice of nations;

Declare:

That the High Contracting Parties, so far as they are not already Parties to Treaties prohibiting such use, accept this prohibition, agree to extend this prohibition to the use of bacteriological methods of warfare and agree to be bound as between themselves according to the terms of this declaration.

The High Contracting Parties will exert every effort to induce other States to accede to the present Protocol. Such accession will be notified to the Government of the French Republic, and by the latter to all signatory and acceding Powers, and will take effect on the date of the notification by the Government of the French Republic.

Document 4.9

Maxim Litvinov: General and Complete Disarmament

From the statement of 30 November 1927

In now sending its delegation to the fourth session of the Preparatory Commission on Disarmament, the Government of the USSR has authorized it to present a scheme for general and complete disarmament.

The USSR Delegation is authorized by its Government to propose the complete abolition of all land, sea and air forces. . . .*

The Delegation of the USSR is empowered to propose the execution of the above programme of complete disarmament as soon as the Convention in question comes into force, in order that all the necessary measures for the destruction of military stores be completed in a year's time. . . .

In the case, however, of capitalist States rejecting immediate actual abolition of standing armies, the Soviet Government . . . is prepared to make a proposal for complete disarmament to be carried out . . . by gradual stages, during a period of four years. . . .

While insisting upon the views just stated, the USSR delegation is nevertheless ready to participate in any and every discussion of the question of the limitation of armaments whenever practical measures really leading to disarmament are proposed.

I confess that on acquainting myself with the findings of this Commission, I was aghast at the complexity, confusion and multiplicity of the questions with which that of disarmament had become involved. . . .

---

* Litinov specified the dissolution of all military forces; destruction of all weapons, including warships and airplanes; and national legislation to abolish all military training and service, including trained reserves, to destroy fortresses, and to prohibit arms manufacturing and military budgets.

Unanimity has only been achieved with regard to certain trivial and common points. . . . [If these issues should be] reconciled, the Commission will still only be at the threshold of its real difficulties. The Commission will have to agree to the satisfaction of all as to what constitutes security. . . .

Document 4.10

Herbert Hoover: Simple and Complete Disarmament

From the message of 22 June 1932

The time has come when we should cut through the brush and adopt some broad and definite method of reducing the overwhelming burden of armament which now lies upon the toilers of the world. This would be the most important world step that could be taken to expedite economic recovery. We must make headway against the mutual fear and friction arising out of war armaments which kill human confidence throughout the world. We can still remain practical in maintaining self-defense among all nations. We can add to the assurances of peace and yet save the people of the world from ten to fifteen billions of wasted dollars during the next ten years.

I propose that the following principles should be our guide.

First: The Briand-Kellogg Pact to which we are all signatories can only mean that the nations of the world have agreed that they will use their arms solely for defense.

Second: This reduction should be carried out, not only by broad general cuts in armaments, but by increasing the comparative power of defense through decreases in the power of the attack.

Third: The armaments of the world have grown up in mutual relation to each other; and, speaking generally, such relativity should be preserved in making reductions.

Fourth: The reductions must be real and positive. They must effect economic relief.

Fifth: There are three problems to deal with—land forces, air forces, and naval forces. They are all inter-connected. No part of the proposals which I make can be dissociated one from the other.

Based on these principles, I propose that the arms of the world should be reduced by nearly one-third.

Land Forces. In order to reduce the offensive character of all land forces as distinguished from their defensive character, I propose the

adoption of the presentation already made at the Geneva Conference*
for the abolition of all tanks, all chemical warfare, and all large mobile
guns. This would not prevent the establishment or increase of fixed fortifications of any character for the defense of frontiers and seacoasts. It
would give an increased relative strength to such defense as compared
with attack.

I propose, furthermore, that there should be a reduction of one-third
in the strength of all land armies over and above the so-called police
component.†

Air Forces. All bombing-planes to be abolished. This will do away
with the military possession of types of planes capable of attacks upon
civil populations and should be coupled with the total prohibition of all
bombardment from the air.

Naval Forces. I propose that the treaty number and tonnage of battleships shall be reduced by one-third; that the treaty tonnage of aircraft-
carriers, cruisers, and destroyers shall be reduced by one-fourth; that the
treaty tonnage of submarines shall be reduced by one-third, and that no
nation shall retain a submarine tonnage greater than 35,000 tons. . . .§

These proposals are simple and direct. They call upon all nations to
contribute something. The contribution here proposed will be relative
and mutual. I know of nothing that would give more hope for humanity
today than the acceptance of such a programme with such minor changes
as may be necessary. It is folly for the world to go on breaking its back
under military expenditure, and the United States is willing to take its
share of the responsibility, by making definite proposals that will relieve
the world.

Document 4.11

The Women's International League: Disarmament

From the resolution of the WILPF at Lille, April 1931

The WIL as an International organization stands on the basis of total
and universal disarmament as an obligation involved in the Kellogg-

---

* Meeting of the preparatory commission, 1927.

† Those forces required to maintain internal order in conjunction with civilian police.

§ The relative strength of battleships and aircraft carriers of the five leading naval
powers had been fixed in Washington in 1922; the London Naval Treaty of 1930 extended
the Washington agreement to cruisers, destroyers, and submarines.

Briand pact but urges as a first step towards this goal, to be taken within a definite period, that the General Disarmament Conference of 1932 accept a convention for definite and drastic measures of disarmament on sea and land by budgetary and other means, and for international control of civil aviation including the abolition of air warfare.*

Document 4.12

Charles Evans Hughes: Arms Limitation

From the statement of 12 November 1921
and the Treaty of 6 February 1922

The Statement by Secretary of State Hughes

The world looks to this conference to relieve humanity of the crushing burden created by competition in armament, . . . and it is the view of the American Government that we should meet that expectation without any unnecessary delay. . . .

The proposal to limit armament by agreement of the powers is not a new one, and we are admonished by the futility of earlier effort. It may be well to recall the noble aspirations which were voiced twenty-three years ago in the imperial rescript of his Majesty the Emperor of Russia. It was then pointed out with clarity and emphasis that the intellectual and physical strength of the nations, labor, and capital are for the major part diverted from their natural application and unproductively consumed. . . .

. . . If we are warned by the inadequacy of earlier endeavors for limitation of armament. we cannot fail to recognize the extraordinary opportunity now presented.

We not only have the lessons of the past to guide us, not only do we have the reaction from the disillusioning experiences of war, but we must meet the challenge of imperative economic demands. What was convenient or highly desirable before is now a matter of vital necessity. If there is to be economic rehabilitation, if the longings for reasonable progress are not to be denied, if we are to be spared the uprisings of

---

* The WILPF organized a massive petition campaign in connection with the Geneva Conference. Petitions circulated in Europe and the United States obtained over three million signatures by the end of 1931. Referring to the Briand-Kellogg Pact, they read, in part, "War is Renounced–Let Us Renounce Armaments."

peoples made desperate in the desire to shake off burdens no longer endurable, competition in armament must stop. . . .

The Treaty on Limitation of Naval Armament

ARTICLE 3. . . . the Contracting Powers shall abandon their respective capital ship building programs and no new capital ships shall be constructed or acquired by any of the Contracting Powers except replacement tonnage. . . .

ARTICLE 4. The total capital ship replacement tonnage of each of the Contracting Powers shall not exceed in standard displacement, for the United States, 525,000 tons . . . ; for the British Empire, 525,000 tons . . . ; for France, 175,000 tons . . . ; for Italy, 175,000 tons . . . ; for Japan, 315,000 metric tons.*

ARTICLE 5. No capital ship exceeding 35,000 tons . . . standard displacement shall be acquired by, or constructed by, for, or within the jurisdiction of any of the Contracting Powers.

ARTICLE 6. No capital ship of any of the Contracting Powers shall carry a gun with a caliber in excess of 16 inches. . . .

ARTICLE 7. The total tonnage for aircraft carriers of each of the Contracting Powers shall not exceed in standard displacement, for the United States 135,000 tons . . . ; for the British Empire, 135,000 tons . . . ; for France, 60,000 tons . . . ; for Italy, 60,000 tons . . . ; for Japan, 81,000 tons. . . .

ARTICLE 12. No vessel of war of any of the Contracting Powers, hereafter laid down, other than a capital ship, shall carry a gun with a caliber in excess of 8 inches. . . .

ARTICLE 13. Except as provided in Article 9, no ship designated in the present Treaty to be scrapped may be reconverted into a vessel of war.

ARTICLE 19. The United States, the British Empire and Japan agree that the status quo at the time of the signing of the present Treaty, with regard to fortifications and naval bases, shall be maintained in their respective territories and possessions. . . .

---

* This fixed the ratio for the respective powers at 5:5:1.75:1.75:3. A capital ship was defined in terms of standard displacement and size of gun carried. A separate chapter of the treaty designated specific ships to be retained by each country.

Moral Disarmament

In the midst of its technical debates, the Conference for the Reduction and Limitation of Armaments established a Committee on Moral
Disarmament. Wars begin in people's minds and political cultures, it
was assumed, and peace requires the transformation of social attitudes
(document 4.13). Campaigns for moral disarmament and peace education in the 1920s were united by that idea, but they divided over the
issues of collective security when the international order collapsed.

Efforts to educate people for peace, begun in the nineteenth century,
were revived following World War I and became international in scope.
Their main goal was to create a well-informed public, knowledgeable
about issues and tolerant of national differences. In 1925 the League of
Nations authorized a program of peace education to "train the younger
generation to regard international co-operation as the normal method of
conducting world affairs."[17] By then there was a loose international
campaign to challenge national chauvinism and the glorification of war.
A British analyst, Caroline Playne, defined "moral disarmament" as "the
transformation of the aggressive, vindictive and revengeful mentality into
a conciliatory mentality. . . . , the sacrifice of national interests in favor
of interests not less real of the large human family, . . . altruism substituted for egoism . . . , reason and equity applied instead of passion and
injustice."[18]

The idea of moral disarmament described by Playne reflected the
evolution of absolute pacifism in the twentieth century. From the evolution of the early Christian church to the emergence of modern nonresistant sects, absolute pacifism had been associated with a distinctive
religious way of life: spiritual peace implied personal behavior based on
a higher moral law than that which prevailed in the world. This orientation had led pacifists to some degree of separation from society. In the
crisis of World War I, however, absolute pacifism became increasingly
associated with forms of social activism. Working for peace necessitated
the transformation of attitudes, not only in isolated communities but
among the general public.

The Protestant churches were the most significant venue for this
reorientation during the interwar period, most notably in Great Britain
and the United States but also on the European continent (especially in
Germany and Czechoslovakia). Peace and social justice were interpreted
as corollaries to ecumenism, or Christian unity. Reiterated in countless
sermons, speeches, tracts, and books, that message was put succinctly by
the American lay evangelist Kirby Page, who insisted that "war is sin"

(document 4.14). For Page and his generation of Christian pacifists, this was a moral judgment with practical consequences: commitment to peace should lead to action; pacifists should engage their society on political issues.

Immediately after the war, groups of pacifists sponsored exchanges of people from belligerent states—Germans and French, for example—to dissolve hostile stereotypes and foster creative empathy. Similarly, Pierre Ceresole, a Swiss educator, organized an International Civilian Service that brought together people from various countries for work projects. In Britain the publicist Gerald Heard stressed meditation and group training through which, he thought, small bands of dedicated persons could help to resolve conflict within nations and between them. Like traditional nonresistance, his "new pacifism" was based on the transformation of behavior by a disciplined nonviolence; but unlike it, Heard's brand of pacifism projected pacifists into worldly conflicts, seeing the "initiative of social creativeness" as the cure for "a diseased individualized civilization."[19] The prominent Italian educational reformer Maria Montessori also sought to liberate people from a coercive culture (document 4.15).

Other peace advocates shared her concern. Behind the terrible carnage on the front lines, they found pathological emotions that had been manipulated on a mass scale. Governments had tapped primitive, dangerous, and irrational impulses that existed on the subconscious level. Could national conflicts be resolved by reason if chauvinism and violence were deeply held feelings reinforced by the structure of power? This question had been raised during World War I, notably by women in the antiwar movement. It became ever more urgent as militarism and fascism grew bolder in the 1930s, presaging another war.

The ideology of nationalism itself was questioned. Thus, the German theologian Martin Buber (later an Israeli) sought to introduce moral principles into the political and emotional reality of nationalism. As leader of the pacifist wing of the Zionist movement, he championed a binational state in Palestine, where Jews and Arabs would enjoy political and national equality. In October 1929, shortly after violent Arab attacks on Jews in Jerusalem and Hebron, Buber appealed for reconciliation between the two peoples as part of the Zionist mission (document 4.16).

Some analysts explored the sources of violence with the new science of social psychology. Caroline Playne portrayed World War I as the product of growing mental derangement in the western world (document 4.17). She argued that the stresses of modern life had resulted in the

inhibition of reason, and consequently in war. Playne hoped that Freud-
ian and other behavioral concepts might help to develop a kind of social
psychiatry that would prevent new catastrophe.

Freud himself, the Austrian founder of psychoanalysis, was not at all
sure that was possible. He had expressed doubts in 1930–31, and when
the physicist Albert Einstein queried him the following year about the
immediate prospects for controlling aggressive impulses, Freud responded that social order might require the imposition of force (document 4.18). But he also pointed to indirect ways of dealing with violence,
and to the emergence of a new, pacifist type of individual whose existence
offered hope for the future.

The connection between unconscious social attitudes and cultural
repression was the key issue for writers and artists of the Surrealist
movement that arose in France shortly after World War I. Their experience was instructive. At first they believed that humanity could be liberated by a vision of what is possible, together with awareness of the
repression of militarism, bellicose patriotism, and economic materialism.
When the French army opened hostilities in Morocco in 1925, Surrealists
became political. For a decade some of them pursued cultural and political revolution by trying to align with the French communist party, only
to be disillusioned by the party's rigid discipline and submission to Soviet
Russia, and by the blatant repression of Stalinism there. The 1930s were
intensely frustrating for those whose vision of peace depended on the
transformation of social attitudes.

Those were the people whom the American theologian Reinhold
Niebuhr called the "children of light"—idealists who neglected the real
force of evil, in themselves and others, and were vulnerable to the "children of darkness"—those who understood power and were cynical
about ideals. Probably Niebuhr characterized peace advocates unfairly.
Some of them personally faced the fascist evil, and many of them had
wrestled with the same problem he addressed: the relationship between
personal morality and social ethics. If it was necessary to change basic
social attitudes in order to achieve peace, then it was important to get
beyond public information and understanding to the deeper level of
learned behavior and subconscious emotions. But moral disarmament in
this sense led back to a political question: what if the attitudes and
behavior conducive to violence were reinforced by social institutions and
public policy?

In response to that concern, numerous pacifist reformers combined
total rejection of warfare on the personal level with activism in political
and social affairs. Implicitly, they distinguished between the values gov-

erning individual morality and the criteria for making social and political choices: an individual might make personal choices on the basis of personal values that are absolute and intrinsic (good in themselves) but at the same time advocate political values that are relative and conditional (good in terms of their consequences). That is to say, one might pursue the peace of spiritual tranquillity for oneself, while advocating peace in the sense of order and justice for society.

This way of thinking transformed interwar peace advocacy, especially in Great Britain and the United States. Together, the pacifist organizations that emerged from the war (notably the Fellowships of Reconciliation, the Women's International League for Peace and Freedom, the American Friends Service Committee, and, in Britain, the Friends Service Council) formed a pacifist international. Small groups of people who were committed to nonviolence helped to mobilize large coalitions on foreign policy issues. They cooperated with other peace advocates in public campaigns for peace education, disarmament, international organization, international economic justice, and dispute settlement. In the 1930s they participated in the great debates over neutrality, appeasement, and collective security.

Document 4.13

The Committee on International Cooperation: Moral Disarmament

From the draft text of 17 November 1933

The High Contracting Parties,

Considering that moral disarmament is one of the essential aspects of the general work of disarmament;

Considering that the reduction and limitation of armaments depend to a large extent upon the increase of mutual confidence between nations;

Considering that as far as public opinion is concerned, a sustained and systematic effort to ease tension may contribute to the progressive realization of material disarmament;

Considering that the interdependence of States calls, not only for their co-operation in the political sphere, but also for an effort of mutual understanding between the peoples themselves;

Being resolved to do whatever lies in their power to induce their nationals to display in any public discussion a spirit of tolerance and mutual respect;

Being convinced that the success of the measures adopted in one country to ensure moral disarmament is largely dependent on the application of similar measures in other countries . . . :

ARTICLE 1. The High Contracting Parties undertake to use their powers or their influence to see that education at every stage, including the training of teachers, is so conceived as to inspire mutual respect between peoples and to emphasize their inter-dependence, which makes international collaboration a necessity.

ARTICLE 2. The High Contracting Parties . . . agree to recommend to their competent authorities the inclusion of the following subjects in the syllabus prescribed for entrance examinations to official posts which entail relations with other countries: fundamental principles of international law, legal bases of international relations, and outlines of the efforts made to consolidate peace between nations.

They undertake to recommend to their competent authorities that their country's history is taught in relation to the history of other countries.

ARTICLE 3. The High Contracting Parties undertake to encourage . . . the use of the cinematograph and broadcasting with a view to increasing the spirit of goodwill between nations . . . [and] to avoid the showing of films, the broadcasting of programmes and the organization of performances obviously calculated to wound the legitimate sentiments of other nations.

ARTICLE 4. The High Contracting Parties will endeavor to facilitate . . . co-operation in the work of moral disarmament of Government departments, intellectual circles, and others working for peace on a larger scale.

Document 4.14

Kirby Page: War is Sin

From *If War is Sin*, 1935

"War is sin." This conviction has been expressed in scores of resolutions passed by religious assemblies and broadcast in various proclamations signed by eminent leaders of religious institutions. . . . The commission on world peace of the general conference of the Methodist Episcopal church, for example, says: "Our fundamental conviction is that war is sin . . . because it involves (a) the slaughter of human beings, (b) violation of personality, (c) lying propaganda, (d) deliberate breeding of the spirit of hate, (e) vast destruction of property, (f) it puts in the place of moral law the doctrine of military necessity, (g) it distorts the religion of Jesus into the religion of a war god."

The Lambeth conference of the Anglican communion in 1930 declared: "We affirm that war as a method of settling international disputes is incompatible with the teaching and example of our Lord Jesus Christ." The commission on international justice and goodwill of the Federal Council of the Churches of Christ in America issued a manifesto from which these words are taken: "The war-system of the nations is the outstanding evil of the present-day civilization. It is the most ominous anti-Christian phase of modern life."

That these emphatic pronouncements are warranted is apparent from an examination of the nature of modern war. Much confusion may easily be avoided by remembering that *war is a method.* It is not an end, nor is it a spirit. War has ends in view and is waged in a certain spirit, but war is not noble objectives and it is not the spirit of courage and sacrifice. War is method, the method of military necessity. . . .

Therefore—what? . . .

1. The agencies of religious education should teach that since war is sin, no Christian may legitimately engage in it. . . .

2. If war is sin, no candidate for ordination to the ministry of the Christian church who professes a willingness to sanction war or to participate in it should be accepted as a minister of the Prince of Peace. . . .

3. If war is sin, official chaplains of religion should be withdrawn from this sinful business, and arrangements made for serving soldiers and sailors in non-official and non-sinful ways. . . .

4. If war is sin, young Christians should be taught that they must not take military training in high school or college. . . .

5. If war is sin, the churches must advocate total disarmament and must cease to place any reliance whatever in armed preparedness against other nations. . . .

6. If war is sin, the churches should demand a friendly and cooperative foreign policy on the part of their government. . . .

7. If war is sin, the churches must seek to create public opinion in behalf of international agencies of justice. . . .

8. If war is sin, the churches should seek to transform the economic and political systems out of which war emerges. . . .

If war is sin, and if the churches act as if war is sin, a revolution in thought will be accompanied by a revolution in policy with regard to economic and political systems. . . .

Document 4.15

Maria Montessori: Educating for Peace

From "Educate for Peace," 1937

It is obvious that education as the cornerstone of peace cannot consist only in attempting to prevent children from becoming fascinated by war. It is not enough to keep the child from playing with toy weapons, to stop making him study the history of mankind as a succession of feats of arms, and to stop teaching him that victory on the battlefield is a supreme honor. It is not even enough to instill in the child a love and a respect for all living beings and all the things that human beings have built through the centuries. . . .

An education capable of saving humanity is no small undertaking; it involves the spiritual development of man, the enhancement of his value as an individual, and the preparation for young people to understand the times in which they live.

The secret is this: making it possible for man to become the master of the mechanical environment that oppresses him today. Man the producer must become the master of production. Production today has been intensified by science and has become highly organized all over the world. It has therefore become necessary both to enhance human energies scientifically and to organize humanity proportionately. Men can no longer remain ignorant of their own natures and the world in which they live. The real scourge that threatens them today is precisely this sort of ignorance. We must organize our efforts for peace and prepare the way for it scientifically, through education. Education points the way to a new world to conquer: the world of the human spirit.

In our experience with children, we observed that the human child is a spiritual embryo, endowed with mysterious sensitivities that guide him with creative energies that tend to construct a sort of marvelous instrument in men's souls. . . . It is this sensitivity that makes man uniquely valuable. . . .

The child is also capable of developing and giving us tangible proof of the possibility of a better humanity. He has shown us the true process of construction of the normal human being. We have seen children totally change as they acquire a love for things and as their sense of order, discipline, and self-control develops within them as a manifestation of their total freedom. We have seen them labor steadily, drawing on their own energies and developing them as they work. . . .

Today those energies are scattered; or, rather, they are repressed and misdirected through the errors perpetuated by a kind of education that still holds sway all over the world. The adult does not understand the child. Parents unconsciously battle with their children. . . . And this lack of understanding is man's undoing; it leads him astray, sickens his spirit, impoverishes him, and makes him fail to realize his potential. The lack of understanding between children and adults precipitates the tragedy of the human heart, which in later life manifests itself in a lack of sensitivity, in sloth, and in criminality. Those who have been humiliated are ashamed of themselves; the timid withdraw into their shells; the fearful seek their own personal comfort. All the potential wealth of man's personality comes to nothing.

Education must take advantage of the value of the hidden instincts that guide man as he builds his own life. Powerful among these instincts is the social drive. It has been our experience that if the child and the adolescent do not have a chance to engage in a true social life, they do not develop a sense of discipline and morality. These gifts in their case become end products of coercion rather than manifestations of freedom. The human personality is shaped by continuous experiences; it is up to us to create for children, for adolescents, for young people an environment, a world that will readily permit such formative experiences. . . .

Today we have an organization of machines. What is needed are men capable of using machines to carry out a lofty mission that each of them will be aware of and feel responsibility for.

Document 4.16

Martin Buber: Humanitarian Nationalism

From "The National Home and National
Policy in Palestine," 1929

We are now faced . . . with the added responsibility for that nation which has become our neighbor in Palestine and which in so many respects shares a common fate with us. No contradiction could be greater, if we continue to preserve the idea of our internal mission, than for us to build a true communal life within our own community, while at the same time excluding the other inhabitants of the country from participation, even though their lives and hopes, like ours, are dependent upon the future of the country. . . .

It is indeed true that there can be no life without injustice. The fact that there is no living creature which can live and thrive without destroying another existing organism has a symbolic significance as regards our human life. But the human aspect of life begins the moment we say to ourselves: we will do not more injustice to others than we are forced to do in order to exist. Only by saying that do we begin to be responsible for life. This responsibility is not a matter of principle and is never fixed; the extent of the injustice that cannot be determined beforehand but must be reassessed each time, must be recognized anew in the inner recesses of the mind, whence the lightning of recognition flashes forth. Only he who acknowledges it, as the result of serious examination which leaves no room for pricks of conscience, only he can live a human life; and a nation that does so—its life is that of a humanitarian nation. The group's responsibility for life is not qualitatively different from that of the individual; for if this were not the case the members of the group would truly fulfill their responsibility only as individuals. The collective element within them would necessarily oppose the individual aspect within them, and would undermine and even destroy it; anyone who is [morally] severe with himself as an individual and lenient with himself as a member of a group will eventually, whether consciously or not, falter when he has to fulfill personal responsibility.

Every responsible relationship between an individual and his fellow begins through the power of a genuine imagination, as if we were the residents of Palestine and the others were the immigrants who were coming into the country in increasing numbers, year by year, taking it away from us. How would we react to events? Only if we know this will it be possible to minimize the injustice we must do in order to survive and to live the life which we are not only entitled but obliged to live, since we live for the eternal mission, which has been imbedded within us since our creation.

Document 4.17

Caroline Playne: Neurosis and War

From The Neuroses of the Nations, 1925

The special limitation of human nature which hindered the progress of this generation was the failure of men's nervous systems to adjust themselves to the ever-increasing strain of life under highly stressed and complicated conditions of existence. Out of this failure of adjustment arose nervous excitement, nervous depression, general irritation, resulting in anger and passion. Primitive passions burst forth, accompanied by emotions of instinctive type. The effect of this upthrust of ancient and obsolete furies into the newer order was so turbulent, that, as has been said, they swept the masses out of the path of reasonable advancement and plunged them into a series of group-neuroses.

Some contemporary theories of knowledge and some social conditions conspired to promote the unhealthy mind of society. Among these was the particular turn which the trend of scientific thought had taken, in consequence of the theory of evolution. . . .

In this case, the theory of the descent of man from the animals led to the exaltation of the animal side of man's nature. The whole subsequent mental and spiritual development was apt to be minimized or overlooked. Primitive passions were exalted and the moral and social inheritance of mankind was disregarded. Reasoned thought and right action were too much to be asked of human nature. The instinctive will to power must needs triumph over the will to do good. The thought of the day which had seemed to clarify and explain, was degraded to do duty in excusing and denying.

If the evolutionary theories favored the reversion to earlier stages of thought and conception, the social conditions, established at the time, added to the sense of confusion and to its anxieties and stresses. A certain hollowness in the credit-system rang through the mighty edifice, built upon it. The rich . . . half-sensed the fact that there was apt to be nothing tangible at the back of the credits which supplied them with money in the shape of interest.

The poor among the congested masses of town-dwellers had the specter of unemployment ever before them. Obscure movements of production were apt to bring them face to face with the thing itself. Men were none too secure in their birthright of labor and its due reward; for thousands any week-end might plunge them into penury. Harassing uncertainty was their lot through life. "I am tired of living on the edge of a precipice," as a wage-earner put it once long ago.

The armed peace, the idea of keeping peace by endless preparations for war, was the perverse and excessive effort made by the various groups to meet the unwarranted fear which possessed them and to cover up the shame they felt at being afraid. . . .

All the strutting, all the parading, all the glorified maneuvers, all the vaunted naval reviews, indeed the whole complex, which exalted military life above civil life during decades before the war, was a forced and stultifying effort to meet the fear that assaulted over-stimulated and over-anxious, unstrung human beings. . . .

. . . Does not every historical period exhibit group-mental maladies?

Why speak of a special mental malady displayed at this particular period? Mass-aberrations might certainly be traced in almost every age throughout the history of the human race. The contention maintained is, however, that particular mass-neurosis developed more generally during the pre-war decades, that it probably spread to larger proportions than previous group-psycho-neurosis attained. . . . . If conflict is to be allayed, time is needed to obtain balance, to establish control. But conflict was present in an acute form, there was an uprush of primitive instincts, a rebound of natural tendencies, upsetting restrictions and suppressions. Artificialities were probably greater and more established than ever before, and the uprush, the urge for liberation, was more unwitting and stark. The consequent conflict heaved and swelled till it threw society off the tracks. For the fullness and complexity of life allowed no time for the solving of conflict on reasonable, intelligent lines. The richness of circumstance, the rush of events prompted distraction, the dodging of conflict rather than its patient solution. Wise balancing requires time for thought and quietness of mood. A distracted world knew neither. Hence the inroads of mass-hysteria and a further rolling-back into barbarism. . . .

The antithesis of the belief and practice which characterized the fatal years of conflict may be put thus: only in peace and confidence may men possess their souls. From the time when the world turned away from the chance of establishing international peace and of founding it in courageous moral confidence, . . . intrigues, jealousies, fears, warlike preparations, and widening antagonism increased with such rapidity that they barred the way of escape. The doom of the nations was the same as the doom of the individual who sees—but spurns—the way of salvation, preferring to follow the dictates of his baser nature. Considered plans for reaching security and insuring confidence were scorned and stigmatized as merely idealistic by a generation of men whose overwrought nerves craved, above all, for some vast excitement. Their nervous restlessness hindered the exercise of sustained effort, without which radical changes in world-government cannot be successfully established.

Document 4.18

Sigmund Freud: Psychic Dimensions of War and Peace

From *Civilization and Its Discontents,* 1930, and
letter to Albert Einstein, 1932

Civilization and Its Discontents

The fateful question for the human species seems to me to be
whether and to what extent their cultural development will succeed in
mastering their disturbance of their communal life by the human instinct
of aggression and self-destruction. It may be that in this respect precisely
the present time deserves a special interest. Men have gained control over
the forces of nature to such an extent that with their help they would
have no difficulty in exterminating one another to the last man. They
know this, and hence comes a large part of their current unrest, their
unhappiness and their mood of anxiety. And now it is to be expected
that the other of the two "Heavenly Powers," eternal Eros, will make
an effort to assert himself in the struggle with his equally immortal
adversary. But who can foresee with what success and with what
result? *

Letter to Albert Einstein

. . . You are amazed that it is so easy to infect men with the war
fever, and you surmise that man has in him an active instinct for hatred
and destruction, amenable to such stimulations. I entirely agree with
you. I believe in the existence of this instinct and have been recently at
pains to study its manifestations. In this connection may I set out a
fragment of that knowledge of the instincts, which we psychoanalysts,
after so many tentative essays and gropings in the dark, have compassed?
We assume that human instincts are of two kinds: those that conserve
and unify, which we call "erotic" (in the meaning Plato gives to Eros in
his Symposium), . . . and, secondly, the instincts to destroy and kill,
which we assimilate as the aggressive or destructive instincts. These are,
as you perceive, the well-known opposites, Love and Hate, transformed
into theoretical entities. . . . But we must be chary of passing overhastily
to the notions of good and evil. Each of these instincts is every whit as

* According to the translator, James Strachey, the last sentence was added in 1931
"when the menace of Hitler was already beginning to be apparent." For the sense in which
Freud here refers to Eros and its antithesis, see his letter to Einstein below.

indispensable as its opposite, and all the phenomena of life derive from their activity, whether they work in concert or in opposition. It seems that an instinct of either category can operate but rarely in isolation; it is always blended ("alloyed," as we say) with a certain dosage of its opposite, which modifies its aim or even, in certain circumstances, is a prime condition of its attainment. . . . It is the difficulty of isolating the two kinds of instinct in their manifestations that has so long prevented us from recognizing them.

If you will travel with me a little further on this road, you will find that human affairs are complicated in yet another way. Only exceptionally does an action follow on the stimulus of a single instinct, which is per se a blend of Eros and destructiveness. As a rule several motives of similar composition concur to bring about the act. . . . Thus, when a nation is summoned to engage in war, a whole gamut of human motives may respond to this appeal—high and low motives, some openly avowed, others slurred over. The lust for aggression and destruction is certainly included; the innumerable cruelties of history and man's daily life confirm its prevalence and strength. The stimulation of these destructive impulses by appeals to idealism and the erotic instinct naturally facilitate their release. Musing on the atrocities recorded on history's page, we feel that the ideal motive has often served as a camouflage for the lust of destruction. . . .

. . . this destructive instinct . . . is seldom given the attention that its importance warrants. With the least of speculative efforts we are led to conclude that this instinct functions in every living being, striving to work its ruin and reduce life to its primal state of inert matter. Indeed, it might well be called the "death instinct"; whereas the erotic instincts vouch for the struggle to live on. . . . The living being, that is to say, defends its own existence by destroying foreign bodies. . . . Here is then the biological justification for all those vile, pernicious propensities which we are now combating. We can but own that they are really more akin to nature than this our stand against them. . . .

The upshot of these observations, as bearing on the subject in hand, is that there is no likelihood of our being able to suppress humanity's aggressive tendencies. In some happy corners of the earth, they say, where nature brings forth abundantly whatever man desires, there flourish races whose lives go gently by, unknowing of aggression or constraint. This I can hardly credit; I would like further details about these happy folk. The Bolshevists, too, aspire to do away with human aggressiveness by insuring the satisfaction of material needs and enforcing equality between man and man. To me this hope seems vain. Meanwhile they busily perfect their armaments, and their hatred of outsiders is not the least of the factors of cohesion among themselves. In any case, as you too have observed, complete suppression of man's aggressive tendencies is not in issue; what we may try is to divert it into a channel other than that of warfare.

From our "mythology" of the instincts we may easily deduce a formula for an indirect method of eliminating war. If the propensity for war be due to the destructive instinct, we have always its counter-agent, Eros, to our hand. All that produces ties of sentiment between man and man must serve us as war's antidote. These ties are of two kinds. First, such relations as those toward a beloved object, void though they be of sexual intent. The psychoanalyst need feel no compunction in mentioning "love" in this connection; religion uses the same language: Love thy neighbor as thyself. A pious injunction, easy to announce, but hard to carry out! The other bond of sentiment is by way of identification. All that brings out the significant resemblances between men calls into play this feeling of community, identification, whereon is founded, in large measure, the whole edifice of human society. . . .

. . . Why do we, you and I and many another, protest so vehemently against war, instead of just accepting it as another of life's odious importunities? . . . We cannot do otherwise than hate it. Pacifists we are. . . . The cultural development of mankind (some, I know, prefer to call it civilization) has been in progress since immemorial antiquity. . . . Sensations which delighted our forefathers have become neutral or unbearable to us; and, if our ethical and aesthetic ideals have undergone a change, the causes of this are ultimately organic. On the psychological side two of the most important phenomena of culture are, firstly, a strengthening of the intellect, which tends to master our instinctive life, and, secondly, an introversion of the aggressive impulse, with all its consequent benefits and perils. Now war runs most emphatically counter to the psychic disposition imposed on us by the growth of culture; we are therefore bound to resent war, to find it utterly intolerable. . . .

How long have we to wait before the rest of men turn pacifist? Impossible to say, and yet perhaps our hope that these two factors— man's cultural disposition and a well-founded dread of the form that future wars will take—may serve to put an end to war in the near future, is not chimerical. But by what ways or byways this will come about, we cannot guess. Meanwhile we may rest on the assurance that whatever makes for cultural development is working also against war.

Nonviolent Action

Organized nonviolence evolved in two forms: nonviolent resistance and war resistance. Both of them were innovations in citizen peace strategy, and each presented absolute pacifists with the dilemmas that divided other elements of society and paralyzed their governments between the two world wars.

Nonviolent Resistance

Nonviolent resistance, or nonviolent direct action, emerged as a way to conduct active struggle without violence. It was a way of resolving an ancient dilemma: defending justice by force would betray the absolute commitment to peace, but remaining totally nonviolent would leave injustice triumphant. Nonviolent resistance seemed to cut through that dilemma.

There were antecedents of this strategy in Henry David Thoreau's civil disobedience, Tolstoy's nonresistance, the socialists' general strike, and Finnish noncooperation. But nonviolent resistance as a movement owed most to Mohandas Gandhi. He first led a struggle for Indian civil rights in South Africa, where he had gone as a lawyer in 1893. His campaign of nonviolent civil disobedience there stemmed racist legislation against the Indian community. Returning to India as a hero in 1915, Gandhi became the leader of the Hindu nationalist movement. He also established commune-like centers called *ashrams,* where his disciples were trained in nonviolent resistance, which he called *satyagraha* (truth force).

Gandhi orchestrated both compromise and confrontation as he challenged British imperialism and religious and caste discrimination among Indians. He employed negotiation, political organization, economic boycotts, nonviolent strikes, work-stoppages, mass civil disobedience, and personal fasts. He also explained and publicized nonviolent resistance through two newspapers, *Young India* and *Navajivan.* He not only employed direct action but also articulated the principles of satyagraha (document 4.19).

Although Gandhi was originally cast in the role of a saint by American pacifists, he was reinterpreted as a practical reformer by Richard Gregg. Work in labor relations gave Gregg an interest in conflict resolution, and in 1925 he went to India to live and work with Gandhi. Upon his return he interpreted the pragmatic aspects of nonviolent resistance in terms of western social psychology and military theory (document

4.20). His writing influenced the thinking of American activists, including civil rights leader Martin Luther King, Jr.

The Indian Mahatma was introduced to Europe mainly through a 1924 biography by Romain Rolland, a famous French radical author and pacifist. Rolland feared that a Bolshevik-style violent revolution would only substitute a new form of coercion for the old ones. He saw in the satyagraha campaign an alternative to either acquiescing in the coercive structures of the status quo or employing violence for change. "The way to peace is not through weakness . . . ," Rolland wrote. "Nothing is worthwhile without strength. . . . Whining pacifism is fatal for peace."[20]

In the Soviet Union the commitment to total nonviolence presented a dramatic case of the struggle for social justice. The Russian followers of Leo Tolstoy had formed colonies that continued to attract adherents after the Bolshevik revolution. At least a hundred Tolstoyan agricultural communes persisted in the 1920s, loyal to their own principles but not overtly challenging the new regime. In 1929 the Soviet government closed down the Tolstoyan Society in Moscow and then prosecuted members of the communes. During his trial at Kuznetsk in May 1936, a Tolstoyan insisted that, by contrast with violence, nonviolence is truly revolutionary (document 4.21).

The French writer Simone Weil came to a similar conclusion by 1933. Convinced that genuine social revolution would be subverted by war—even revolutionary war—Weil sharply criticized Marxist-Leninist formulas for revolutionary or antifascist violence (document 4.22). Although she did not specifically advocate nonresistance, she identified its political significance. In this respect, the idea of nonviolent resistance became enmeshed in the bitter debates among socialists and communists over how to respond to fascist aggression.

Document 4.19

Mohandas Gandhi: Nonviolent Resistance

From "The Doctrine of the Sword," 1920, and
"War or Peace," 1926

Beyond the Doctrine of the Sword

. . . I believe that non-violence is infinitely superior to violence. . . . I do not believe India to be helpless. I do not believe myself to be a helpless creature. Only I want to use India's and my strength for a better purpose.

Let me not be misunderstood. . . . Strength does not come from physical capacity. It comes from indomitable will. . . .

I am not a visionary. I claim to be a practical idealist. The religion of nonviolence is not meant merely for the Rishis and saints. It is meant for the common people as well. Non-violence is the law of our species as violence is the law of the brute. The spirit lies dormant in the brute and he knows no law but that of physical might. The dignity of man requires obedience to a higher law—to the strength of the spirit.

I have therefore ventured to place before India the ancient law of self-sacrifice. For Satyagraha and its offshoots, non-cooperation and civil resistance, are nothing but new names for the law of suffering. The Rishis, who discovered the law of non-violence in the midst of violence, were greater geniuses than Newton. They were themselves greater warriors than Wellington. Having themselves known the use of arms, they realized their uselessness and taught a weary world that its salvation lay not through violence but through non-violence.

Non-violence in its dynamic condition means conscious suffering. It does not mean meek submission to the will of the evil-doer, but it means the putting of one's whole soul against the will of the tyrant. Working under this law of our being, it is possible for a single individual to defy the whole might of an unjust empire to save his honor, his religion, his soul and lay the foundation for that empire's fall or its regeneration.

And so I am not pleading for India to practice non-violence, because it is weak. I want her to practice non-violence being conscious of her strength and power. No training in arms is required for realization of her strength. . . .

. . . I invite even the school of violence to give this peaceful non-cooperation a trial. It will not fail through its inherent weakness. It may fail because of poverty of response. Then will be the time for real danger. The high-souled men, who are unable to suffer national humiliation any longer, will want to vent their wrath. They will take to violence. So far as I know, they must perish without delivering themselves or their country from the wrong. If India takes up the doctrine of the sword, she may gain momentary victory. Then India will cease to be the pride of my heart. . . . I believe absolutely that she has a mission for the world. She is not to copy Europe blindly.

Truth and Nonviolence

No war of which history has any record took so many lives as this did.* Moral loss was greater still. Poisonous forces destructive of the soul (lying and deception) were brought to perfection as much as the forces destructive of the body. The moral results have been as terrible as the physical. . . . The brute in man has for the time being gained supremacy.

The after-effects are, perhaps, more terrible than the actual and immediate effects. There is no stability about the government of any single state of Europe. No class is satisfied with its own condition. Each wants to better it at the expense of the rest. War between the states has now become a war within each state.

India has to make her choice. She may try, if she wishes, the way of war and sink lower than she has. . . .

But the way of peace is open to her. Her freedom is assured if she has patience. That way will be found to be the shortest even though it may appear to be the longest to our impatient nature. The way of peace insures internal growth and stability. We reject it because we fancy that it involves submission to the will of the ruler who has imposed himself upon us. But the moment we realize that the imposition is only so-called and that through our unwillingness to suffer loss of life or property, we are party to the imposition, all we need do is to change that negative attitude of passive endorsement. The suffering to be undergone by the change will be nothing compared to the physical suffering and the moral loss we must incur in trying the way of war. And the sufferings of war harm both the parties. The sufferings in following the way of peace must benefit both. They will be like the pleasurable travail of a new birth. . . .

The way of peace is the way of truth. Truthfulness is even more important than peacefulness. Indeed, lying is the mother of violence. A truthful man cannot long remain violent. He will perceive in the course of his search that he has no need to be violent and he will further discover that so long as there is the slightest trace of violence in him, he will fail to find the truth he is searching.

There is no half way between truth and nonviolence on the one hand and untruth and violence on the other. We may never be strong enough to be entirely nonviolent in thought, word and deed. But we must keep nonviolence as our goal and make steady progress towards it. The attainment of freedom, whether for a man, a nation or the world, must be in

---

* Gandhi refers here to World War I.

exact proportion to the attainment of nonviolence by each. Let those, therefore, who believe in nonviolence as the only method of achieving real freedom, keep the lamp of nonviolence burning bright in the midst of the present impenetrable gloom. The truth of a few will count, the untruth of millions will vanish even like chaff before a whiff of wind.

Document 4.20

Richard Gregg: Nonviolent Power

From *The Power of Non-Violence*, 1934

[Nonviolent resistance] does not avoid hardships, suffering, wounds or even death. In using it men and women may still risk their lives and fortunes and sacrifice all. Nevertheless, the possibilities of casualties and death are greatly reduced under it, and they are all suffered voluntarily and not imposed by the non-violent resisters.

It is more efficient than war because it cost[s] far less in money as well as in lives and suffering. Also usually it permits a large part of the agricultural and industrial work of the people to go on, and hence the life of the country can be maintained during the struggle.

It is again more efficient than war because "the legitimate object of war is a more perfect peace." If the peace after the war is to be better than that which preceded it, the psychological processes of the conflict must be such as will create a more perfect peace. . . . Mutual violence inevitably breeds hatred, revenge and bitterness,—a poor foundation for a more perfect peace. The method of non-violent resistance, where there really is resistance, so as to bring all the issues out into the open, and a really new settlement worked out as nearly as possible in accord with the full truth of the issues at stake,—this method does not leave a sense of frustration and will bring a more perfect peace.

Considering the completeness of its effects, non-violent resistance is as quick and probably quicker than war by violence. It is a weapon that can be used equally well by small or large nations, small or large groups, by the economically weak and by the apparently strong, and even by individuals. It compels both sides and neutrals to seek the truth, whereas war blinds both sides and neutrals to the truth.

. . . Non-violent resistance certainly produces less ill-effect, if any, than does violent war, and this decrease of ill-effects applies to the users of non-violence, to the opposing side, and to society and the world at large.

May we not then fairly describe non-violent resistance as an effective substitute for war?

It is realistic in that it does not eliminate or attempt to eliminate possibilities of conflict and differences of interest, and includes *all* factors in the situation both material and imponderable, physical and psychological.

It does not require any nation to surrender any part of its real sovereignty or right of decision, as a real league of nations might. It does not surrender the right of self-defense, although it radically alters the nature of defense. It requires no expensive weapons or armament, no drill grounds or secrecy. It does not demoralize those who take part in it, but leaves them finer men and women than when the struggle began.

Moreover, the method does not require the machinery of a government or a large wealthy organization. It may be practiced and skill may be acquired in it in every situation of life, at home and abroad, by men and women of any and all races, nations, tribes, groups, classes, or castes, young and old, rich and poor.

Document 4.21

Yakov Dragunovsky: Violence Contradicts Reason

From his address to the Soviet Government, 1936

Dear accused Tolstoyan friends! It is not you they have put on trial, because you have committed no crime; they have put on trial the idea you wanted to support! What is on trial is the philosophy of life based on reason. What is on trial is your higher consciousness. What is on trial is your reason. And so much the better for the people who are putting this idea on trial. They will understand sooner when they try and examine than when they don't think about it at all.

Friends! The reproach is made against us that Tolstoyans do not understand, value, and take part in the building of socialism, the building of a classless, communist society. "The Tolstoyans are counterrevolutionaries!" Such an accusation is absolutely untrue. The Tolstoyans see and value the enormous efforts and exertion of people who wish to build life on new, reasonable principles. How much heroism has been shown here, how much self-sacrifice has it taken to prove the falsity of the existing irrational class society, the irrationality of the feudal and capitalist system. . . .

But when our revolutionary friends took the helm of our new, reasonable life, when the theoreticians of those great ideas of equality, brotherhood, and classlessness began applying the outdated, conservative, and counterrevolutionary methods of violence, here the Tolstoyans categorically parted company with them. And in their disagreement they see nothing conservative or counterrevolutionary; on the contrary, they feel themselves to be pioneers of that great and rational life which is the desire of all thoughtful, reasonable people.

Are the Communists aware of their own contradiction, that their beautiful theory about the ideal society is the positive side, but their method of violence for the attainment of their reasonable goal is something else entirely—the negative side?

In theory the idea of communism is in harmony with our reason; the method of violence contradicts reason. The idea, based on reason, is a world internationalism; the method of violence is egotistical, divisive despotism. What is there in common between these two ideas?

Document 4.22

Simone Weil: Revolutionary War

From "Reflections on War," 1933

Revolutionary war is the grave of revolution. . . . Revolution engaged in war has only the choice of either succumbing under the murderous blows of counterrevolution or transforming itself into counterrevolution through the very mechanism of the military struggle.

The perspectives of a revolution seem therefore quite restricted. For can a revolution avoid war? It is, however, on this feeble chance that we must stake everything or abandon all hope. An advanced country will not encounter, in case of revolution, the difficulties which in backward Russia served as a base for the barbarous regime of Stalin. But a war of any scope will give rise to others as formidable.

For mighty reasons a war undertaken by a bourgeois state cannot but transform power into despotism and subjection into assassination. If war sometimes appears as a revolutionary factor, it is only in the sense that it constitutes an incomparable test for the functioning of the state. In contact with war, a badly organized apparatus collapses. But if the war does not end soon, or if it starts up again, or if the decomposition of the state has not gone far enough, the situation results in revolutions, which, according to Marx's formula, perfect the state apparatus instead of shattering it. That is what has always happened up to now. . . .

The absurdity of an anti-fascist struggle which chooses war as its means of action thus appears quite clear. Not only would this mean to fight barbarous oppression by crushing peoples under the weight of even more barbarous massacre. It would actually mean spreading under another form the very regime that we want to suppress. It is childish to suppose that a state apparatus rendered powerful by a victorious war would lighten the oppression exercised over its own people by the enemy state apparatus. It is even more childish to suppose that the victorious state apparatus would permit a proletarian revolution to break out in the defeated country without drowning it immediately in blood. . . .

It seems that, generally speaking, history is more and more forcing every political actor to choose between aggravating the oppression exercised by the various state apparatuses and carrying on a merciless struggle against these apparatuses in order to shatter them. Indeed, the almost insoluble difficulties presenting themselves nowadays almost justify the pure and simple abandonment of the struggle. But if we are not to renounce all action, we must understand that we can struggle against the state apparatus only inside the country. And notably in the case of war, we must choose between hindering the functioning of the military machine of which we are ourselves so many cogs and blindly aiding that machine to continue to crush human lives. . . .

Whether the mask is labeled fascism, democracy, or dictatorship of the proletariat, our great adversary remains The Apparatus—the bureaucracy, the police, the military. Not the one facing us across the frontier or the battle lines, which is not so much our enemy as our brothers' enemy, but the one that calls itself our protector and makes us its slaves. No matter what the circumstances, the worst betrayal will always be to subordinate ourselves to this Apparatus, and to trample underfoot, in its service, all human values in ourselves and in others.

War Resistance

The activist strategy of war resistance was, quite simply, the organized refusal to do military service: people pledged to withhold their support from any war that might be undertaken. In the past, conscientious objection to military service had reflected an *individual's* choice of principle, but war resistance was a collective political strategy. It resembled the strategy of the general strike, which socialists had popularized prior to World War I, except that it envisioned a revolt against war of potential soldiers from all classes.

The main proponent of this strategy was the War Resisters' International (WRI) which was formed in Bilthoven, Holland (1919) around the statement, "War is a crime against humanity. We therefore are determined not to support any kind of war and to strive for the removal of all causes of war" (document 4.23). Using the image of a broken rifle as its symbol, the WRI publicized the slogan, "Wars will cease when men refuse to fight." Small national branches were established, often together with socialists. The most famous convert to war resistance was the German physicist Albert Einstein, who emerged from World War I as a pacifist.

Shortly before the beginning of World War II, the WRI claimed 54 affiliated sections in 24 countries, most of them quite small. Britain was a special case, because the idea of a pledge to refuse war service was taken up by students at Oxford University in 1933 (the so-called Oxford Pledge), and subsequently by the Peace Pledge Union, which claimed some 150,000 members in 1939. By then war resistance had became part of the larger debate over how to maintain peace in the face of aggression.

That problem was explored especially by a leading Dutch pacifist and anarchist, Barthelemy (Bart) de Ligt. Like Rolland, de Ligt respected the human "impulses to struggle, to conquer, to sacrifice" as long as they did not make people the instruments of inhuman violence.[21] In the late 1930s he developed a detailed strategy for resisting military aggression and totalitarian authority through tactics of non-cooperation. Many of those techniques were appropriated to combat Nazi occupation during World War II, and the concept later evolved into the strategy of civilian nonviolent defense.

Document 4.23

The War Resisters' International: War Resistance

From "Statement of Principles," 1925

WAR IS A CRIME AGAINST HUMANITY. It is a crime against life, and uses human personalities for political and economic ends.

WE, THEREFORE, actuated by an intense love of mankind, ARE DETERMINED NOT TO SUPPORT either directly by service of any kind in the army, navy, or air forces, or indirectly by making or consciously handling munitions or other war material, subscribing to war loans or using our labor for the purpose of setting others free for war service—ANY KIND OF WAR, aggressive or defensive, remembering that modern wars are invariably alleged by Governments to be defensive.

Wars would seem to fall under three heads:

(a) Wars to defend the State to which we nominally belong and wherein our home is situated. To refuse to take up arms for this end is difficult: (1) because the State will use all its coercive powers to make us do so; (2) because our inborn love for home has been deliberately identified with love of the State in which it is situated.

(b) Wars to preserve the existing order of society with its security for the privileged few. That we would never take up arms for this purpose goes without saying.

(c) Wars on behalf of the oppressed proletariat, whether for its liberation or defense. To refuse to take up arms for this purpose is most difficult: (1) because of the proletarian regime, and, even more, the enraged masses, in time of revolution would regard as a traitor anyone who refused to support the new order by force; (2) because our instinctive love for the suffering and the oppressed would tempt us to use violence on their behalf.

However, we are convinced that violence cannot really preserve order, defend our home, or liberate the proletariat. In fact, experience has shown that in all wars, order, security, and liberty disappear, and that . . . the proletariat always suffer most. We hold, however, that consistent pacifists have no right to take up a merely negative position, but must recognize AND STRIVE FOR THE REMOVAL OF ALL THE CAUSES OF WAR.

We recognize as causes of war not only the instinct of egoism and greed, which is found in every human heart, but also all agencies which create hatred and antagonism between groups of people. . . .

. . . we see an important cause of war in the prevalent misconception of the State. The State exists for man, not man for the State. The recognition of the sanctity of human personality must become the basic principle of human society. Furthermore, the State is not a sovereign self-contained entity, as every nation is a part of the great family of mankind. We feel, therefore, that consistent pacifists have no right to take up a merely negative position, but must devote themselves to abolishing classes, barriers between the peoples, and to creating a world-wide brotherhood founded on mutual service.

War Resistance is not an end in itself, it is a way of life to achieve an end. The goal, in the expression of the Socialist is, Liberty Equality, Fraternity; in that of the Christian it is, Truth, Beauty, Love, a world where all can and will desire to co-operate for the common good.

Socialist Approaches

Announcing his new journal, *Clarté,* Henri Barbusse (1873–1935) expressed the idealism of leading French socialists in 1919, as he had distilled two years of trench life in his antiwar novel, *Le Feu* (*Under Fire*) three years before. Barbusse was the most visible communist intellectual in France in the interwar period. A loyal activist and writer for the Third International, he translated his deep aversion for injustice and war into an uncritical enthusiasm for the Soviet experiment. *Clarté* was a journal and also an association of French intellectuals and artists whose humanitarian idealism was expressed as political culture more than as political action. The journal and its sponsors stood against capitalism and war, Barbusse wrote; they were in the vanguard of an "invincible" movement for democracy, socialism, internationalism, and peace.[22] That equation was formulated in quite different ways in the last fifteen years of his life, ways that reflected the changing currents of socialism.

Before World War I the Second International, established in 1889, had affiliated most socialist and labor organizations and had accommodated most of their differences. But in 1914 almost all socialists in the belligerent nations supported their governments and, as wartime pressure mounted, their movements were torn between national loyalty and allegiance to international solidarity. The Second International and the International Federation of Trade Unions, established in 1913, disintegrated.

By the end of the war, a new base of influence existed in Bolshevik Russia, and international socialism was further divided between democratic socialism and communism. That polarity was fixed by the formation of the Third, or Communist, International in March 1919, which created its own Red Trade Union International in 1921. Henceforth, alternative ideas about war and peace were integral to the disputes among socialists and between socialists and communists over organization and policy.

Social Democratic parties and unions regrouped in the International Trade Union Federation of independent unions, in 1919, and the Labor and Socialist International of 1923, a federation of autonomous parties. The organizations aligned in these two internationals divided into myriad factions that faced distinctive challenges in their own nations. They nonetheless shared a rough, minimal consensus (1) existing social and political structures could be modified and that socialism achieved incrementally by broadening political and economic power; (2) the democratic process of participation in decision-making was essential; and (3) because war reinforced the hierarchical structure of capitalism, the international system should be reformed to prevent warfare. This general consensus was developed in formal works such as that of British economist Harold Laski, professor at the London School of Economics and member of the executive committees of the Fabian Society and Labour party (document 4.24). A similar position was expressed in the political statements of the German socialist Rudolf Hilferding, a leader in the right wing of the Independent Social Democratic party (USPD) who rejected the Third International and was repudiated by it (document 4.25). The consensus shared by Social Democrats became a means of distinguishing them from the Communist International, at least until 1935, and defined their program for *realistic* or *reformist* peace (document 4.26).

The program for *Revolutionary* peace, in contrast, had been proclaimed by Lenin during World War I. Assuming that capitalism inevitably produced war, he argued that peace required a victorious socialist revolution. The success of the Bolshevik Revolution in Russia—and the necessity of consolidating it—confirmed his faith in revolutionary strategy and in mass organization under an elite vanguard. Accordingly, the Communist International was organized on the model of Russian Bolshevism and was subservient to its Soviet patron. It operated on the assumptions that (1) Social Democrats were enemies because social and political reform only impeded the workers' revolution; (2) democratic participation in decision making would only weaken the revolutionary movement, which required disciplined leadership; and (3) pacifists should be considered reactionaries because international cooperation was a conspiracy for capitalist control, whereas imperialist war would unleash a workers' revolution.

The repeated failure of Lenin's revolutionary strategy in western nations during the 1920s only intensified communist allegiance to Russia as the bastion of the true revolution. Indeed, the International became an instrument of Soviet policy, which was aimed as much against Social Democrats and pacifists as capitalists (document 4.27). The result was to divide the socialist and labor movement, sometimes with disastrous results, as in Germany.

Joseph Stalin forced the Third International to take a rigid ideological line that sometimes contradicted his own foreign policy. While the Soviet Union stabilized its relationship with capitalist countries, endorsed the Briand-Kellogg Pact, participated in the Geneva disarmament conference, and entered the League of Nations in 1934, the International was ordered to oppose Social Democrats along with the international reform and cooperation they advocated. Moreover, from the 1922 treaty of Rapallo until 1934, the Soviet Union maintained a working relationship with Germany, where the communist party was ordered to support the rising National Socialists, or Nazis, against the Social Democrats.

As National Socialism revealed its aggressive character after 1933, some loyal British and French communists joined with Social Democrats to fight it. By mid-1934 the Communist International reversed itself and authorized cooperation with parallel "anti-fascist" movements. At its Seventh Congress a year later, it formally declared for a United Front against war *and* fascism (document 4.28), a policy that Henri Barbusse had urged upon Stalin and the highest party leaders just before his death on 30 August. The International was brought into line with the new foreign policy of Soviet Russia, which courted the democracies, concluded an alliance with France, and endorsed collective action by the League. Communist parties lined up with Social Democrats and even bourgeois democratic governments.

The idea of a United Front nevertheless remained controversial. For some communists it did not seem consistent with the idea of revolutionary peace. For Social Democrats it was suspect because of their doubts about communist motives, their vulnerability in being associated with communists, and their rejection of Stalin's dictatorial style—notably his extraordinary use of terror against Russians in the purges culminating in 1937. The Front collapsed in 1939 when Stalin negotiated a nonaggression pact with Hitler and joined Germany in the invasion and partition of Poland. That diplomatic revolution confirmed the fact that even the revolutionary position on war and peace was related to issues of national security.

Document 4.24

Harold Laski: Economic Foundations of Peace

From "The Economic Foundations of Peace," 1934

The Movement towards Equality. Upon this view, the high road to peace lies in the reconstruction of the present social order in the direction of equality. The more effectively this is achieved the less interest states possess in the pursuit of an imperialist policy. To develop the productive power of the community so that men share equally in its results is to prevent the perversion of its political authority in the interest of a small number of its members. Its sovereignty is then no longer a cloak for that interest. Its direction of capital investment is no longer a technique of exploitation abroad which pays no adequate attention to domestic need.

Its foreign relations express a commercial connection which does not require the inherent militarism of a policy built upon the ideal of economic empire. A society of Socialist states is in a position, to which no other order of life can pretend, to consider its economic problems upon a basis of genuine mutuality and goodwill. For such a society can plan its life in a deliberate and coherent way. It is not pressed by those problems of prestige which are inherent in the structure of capitalism. Its interest in peace is the more direct since it is not perverted from allegiance to peace by the peculiar psychology of patriotism which a capitalist society is driven to invent for its own preservation. . . .

Economic Democracy the Road to Peace. The way of peace is the way of economic democracy; for there is no other method of building social organization upon the basis of reason and justice. In any other form of society, it is the power of the privileged class which determines the habits of the state; and they are bound to use that power in the international field both to consolidate and to reinforce their authority. Desire then becomes the parent of principle, and reason the servant of prestige. Such a society may even will to do justice; but it cannot help equating its substance with the maintenance of its own authority. The character and technique of international institutions then becomes adapted to the needs of this atmosphere. The international community cannot find the unity that it requires to plan its life coherently; its power to act rationally is constantly frustrated by vested interests. . . . The consequence is the inherent inability of instruments like the League to secure an allegiance from its more powerful members which makes observance of peace the highest consideration they can desire.

In an equal society, the emphasis is a different one. . . . Because it is not wedded to imperialism, it does not find the same need for *machtpolitik* as alternative forms; and this makes its attitude to disarmament wholly different again in character. It is able, moreover, by reason of its egalitarian atmosphere, to develop psychological habits among its members which recognize and sharpen the relation between peace and well-being. For such a society, pacifist institutions are a guarantee of progress; where, in an unequal society, they are always a contingent threat to privilege. An economic democracy, moreover, by reason of its control of the instruments of production, and the equal disposal of their results, is . . . in a position where its advantage lies in the organized planning of international life. The conception of a world state is directly related to its own interests as a society. It can see that while war, as an instrument of policy, may benefit a few, it means nothing but material and spiritual loss for the kind of society it is. . . .

Document 4.25

Rudolf Hilferding: Realistic Pacifism

From "The Struggle of Workers Against
the Military Menace," 1925

. . . With the winning of political democracy, the phase of utopian pacifism can come to an end; the time of real pacifism has begun because we are no longer appealing to humanity, nor to common sense, nor to the feeling of indignation at the horrors of war; but rather we are leaning on the real growing force of the proletariat, on its growing hostility to war, on the political force of the workers' movement. Here is this new phase in which we now find ourselves. Because of that, for us, this struggle for pacifism—our struggle for pacifism—is nothing else but a part of the whole class struggle of the proletariat against the war tendencies of capitalism. Therefore, I emphasize that the new point of view of the International regarding the problems of war is essentially not new. . . . Its irreconcilable enmity to war . . . was always part of the *raison d'etre* of the International. But the method of our struggle is new.

We shall have to lead this struggle for peace with the determination to surmount international anarchy. We are going to have to oppose the concept of the bourgeoisie, oppose their view on the incessant rivalry and conflict of various nations for domination, with the concept of the proletariat, the spirit of solidarity and cooperation. . . . The question can now be only about the defense of the whole against a part. . . . Therefore, we demand that the League of Nations be completed. We demand absolutely and unconditionally the entry of Germany into the League of Nations. We are of the opinion that each nation not included in the League is a break with the principle of the solidarity of peoples. Therefore, we propose that, besides Germany, it is no less important that Russia enter the League of Nations. We demand, and call . . . upon all democratic factions in the United States to reject its isolation . . . and apply all of their efforts to get the United States into the League of Nations. Once it is a union of all nations, the League of Nations will be in a position to broaden its political program.

. . . The politics of the League of Nations is a function of our politics . . . of class struggle, a function of that force with which we will be able to achieve the victory of our ideas in individual countries. It is necessary to develop the politics of the League of Nations [and to realize] the principles: security, courts of arbitration, disarmament.

Document 4.26

The Labor and Socialist International: War and the Workers

From the Third Congress, Brussels, 1928

To the Workers of the World

Ten years have passed since the end of the war.

Despite all solemn promises which the governments made to their peoples, peace has not yet been assured; competition in armaments has again begun; the nations have not yet that feeling of security which indeed Socialism alone can bring them completely by abolishing class domination which is the source of national conflicts. . . .

As against the disastrous, arbitrary and violent solutions proposed, the Labor and Socialist International has been the first to indicate pacific solutions of the reparations problem. At this very moment the International is trying to force from the governments fulfillment of their promises regarding compulsory arbitration, general disarmament of all peoples and a complete liquidation of war. . . .

The text of the Kellogg Pact, which the governments intend to sign, contains an absolute renunciation of war, but it is distorted by the unacceptable reservations of certain governments and will be still more weakened by the exclusion of the Soviet Union. It will indeed remain a dead letter unless the workers unite and conquer political power so as to extend the pact without any exception to the entire world, to organize peace after having proclaimed it. . . .

The International's activity, the action of the international proletariat for its emancipation and for peace, will be rendered complete and efficacious only by political liberty. Of course, democracy, when connected with a class system, is not an aim in itself for the working class. But it constitutes an important means of obtaining social equality besides political equality. The working class will attain this aim only if it tenaciously fights within the bourgeois democracy, if it extends its position of power by the use of political rights and liberties, thus creating the essential conditions for erecting the proletarian democracy. . . .

The last Congress of the Communist International, by declaring that a recurrence of imperialist wars is inevitable, has again set all its hopes on a world war which would give birth to a revolution of violence. How is it possible adequately to describe and condemn such insanity, which directs the thoughts and hopes of the workers towards new wars, when on the contrary it should be the passionate endeavor of all human beings who suffer and think, to unite without delay all the workers of the world in a common effort against a frightful repetition of the barbarous years of bloodshed? . . .

The division of the proletariat diminishes its power. The unity of the workers would be a fresh stimulus, which would render its fight for peace and social emancipation irresistible.

Document 4.27

The Communist International:
Struggle Against Imperialist War

From the Sixth World Congress, Moscow, 1928

Ten years after the world war, the big imperialist powers solemnly conclude a pact for outlawing war: they talk about disarmament; they seek, with the support of the leaders of international Social Democracy, to delude the workers and toiling masses into the belief that the rule of monopoly capitalism assures peace to the world.

The Sixth World Congress of the Communist International condemns all these maneuvers as vile deception of the working masses. . . .

The speeches of the bourgeoisie and their Social Democratic and petty bourgeois pacifist accomplices, about disarmament security, arbitration courts, outlawry of war as an instrument of national policy, etc., are examples of the worst hypocrisy.

The League of Nations, founded nine years ago as an imperialist alliance in defense of the robber "peace" of Versailles, and for the suppression of the revolutionary movement of the world, is itself more and more becoming a direct instrument for war against the Soviet Union. . . .

War is inseparable from capitalism. From this it follows that the "abolition" of war is possible only through the abolition of capitalism, i.e. through the overthrow of the bourgeois class of exploiters, through the proletarian dictatorship, the building of Socialism, and the elimination of classes. All other theories and proposals, however "realistic" they may claim to be, are nothing but a deception calculated to perpetuate exploitation and war. . . .

The first duty of Communists in the fight against imperialist war is to tear down the screen by which the bourgeoisie conceal their preparations for war. . . . This duty implies above all a determined political and ideological fight *against pacifism*. In this fight the Communists must take careful note of the various shades of pacifism . . . :

(a) Official pacifism . . . (League of Nations, Locarno, Disarmament Conferences, "outlawry of war," etc.)

(b) The pacifism of the Second International (Hilferding, Paul Boncour, MacDonald), which is but a branch of official government pacifism. . . .

(c) "Radical" or "revolutionary" pacifism, advocated by certain "Left" Socialists who admit the danger of war, but strive to combat this danger frequently by meaningless phrases against war. . . .

(d) Semi-religious pacifism, which has its basis in the church movement. . . .

Imperialist war against the Soviet Union is open, bourgeois, counterrevolutionary class war. . . . The basis for the tactics of the proletariat in capitalist countries in the struggle against such a war is furnished by the Bolshevik program [to] turn the war into civil war. . . .

. . . In the event of a war against the Soviet Union, the workers in capitalist countries must not allow themselves to be scared from supporting the Red Army and fighting against their own bourgeoisie. . . .

The international policy of the U.S.S.R. is a *peace policy*, which conforms to the interests of the ruling class in the Soviet Russia, *viz.*, the proletariat, and to the interest of the international proletariat. . . . In regard to the capitalist States . . . this policy implies: opposition to imperialist war, to predatory colonial campaigns, and to pacifism, which camouflages these campaigns. . . .

Document 4.28

The Communist International: The United Front

From the Seventh Communist International,
Moscow, August 1935

The Seventh World Congress of the Communist International, confirming the decisions of the Sixth Congress on the struggle against imperialist war, sets the following main tasks before the Communist Parties, revolutionary workers, toilers, peasants and oppressed peoples of the whole world:

1. *The struggle for peace and for the defense of the U.S.S.R.* In face of the war provocations of the German fascists and Japanese militarists,

and the speeding up of armaments by the war parties in the capitalist countries, in face of the immediate danger of a counter-revolutionary war breaking out against the Soviet Union, the *central slogan* of the Communist Parties must be: struggle for peace.

2. *The united people's front in the struggle for peace and against the instigators of war.* The struggle for peace opens up before the Communist Parties the greatest opportunities for creating the broadest united front. All those interested in the preservation of peace should be drawn into this united front. The concentration of forces against the chief instigators of war at any given moment (at the present time—against fascist Germany, and against Poland and Japan which are in league with it) constitutes a most important tactical task of the Communist Parties. . . .

The formation of a united front with *Social-Democratic and reformist organizations* for the struggle for peace necessitates a determined ideological struggle against reactionary elements within the Social-Democratic Parties which . . . by their campaigns of slander against the Soviet Union directly aid the preparations for an anti-Soviet war. It necessitates close collaboration with those . . . whose position is approaching ever closer to that of revolutionary struggle against imperialist war.

The drawing of pacifist organizations and their adherents into the united front of [the] struggle for peace acquires great importance in mobilizing the petty bourgeois masses, progressive intellectuals, women and youth . . . that are prepared to go with them even if only part of the way. . . .

3. *The combination of the struggle against imperialist war with the struggle against fascism.* The anti-war struggle of the masses striving to preserve peace must be very closely combined with the struggle against fascism and the fascist movement. . . .

4. *The struggle against militarism and armaments.* The Communist Parties of all capitalist countries must fight: against military expenditures (war budgets), for the recall of military forces from the colonies and mandated territories, against militarisation . . . of the youth, women and the unemployed, against emergency decrees restricting bourgeois-democratic liberties . . . ; against restricting the rights of workers employed in war industry plants; against subsidizing the war industry and against trading in or transporting arms. . . .

5. *The struggle against chauvinism.* In the struggle against chauvinism the task of the Communists consists in educating the workers and the whole of the toiling population in the spirit of *proletarian internationalism*. . . .

6. *The national liberation struggle and the support of wars of na-*

tional liberation. . . . It is the task of the Communists . . . to be in the front ranks of the fighters for national independence and to wage a war of liberation to a finish. . . .

The Problem of Change and Security

Throughout the interwar period, the relationship between security and peace was in constant flux. Security requirements differed from nation to nation, and there were dramatic changes from one decade to the next. In general, security came to be defined in terms of four broad strategies: peaceful change, neutrality, appeasement, and collective security. Because neutrality and appeasement were subsequently blamed for World War II, scholars have been reluctant to take them seriously. Nonetheless, it is important to do so in order to appreciate all four policies, as well as the difficulties of those who tried to formulate a coherent idea of peace in the 1920s and 1930s.

The terrible dilemma of the interwar generation, between strict observance of the peace treaties and the possibility of peaceful revision, was summarized by a French delegate to the League Assembly in 1921: "We are spectators of a strange duel, a duel between the spirit of war and revenge on the one hand, and the spirit of work and peace on the other —a struggle between the Junkers and the democrats. We can only feel secure . . . when the German Republic is established on a stable foundation, and when it is filled with the idea of justice, dignity and liberty, which are the ideals of the League of Nations. But, unfortunately, this duel is not yet concluded, and meanwhile we must keep our weapons in readiness."[23] This "strange duel" was translated into the twin necessities for change and order.

The goal of orderly, *peaceful change* was assumed in Article 19 of the League Covenant, which authorized "the reconsideration . . . of treaties which may have become inapplicable and the consideration of international conditions whose continuance might endanger the peace of the world." Much of the diplomacy of the 1920s was devoted to the problem of reconciling revision of the peace terms with the requirements of security. Failure to do so accounts for much of the anguish of the 1930s. Some observers understood that at the time. Maurice Bourquin, a professor at the Graduate Institute of International Studies, Geneva, summarized the deliberations of the Tenth International Studies Conference (1937) by observing that the polarization of movement and order, change and stability, reflected a "moral crisis" in western civilization.[24]

According to the American lawyer John Foster Dulles, Article 19 was a vital step in stabilizing international change (document 4.29).

Collective security, in the broadest sense, implies a defensive alliance system—the joint response of several powers to a military threat against any one of them. In the special, innovative sense of the League Covenant (articles 10–17), however, collective security suggested something different. It meant an obligation binding on all members of the League of Nations to act together against any nation which engaged in warfare prior to attempting a pacific settlement. In several respects, however, the Covenant left unanswered questions: Under what conditions and under whose direction would collective force be applied? How binding was the obligation to use it? From 1921 to 1936 there were futile efforts to refine, institutionalize, and apply collective security in this sense of the Covenant.

In 1923 the Assembly of the League adopted a Treaty of Mutual Guarantee that made binding collective action contingent on general disarmament. It was not ratified. The following year the Assembly unanimously adopted the Protocol for the Pacific Settlement of International Disputes (document 4.30). This measure explicitly linked collective sanctions and general disarmament to a prescribed procedure for the judicial and arbital settlement of disputes. It, too, failed of ratification. Although the concept of collective security remained codified in the Covenant, it was considered too ambiguous to be binding.

Toward the end of the decade, French foreign minister Aristide Briand and U.S. secretary of state Frank B. Kellogg drafted an antiwar pact open to all states. Widely endorsed, the 1928 Pact of Paris (document 4.31) repudiated warfare "as an instrument of national policy."[25] Although it contained no provisions for enforcement and although signatory states reserved the right of military defense, the pact did extend the Covenant's rejection of war to non-League states, and was the basis for a Soviet-sponsored convention that defined aggression (document 4.32). The Briand-Kellogg Pact and the Covenant were often cited together to brand aggression a crime under international law. For a brief time the universality of that principle obscured the special interests of the states that enunciated it.

Clarity came from a series of events that tested the League's capacity for collective responses: notably: Japanese aggression in Manchuria (1931); Italian aggression in Ethiopia (1935–36); German reoccupation of the Rhineland (1936); and external intervention in the Spanish Civil War (1936–38). Only in the Ethiopian case was there a real effort to apply collective sanctions, and that was undercut by French and British appeasement of Italy, if not also by the neutrality of the United States. At this point there emerged a major citizen campaign to restore credibility to the League, the International Peace Campaign (document 4.33). Between 1936 and 1939, it acquired national committees in forty-three countries and coordinated the efforts of professional, left-wing, trade-union, religious, peace, women's, and veterans' associations.

The campaign became controversial, in part because its goals coincided with those of the Soviet Union, which at that time supported joint action against aggression. Litvinov eloquently appealed to the League in July 1936 to strengthen the concept of collective security (document 4.34). It was too late, and the idea of binding joint action was abandoned, just when Italy and Germany were about to form an Axis, to be joined by Japan a year later. By then the idea of collective security in the innovative sense of the League Covenant was obsolete. Implicitly, at least, it became understood as an antifascist alliance system.

Neutrality meant at least the rejection of any obligation to intervene in international disputes not directly related to a nation's interests and sovereignty over its own affairs. This approach was fairly consistent for the Netherlands, Switzerland, and the Scandinavian countries, which had not participated in World War I but did join the League of Nations. It was the fixed policy of the United States, which repudiated the League along with the security guarantee that Woodrow Wilson had pledged, with Britain, to France. A spirit of neutrality also characterized the British commonwealth dominions and exerted a restraining influence on British foreign policy.

At the very least, the neutral states perceived that intervention would threaten their own economic or political security or would incur risks disproportionate to those of other powers (document 4.35). At most, they argued that the existence of neutrals was useful to mediate conflict, provide practical and humanitarian assistance to belligerents, and prevent war from becoming general (in some measure, a view reflecting the experience of World War I).[26] Basically, the strategy of neutrality reflected the idea that war could be localized, that peace could exist in islands of sanity.

The collective obligation to apply economic and military sanctions against an aggressor state was perceived to threaten neutrality. Canada and the British dominions discretely resisted attempts to strengthen League sanctions. So did the Scandinavian nations, except in the case of Italy's invasion of Ethiopia; and thereafter they concluded: "under present conditions and the practice followed during the last years the system of sanctions has acquired a non-obligatory character . . . that applies not only to a particular group of States, but to all Members of the League. They are convinced that it is in the interests of the League itself that this liberty of decision is expressly acknowledged."[27]

The United States bristled at the barest hint of binding obligations. Its vaunted neutrality was cited by Europeans as an obstacle to collective security, despite the Roosevelt administration's assurance in 1932 that it would not obstruct collective sanctions against an aggressor. American neutrality legislation of the late 1930s authorized embargoes of war-related material against all belligerents, and these might have been coordinated with selective sanctions imposed by other democratic powers; but the apparent vacillation of those states reinforced the U.S. commitment to neutrality in the hope that war and peace could be isolated.

Appeasement was a strategy no less grounded in national interest than neutrality, and it was influenced by the idea of peaceful change as well as by practical considerations. Revisionist interpretations reinforced the impression that the responsibility for World War I had been distributed almost equally among the various powers. Article 231 of the Treaty of Versailles, which assigned sole guilt to Germany, became an embarrassment. Sentiment grew for revising the peace terms, which had redrawn boundaries along strategic as much as national principles, severely restricted German economic and military capacity, and distorted colonial and economic systems.

This conviction, as well as certain economic and ideological concerns, contributed to the appeasement of Japan, Fascist Italy, and Nazi Germany in the 1930s. The French accepted a readjustment in northern China when the Japanese army invaded Manchuria in 1931. The British reluctantly accepted Italian expansion in Ethiopia five years later, and even the German reoccupation of the Rhineland. But by that time the practice of appeasement had shifted, from accommodating reasonable change to conciliating expansionist powers. In the old spirit of conciliation and the new realities of the 1930s, Britain and France accepted Germany's reunification, or Anschluss, with Austria and facilitated her takeover of Czechoslovakia in 1938–39. It was perhaps also in this sense that the Soviet Union abandoned collective security and concluded a nonaggression pact with Germany in 1939, together with a secret protocol dividing control of Poland and the Baltic states between them.

In some cases the Great Powers opted for appeasement because there seemed be no alternative to nonintervention (document 4.36). In others, appeasement was based on the hope that conflict could be localized, that differences among the Great Powers could be composed, that the ambitions of aggressive states would be satiated when a new balance of power emerged (document 4.37), or that precious time could be won to hold a line elsewhere. On the ruins of collective security, a balance-of-power system appeared attractive to leaders like Britain's Neville Chamberlain, but only as long as aggression did not threaten the balance itself. The League could only appeal to that hope (document 4.38).

When Germany and the Soviet Union invaded Poland in 1939, they clearly threatened British and French security, and European war ensued. There were anguished calls for peace at that moment: "This time there are no flowers decorating the guns; no heroic songs; no bravos for the departing soldiers," one appealed. "From the first day, the war was condemned by its participants on the front and at home. Therefore let us make peace quickly."[28] Appeals could not stem the bloody tide, but they presaged a continuing struggle against international violence.

Document 4.29

John Foster Dulles: Peaceful Change

From *War, Peace and Change*, 1939

There are inherent in Article 19 [of the League of Nations Covenant] the elements essential to an effectively functioning authority, namely: (a) the objective—avoidance of violence; (b) the means—a periodic but measured alteration of the *status quo,* designed to strike an acceptable balance between the dynamic and static desires of the national groups; and (c) the placing of responsibility for achieving this balance in the hands of an impartial and continuous body owing a responsibility to all. By another Article [16], sanctions were provided.

It may be impractical to put this particular provision (Article 19) to work. The League is to some extent dismembered and to a considerable extent discredited. Perhaps Article 19 has at all times constituted too ambitious a beginning. But the basic concept of this Article must sooner or later be given practical application.* Without it we cannot have a

---

* In his book Dulles applied the abstract principle described in this excerpt to specific issues, especially U.S. policy on Japan. A future U.S. secretary of state, Dulles was a leader in the Peace Commission of the Federal Council of Churches and in the American Co-ordinating Committee for International Studies.

peace which is other than an armed and precarious truce. We cannot have a peace which is predicated upon principle or which is other than a matter of expediency.

Before considering how the concept of Article 19 might be implemented, it will be well to consider in the abstract certain general characteristics of "change." . . .

There are certain general laws of change which we should be aware of and take into account. Change is the result of the dynamic prevailing over the static. There is always resistance to change, just as there is always the impulse to change. . . . Obviously there are some forms of change which should be and can be resisted. There are existing institutions which deserve to be preserved. However, by and large, the dynamic prevails over the static. That is why we have a world which, in all its phases, is a changing world. If, however, man cannot prevent change from occurring, he can . . . influence the form which change assumes and the rate at which it occurs. . . .

. . . the impulse for change is usually moderate and malleable at an early stage. It is then disposed to adapt itself to and accept such openings as may be offered. If, however, the impulse to change is of a character destined to become increasingly intense, then with delay it becomes a force which masters, rather than a force which can be controlled and directed. As dynamic pressure grows, there develops a momentum behind a given form of change; its direction cannot at that time be readily altered. Furthermore, resistance or delay serves to pile up forces which make the change, when it occurs, violent in character. . . .

In international affairs—as indeed elsewhere—we should seek to abolish any sense of finality. "Never" and "forever" are words which should be eliminated from the vocabulary of statesmen.

Document 4.30

The League of Nations: Pacific Settlement of Disputes

From the Protocol for the Pacific Settlement of
International Disputes, 1924

ARTICLE 2. The signatory States agree in no case to resort to war either with one another or against a State which, if the occasion arises, accepts all the obligations herein set out, except in case of resistance to acts of aggression or when acting in agreement with the Council or the

Assembly of the League of Nations in accordance with the provisions of the Covenant and of the present Protocol.*

ARTICLE 10. Every State which resorts to war in violation of the undertakings contained in the Covenant or in the present Protocol is an aggressor. Violation of the rules laid down for a demilitarized zone shall be held equivalent to resort to war.

In the event of hostilities having broken out, any State shall be presumed to be an aggressor, unless a decision of the Council, which must be taken unanimously, shall otherwise declare:

1. If it has refused to submit the dispute to the procedures of pacific settlement provided . . . or to comply with a judicial sentence or arbital award or with a unanimous recommendation of the Council. . . .

2. If it has violated provisional measures enjoined by the Council for the period while the proceedings are in progress. . . .

. . . if the Council does not at once succeed in determining the aggressor, it shall be bound to enjoin upon the belligerents an armistice, and shall fix its terms, acting, if need be, by a two-thirds majority and shall supervise its execution.

Any belligerent which has refused to accept the armistice or has violated its terms shall be deemed an aggressor.

The Council shall call upon the signatory States to apply forthwith against the aggressor the sanctions provided by Article 11 of the present Protocol. . . .

ARTICLE 11. As soon as the Council has called upon the signatory States to apply sanctions, . . . the obligations of the said States . . . will immediately become operative in order that such sanctions may forthwith be employed against the aggressor.

These obligations shall be interpreted as obliging each of the signatory States to co-operate loyally and effectively in support of the Covenant of the League of Nations, and in resistance to any act of aggression, in the degree which its geographical position and its particular situation as regards armaments allow.

. . . the signatory States [pledge collectively] to come to the assistance of the State attacked or threatened, and to give each other mutual support. . . .†

---

* Article 1 obligated the signatories to respect the protocol under the League's authority; Articles 3–9 provided detailed formulas for referring disputes alternately to the World Court or to arbitration under the aegis of the League Council of Assembly, and authorized the Council to supervise demilitarized zones under certain conditions.

† Articles 12–15 provided for the administration of sanctions, empowered the Council to end them, and placed the burden of their cost upon the aggressor.

ARTICLE 16. The signatory States agree that in the event of a dispute between one or more of them and one or more States which have not signed the present Protocol and are not Members of the League of Nations, such non-Member States shall be invited . . . to submit, for the purpose of a pacific settlement, to the obligations accepted by the . . . signatories. . . .

If the State so invited, having refused to accept the said conditions and obligations, resorts to war against a signatory State, the provisions of Article 16 of the Covenant, as defined by the present Protocol, shall be applicable against it.

ARTICLE 17. The signatory States undertake to participate in an International Conference for the Reduction of Armaments. . . . All other States, whether Members of the League or not, shall be invited to this Conference.

ARTICLE 21. . . . So soon as the majority of the permanent Members of the Council and ten other Members of the League have deposited or effected their ratifications . . . the Protocol shall come into force as soon as the plan for the reduction of armaments has been adopted by the Conference provided for in Article 17.

If within such period after the adoption of the plan for the reduction of armaments as shall be fixed by the said Conference, the plan has not been carried out, the Council shall make a declaration to that effect; this declaration shall render the present Protocol null and void.

Document 4.31

The Briand-Kellogg Pact: Renunciation of War

From *The General Pact for the Renunciation of War*, 1928

ARTICLE 1. The High Contracting Parties solemnly declare in the names of their respective peoples that they condemn recourse to war for the solution of international controversies, and renounce it as an instrument of national policy in their relations with one another.

ARTICLE 2. The High Contracting Parties agree that the settlement or solution of all disputes or conflicts of whatever nature or of whatever origin they may be, which may arise among them, shall never be sought except by pacific means.*

---

* A third article provided for ratification and opened the treaty to all nations.

Document 4.32

The Convention for the Definition of Aggression

From the Convention of 4 July 1933

Desirous of strengthening the peace existing between their countries,

Believing that the Briand-Kellogg Pact, of which they are signatories, forbids all aggression,

Deeming it necessary in the interests of general security to define as precisely as possible the conception of aggression, in order to eliminate every pretext for its justification,

Declaring that every state has an equal right to independence, security, defense of its territories, and the free development of its institutions, . . .

ARTICLE 1. Each of the high contracting parties undertakes to recognize in its relations with each of the other parties . . . the definition of aggressor . . . based upon the proposal of the Soviet delegation.*

ARTICLE 2. Therefore, the aggressor in an international conflict . . . will be considered the state which is the first to commit any of the following acts:

(1) Declaration of war against another state;

(2) Invasion by armed forces, even without a declaration of war, of the territory of another state;

(3) An attack by land, naval, or air forces, even without a declaration of war, upon the territory, naval vessels, or aircraft of another state;

(4) Naval blockade of the coasts or ports of another state;

(5) Support to armed bands formed on the territory of a state and invading the territory of another state, or refusal, in spite of the demand of the invaded state, to take all possible measures on its own territory to deprive the said bands of any aid or protection.

ARTICLE 3. No consideration of a political, military, economic or any other nature may serve as an excuse or justification for aggression as specified in Article 2.

---

* Signatories were the USSR, Rumania, Czechoslovakia, Turkey, and Yugoslavia. Similar conventions were signed by Persia, Afghanistan, Poland, and the Baltic states.

Document 4.33

The International Peace Campaign: Peace in Danger

From "First Appeal: Peace in Danger," 1936

The most precious possession of humanity, peace, is endangered.*

The League of Nations, an instrument of international politics, created after the bloody war to resolve all conflicts peacefully, is in a very grave crisis.

Governments have taken it upon themselves to violate openly the constitution of the League and international treaties.

War, that shame of humanity, is celebrated by some as the greatest human glory.

Given this situation, we call on all the peoples of the earth, on all organizations which have inscribed the defense of peace on their programs, to coordinate their efforts.

Under what circumstances can peace be preserved?

Peace can only be saved if the following four principles are applied:

1. Recognition of the inviolability of obligations imposed by treaties;

2. Reduction and limitation of armaments by international agreement and suppression of the profits resulting from the manufacture and trade in arms;

3. Revival of the League of Nations to prevent and stop wars through the organization of collective security and mutual aid;

4. Creation of an effective mechanism within the League of Nations to address international situations that can provoke war.

None of these principles is aimed against a people. The absolute equality of all peoples and their representatives is what our movement seeks to achieve. An indivisible peace for all nations of our planet is the only path to a constructive and fruitful collaboration among peoples.

---

* This appeal was issued early in 1936, in anticipation of the Universal Congress of Brussels.

Document 4.34

Maxim Litvinov: Collective Security

From a speech of 1 July 1936

We have met here to complete a page in the history of the League of Nations, a page in the history of international life, which it will be impossible for us to read without a feeling of bitterness. We have to liquidate a course of action which was begun in fulfilment of our obligations as Members of the League to guarantee the independence of one of our fellow-Members, but which was not carried to its conclusion. . . .

I speak of the necessity of every Member of the League now to realize its individual responsibility for the lack of success of the common action . . . because both inside the League and outside it, there have been attempts to ascribe this lack of success to the League Covenant, to its defects, and to the present composition of the League.* From this are drawn far-reaching conclusions, which may lead to the result that, together with Ethiopian independence, the League itself may turn out to have been buried as well. Such attempts and conclusions must be decisively rejected.

We find ourselves face to face with the fact that the League of Nations has proved unable to secure for one of its Members the territorial integrity and political independence provided for by Article 10 of the Covenant, and today is able only to express to that Member its platonic sympathy. We cannot tranquilly and indifferently pass by this crying fact; we must analyze it, and draw from it all the lessons requisite to prevent similar cases for the future.

Some, however, are proposing too simple a remedy. They tell us: eliminate Article 10 altogether, free yourselves from obligations in respect of guaranteeing the integrity of the territory and the independence of League Members, and then it will never be possible to accuse the League of Nations of being bankrupt. They even consider it a mistake for the League of Nations to stop aggression and defend its Members. Only those can hold such views who deny the very principle of collective security, who deny the principle function of the League and the whole *raison d'être* of its creation and existence. It is therefore not worth while arguing with such people.

But those who recognize the principle of collective security, who

---

* The purpose of this meeting of the Assembly was to review the lessons of the Italian-Ethiopian war and to "reform" the League Covenant in that light.

continue to regard the League Covenant as an instrument of peace, might blame the Covenant only if they could show either that the Covenant does not provide sufficiently effective means in support of Article 10, or that, in this particular case, all such means were utilized to the full, yet failed to achieve their aim. But they will not be able to prove that.

I assert that Article 10 equipped the League of Nations with such powerful weapons that, in the event of their being fully applied, every aggression can be broken. Moreover, the very conviction that they may be applied may rob the aggressor of his zeal to put his criminal intentions into practice. The melancholy experience of the Italo-Ethiopian conflict does not contradict this assertion: on the contrary. In this particular case, whether because this was the first experiment in the application of collective measures; whether because some considered that this case has particular characteristics; whether because it coincided with the preparations elsewhere for aggression on a much larger scale, to which Europe had to devote special attention; whether for these or other reasons, it is a fact that, not only was the whole terrible mechanism of Article 16 not brought into play, but from the very outset there was a manifest striving to confine the action taken to the barest minimum. Even economic sanctions were limited in their scope and their function, and even in this limited scope sanctions were not applied by all Members of the League. . . .

Some are inclined to attribute the failure of League action to the absence from it of some countries, or its insufficiently universal character. We see, however, that not every Member of the League took part in sanctions. . . . On the other hand, we see from the example of the United States of America that the League of Nations may reckon on non-members of the League in applying Article 16, and reckon with them all the more, the more energetically it acts itself. . . .*

. . . To whose state of mind, then, should the Covenant be adapted?

Of those who take their stand on the consistent and collective defense of security, who see the highest interest of all nations in the maintenance of universal peace, who consider that, in the long run, this is required by the interests of every State, that it can be achieved only by sacrificing temporary interests to the community of nations, and who are ready even to place part of their own armed forces at the disposal of that community?

Or of those who, in principle, swear allegiance to collective security

---

* The United States independently embargoed arms shipments to Italy, as well as to Ethiopia, in accordance with its own neutrality legislation.

but, in practice, are ready to apply it only when it coincides with the interests of their own country?

Or, again, of those who reject the very principle of collective security, replace international solidarity with the watchword "Sauve qui peut" [stampede], preach the localization of war and proclaim war itself to be the highest manifestation of the human spirit?

I fear that is precisely the last category of persons whom people have in mind when they argue the necessity of adapting—or, as I would call it, degrading—the Covenant, since they reinforce their argument by asserting that in this way States which have left the League may be brought back.* Thus we are asked at all costs to restore to the League States which left it only because they see obstacles to the fulfillment of their aggressive intentions in the Covenant, in Articles 10 and 16, in sanctions. We are told: "Throw Article 10 out of the Covenant, throw out Article 16, renounce sanctions, reject collective security, and then former Members of the League may return to our ranks, and the League will become universal." In other words: "Let us make the League safe for aggressors."

I say that we don't need such a League, we don't need a League which, with all its universality, is safe for aggressors, since such a League, from an instrument of peace, will turn itself into its very opposite. . . .

It is not the Covenant which we have to degrade, but people whom we have to educate and bring up to the level of its lofty ideas. We must strive for the universality of the League, but not make it safe for the aggressor for the sake of that universality. On the contrary, every new Member, every old Member wishing to return to it, must read over its doorway, "All hope of aggression with impunity abandon, ye who enter here." . . .

I am far from idealizing the Covenant. Its imperfections consist, not so much in its articles as in its omissions and obscurities. Therefore, one has to speak, not of reforming the Covenant, but of making it more precise and of reinforcing it. I consider it, for instance, a serious omission that a definition of aggression is absent from the Covenant, a fact which, in the Italo-Ethiopian conflict, enabled some Members of the League to refuse to participate in sanctions from the very beginning. There is no clarity on the question of what organ of the League registers the fact of aggression. There is no clarity as to the binding character of decisions taken by League organs in the matter of sanctions. . . .

What is necessary is confidence that in all cases of aggression, independent of the degree of interest in the particular conflict, sanctions will

---

* Japan and Germany; Italy left in December 1937.

be applied by all, and this can be attained only when sanctions are obligatory. . . . In the ideal League of Nations, military sanctions as well as economic sanctions ought to be binding on all. . . .

. . . You cannot strengthen the League of nations if you do not stick to the principle of collective security, which is not at all a product of idealism, but a practical measure for ensuring the security of all peoples; if you do not stick to the principle of the indivisibility of peace. . . . *

Document 4.35

Sweden: Neutrality

From the League of Nations *Documents*, 1923,
and *Records*, 1930

The Swedish Government, 1923

. . . in the case of Sweden, whose geographical position affords her a fair degree of protection, and whose relations with other States are normal, the obligation arising out of a joint guarantee would increase the danger of her being drawn into war to an extent entirely out of proportion to the increased risk incurred, from the same cause, by certain other countries.† There is, no doubt, hope that the day will come when all States will agree to regard any disturber of the peace as a common enemy, against whom they will be prepared to take up arms immediately. But . . . we have not yet reached that stage, and there is no reason to suppose that we shall reach it in the near future. In the present disturbed conditions of the world, no Swedish Government could ask the representatives of the nation to undertake international obligations possibly involving Sweden in warlike operations, which might appear to the nation to be in no way connected with the vital interests and independence of the country.

Bo Östen Undén, 1930

My government is not one of the main adversaries of penalties [sanctions] themselves. On the contrary, it holds that the members of the

---

* This theme reflected not only Litvinov's views but also Soviet policy perhaps as late as May 1939, when he was dismissed from the foreign office.

† Shared by other Scandinavian countries, this view was also repeatedly voiced by Canada.

League are bound to take joint action against any State which threatens the peace. . . . But the system of penalties as conceived by the Covenant has certain serious drawbacks, one of which is that there is no guarantee that the members of the League will, at a critical moment, agree as to who is the aggressor. If a serious divergence of views occurred among the members of the League, and if they were thereby divided into two hostile camps of about equal strength, and war broke out, I confidently affirm that it would be cynical in the extreme to call such a war "the joint enforcement of penalties by the League of Nations." . . . The Swedish Government is of opinion that the best method of rendering the system of security more effective at the moment—apart from the possibility of international disarmament—is to perfect the preventative means which the League can employ in times of crisis.

Document 4.36

Léon Blum: Nonintervention

From a speech of 6 September 1936

. . . In so far as it is possible I want to try to make you understand . . . , speaking to you face to face, I as Head of the Government and you as militants in the Popular Front. . . .*

I know that the support of the legal Government of the Spanish Republic would guarantee to France, in case of European complications, the security of her Pyrenean frontier, the security of her communications with North Africa, and . . . from the military Government it is impossible, on the contrary, for us to foresee with certainty what either the obligations or the ambitions of its chiefs would be. . . .

The question of public right is no more doubtful than the question of the direct national interest of France. As we ourselves have said in a public document, the Government formed by the President of the Republic, Azãna, in accordance with the directives established by consultation with universal suffrage, is the regular Government of a friendly nation. . . .

. . . There is no doubt that if we place ourselves on the strict ground

---

* Because Blum headed the Popular Front government in France, his profound impulse was to take direct action on behalf of the Spanish Popular Front, which was fighting for the republic against the forces of General Francisco Franco, who was supported by Germany and Italy.

of international law, of public law, only the legal government would have the right to receive deliveries of arms from abroad, while this right should be severely denied to the chiefs of the military revolt. . . .

Comrades, I speak to you gravely, I know, I have come here for that. I well know what each of you desires in the bottom of his heart. I know it very well. I understand it very well. You would like to get to a point where arms deliveries could be made to the advantage of the rebel forces. In other countries, the exact opposite is desired. . . .

. . . Do not hope in the possibility of any arrangement which, on a European basis, would permit aid to one side and deny it to the other.

Ask yourselves also who can best supply, as far as the secrecy, the concentration of powers, the intensity of armaments, [and] industrial potential are concerned, ask yourselves who can insure for himself the advantage in such a competition? Once competition in armaments begins, for it is fatal in such a hypothesis, it will never become unilateral. Once competition in the supply of arms begins on Spanish soil, what might be the consequences for all of Europe in its present situation? . . .

Do not be surprised if we have arrived at this idea: the solution which might perhaps insure at the same time the welfare of Spain and the maintenance of peace is the conclusion of an international convention through which all the Powers bind themselves, not to neutrality—it is not a question of that word which has nothing to do with the case— but to abstention from all that concerns deliveries of arms and to the prohibition of shipments of war materials to Spain. . . .

Document 4.37

Neville Chamberlain: Appeasement

From his speeches of 1936 and 1938

June 1936

. . . Surely it is time that the nations who compose the League should review the situation and should decide so to limit the functions of the League in future that they may accord with its real powers.* If that policy were to be pursued and were to be courageously carried out, I

---

* Chamberlain, a Conservative leader in the House of Commons, was reflecting on the Italian-Ethiopian conflict. His views were among those to which Maxim Litvinov objected half a month later (document 4.33).

believe that it might go far to restore the prestige of the League and the moral influence which it ought to exert in the world. But if the League be limited in that sort of way it must be admitted that it could no longer be relied upon by itself to secure the peace of the world.

That leads me to the second conclusion which I wish to suggest to your minds. Is it not apparent that the policy of sanctions involves, I do not say war, but a risk of war? Is it not apparent that that risk must increase in proportion to the effectiveness of the sanctions and also by reason of the incompleteness of the League? Is it not also apparent from what has happened that in the presence of such a risk nations cannot be relied upon to proceed to the last extremity of war unless their vital interests are threatened?

That being so, does it not suggest that it might be wise to explore the possibilities of localizing the danger spots of the world and trying to find a more practical method of securing peace by means of regional arrangements which could be approved by the League, but which should be guaranteed only by those nations whose interests were vitally connected with those danger zones? . . .

February 1938

In order that the House may have before it as complete a picture as possible of the events which have led up to the present situation, I must ask for their indulgence while I endeavor to state once again my own views upon certain aspects of foreign policy. . . .* On a former occasion I described that policy as being based upon three principles—first, on the protection of British interests and the lives of British nationals; secondly, on the maintenance of peace, and, as far as we can influence it, the settlement of differences by peaceful means and not by force; and, thirdly, the promotion of friendly relations with other nations who are willing to reciprocate our friendly feelings and who will keep those rules of international conduct without which there can be neither security nor stability.

It is not enough to lay down general principles. If we truly desire peace, it is, in my opinion, necessary to make a sustained effort to ascertain, and if possible remove, the causes which threaten peace and which now, for many months, have kept Europe in a state of tension and

---

* Chamberlain became prime minister in May 1937. He refers here to the resignation of Anthony Eden as foreign secretary in February 1938 in opposition to the government's conciliation of dictatorial states, specifically of Italy's intervention in Spain.

anxiety. . . . I cannot believe that, with a little good will and determination, it is not possible to remove genuine grievances and to clear away
suspicions which may be entirely unfounded.

For these reasons, then, my colleagues and I have been anxious to
find some opportunity of entering upon conversations with the two European countries with which we have been at variance, namely Germany
and Italy, in order that we might find out whether there was any common
ground on which we might build up a general scheme of appeasement in
Europe. . . .

The peace of Europe must depend upon the attitude of the four
major Powers—Germany, Italy, France, and ourselves. For ourselves, we
are linked to France by common ideals of democracy, of liberty and
Parliamentary government. . . . On the other side we find Italy and Germany linked by affinities of outlook and in the forms of their government. The question that we have to think of is this: Are we to allow
these two pairs of nations to go on glowering at one another across the
frontier . . . until at last the barriers are broken down and the conflict
begins which many think would mean the end of civilization? Or can we
bring them to an understanding of one another's aims and objects, and
to such discussion as may lead to a final settlement? If we can do that, if
we can bring these four nations into a friendly discussion, into a settling
of their differences, we shall have saved the peace of Europe for a generation. . . .

September 1938

I can well understand the reasons why the Czech Government have
felt unable to accept the terms which have been put before them in the
German memorandum. Yet I believe after my talks with Herr Hitler that,
if only time were allowed, it ought to be possible for the arrangements
for transferring the territory that the Czech Government has agreed to
give to Germany to be settled by agreement under conditions which
would assure fair treatment to the population concerned.

You know already that I have done all that one man can do to
compose this quarrel. After my visits to Germany I have realized vividly
how Herr Hitler feels that he must champion other Germans, and his
indignation that grievances have not been met before this. He told me
privately, and last night he repeated publicly, that after the Sudeten
German question is settled, that is the end of Germany's territorial claims
in Europe. . . .

However much we may sympathize with a small nation confronted by a big and powerful neighbor, we cannot in all circumstances undertake to involve the whole British Empire in war simply on her account. If we have to fight it must be on larger issues than that. I am myself a man of peace to the depths of my soul. Armed conflicts between nations is a nightmare to me; but if I were convinced that any nation had made up its mind to dominate the world by fear or its force, I should feel that it must be resisted. Under such a domination life for people who believe in liberty would not be worth living; but war is a fearful thing, and we must be very clear, before we embark on it, that it is really the great issues that are at stake, and that the call to risk everything in their defense, when all the consequences are weighed, is irresistible.*

Document 4.38

The League of Nations: The Situation in Europe

From a resolution of the Assembly, 29 September 1938

Representatives of forty-nine States meeting as delegates to the Assembly of the League of Nations have watched with deep and growing anxiety the development of the present grave situation in Europe.

The Assembly is convinced that the existing differences are capable of being solved by peaceful means. It knows that recourse to war, whatever be its outcome, is no guarantee of a just settlement and that it must inevitably bring untold suffering to millions of individuals, and imperil the whole structure of civilization in Europe.

The Assembly, therefore, voicing the prayer of the peoples of all countries, expresses the earnest hope that no Government will attempt to impose a settlement by force.

* Two days after this speech, Chamberlain met with Edouard Daladier of France, Benito Mussolini of Italy, and Adolf Hitler of Germany and concluded an accord on the fate of Czechslovakia. It was met with overwhelming approval in France and England, in the belief that, as Chamberlain said, "it is peace for our time."

5

World War II and Peace
1939–1945

War enveloped the world between 1939 and 1945. It was waged on the most massive scale in history by the total mobilization of many peoples. It was fought across the Eurasian land mass, on Pacific islands, on all the seas, and in the air. It was carried directly to civilian populations whose cities were razed by day and night. Violence burned its way around the globe, escalating from German blitzkrieg raids against Poland and France to American fire and atomic bombing of Japan.

The Second World War differed from the First not only in its scale and totality but also in its purpose, for it was fought against military aggression waged by dictatorial regimes and accompanied by the systematic genocide of the Holocaust. The World War I allies against Germany and Austria-Hungary had interpreted their opponents as autocrats and aggressors, but the voices of dissent were then much stronger than a generation later. If ever there was a justifiable cause for war (*jus ad bellum*), it was often said, then it was military resistance to Nazi and Japanese aggression.

This is not to say that World War II was a *simple* case of aggression, dictatorship, and atrocity. It was not. Totalitarianism existed outside the Nazi camp. Atrocities accompanied technological war on all sides. And it was widely believed that the war had resulted from diplomatic and moral failure by a generation of leaders from many nations.

As the Second World War drove home the terrible lesson of the first, it was accompanied by renewed attempts to secure peace. From 1939 to 1945 people brought varied ideas about peace to the problem of war. Some of them gave practical expressions to their commitment to total

283

nonviolence; some reexamined the standards of justifiable war in the light of weapons of indiscriminate destruction; many sought peace through social and economic security; and, at the highest levels, there were renewed efforts to establish international security. The four parts of this chapter document those approaches, through which historic ideals and understandings were given institutional form.

Absolute pacifists, those who repudiated violence on moral and religious grounds, had to reconcile their principles with the terrible reality of clear aggression. Many of them put into practice forms of nonviolent resistance that had been advocated before the war, as illustrated in the first part of the chapter. This approach was adopted by people in occupied countries and in Germany itself for the altogether practical reason that violent resistance was not viable there. To its idealism, therefore, nonviolence added a pragmatic agenda that anticipated proposals for the kinds of civilian-based defense and nonviolent activism that were developed in the second half of the twentieth century.

For religious and humanist peace advocates there was another dilemma: was *any* form of warfare against an aggressor acceptable, or should some restrictions be imposed to spare innocent people as much as possible, in the just war tradition of *jus in bello?* The Nazi slaughter of whole classes of people was clearly intolerable. But what about war from the air, in which fire and explosives were launched against civilians? The challenge of modern, indiscriminate warfare is documented in the second part of this chapter. With the advent of atomic bombs, the issue became acute. Leading nuclear physicists began a campaign to ban nuclear weapons, or at least subject them to international control, which slowly influenced policymaking in the postwar era.

Postwar policy was affected, too, by the belief that totalitarianism and militarism, colonialism and revolution were fueled by social, economic, and cultural insecurity. That perception, which had grown in the nineteenth century, had became especially strong in the interwar period. The anti-Hitler coalition was interpreted as a people's war, and there was a widespread opinion that not only should Nazi barbarism be defeated, but also that such social evils as inequality, undernourishment, poverty, cultural depravation, and the violation of human rights should be addressed in "the age of the common man." Expressions of hope for this kind of postwar peace are represented in the third part of this chapter.

The war against Germany, Italy, and Japan was conducted by imperial powers that spoke in the language of common humanity. Quite naturally, some peace activists concluded that the alliance should be transformed into an international order based on law and cooperation. This ancient ideal was expressed in the simple words "One World," and in a variety of practical proposals documented in the fourth part of the chapter. Suggestions ranged from regional groupings of nations to world government, but they had in common the idea that sovereign states would be accountable to larger collectives.

Some circles in the West considered regionalism as a kind of *cordon sanitaire* against a perceived Russian threat. Soviet leaders, justifiably worried about this strategy, were also concerned to maintain their own Great Power hegemony. Conflicts of national interest within the wartime alliance affected plans for a postwar security system in which the hegemony of the Great Powers was confirmed as a matter of political realism. Accordingly, although the United Nations had some characteristics of a world organization when it was founded in 1945, it also reflected the distribution of national power. The ancient idea of order imposed by a world authority was institutionalized as a confederation of nations in which preeminent influence was vested in the most powerful states. Subsequently the wartime ideal of peace was dimmed by postwar conflict between the Soviet Union and the other Great Powers—the Cold War. Although the United Nations and its related agencies were disrupted by that struggle, they embodied the idea and remained the potential instruments of collective social, economic, and political security.

Nonviolent Responses

With the escalation of World War II, the idea of nonviolence took on increasing significance, although for the most part it was removed from the daily news of military campaigns and civilian mobilization. Nonviolence offered an alternative to militarism. In a vivid reflection on a German air raid, for example, the British novelist Virginia Woolf evoked a sense of female—and human—powerlessness: true victory would overcome militarism itself, not simply defeat the German military machine (document 5.1). This would be a cause "more positive, reviving, healing and creative than the dull dread made of fear and hate." Similarly, A. J. Muste, a Dutch-born minister, labor organizer, and co-secretary of the American Fellowship of Reconciliation, urged pacifists to follow the example of Gandhi and to help the oppressed "develop a nonviolent technique" (document 5.2). Both of them insisted that the only victory worth seeking would be a just and humane peace.

Pacifists and other citizens faced the specific challenge of responding to the brutalities of war and dictatorship. Even within Nazi Germany, nonviolent direct action campaigns against fascist tyranny were conducted by courageous citizens. A small group of students in Munich, for example, launched a campaign designated as the White Rose. From the summer of 1942 to early 1943 they clandestinely distributed thousands of leaflets in several German and Austrian cities (document 5.3), in which they denounced the Nazi war and called upon Germans to engage in "passive resistance."

In countries occupied by the fascist powers, remarkable nonviolent actions complemented the broader, sometimes violent, work of organized resistance movements. Perhaps best known is the effort of the Swedish diplomat Raoul Wallenberg, who rescued some 100,000 Hungarian Jews about to be shipped off to Nazi death camps before he disappeared in Soviet Russia. His effort was unique in its scale, but countless other individuals defied Nazi repression by giving sanctuary to Jewish people. In occupied France, the pacifist minister André Trocmé secretly turned his town of Le Chambon into an important hiding place and way station for thousands of Jews and other refugees fleeing the Nazi terror. Deeply suspicious of him, the authorities placed Trocmé in a concentration camp and, when he was released, threatened him with death. He survived the war by going underground and expressing his pacifist principles in action (document 5.4). In this respect he epitomized an anonymous cadre of nonviolent resisters. Large numbers of them participated in the organized campaigns in occupied Norway (document 5.5) and Denmark.

Outside the war zone, nonviolent action was further developed to deal with oppression. In India, Gandhi launched another independence struggle, the "Quit India" campaign, to which the British government responded by jailing him and other leaders in the Indian National Congress. In the Civilian Public Service camps and in prisons of the United States, where some 18,000 conscientious objectors to military service were held, small groups undertook campaigns of nonviolent resistance against racial segregation, forced labor, and conscription itself. Another group of Americans experimented with nonviolent direct action against racial discrimination, forming a base for the civil rights movement of the 1950s.[1]

By the end of the war, nonviolent resistance to war and oppression had moved, largely unnoticed, from the realm of theory to a body of first-hand experience in numerous nations.

Document 5.1

Virginia Woolf: Thinking Peace into Existence

From "Thoughts on Peace in an Air Raid," 1940

The Germans were over this house last night and the night before that. Here they are again. It is a queer experience, lying in the dark and listening to the zoom of a hornet which may at any moment sting you to death. It is a sound that interrupts cool and consecutive thinking about peace. Yet it is a sound—far more than prayers and anthems—that should compel one to think about peace. Unless we can think peace into existence we—not this one body in this one bed but millions of bodies yet to be born—will lie in the same darkness and hear the same death rattle overhead. Let us think what we can do to create the only efficient air raid shelter while the guns on the hill go pop pop pop and the searchlights finger the clouds and now and then, sometimes close at hand, sometimes far away, a bomb drops. . . .

But to make ideas effective, we must be able to fire them off. We must put them into action. And the hornet in the sky rouses another hornet in the mind. There was one zooming in *The Times* this morning —a woman's voice saying, "Women have not a word to say in politics." There is no woman in the Cabinet; nor in any responsible post. All the idea-makers who are in a position to make ideas effective are men. That is a thought that damps thinking, and encourages irresponsibility. Why not bury the head in the pillow, plug the ears, and cease this futile activity of idea-making? Because there are other tables besides officer tables and conference tables. Are we not leaving the young Englishman without a weapon that might be of value to him if we give up private thinking, tea-table thinking, because it seems useless? Are we not stressing our disability because our ability exposes us perhaps to abuse, perhaps to contempt? "I will not cease from mental fight," Blake wrote. Mental fight means thinking against the current, not with it.

That current flows fast and furious. It issues in a spate of words from the loudspeakers and the politicians. Every day they tell us that we are a free people, fighting to defend freedom. That is the current that has whirled the young airman up into the sky and keeps him circling there among the clouds. Down here, with a roof to cover us and a gas mask handy, it is our business to puncture gas bags and discover seeds of truth. It is not true that we are free. We are both prisoners tonight—he boxed up in his machine with a gun handy; we lying in the dark with a gas mask handy. If we were free we should be out in the open, dancing, at the play, or sitting at the window talking together. What is it that prevents us? "Hitler!" the loudspeakers cry with one voice. Who is Hitler? What is he? Aggressiveness, tyranny, the insane love of power made manifest, they reply. Destroy that, and you will be free.

The drone of the planes is now like the sawing of a branch overhead. Round and round it goes, sawing and sawing at a branch directly above the house. Another sound begins sawing its way in the brain. "Women of ability"—it was Lady Astor speaking in *The Times* this morning— "are held down because of a subconscious Hitlerism in the hearts of men." Certainly we are held down. We are equally prisoners tonight— the Englishmen in their planes, the Englishwomen in their beds. But if he stops to think he may be killed; and we too. So let us think for him. Let us try to drag up into consciousness the subconscious Hitlerism that holds us down. It is the desire for aggression; the desire to dominate and enslave. Even in the darkness we can see that made visible. We can see shop windows blazing; and women gazing; painted women; dressed-up women; women with crimson lips and crimson fingernails. They are slaves who are trying to enslave. If we could free ourselves from slavery we should free men from tyranny. Hitlers are bred by slaves. . . .

The sound of sawing overhead has increased. All the searchlights are erect. They point at a spot exactly above this roof. At any moment a bomb may fall on this very room. One, two, three, four, five, six . . . the seconds pass. The bomb did not fall. But during those seconds of suspense all thinking stopped. All feeling, save one dull dread, ceased. A nail fixed the whole being to one hard board. The emotion of fear and of hate is therefore sterile, unfertile. Directly that fear passes, the mind reaches out and instinctively revives itself by trying to create. Since the room is dark it can create only from memory. It reaches out to the memory of other Augusts—in Bayreuth, listening to Wagner; in Rome, walking over the Campagna; in London. Friends' voices come back. Scraps of poetry return. Each of those thoughts, even in memory, was far more positive, reviving, healing and creative than the dull dread made of fear and hate. Therefore if we are to compensate the young man for the loss of his glory and of his gun, we must give him access to the creative feelings. We must make happiness. We must free him from the machine. We must bring him out of his prison into the open air. But what is the use of freeing the young Englishman if the young German and the young Italian remain slaves?

The searchlights, wavering across the flat, have picked up the plane now. From this window one can see a little silver insect turning and twisting in the light. The guns go pop pop pop. Then they cease. Probably the raider was brought down behind the hill. One of the pilots landed safe in a field near here the other day. He said to his captors, speaking fairly good English, "How glad I am that the fight is over!" Then an Englishman gave him a cigarette, and an Englishwoman made him a cup of tea. That would seem to show that if you can free the man from the machine, the seed does not fall upon altogether stony ground. The seed may be fertile.

Document 5.2

A. J. Muste: Pacifism in Wartime

From "The World Task of Pacifism," 1941

The movement to which alone men might turn with hope in the conviction that the journey into a new day had indeed begun, would need to have certain characteristics. It must be a movement which renounces war and organized violence of all kinds and which had made it clear beforehand that this was its stand. It must be a movement which renounced dictatorship, which summoned men to a life organized around the principle of cooperation and not of coercion or individualism. It must be a profoundly religious movement. For men will no longer be able to believe in the too simple and mechanical notion that if you will only set up a new system, all our problems will be solved. They will not really be able to believe that a new world is possible unless they can believe that new men can be created, that they themselves can be delivered from imprisonment in the self and become conscious of unity with the whole, united with God, with moral reality beyond themselves. They will need a faith that transforms and saves them, gives them eternal resources to live by and values to live for. . . .

A searching question immediately arises. Should the religious pacifist movement think of itself in these large terms as a mass movement for achieving social change by nonviolence? It seems to me increasingly clear that we can no longer evade the responsibility and the challenge. If we do seek to evade it, we shall no longer be able to believe in or respect ourselves. Either we believe our own words when we say that love, nonviolence, community form the basis on which all human association must be founded—and in that case we must do our utmost to achieve such an order . . .—or we do not really believe what we say. . . .

To put it another way, either we ought to resign from the world and abandon political activity altogether—quit voting, quit working against conscription laws or for provisions for conscientious objectors in draft laws, and the like—or else we must resolutely carry out the political task to its end, the organization of all life on true foundations and for worthy ends. . . .

But is not all this a fantastic kind of day dreaming? Is it even remotely possible that the religious pacifist forces, the Christian forces, should measure up to such a challenge? . . .

Several observations may be made in answer to that question. In the first place, the fact that we are now few and that the self-styled realists do not think that they need to take us into political consideration is not at all decisive. In the nature of the case, the revolutionary element remains small, little noticed unless it be to visit persecution upon it, so long as men still hope that the world can go on much as it has done or that they can wake up presently as from a nightmare and find themselves safe in the old bed . . . until the bankruptcy of the forces of the old order can no longer be hidden.

Secondly, we are appreciably stronger than we were a score of years ago, not only in numbers, but in intellectual comprehension and spiritual development. . . .

In the third place, every period of upheaval in history has revealed that there are men and women of great technical, organizing, administrative ability who cannot adjust themselves to a new order and who in one way or another sabotage it. There are, however, not a few such experts and technicians who have long known that the old order was thwarting them and stultifying them in the exercise of their abilities, and many who have no objection to placing their technical and other talents at the disposal of the forces of the new day. . . .

Fourthly, the Gandhi movement in India is giving the world an example of the use of nonviolence on a mass scale. Not only may we pacifists learn much from Gandhi and his followers in building a mass nonviolence movement in this and other Western countries, but we may hope that people generally in the Western world will be impressed by this oriental example, as the futility and waste of violence becomes more obvious. . . .

It may be fruitful to observe in passing those fundamental characteristics of the Gandhi movement which must also, I believe, mark the growing pacifist movement in the United States. First of all, it is a religious movement. It is based upon convictions about the very nature of life and the universe, convictions held not merely by the mind but by a moral commitment of the whole being to the practice of them. . . .

It is an economic and social movement. . . .

Gandhi's movement, finally, is a political movement. It expresses the determination of the masses of India to free themselves from the yoke of British imperialism without violence and without hatred for the oppressor. For our present purpose it is not necessary to elaborate this point except to observe that, in addition to developing mass resistance to war, a Western nonviolence movement must make effective contacts with oppressed and minority groups such as Negroes, share-croppers, industrial workers, and help them to develop a nonviolent technique. . . .

It seems clear to me that we must indeed do our utmost to remain in fellowship with our own countrymen and fellow-churchmen. We must seek to identify ourselves with their need and suffering. If community is temporarily broken, it must be they and not we who do the cutting off, and even then we must harbor no ill will and be on the look-out for opportunities to be helpful to them in simple human ways. It is also clear that we cannot engage in sabotaging the activities of our fellow-citizens who feel called to fight. We seek to wean our fellows from the desire to make war, not to interfere from without with their war-efforts or to destroy their property. . . .

I am, however, equally clear in feeling that in time of conscription and war, we cannot retire for practical purposes from political activity, from attempting to influence the nation's course, especially when there are still certain democratic channels available for doing so. The movement as a whole should not, it seems to me, become quietist and non-political. That might be merely an expression of an isolationist or escapist attitude, neither of which expresses the true spirit of community with our fellows.

For one thing, there will always be concrete issues on which we must speak or run the risk of being traitors to the truth. Civil liberties will be abridged; minorities may be persecuted; labor may be denied its rights and the masses may be made to bear an inordinate share of the costs of war. . . . Periodically, in a war situation, the question comes up as to whether an effort should be made to negotiate a peace or whether the war shall go on until our nation is in a position to dictate a peace. Periodically, the question of war aims or peace terms will or should be raised.

We have already pointed out a more fundamental reason why the pacifist movement cannot, save at peril to itself and mankind, retire from the arena of political discussion. In that arena the process of education and mis-education is going on all the time. Silence may contribute to it as well as speech. The extent to which the masses will have confidence in us . . . after the war will depend upon . . . whether by our analysis and interpretation of events we have demonstrated our intellectual capacity for leadership, our ability to see that war was futile before that became common knowledge, and our courage to speak the truth when it is unpleasant and dangerous to do so. . . .

Here I think we have put our fingers on what must be foremost and basic in our shaping of pacifist policy in time of crisis. Probably we are not all called upon to bear our witness in the same way. Some will be led to a more militant course, others to a quieter form of witness. The former must take especial pains to make sure their only motive is love; the latter that they are not unwittingly influenced by fear or a tendency to avoid difficult and complicated issues. All who have committed themselves to a way of love and nonviolence must remain in fellowship and unity with each other, not thinking of themselves as more orthodox or honest or useful pacifists than those who put the emphasis in a different place. . . .

The problem which confronts us at any moment is never: to what extent can we compromise with existing economic and political institutions, adapt ourselves to the demands of the world? Our problem always is to bring the state and other institutions of the world to adjust themselves to the demands of the Christ spirit, to the way of life which His truest followers incarnate, though in order to accomplish this we have no weapons but those of reason, love, humility, prayer, and willingness to die for our faith.

Document 5.3

The White Rose: Passive Resistance in Germany

From leaflets of The White Rose, 1942

The First Leaflet

Nothing is so unworthy of a civilized nation as allowing itself to be "governed" without opposition by an irresponsible clique that has yielded to base instinct. . . .

. . . If everyone waits until the other man makes a start, the messengers of avenging Nemesis will come steadily closer; then even the last victim will have been cast senselessly into the maw of the insatiable demon.* Therefore every individual, conscious of his responsibility as a

---

* Many leaders of the White Rose were arrested and executed by the Nazi regime, including initators Hans Scholl (1918–43), Sophie Scholl (1921–43), and Christoph Probst (1919–43).

member of Christian and Western civilization, must defend himself as best he can at this late hour, he must work against the scourges of mankind, against fascism and any similar system of totalitarianism. Offer passive resistance—*resistance*—wherever you may be, forestall the spread of this atheistic war machine before it is too late, before the last cities, like Cologne, have been reduced to rubble, and before the nation's last young man has given his blood. . . .

The Second Leaflet

We are not in a position to draw up a final judgment about the meaning of our history. But if this catastrophe can be used to further the public welfare, it will be only by virtue of the fact that we are cleansed by suffering; that we yearn for the light in the midst of deepest night, summon our strength, and finally help in shaking off the yoke which weighs on our world. . . .

. . . Why do the German people behave so apathetically in the face of all these abominable crimes, crimes so unworthy of the human race? Hardly anyone thinks about that. It is accepted as fact and put out of mind. The German people slumber on in their dull, stupid sleep and encourage these fascist criminals; they give them the opportunity to carry on the depredations; and of course they do so. Is this a sign that the Germans are brutalized in their simplest human feelings, that no chord within them cries out at the sight of such deeds, that they have sunk into a fatal consciencelessness from which they will never, never awake? It seems to be so, and will certainly be so, if the German does not at last start up out of his stupor, if he does not protest wherever and whenever he can against this clique of criminals, if he shows no sympathy for these hundreds of thousands of victims. He must evidence not only sympathy; no, much more: a sense of *complicity* in guilt. For through his apathetic behavior he gives these evil men the opportunity to act as they do. . . . It is not too late, however, to do away with this most reprehensible of all miscarriages of government, so as to avoid being burdened with even greater guilt. . . .

The Third Leaflet

Many, perhaps most, of the readers of these leaflets do not see clearly how they can practice an effective opposition. They do not see any avenues open to them. We want to try to show them that everyone is in a position to contribute to the overthrow of this system. . . . [It] can be done only by the cooperation of many convinced, energetic people—

people who are agreed as to the means they must use to attain their goal. We have no great number of choices as to these means. The only one available is *passive resistance*. The meaning and the goal of passive resistance is to topple National Socialism, and in this struggle we must not recoil from any course. . . . We must soon bring this monster of a state to an end. A victory of fascist Germany in this war would have immeasurable, frightful consequences. The military victory over Bolshevism dare not become the primary concern of the Germans. The defeat of the Nazis must *unconditionally* be the first order of business. . . .

Sabotage in armament plants and war industries, sabotage at all gatherings, rallies, public ceremonies, and organizations of the National Socialist Party. Obstruction of the smooth functioning of the war machine (a machine for war that goes on solely to shore up and perpetuate the National Socialist Party and its dictatorship). *Sabotage* in all the areas of science and scholarship which further the continuation of the war—whether in universities, technical schools, laboratories, research institutes, or technical bureaus. *Sabotage* in all cultural institutions which could potentially enhance the "prestige" of the fascists among the people. *Sabotage* in all branches of the arts which have even the slightest dependence on National Socialism or render it service. *Sabotage* in all publications, all newspapers, that are in the pay of the "government" and . . . aid in disseminating the brown lie. Do not give a penny to public drives . . . . Do not contribute to the collections of metal, textiles, and the like. Try to convince all your acquaintances, including those in the lower social classes, of the senselessness of continuing, of the hopelessness of this war; of our spiritual and economic enslavement at the hands of the National Socialists; of the destruction of all moral and religious values; and urge them to *passive resistance!*

Document 5.4

André Trocmé: Moral Resistance in France

From "A Note about My Attitude in Time of War,"
5 September 1939

Today, I am again disposed to serve my country, with all my strength, as long as it does not ask of me that which God refutes: collaboration in a war.

I have tried, like so many others, to imagine collaboration in another form: like stretcher-bearer, chaplain, or nurse. Each time I have been stopped by my conscience. The Army is a single entity. If war is at certain times just and necessary, if God allows it, I will better be a soldier . . . in order to serve as best I can a good cause.

But if war, as I believe, is never desirable, nor permitted by God, then I am constrained to not serve on the front or behind the lines. . . .

I have none of the pride of a revolutionary. . . . I am not a fanatic. I have never had visions. All is in place in my life and in my head. . . .

I don't believe that I am better than others. Like everyone, I have a part of the responsibility in the war. I do not excuse Hitler. He is precisely the incarnation of the Evil I detest. I don't accuse Daladier or Chamberlain, because I don't know what I would have done in their places. . . .

I do not wish to remain in the rear, in security. I ask only to be able to serve, in danger, the most pitiable victims of the war: the women and children from bombed-out towns.* I ask that this service be of a strictly civilian nature.

Document 5.5

Diderich Lund: Nonviolent Resistance in Norway

From *Resistance in Norway*, 1945

When the tide of destruction flowed over us the stand of the Norwegian pacifists was, on the whole, good.† Many took up the fight against injustice. The Chairman of the War Resisters' International, Olaf Kullman, was soon imprisoned. . . . When he was sent to the huge Concentration Camp of Oranienburg, near Berlin, we lost touch with him, and we do not know how he died there in 1942. Many other members of the W.R.I. are to-day in prison in Norway, or in Germany; some have been, or are perhaps, undergoing torture. Thousands of unknown persons spread over the whole country, who have been influenced by pacifist teaching, have courageously taken up the struggle in one or other of the many forms in which it has been carried on. The result has been varied:

---

* Trocmé initially asked the International Red Cross to support his humanitarian service; rejected, he embarked on his independent, dangerous career.

† Lund was active in the prewar Norwegian WRI group and headed the pacifist wing of the resistance movement in wartime. To elude imminent capture by the Nazis, he escaped to Sweden in 1944; the next year he returned to liberated Norway to help supervise reconstruction efforts.

for most, prison and suffering; for all, certainly a sure conviction that our struggle was the one which gives lasting victory.

None of our members have gone into Quisling's service.* But it cannot be denied that very many have interpreted pacifism as a lazy passive acceptance of the evil power of force without active resistance. They have not understood that it demands a burning, fearless struggle with all appropriate weapons for the worth of man, for truth and for goodness. Some have certainly given up pure pacifism and taken part in the active struggle with outward weapons. . . .

Attitude to the Military Struggle

A few days after Germany attacked us Norway declared war. In a military sense the war in Norway did not effect much, yet it had some significance. If there had been a stronger and more conscious pacifist conviction in Norway we could have achieved the same, or more, by crippling communications, and by refusing every kind of work for the Germans, especially building fortifications. It would have meant great sacrifices and have cost life, but perhaps not more than the war. As it was, we had the feeling that the military struggle was the only way in which we could express our united will to oppose the aggressors. . . .

Our pacifist conviction was not, as already stated, strong enough, or widely enough accepted, to carry through the ideal form of struggle. In these circumstances it seemed to me then, and still seems, to have been a more honest and right answer to the attack by an evil power, for the nation to take up the military struggle, and it would have been cowardly to have tried to avoid resistance. This last has in any case nothing to do with real pacifism. A pacifist's attitude to military struggle is that he accepts and recognizes it as an honest answer to a devilish attack. . . . The pacifist who does not take part in the struggle with outward weapon has, therefore, all the more a duty to take part in other forms of struggle. . . .

Our Attitude to the Two Power Groups

In the above I have used the expression "evil powers" for the Nazis and those who helped them in whatever way. It is necessary to be clear on this point. In every war it has been, up to now, the pacifists' attitude to avoid taking the part of either side. One has been prepared to see the

* Vidkun Quisling (1887–1945) was a puppet administrator for the German regime and recuited his countrymen on its behalf.

complexity of interrelated causes which lie behind a conflict and have created the grounds for the struggle. Even the outbreak of war one has looked upon as almost accidental, but an inevitable consequence of economic or psychological factors. Seen from this point of view we have the feeling that we all bear some part of the blame. It becomes, at a glance, impossible to say who has most.

This point of view is, at least, partly correct. It is always our duty and our right to use all our capacities to understand as clearly as possible what is really going on. . . . We must take care, however, that this does not lead us to unconcern for evil behavior, for a dangerous ideology, if we find it in an individual or in a group, among our own people or among others. We must also guard against a sentimental or unrealistic attitude which all too often has been characteristic of so-called pacifism. On the contrary, it must be the very basis of our attitude that there are both evil and good forces in the world and that evil must be destroyed without compromise.

In this case, what is our position? Fascism, Nazism and the Japanese ideology use in their "social technique" . . . methods which we pacifists must fight against as vigorously as possible. They use every means to break the independent personality and smother spiritual consciousness. Social justice with equality before the law is not found, or is only for limited groups and is, in fact, an illusion. Only in the economic sphere is there shown a certain attempt to put the common good before individual interests, but even here it is somewhat of a caricature. . . . For the Axis Powers, spiritual terror and suppression by force of political opponents are recognized as regular principles in their ideology. Their aggressive attitude towards others . . . forces us all to oppose, to struggle, even while we pacifists seek to carry it through without weapons. . . .

Economic Co-operation with the Germans during the Occupation

When the military forces in Norway had capitulated to the Germans we were faced with the question as to what attitude we should take in relation to the resistance. Should every form of co-operation be refused and no work be done for them; should a general strike be declared and economic chaos be created? . . . The great majority were not prepared, nor were they willing, to make the sacrifices which such a method would have demanded, and there was, therefore, nothing to do but accept economic co-operation. . . .

It is a dark page in our history, and it would not have been written in this way if a strong pacifism had taken deep root among us.

Resistance to Violence

Neither in the military nor in the economic field was a serious struggle made against the Germans, but it was the more vigorous in other respects. In legal circles, in the administration, in the schools, Church and press, in theatrical and musical life, among athletes and trade and professional organizations, in fact on all sides of the cultural life, resistance is strong and usual. It was soon shown that where the struggle was taken up whole-heartedly with intelligence and with a readiness to sacrifice, it was possible to carry it through to complete victory. The Germans were helpless in the face of serious resistance. In most of these areas of public life the struggle was carried through *openly*, and where this was the case the results were the best. Nothing woke such enthusiasm as the teachers' and the Church's fearless and open resistance, and there was certainly no better witness for our cause among the Germans. In some cases we felt ourselves forced to work in secret, as, for example, in spreading information, and in the support of our comrades in the struggle and their dependents. I am sure that even here we could have achieved greater results with a more open resistance. By this means we should also have had a large circle taking part. . . .

There are obviously a number of situations in which a secret struggle was absolutely necessary. When it came to rescuing the prosecuted, for example the Jews, and bringing them to safety, it is impossible to see how the organization could work openly. It was not just a question of going into the breach ourselves, it was the welfare and lives of others which were at stake.

Sabotage

Sabotage in its active form, such as the destruction of factories and other works, . . . must be regarded, more or less, as part of the military struggle. It has been carried on to a considerable extent in Norway. We pacifists have not found it to be a form of struggle in which we felt at home. On the other hand we have gone in for the form of sabotage in factories or the administration which hinders, stops or makes impossible the Germans' war effort or their other attempts to suppress us. . . . Sabotage is fundamentally a secondary weapon. If one cannot achieve open opposition or circumstances make it impossible, then sabotage can be a last resort.

Our Attitude to the Germans

Our attitude to the Germans is determined on the one hand by our hatred of the brutality, the inhuman gruesomeness which they daily practise on us and others, a hatred of their whole political and ideological system. On the other hand, our attitude is determined by our understanding of the fact that we have not the right to make the individual responsible for all the actions done in the name of the system. We know that there are many Germans, both military and civilian, who have been responsible for the worst of crimes. They must be punished in the way which is the healthiest for our society and for themselves. But it was also obvious to everyone in Norway who used their intelligence that there were thousands of German soldiers who were in reality opponents of the system. One . . . understood that they felt themselves powerless in the grip of a demonic force. . . .

The average Norwegian usually adopts a cold, hostile attitude towards the Germans he accidentally meets. This is often the only way he can find to show his dislike of the system which the German represents. Unfortunately the same Norwegian is often all too willing at the same time to obey the German's orders which results in assistance to the German war effort. I am, therefore, prepared to suggest: More friendliness towards the individual German and less obedience in face of him and his régime.

The Meaning of Mass Destruction

World War II was the most destructive war in history, primarily because of the impact of science and technology. Earlier breakthroughs in weaponry were surpassed by new techniques of mass slaughter, often involving the widespread destruction of civilians. Typical of military developments were those in aerial bombardment. During the Spanish Civil War the bombing of noncombatants was still uncommon enough to be regarded as a sign of fascist barbarism, a view portrayed in Pablo Picasso's *Guernica*.[2] Only a few years afterward, democracies as well as dictatorships made the practice routine, sending off daily air armadas to blast enemy or occupied cities into charred rubble. The toll in human lives mounted to a terrible sixty million dead and many more wounded or crippled, most of them civilians.

This slide into mass destruction was epitomized by the development and use of the atomic bomb. All major powers initiated atomic bomb projects, but only the Anglo-American venture—the Manhattan project —had sufficient resources to reach fruition. Although the scientists who initiated the project regarded the bomb as a deterrent to Nazi atomic attack, Allied leaders did not hesitate to use it twice without warning against a largely defeated Japan. Their action was supported by overwhelming majorities of American, British, Canadian, and French citizens in the belief that it had shortened the war.

Nevertheless, the new levels of mass destruction did draw sharp, although not widespread, criticism. Absolute pacifists, in particular, condemned aerial bombardment of cities. Perhaps the best-known critic of saturation bombing during the war was the English writer and lecturer Vera Brittain. Horrified by World War I, in which she served as a nurse, Brittain had supported the League of Nations Union and, after becoming a pacifist in 1936, the Peace Pledge Union. Her autobiographical best-seller, *Testament of Youth* (1933), did much to popularize the cause of peace. Her critique of bombing, *Massacre by Bombing,* aroused public controversy in the United States, where it was distributed in article and pamphlet form; in contrast, its British version, *Seed of Chaos* (document 5.6), was studiously ignored.

Meanwhile, within the narrow circles that knew of the Manhattan project, concerned scientists began to warn of the dangers of nuclear weapons. The Danish physicist Niels Bohr tried to persuade Allied leaders in Great Britain and the United States that international agreement was necessary to prevent a postwar arms race. A group of Manhattan Project scientists in Chicago warned the government in June 1945 about the postwar dangers of atomic power and tried to head off the use of atomic bombs against Japan. Although they all responded to moral considerations, they emphasized practical concerns (document 5.7).

Surmising that the bomb was about to be tested and that government officials would use it, the physicist Leo Szilard persuaded scientists at the Chicago laboratory to sign a petition in opposition (document 5.8). A similar document was circulated among Oak Ridge scientists. Elsewhere petitions were blocked by Army officials, who also saw to it that they did not reach the president until after the bombings of 6 and 9 August.

On the night after Hiroshima was leveled, Norman Cousins, the young American editor of the *Saturday Review* and a strong supporter of the war effort, wrote what became his most famous editorial, "Modern Man is Obsolete" (document 5.9). Arguing that nuclear weapons had made modern war suicidal, Cousins insisted that human survival could be assured only by drastic changes in international behavior—in particular, the establishment of world government. The statement reflected a growing feeling that there would be "one world or none." It became the most widely quoted editorial of its time, and Cousins emerged as an influential critic of nuclear weapons and a leading advocate of world federation.

The advent of nuclear weapons infinitely raised the stakes of modern war and dramatized questions raised earlier by the saturation bombing of civilians with conventional weapons: Even granting a justifiable cause, is it possible any longer to wage warfare within moral or practical bounds? If war has become total, in its mobilization and destruction of populations, is there an alternative to total peace? What is the meaning of mass destruction for the tradition of justified war?

Document 5.6

Vera Brittain: Seed of Chaos

From *Seed of Chaos: What Mass Bombing Really Means*, 1944

The purpose of this book is to inquire how far the British people understand and approve of the policy of "obliteration bombing" now being inflicted upon the civilians of enemy and enemy-occupied countries (including numbers of young children born since the outbreak of war) by ourselves and the United States. The propagandist press descriptions of this bombing and its results skilfully conceal their real meaning from the normally unimaginative reader by such carefully chosen phrases as "softening-up" an area, "neutralizing the target," "area bombing," "saturating the defences," and "blanketing an industrial district."

Up to the summer of 1943 the short paragraphs which gave more factual descriptions of our raids and their consequences were apt to appear in small print on the back pages of newspapers or at the foot of main columns. Since that time one or two newspapers . . . have begun to report R.A.F. [Royal Air Force] bombing in a franker and more conspicuous fashion, and even to carry special articles by air experts or pilots, while the gigantic raids on Berlin which began in November, 1943, were apparently treated as gala occasions on which the whole Press was permitted to let itself go. But it is only when the facts are collected, and the terrible sum of suffering which they describe is estimated as a whole, that we realize that, owing to the R.A.F. raids, thousands of helpless and innocent people in German, Italian, and German-occupied cities are being subjected to agonizing forms of death and injury comparable to the worst tortures of the Middle Ages.

From the extreme discomfort of this realization, the British citizen seeks to escape by two main arguments. In the first place, he maintains, mass bombing will "shorten the war"—a contention now much favored by ministers, officials, members of Parliament, and some leading churchmen.

In reply it can justly be stated, *first,* that there is no *certainty* that such a shortening of the war will result; and that nothing less than absolute certainty entitles even the most ardent of the war's supporters to use these dreadful expedients.*

... What does appear certain is the downward spiral in moral values, ending in the deepest abysses of the human spirit, to which this argument leads. Those who remember the first Great War will recall that precisely the same excuse—that it would "shorten" the period of hostilities—was given by the Germans for their policy of *Schrecklichkeit* (terror), and was used in connection with their submarine campaign. We ourselves refused to accept the argument as valid when the Nazis revived it in this war to justify the bombing of Warsaw, Rotterdam, Belgrade, London and Coventry.

Secondly, when the word "shorten" is used, it generally implies the limiting or reduction of the total amount of human suffering and destruction. Such a time test or standard is misleading. In a vast, concentrated raid, lasting a few minutes, more persons may be killed or injured than in a modern major battle lasting two or three weeks, in addition to the destruction of an irreplaceable cultural heritage of monuments, art treasures and documents, representing centuries of man's creative endeavor. In fact, the mass bombing of great centers of population means *a speed-up of human slaughter, misery and material destruction superimposed on that of the military fighting fronts.*

Thirdly, the "experiment" has demonstrated, so far, that mass bombing does not induce revolt or break morale. The victims are stunned, exhausted, apathetic, absorbed in the immediate tasks of finding food and shelter. But when they recover, who can doubt that there will be, among the majority at any rate, the desire for revenge and a hardening process, even if, for a time, it may be subdued by fear? ...

The second main argument brought forward to excuse our present policy of obliteration bombing is that we too have suffered—as indeed

---

* Postwar analyses conducted by the Royal Air Force and U.S. Air Force led to the conclusion that air raids against civilian targets had *not* shortened the war, either by destroying war-making capacity or by demoralizing the population.

we have—and that therefore we are fully entitled to pay back what we have endured. . . .

There are three . . . replies which should . . . be carefully considered by all rational people.

In the first place, investigations into the origins of *civilian* bombing far from the fighting lines (as distinct from the bombing which forms part of a military campaign) makes clear the difficulty of justly assessing with whom lay the fault of starting it. The cumulative growth of civilian bombing to its present nightmare stage seems on present information to be an outstanding instance of the tragic fashion in which war-time cruelty grows like a snowball by its own momentum once the power of Juggernaut has taken control. Some accidental violation of international law, assumed to be deliberate, is repaid by a reprisal "in kind." The enemy "hits back"; we retaliate harder still. . . . So the grim competition goes on, until the mass-murder of civilians becomes part of our policy— a descent into barbarism which we should have contemplated with horror in 1939.

Secondly, it is a fact . . . that though parts of Britain suffered cruelly in the "blitz," some of the terrible inventions and tactics now being used were not known or practised at that stage of the war. Even in those early days, the knowledge of our distress and confusion was limited to areas which endured them, and particularly to the surviving victims and to civil defence and rescue workers, who had actually to deal with the shambles to which German bombs reduced many humble homes. It is, I believe, the comparative study of first-hand experience among the majority of the British people which accounts for their supine acquiescence in obliteration bombing as a policy.

My own experience is relatively small, but as a Londoner who has been through about 600 raid periods and has spent 18 months as a volunteer fireguard, I have seen and heard enough to know that I must vehemently protest when this obscenity of terror and mutilation is inflicted upon the helpless civilians of another country. Nor do I believe that the majority of our airmen who are persuaded that mass bombing reduces the period of their peril really want to preserve their own lives by sacrificing German women and babies, any more than our soldiers would go into action using "enemy" mothers and children as a screen.

In the third place, retaliation "in kind" and worse means the reduction of ourselves to the level of our opponents, whose perverted values have induced us to fight. However anxious we may be to win the war, the way in which we win it will also determine our future standing as a nation. If we imitate and intensify the enemy's methods, we shall actually have been defeated by the very evils which we believe ourselves to be fighting.

Document 5.7

The Franck Committee: Report on the Atomic Bomb

From James Franck et al., "A Report to the Secretary of War," June 1945*

. . . The scientists on this project do not presume to speak authoritatively on problems of national and international policy. However, we found ourselves, by the force of events during the last five years, in the position of a small group of citizens cognizant of a grave danger for the safety of this country as well as for the future of all other nations, of which the rest of mankind is unaware. . . .

In the past, science has often been able to . . . provide new methods of protection against new weapons of aggression it made possible, but it cannot promise such efficient protection against the destructive use of nuclear power. This protection can come only from the political organization of the world. . . .

The development of nuclear power not only constitutes an important addition to the technological and military power of the United States, but also creates grave political and economic problems for the future of this country.

Nuclear bombs cannot possible remain a "secret weapon" at the exclusive disposal of this country for more than a few years. The scientific facts on which their construction is based are well known to scientists of other countries. Unless an effective international control of nuclear explosives is instituted, a race for nuclear armaments is certain to ensue following the first revelation of our possession of nuclear weapons to the world. . . . In the war to which such an armaments race is likely to lead, the United States, with its agglomeration of population and industry in comparatively few metropolitan districts, will be at a disadvantage compared to nations whose population and industry are scattered over large areas.

---

* This report was produced by a committee chaired by James Franck, a distinguished chemist who had resigned his German university post rather than serve under fascism, and was written largely by Eugene Rabinowitch, a Soviet emigré biophysicist.

We believe that these considerations make the use of nuclear bombs for an early unannounced attack against Japan inadvisable. If the United States were to be the first to release this new means of indiscriminate destruction upon mankind, she would sacrifice public support throughout the world, precipitate the race for armaments, and prejudice the possibility of reaching an international agreement on the future control of such weapons.

Much more favorable conditions for the eventual achievement of such an agreement could be created if nuclear bombs were first revealed to the world by a demonstration in an appropriately selected uninhabited area.

In case chances for the establishment of an effective international control of nuclear weapons should have to be considered slight at the present time, then not only the use of these weapons against Japan but even their early demonstration may be contrary to the interests of this country. A postponement of such a demonstration will have in this case the advantage of delaying the beginning of the nuclear armaments race as long as possible.

If the government should decide in favor of an early demonstration of nuclear weapons, it will then have the possibility of taking into account the public opinion of this country and of the other nations before deciding whether these weapons should be used against Japan. In this way, other nations may assume a share of responsibility for such a fateful decision.

Document 5.8

Leo Szilard: A Petition Against the Atomic Bomb

From "A Petition to the President of the United States,"
17 July 1945

Discoveries of which the people of the United States are not aware may affect the welfare of this nation in the near future. The liberation of atomic power which has been achieved places atomic bombs in the hands of the Army. It places in your hands, as Commander-in-Chief, the fateful decision whether or not to sanction the use of such bombs in the present phase of the war against Japan.

We, the undersigned scientists, have been working in the field of atomic power. Until recently we have had to fear that the United States might be attacked by atomic bombs during this war and that her only defense might lie in a counterattack by the same means. Today, with the defeat of Germany, this danger is averted and we feel impelled to say what follows:

The war has to be brought speedily to a successful conclusion and attacks by atomic bombs may very well be an effective method of warfare. We feel, however, that such attacks on Japan could not be justified, at least not unless the terms which will be imposed after the war on Japan were made public in detail and Japan were given an opportunity to surrender.

If such public announcement gave assurance to the Japanese that they could look forward to a life devoted to peaceful pursuits in their homeland and if Japan still refused to surrender, our nation might then, in certain circumstances, find itself forced to resort to the use of atomic bombs. Such a step, however, ought not to be made at any time without seriously considering the moral responsibilities which are involved.

The development of atomic power will provide the nations with new means of destruction. The atomic bombs at our disposal represent only the first step in this direction and there is almost no limit to the destructive power which will become available in the course of their future development. Thus a nation which sets the precedent of using these newly liberated forces of nature for purposes of destruction may have to bear the responsibility of opening the door to an era of devastation on an unimaginable scale.

If after this war a situation is allowed to develop in the world which permits rival powers to be in uncontrolled possession of these new means of destruction, the cities of the United States as well as the cities of other nations will be in continuous danger of sudden annihilation. All the resources of the United States, moral and material, may have to be mobilized to prevent the advent of such a world situation. Its prevention is at present the solemn responsibility of the United States—singled out by virtue of her lead in the field of atomic power.

The added material strength which this lead gives to the United States brings with it the obligation of restraint, and if we were to violate this obligation our moral position would be weakened in the eyes of the world and in our own eyes. It would then be more difficult for us to live up to our responsibility of bringing the unloosened forces of destruction under control.

In view of the foregoing, we, the undersigned, respectfully petition: first, that you exercise your power as Commander-in-Chief to rule that the United States shall not resort to the use of atomic bombs in this war unless the terms which will be imposed upon Japan have been made public in detail and Japan, knowing these terms, has refused to surrender; second, that in such an event the question whether or not to use atomic bombs be decided by you in the light of the considerations presented in this petition as well as all the other moral responsibilities which are involved.

Document 5.9

Norman Cousins: War Is Obsolete

From "Modern Man Is Obsolete," 18 August 1945

Whatever elation there is in the world today because of final victory in the war is severely tempered by fear. It is a primitive fear, the fear of the unknown, the fear of forces man can neither channel nor comprehend. This fear is not new; in its classical form it is the fear of irrational death. But overnight it has become intensified, magnified. It has burst out of the subconscious and into the conscious, filling the mind with primordial apprehensions. It is thus that man stumbles fitfully into a new age of atomic energy for which he is as ill equipped to accept its potential blessings as he is to counteract or control its present dangers. . . .

. . . On August 6, 1945, a new age was born. When on that day a parachute containing a small object floated to earth over Japan, it marked the violent death of one stage in man's history and the beginning of another. Nor should it be necessary to prove the saturating effect of the new age, permeating every aspect of man's activities, from machines to morals, from physics to philosophy, from politics to poetry; in sum, it is an effect creating a blanket of obsolescence not only over the methods and the products of man but over man himself. . . .

In the most primitive sense, war in man is an expression of his competitive impulses. Like everything else in nature, he has had to fight for existence; but the battle against other animals, once won, gave way in his evolution to battle against his own kind. . . .

What does it matter, then, if war is not in the nature of man so long as man continues through the expression of his nature to be a viciously competitive animal? The effect is the same, and therefore the result must be as conclusive—war being the effect, and complete obliteration of the human species being the result.

If this reasoning is correct, then modern man is obsolete, a self-made anachronism becoming more incongruous by the minute. He has exalted change in everything but himself. He has leaped centuries ahead in inventing a new world to live in, but he knows little or nothing about his own part in that world. He has surrounded and confounded himself with gaps—gaps between revolutionary science and evolutionary anthropology, between cosmic gadgets and human wisdom, between intellect and conscience. . . . Given time, man might be expected to bridge those gaps normally; but by his own hand, he is destroying even time. Communication, transportation, war no longer wait on time. Decision and execution in the modern world are becoming virtually synchronous. Thus, whatever bridges man has to build and cross he shall have to build and cross immediately. . . .

Man is left, then, with a crisis in decision. The main test before him involves his will to change rather than his ability to change. That he is capable of change is certain. For there is no more mutable or adaptable animal in the world. We have seen him migrate from one extreme clime to another. We have seen him step out of backward societies and join advanced groups. . . . Once the instinct for survival is stimulated, the basic condition for change can be met.

That is why the quintessence of destruction as potentially represented by modern science must be dramatized and kept in the forefront of public opinion. The full dimensions of the peril must be seen and recognized. Then and only then will man . . . be prepared to make the decisions necessary to assure that survival. . . .

The first adjustment or mutation needed . . . is his savage competitive impulses. In the pre-Atomic Age, those impulses were natural and occasionally justifiable, though they often led to war. But the rise of materialistic man had reasons behind it and must be viewed against . . . an insufficiency of the goods and the needs of life. From Biblical history right up through the present, there was never time when starvation and economic suffering were not acute somewhere in the world.

This is only part of the story, of course, for it is dangerous to apply an economic interpretation indiscriminately to all history. Politics, religion, force for force's sake, jealousy, ambition, love of conquest, love of reform—all these and others have figured in the equations of history and war. But the economic factor was seldom if ever absent, even when it was not the prime mover. . . .

Yet all this has been—or can be—changed by the new age. Man now has it within his grasp to emancipate himself economically. If he wills it, he is in a position to refine his competitive impulse; he can take the step from competitive man to cooperative man. He has at last unlocked enough of the earth's secrets to provide for his needs on a world scale. . . . There is power enough and resources enough for all.

It is here that man's survey of himself needs the severest scrutiny, for he is his own greatest obstacle to the achievement of those attainable and necessary goals. While he is willing to mobilize all his scientific and intellectual energies for purposes of death, he is unwilling to undertake any comparable mobilization for purposes of life. . . .

We have saved for last the most crucial aspect . . . : the transformation or adjustment from national man to world man. Already he has become a world warrior; it is but one additional step—though a long one—for him to develop a world conscience. This is not vaporous idealism, but sheer driving necessity. It bears directly on the prospects of his own survival. He shall have to recognize the flat truth that the greatest obsolescence of all in the Atomic Age is national sovereignty. Even back in the old-fashioned rocket age before August 6, 1945, strict national sovereignty was an anomalous and preposterous hold-over from the tribal instinct in nations. If it was anomalous then, it is the quintessence of anomaly now. The world is a geographic entity. This is not only the basic requisite for world government but the basic reason behind the need. A common ground of destiny is not too large a site for the founding of any community.

Reject all other arguments for *real* world government—reject the economic, the ideological, the sociological, the humanitarian arguments, valid though they may be. Consider only the towering problem of policing the atom—the problem of keeping the smallest particle of matter from destroying all matter. . . . In all history, there is not a single instance of a new weapon being kept exclusively by any power or powers; sooner or later either the basic principles become generally known or parallel devices are invented. Before long, the atomic bomb will follow the jet plane, the rocket bomb, radar, and the flame thrower into general circulation. . . .

Nor can we rely on destructive atomic energy to take care of itself. Already there is the tempting but dangerous notion to the effect that the atomic bomb is so horrible and the terror of retaliation so great that we may have seen the last great war. . . .

Far from banishing war, the atomic bomb will in itself constitute a cause of war. In the absence of world control as part of world government, it will create universal fear and suspicion. Each nation will live nervously from one moment to the next, not knowing whether the designs or ambitions of other nations might prompt them to attempt a lightening blow of obliteration. . . .

There is no need to discuss the historical reasons pointing to and arguing for world government. There is no need to talk of the difficulties in the way of world government. There is need only to ask whether we can afford to do without it. All other considerations become either secondary or inconsequential.

It would be comforting to know that the world had several generations in which it might be able to evolve naturally and progressively into a single governmental unit. . . . But the time factor has been shattered. We no longer have a leeway of fifteen or twenty years; whatever must be done must be done with an immediacy which is in keeping with the urgency. . . .

In meeting this need, man need not be frightened by the enormity of the difference which shall have to be accommodated within the world structure. . . .

. . . The differences [among peoples] point up the problem, not the problem the differences. The important question is not how great an obstacle the differences may be to the setting up of a closely knit world structure, but whether man will be in a better position to reconcile those differences within world government than without it.

Man must decide, moreover, what is more important—his differences or his similarities. If he chooses the former, he embarks on a path that will, paradoxically, destroy the differences and himself as well. If he chooses the latter, he shows a willingness to meet the responsibilities that go with maturity and conscience. . . .

True, in making the jump to world government, man is taking a big chance. Not only does he have to create the first world authority, but he shall have to make sure that this authority is wisely used. The world institution must be compatible with—indeed, must promote—free institutions. This challenge is not less important than the challenge to establish world government itself, for all through history there has been too great a contradiction between ideals and institutions and the forces which have taken over those ideals and institutions. . . .

That is the double nature of the challenge: to bring about world government and to keep it pure. It is a large order, perhaps the largest order man has had to meet in his 50,000-odd years on earth, but he himself has set up the conditions which have made the order necessary.

Social and Economic Security

The belief that peace requires orderly change to deal with economic and social disparities was developed further during World War II. The conviction grew that, with the defeat of the Axis powers, reactionary governments and institutions should be replaced by democratic ones, and that national security should be supplemented by fairness and protection for both sexes, and all races, groups, and classes. The declaration by Laurence Housman, then chair of the War Resisters' International, typified this view: "If we are not of a mind to abolish the injustices and inequalities of [the interwar] social system, neither are we of a mind— nor shall we be able, however victorious—to abolish war."[3]

Even before the United States entered the war, President Roosevelt identified the universal "Four Freedoms": freedom of speech and expression, freedom of worship, freedom from want, and freedom from fear.[4] After the nation became a belligerent, Vice President Henry A. Wallace called for a "century of the common man." The "freedom loving people" were on the march, he proclaimed. They would "smoke the Hitler stooges out" and "manifest here on earth the dignity that is in every human soul" (document 5.10). The black historian and activist W. E. B. Du Bois attacked economic as well as political colonialism throughout the war. On an official visit to Haiti in the summer of 1944, he called for non-European leadership in a global campaign to eliminate colonialism and poverty (document 5.11).

Peace as economic, social, and cultural security—elements of this idea were institutionalized on an historic scale during World War II with programs undertaken in the name of the wartime alliance, the United Nations. In the spring of 1943, the United States invited representatives of forty-four governments to Hot Springs, Virginia, to consider united action in the fields of food and agriculture. The result was the United Nations Food and Agriculture Organization, which was charged to lay foundations for improved standards of nutrition and conditions of economic stability to help prevent future wars (document 5.12). A week later the United States circulated among its allies a draft charter for the formation of the United Nations Relief and Rehabilitation Agency (UNRRA) to relieve liberated areas and help them reestablish economic productivity. Herbert A. Lehman, a former businessman and governor of New York, was elected the first director-general of UNRRA on November 11, 1943. He expressed the principles of coordinated international relief coupled with self-help by the recipients, of freedom balanced with regulation, of the mutual interests of producers and consumers (document 5.13).

Meanwhile, international conferences laid the foundations of the World Health Organization, the International Monetary Fund, the International Bank for Reconstruction and Development, and the United Nations Educational, Scientific and Cultural Organization (UNESCO,

1945). Holding that "wars began in the minds of men," the UNESCO constitution created an agency through which the United Nations Organization might build peace and security by advancing the ideas of international equality, respect for diversity, and cooperation in the fields of education, science, and culture (document 5.14).

Each of these new institutions built upon League of Nations experience. All of them achieved a global scale of involvement, constituting a new international civil service and penetrating nations through professional networks that addressed common problems. Several of them were semiautonomous—created by separate treaties with their own memberships—but all were functionally related to the United Nations Organization, as were other intergovernmental agencies that predated the war. They shared the assumptions that economic and social welfare is related to political order, and that problem solving contributes to peace. In this respect, the functionalist idea of peace became fully institutionalized.

Document 5.10

Henry Wallace: The Century of the Common Man

From the speech of 8 May 1942

Everywhere the common people are on the march. Thousands of them are learning to read and write, learning to think together, learning to use tools. These people are learning to think and work together in labor movements, some of which may be extreme or impractical at first, but which eventually will settle down to serve effectively the interests of the common man.

When the freedom-loving people march, when the farmers have an opportunity to buy land at reasonable prices and to sell the produce of their land through their own organizations, when workers have the opportunity to form unions and bargain through them collectively, and when the children of all the people have an opportunity to attend schools which teach them truths of the real world in which they live—when these opportunities are open to everyone, then the world moves straight ahead.

Document 5.11

W. E. B. Du Bois: Democracy, Well-Being, and Peace

From "Democracy and Peace," 1944

Europe today with an accumulation of knowledge of this universe, built up laboriously and triumphantly over five long centuries, is unable to redeem mankind because most men, bound mind and body in the shackles of European profit, are too ignorant to appreciate and help preserve and extend this priceless treasure. Rolling in unprecedented wealth and capable by her miraculous technique, of indefinitely extending and multiplying this wealth, Europe finds herself bankrupt because of wars waged to defend this wealth and make more; and weighed down in every part of the world by an array of sheer sordid poverty on the part of the very people whose work rightly directed would give every human being a decent living. With a knowledge of the human brain and body capable of prolonging life twenty years beyond the biblical three-score-and-ten, Europe faces a world swept by preventable disease among colonial millions; her own birthrate declining because of luxury and indulgence. . . .

We do not here have a simple case of right and wrong, of good and evil. We have a complicated intricate pattern of human life which through no one fault and no one mistake has gone grievously astray. The modern world's mistakes need not necessarily be fatal, but certainly every hour lost in righting wrong, piles up enormous cost.

What then must be done? It is natural for us who belong to the disinherited of modern culture to think that all initiative toward righting the world must come from those who now so largely own and rule the world. I want to point out that while without cooperation from the white world, the present colored world cannot successfully undertake the whole program of reform, yet there is not only an opportunity but a duty for the colored world today to lead in reform.

In other words, the level of culture in the world has got to be raised if we are going to have the possibility of democracy and if that democracy is going to bring universal peace because it spells universal contentment. Most persons would immediately admit that if the abolition of extreme poverty were possible, it would be the greatest boon to mankind imaginable; it would make ignorance rare, curable disease non-existent and crime at a minimum. They doubt the possibility of the abolition of poverty because of the cost. I am pointing out that modern miracles of technique make a world without poverty possible if industry is carried on not simply for private profit but primarily for public welfare. . . .

I can easily see that in the tenth century, in the fifteenth and even in the eighteenth the prospect of the abolition of poverty seemed beyond human possibility. But today because of the very things of which we boast, the possibility of the out-and-out attack upon poverty lies in our hands. It is the consensus of scientific opinion that the technical mastery over the forces of the world can be used not simply for profit or for war but for making poverty a thing of the past. If we can do this then we can make this a world of educated men who include not simply men of leisure, lawyers, physicians, writers and artists, but also, and in far larger numbers, highly trained farmers, mechanics, engineers, homemakers and laborers equally well paid and respected. . . .

Before you dismiss a picture of this sort as a mere dream, stop and study what agriculture has accomplished and can accomplish, what chemistry is able to do, the immense and incalculable power which lies in the physical forces about us, and above all how much we now spend in waste and war which might be spent in education, clothes, food and medicine. I maintain that this is the outlook for peace, made certain through permitting the mass of men to have a voice in their own government; that any attempt to accomplish this aim simply through political organization, or organized force, or technical superiority of one group over another, is absolutely hopeless and will be simply a prolongation of the blood, sweat and tears which mark the path of attempted world progress.

Document 5.12

The Food and Agriculture Organization: Freedom from Want

From the Conference on Food and Agriculture, "Final Act," 1943

I. Declaration

This Conference, meeting in the midst of the greatest war ever waged, and in full confidence of victory, has considered the world problems of food and agriculture and declares its belief that the goal of freedom from want of food, suitable and adequate for the health and strength of all peoples, can be achieved.

1. The first task is to complete the winning of the war and to deliver millions of people from tyranny and from hunger. During the period of critical shortage in the aftermath of war, freedom from hunger can be achieved only by urgent and concerted efforts to economize consumption, to increase supplies and distribute them to the best advantage.

2. Thereafter we must equally concert our efforts to win and maintain freedom from fear and freedom from want. The one cannot be achieved without the other.

3. There has never been enough food for the health of all people. This is justified neither by ignorance nor by the harshness of nature. Production of food must be greatly expanded; we now have knowledge of the means by which this can be done. It requires imagination and firm will on the part of each government and people to make use of that knowledge.

4. The first cause of hunger and malnutrition is poverty. It is useless to produce more food unless men and nations provide the markets to absorb it. There must be an expansion of the whole world economy to provide the purchasing power sufficient to maintain an adequate diet for all. With full employment in all countries, enlarged industrial production, the absence of exploitation, an increasing flow of trade within and between countries, an orderly management of domestic and international investment and currencies, and sustained internal and international economic equilibrium, the food which is produced can be made available to all people.

5. The primary responsibility lies with each nation for seeing that its own people have the food needed for life and health; steps to this end are for national determination. But each nation can fully achieve its goal only if all work together. . . .

The United Nations Conference on Food and Agriculture Recommends:

1. That the governments and authorities here represented recognize and embody in a formal declaration or agreement the obligation to their respective peoples and to one another, henceforth to collaborate in raising levels of nutrition and standards of living of their peoples. . . .

2. That the governments and authorities here represented establish a permanent organization in the field of food and agriculture. . . .*

---

* The FAO was the first permanent agency of the United Nations to come into operation. This conference of representatives of 44 nations, meeting in Hot Springs, Virginia, between 18 May and 3 June 1943, set up an interim commission that led in 1945 to the permanent Food and Agriculture Organization, with headquarters in Rome.

Document 5.13

Herbert Lehman: Relief for the War-Stricken

From the Address on Relief and Rehabilitation, 1943

The peace which we all seek must be rooted in the first hurried work of rehabilitation and reconstruction. The dimensions of this task can best be measured by the dimensions of the disaster which has overtaken the world. The Axis has extended its despotism over the peoples of some 35 countries and hundreds of islands, the dwelling-places of more than half a billion men, women, and children. Almost all Europe lies under the dark cloud of Nazi rule; Japan has overrun the rich islands of the western Pacific and has penetrated deep toward the heart of heroic China. In occupied Europe and in enslaved Asia the picture is universally the same —starving people, impoverished land, and nations whose whole economies have been wrecked. . . .

A problem so vast and so world embracing, obviously, does not lend itself to piecemeal solution. The problem is to devise means to harness world production, already greatly taxed by war needs, to total world want during the coming months of tremendous human crisis. We must see to it that relief flows smoothly and swiftly into measures to remove the need of relief, and that rehabilitation measures are so devised as to enable suffering nations to begin their own reconstruction at the earliest possible moment. Our objective is to *help people* to help *themselves* and thereby to help ourselves, by making possible a world in which the four freedoms can have a chance of realization.

. . . There is fortunately a strong disposition among the nations to recognize that this problem is without parallel in history and that its solution must lie in joint and concerted efforts by all nations. It is proposed that each nation in making its greatest possible contribution to the task, shall within its resources make not only a financial contribution but shall contribute further in the form of supplies, shipping and other transportation, personnel and services. It is, as yet, too early to predict what total amounts or what proportion any government will be called upon to supply to the joint enterprise. There are, however, precedents for action in this direction. Under the terms of the International Wheat Agreement, for example, Canada and the United Kingdom, Australia, Argentina, and the United States have undertaken to contribute large quantities of wheat for use in a major offensive against starvation. There are supplies in other area which, when fully drawn upon, will distribute the burden of world relief over many countries.

Document 5.14

The United Nations Educational, Social, and Cultural Organization

From the UNESCO Constitution, 1945

The Governments of the States parties to this Constitution on behalf of their peoples declare:

That since wars began in the minds of men, it is in the minds of men that the defences of peace must be constructed;

That ignorance of each other's ways and lives has been a common cause, throughout the history of mankind, of that suspicion and mistrust between the peoples of the world through which their differences have all too often broken into war;

That the great and terrible war which has now ended was a war made possible by the denial of the democratic principles of the dignity, equality and mutual respect of men, and by the propagation, in their place, through ignorance and prejudice, of the doctrine of the inequality of men and races;

That the wide diffusion of culture, and the education of humanity for justice and liberty and peace are indispensable to the dignity of man and constitute a sacred duty which all the nations must fulfil in a spirit of mutual assistance and concern;

That a peace based exclusively upon the political and economic arrangements of governments would not be a peace which could secure the unanimous, lasting and sincere support of the peoples of the world, and that the peace must therefore be founded, if it is not to fail, upon the intellectual and moral solidarity of mankind.

For these reasons, the States parties to this Constitution, believing in full and equal opportunities for education for all, in the unrestricted pursuit of objective truth, and in the free exchange of ideas and knowledge, are agreed and determined to develop and to increase the means of communication between their peoples and to employ these means for the purposes of mutual understanding and a truer and more perfect knowledge of each others' lives;

In consequence whereof they do hereby create the United Nations Educational, Scientific and Cultural Organization for the purpose of advancing, through the educational, scientific and cultural relations of the peoples of the world, the objectives of international peace and of the common welfare of mankind for which the United Nations Organization was established and which its Charter proclaims.

Purposes and functions

Art. I.(I) The purpose of the Organization is to contribute to peace and security by promoting collaboration among the nations through education, science and culture in order to further universal respect for justice, for the law and for the human rights and fundamental freedoms which are affirmed for the peoples of the world, without distinction of race, sex, language or religion, by the Charter of the United Nations.

(2) To realize this purpose the Organization will:

(a) Collaborate in the work of advancing the mutual knowledge and understanding of peoples, through all means of mass communication and to that end promote such international agreements as may be necessary to promote the free flow of ideas by word and image;

(b) Give fresh impulse to popular education and to the spread of culture;

By collaborating with members, at their request, in the development of educational activities;

By instituting collaboration among the nations to advance the ideal of equality of educational opportunity without race, sex or any distinctions, economic or social;

By suggesting educational methods best suited to prepare the children of the world for the responsibilities of freedom;

(c) Maintain, increase and diffuse knowledge;

By assuring the conservation and protection of the world's inheritance of books, works of arts and monuments of history and science, and recommending to the nations concerned the necessary international conventions;

By encouraging co-operation among the nations in all branches of intellectual activity, including the international exchange of persons active in the fields of education, science and culture, and the exchange of publications, objects of artistic and scientific interest and other materials of information;

By initiating methods of international co-operation calculated to give the people of all countries access to the printed and published materials produced by any of them.

(3) With a view to preserving the independence, integrity and fruitful diversity of the cultures and educational systems of the member States of this Organization, the Organization is prohibited from intervening in matters which are essentially within their domestic jurisdiction.

Political Security

During the war, the countries of the antifascist military coalition were designated the "United Nations," and the effort to conduct a successful war against Germany, Italy, and Japan dominated their foreign policies.[5] Part of that effort was to state war aims that would unite them on the principles of peace and international security. Gradually, proposals evolved that sought security through regional unity and world organization.

War Aims

The first official statement of war aims by the emerging coalition was the "Atlantic Charter," promulgated by the British and U.S. heads of state, Winston Churchill and Franklin D. Roosevelt, 14 August 1941 on board the warship *Prince of Wales* in the Atlantic near Newfoundland (document 5.15). The United States was then technically neutral, but it was cooperating in the defense of Britain. The joint declaration set the general terms for that cooperation: territorial integrity of soveriegn nations, illegality of aggression, self-determination of peoples, economic and social security, and commercial freedom. Churchill and Roosevelt avoided specific questions of colonialism, territorial adjustments, or collective security obligations, but they pledged to disarm aggressor nations, "pending the establishment of a wider and permanent system of general security."[6]

Joseph Stalin and General Wladyslaw Sikorski, the prime minister of the Polish government in exile, also ignored concrete, divisive issues when they negotiated a declaration of mutual assistance in December, following Germany's invasion of the Soviet Union (22 June). Polish exiles were pressing Sikorski to make specific demands, frontiers were unsettled, and rumors of the Katyn massacre poisoned the atmosphere.[7] The two leaders framed their goals in general terms, explicitly including a postwar international organization "of the democratic countries" that would enforce international law with "collective armed force" (document 5.16).

Less than a week after the Stalin-Sikorski pact, the United States was attacked by Japan and entered the war, thus completing the United Nations alliance. On 1 January 1942, the coalition pledged itself to a common war and peace, specifically endorsing the Atlantic Charter and adding the protection of "human rights" to its goals (document 5.17).

During the next three years, while war raged around the world, the postwar configuration of the world was the subject of planning in government offices and of proposals from the peoples of the United Nations. Ideas about peace as political security reflected both interwar experience and the distribution of power in World War II.

Document 5.15

Franklin Roosevelt and Winston Churchill: The Atlantic Charter

From their Joint Declaration, 14 August 1941

Joint declaration of the President of the United States of America and the Prime Minister, Mr. Churchill, representing His Majesty's Government in the United Kingdom, being met together, deem it right to make known certain common principles in the national policies of their respective countries on which they base their hopes for a better future for the world.

First, their countries seek no aggrandizement, territorial or other;

Second, they desire to see no territorial changes that do not accord with the freely expressed wishes of the peoples concerned.

Third, they respect the right of all peoples to choose the form of government under which they will live, and they wish to see sovereign rights and self-government restored to those who have been forcibly deprived of them;

Fourth, they will endeavor, with due respect for their existing obligations, to further the enjoyment by all States, great or small, victor or vanquished, of access, on equal terms, to the trade and to the raw materials of the world which are needed for economic prosperity;

Fifth, they desire to bring about the fullest collaboration between all nations in the economic field with the object of securing, for all, improved labor standards, economic advancement and social security;

Sixth, after the final destruction of the Nazi tyranny, they hope to see established a peace which will afford to all nations the means of dwelling in safety within their own boundaries, and which will afford assurance that all the men in all the lands may live out their lives in freedom from fear and want;

Seventh, such a peace should enable all men to traverse the high seas and oceans without hindrance;

Eighth, they believe that all of the nations of the world, for realistic as well as spiritual reasons must come to the abandonment of the use of force. Since no future peace can be maintained if land, sea or air armaments continue to be employed by nations which threaten, or may threaten, aggression outside of their frontiers, they believe, pending the establishment of a wide and permanent system of general security, that the disarmament of such nations is essential. They will likewise aid and encourage all other practicable measures which will lighten for peace-loving peoples the crushing burden of armaments.

Document 5.16

Josef Stalin and Wladyslaw Sikorski: Mutual Assistance

From their Declaration of Friendship and Mutual Assistance,
4 December 1941

The Government of the Polish Republic and the Government of the Union of Soviet Socialist Republics, animated by the spirit of friendly understanding and fighting collaboration, declare:

1. German Hitlerite imperialism is the worst enemy of mankind—no compromise with it is possible.

Both States together with Great Britain and other Allies, supported by the United States of America, will wage war until complete victory and final destruction of the German invaders.

2. Implementing the Treaty concluded on July 30, 1941, both Governments will render each other during the war full military assistance, and troops of the Republic of Poland located on the territory of the Soviet Union will wage war against the German brigands shoulder to shoulder with Soviet troops.

In peace-time their mutual relations will be based on good neighborly collaboration, friendship and reciprocal honest fulfillment of the obligations they have taken upon themselves.

3. After a victorious war and the appropriate punishment of the Hitlerite criminals, it will be the aim of the Allied States to ensure a durable and just peace. This can be achieved only through a new organization of international relations on the basis of unification of the democratic countries in a durable alliance. Respect for international law backed by the collective armed force of the Allied States must form the decisive factor in the creation of such an organization. Only under this condition can a Europe destroyed by German barbarism be restored and a guarantee be created that the disaster caused by the Hitlerites will never be repeated.

Document 5.17

The Declaration of the United Nations

From the Declaration of 1 January 1942

A Joint Declaration by the United States of America, the United Kingdom of Great Britain and Northern Ireland, the Union of Soviet Socialist Republics, China, Australia, Belgium, Canada, Costa Rica, Cuba, Czechoslovakia, Dominican Republic, El Salvador, Greece, Guatemala, Haiti, Honduras, India, Luxembourg, Netherlands, New Zealand, Nicaragua, Norway, Panama, Poland, South Africa, Yugoslavia.*

The Governments signatory hereto,

Having subscribed to a common programme of purposes and principles embodied in the Joint Declaration of the President of the United States of America and the Prime Minister of the United Kingdom of Great Britain and Northern Ireland, dated August 14th, 1941, known as the Atlantic Charter.

Being convinced that complete victory over their enemies is essential to defend life, liberty, independence and religious freedom, and to preserve human rights and justice in their own lands as well as in other lands, and that they are now engaged in a common struggle against savage and brutal forces seeking to subjugate the world, declare:

(1) Each Government pledges itself to employ its full resources, military or economic, against those members of the Tripartite Pact (Germany, Japan, Italy) 1940 and its adherents with which such Government is at war.

(2) Each Government pledges itself to co-operate with the Governments signatory hereto and not to make a separate armistice or peace with the enemies. The foregoing declaration may be adhered to by other nations which are, or which may be, rendering material assistance and contributions in the struggle for victory over Hitlerism.

Regional Federation

Many Europeans, building on the unity movement of the 1920s, thought in terms of regional organization. European resistance organi-

---

* The declaration was signed by 21 additional states: in 1942, Mexico, the Philippines, and Ethiopia; in 1943, Iraq, Brazil, Bolivia, Iran, and Columbia; in 1944, Liberia, France; in 1945, Ecuador, Peru, Chile, Paraguay, Venezuela, Uruguay, Turkey, Egypt, Saudi Arabia, Lebanon, and Syria.

zations across the whole political spectrum advocated some form of postwar continental federation. A striking example, the "Ventotene Manifesto" (document 5.18), was produced by three left-wing political prisoners who were imprisoned on the rocky island of Ventotene off the coast of Naples.[8] Based somewhat on *The Federalist Papers,* their manifesto was smuggled into Rome and distributed throughout occupied Europe. It had considerable influence on leaders of the underground as well as on the Allies and neutrals. The British political analyst Henry Noel Brailsford, editor of the *New Leader* and a specialist on Russia, the Balkans, and the League of Nations, argued strongly for the regional organization of Europe as a way of dealing with postwar power relationships and the future of Germany (document 5.19).

There were proponents of a North American union, too, and American publicist Clarence Streit broadened the idea of federation to include all democratic states. The British author Leonard Woolf put European unity in a world context, arguing in that it was "common sense" to base a peace system of concrete rules and sanctions upon regional groups and federations (document 5.19). The argument for regional organizations was so compelling that article 52 of the 1945 United Nations Charter explicitly provided for them.

Document 5.18

The Ventotene Manifesto: European Federation

From "For a United Europe," 1941

. . . The many problems which poisoned international relations on the continent—the drawing of borders in the zones of mixed populations, the defense of ethnic minorities, outlets to the seas for landlocked countries, the Balkan question, the Irish question, etc.—are impossible to resolve within the national context. These problems would find their most simple solution in a European federation, as have similar problems in the past. When small states became part of larger national entities, old grievances were largely diffused when they were transformed into problems between different provinces. . . .

The rational organization of the United States of Europe . . . can only be based upon the republican constitution of all the federated states. And, moving beyond the European horizon, when our perspective is extended to all of humankind, we must also recognize that while we await the more distant future when the unity of the entire globe will become possible, a European federation is the only conceivable guarantee that our relations with the Asian and American peoples can evolve on the basis of peaceful cooperation.

Therefore, the dividing line between progressive and reactionary parties no longer is drawn along the traditional criteria of democracy or socialism. It falls along the new, substantive divide that separates those who still direct their political action towards traditional goals, such the conquest of national power, thereby playing unwittingly into the reactionaries' hands by reviving old absurdities and allowing the lava of old-style popular passions to harden; and, on the other side, those who see as their main task the creation of a solid international state, will direct the popular forces towards this end, and, once national power is captured, will use it as a primary instrument for the realization of international unity.

From the beginning, we must seek through our propaganda and action to establish agreements and bonds among the nascent organizations in the various states, to lay the groundwork for a movement that can mobilize the masses, and to bring about the birth of the most magnificent and innovative creation to come out of Europe in centuries. We must seek to constitute a solid federal state that will have at its disposition a European armed force in place of national armies; that will completely dismember the economic autarky that has been the backbone of the totalitarian regimes; that will have adequate institutions and means to see to it that measures of common concern will be carried out by each member state while allowing them sufficient autonomy to apply these measures flexibly and also to develop their own political life according to the particular characteristics of their various peoples.

If sufficient numbers of Europeans understand these things, victory will soon be in their hands. The circumstances and the mood are favorable. The parties and movements who oppose them have been disqualified by the disastrous experience of the past two decades. Because this is the moment for new achievements, it is also the time for new men: for the MOVEMENT FOR A FREE AND UNITED EUROPE.

Document 5.19

Henry Noel Brailsford: The Problem of Power

From *Our Settlement with Germany*, 1944

The tendency of today is to reverse the one-sidedness that marred the settlement after the last war. Then the stress was on politics and on the charters of the jurists. Today it is economics we emphasize, perhaps because we shrink from the problems of power as insoluble. International commissions of a functional type are now in favor, each dealing with a single aspect of our common life—transport, raw materials, currency, investment, labor conditions. This may be a sound prescription for gradual progress. But all the while, behind this useful structure will lurk the unsolved problem of power. Again the smoking volcano will erupt, but not necessarily through the old crater. Planners always know how to avoid the last war, as soldiers know how to win it. Volcanoes, moreover, cast a shadow even when they are inactive. The fear of an eruption may stultify all our efforts to achieve economic cooperation. That will happen if we isolate a defeated Germany. It will happen as certainly if we divide Europe into Russian and Anglo-American spheres of interest. . . .

What, then, have we to suggest? The ideal solution is a United States of Europe, a federation in the true sense of the word. But federations cannot be made by the planning of jurists and politicians. They come into being when great masses of men are so conscious of their solidarity that they crave for it an outward political form. They may arise out of close economic collaboration, but they can hardly precede it. They presuppose some near approach to a common political philosophy. That is lacking between the rest of Europe and the Russians. Spain is still Fascist but may not long remain so. For how long will the hatred the Nazis have earned for the German people exclude it from that friendly collaboration of which federation is the constitutional expression? It may be said that the continental federation will come about piecemeal, by the erection first of all of several partial regional confederations. That is arguable: but the motives which inspire some of the plans are not reassuring. They smell of *cordon sanitaire*. Others are barbed wire against Germany, and some are dual purpose fences. The result is that the Russians, and consequently all Communists, are root and branch opponents both of these partial confederations and of a European Federation. Whether a European Federation will be a danger to the Soviet Union depends on our estimate of the balance of class power within it. Will it be dominated by monopoly capital? What are the Great Powers of tomorrow? Are they a number of classless democracies, which voice their common will to practice an economy of plenty in the English, French and Russian languages? Or are they the Steel Trust, Standard Oil and Imperial Chemicals?

In what form, then, may we hope for the integration of Europe? On the answer to that question depends the restoration of Germany to her due place as a cooperating member of the European family. In some form the United Nations must set up an economic authority for Europe. Boards concerned with production, raw materials, currency, investment, food supply, electricity, railways, civil aviation, navigable rivers and reparations may all come into existence. None of these fields can be rigidly fenced in: each implies some of the others and all together presuppose a master plan. Rather sooner than later we must create a Supreme Economic Council for Europe, which will coordinate the work of the Boards and shape the idea they strive to realize. Its work and its thinking will depend mainly on officials, who should hereafter be trained together at an International University to form a European Civil Service. They must shed their nationalism when they enter it, which they will do the more readily if they study together for a time at a common center.

An Economic Council would be powerless unless its authority sprang from public opinion. In some shape it must represent the interests of the masses in the incessant struggle that will be waged with the great cosmopolitan concentrations of capital round the tables of all these Boards. The best way to compose it would be on a functional basis proportionate to population. The constituent bodies which elect its members in each country are naturally the trade unions, peasants' and farmers' leagues and cooperatives with chambers of commerce and federations of industrialists. The I.L.O. offers a model. . . .

Into a Council of this kind Germans as workers, peasants and consumers will enter much more easily than any delegation which represented Germany as a State. If they enter at all, it can only be with equal rights. But no ingenuity in drawing blueprints will ever create a true European Society. That will come into being only when the masses behind the pioneers realize their solidarity across frontiers. Education, the press and the radio have their part to play. The common man must be helped to perceive that his daily bread depends on the work of the European Council. But the chief formative influences which will make it or mar it are the parties round which the workers, farmers and technicians rally. If the old feud once more divides Socialists from Communists, while peasants and technicians stand aloof, Europe will not come into being in our day as a living society.

So far and no farther we can today grope our way towards a solution of the central issue of the settlement. The problems of power cannot be solved on the basis of a triple alliance between London, Washington and Moscow; nor will it be finally solved while monopoly capital overshadows our economic life and national States retain the ownership of military force. May work and planning in common fit us all for the next difficult step, before the creaking alliance breaks up. In the field of planning for ample production and full employment the Germans have a part to play.

Document 5.20

Leonard Woolf: Regional Federalism and World Organization

From *The War for Peace*, 1940

It follows that, if civilization is not to be destroyed by totalitarian war, human beings must somehow or other create an international system based upon law and co-operation, and with international force as a sanction of international law. But here we reach an impasse not unusual in human affairs. Social psychology has not yet reached the stage, as the history of the League showed, at which there is any possibility that in a world system the obligations of collective security will be carried out. Are we, then, to say with the realist critics of a League system that it must be for ever utopian, because states will not treat an act of war against one as an act of war against all or come to the assistance of the victim of aggression?

I believe that the answer to this question is to be found in common sense, in the ordinary way in which in ordinary life sensible people continually deal successfully with such impasses and difficulties. A goal may be unattainable if you attempt to get to it in one rush, but may be attainable if you are prepared to work towards it in stages. This is true of the international problem. It is possible that at the end of the war . . . we may be able to establish limited geographical federal unions, "peace federations." The federation solves the problem of force so far as the relations of its members are concerned; it solves it in the non-pacifist way, for the federal or communal power is placed as the sanction behind the federal law. As between the federated states, the armed forces are controlled by the federal government. On the other hand, . . . such limited federations are not by themselves adequate guarantees of world peace or even of continental peace. The relations of states are so closely and so widely articulated that some wider and more universal organization for peace and international co-operation is necessary. Thus while in limited geographical areas federal unions or fully developed international systems of law, co-operation, and collective security may be possible, these limited or regional federations or confederations must be combined in a world system in which collective security is not yet possible. . . .

. . . In the world peace system all states would be bound:

(1) Under no circumstances to resort to war;

(2) To institute a regular procedure of judicial settlement or of settlement by other pacific methods and to use this procedure and organization for the settlement of all disputes or differences which may arise between them;

(3) To disarm;

(4) To set up organs and machinery of international government for carrying out the above provisions for making international law and for making those changes in the status quo which changing circumstances from time to time demand, and for promoting the common interests of states by co-operation. In practice that would mean the establishment of an international court of justice and of organs of a deliberative or legislative nature, like the League Council and Assembly. The experience of the League showed that, if progress is to be made in the substitution of law for war and co-operation for conflict, and if provision is really to be made for peaceful change in the world of states where changing conditions make it necessary or equitable, the deliberative or legislative organs of international government must have the power to make laws or take decisions by a majority vote. The *liberum veto* or unanimity rule, the fetish of the nationalist and of his totem, the sovereign state, is the negation of all government.

These should be, with one exception, the only obligations which all states must accept as members of the world peace system. They should not be bound to preserve the independence or territorial integrity of their fellow members against aggression, to treat an act of war against one member as an act of war against all, or to impose "sanctions" against an aggressor. The reason for thus restricting the obligations of states in the world peace system is, as was stated above, psychological. The narrow nationalist psychology is still so strong—and will probably for some time remain so—that there is little chance, in the case of an act of war or aggression, that states all over the world will carry out the obligations of a collective security system demanding immediate, positive, and often dangerous action. It is, however, possible that after the war an important obligation of a less stringent and more negative nature might be accepted and carried out by all the states of the world, namely that they will not aid any state which in any quarter of the world commits an act of aggression or which resorts to war in breach of the fundamental obligations of the peace system.

Within this world peace system, confederation, or commonwealth of nations, which would impose upon its members less stringent or exacting obligations than did the League, there might be regionalized groups and federations of states more closely united by the obligations of collective security. In that case, for instance, the nations of Europe, while each was a member of the world peace system, would collectively be also grouped in a European union or confederation of the kind which [Aristide] Briand proposed. All the states of Europe would be members, it is to be hoped, of this European confederation. It would deal with all international questions which exclusively concerned Europeans and European states and, in order to prevent war in Europe, it would establish a system of collective security for Europe. Its members would therefore be mutually bound to one another by the same obligations as we suggested above for the world peace system, but they would in addition be bound by the obligation to treat an act of war against one as an act of war against all. The European confederation would, therefore, for the affairs of Europe, have its own international organs of government, organs of legislation and of judicial and pacific settlement. It would make European international law and carry through those peaceful changes in the international structure of Europe which must inevitably from time to time become necessary; it would actively promote economic, social and political co-operation in the common interest of all European states. If federal unions were successfully established, . . . [they] would enter the European confederation and the world peace system or commonwealth of nations as units.

World Organization

The global character of the peace for which people hoped was epitomized in the words "One World." That was the title of a popular book by Wendell Willkie, who was a U.S presidential candidate in 1940 and then campaigned for internationalism within the Republican party. The book recounted his 1942 trip around the world, during which he crossed Russia and China. Wilkie's first choice of a title for his book had been, "One War, One Peace, One World." The logic of that phrase was passionately developed by Léon Blum, the French scholar, socialist, and statesman (document 5.21). For Blum, peace had to be based on a collective international morality.

For Emery Reves, however, peace was to be based on universal and enforceable law (document 5.22). Hungarian-born and educated in several European countries, Reves had reported on the major international conferences of the 1930s until he fled the Nazis to Britain and, in 1940, to the United States. He regarded the United Nations Charter as inadequate, and his analysis helped to launch a postwar international movement for world federalism. Even in the last year of the war, international law was being brought to bear on the trial of war criminals (document 5.23). In the process, the *jus in bellum* elements of justifiable war tradition were institutionalized so as to hold individuals as well as states accountable to international standards. Nonetheless, Reves was correct in recognizing limitations in the United Nations organization. As the product of a wartime alliance, the organization was necessarily the product of compromise as well as innovation.

Planning for the postwar order built on assessments of the League of Nations, especially, a concern to make collective security effective. Perhaps mistrusting the cumbersome voting procedures under the League, Franklin Roosevelt suggested to Soviet foreign minister Vyacheslav Molotov in 1942 that authority for collective action might be vested in the four Great Powers of the alliance, acting unanimously and promptly in case of aggression. The idea was not a formal proposal, and it did not divide the world into separate spheres of influence; but it did assign a special responsibility to those powers that had the most to gain from the very world order they would enforce.

That special role was assumed as the respective foreign offices worked out detailed plans for a postwar international organization, which was promised in the 1943 Declaration of Four Nations on General Security (document 5.24). By August 1944, planning was far enough along to warrant a four-power conference at Dumbarton Oaks, near Washington, where agreement was reached on the basic structure of a United Nations organization.[9] Only when critical issues regarding voting procedures and membership were resolved by Churchill, Roosevelt, and Stalin at the Crimean resort of Yalta, early in 1945, were the rest of the nations invited to a general conference at San Francisco, 25 April–26 June, to finalize the UN Charter (document 5.25). There was much give-and-take among the delegations at San Francisco, but the collective security features of the Charter did not depart in essential details from those upon which the three major powers agreed.

The first and foremost goal of the United Nations Organization was to "maintain international peace and security" (Article 1.1). Its Charter went well beyond the League of Nations Covenant in prohibiting the "threat or use of force" (Article 2); in designating sanctions—including military ones; in specifying procedures for their use; and in making their application mandatory on all members under the direction of the Security Council (Articles 39–50). It provided for a permanent Military Staff Committee and pledged members to allocate forces to the Council as necessary to maintain "international peace and security" (Articles 43–47). The Security Council was to include fifteen nations, of which five Great Powers would be permanent members, a distribution of power that reflected the wartime alliance and, it was expected, the postwar world.[10] Council decisions were to be made by majority vote, except that they required the unanimous consent of the permanent members. The ability of those powers to veto Council actions was a concession to their special interests; but it was also designed to prevent the United Nations from undertaking actions that could not command effective support, or degenerating into rival military alliances.

The concept of collective security, as embodied in the UN Charter, was based on the assumptions that peace is indivisible, that war against any member is a threat to all, and that aggression can be contained by the certainty of overwhelming deterrent power against it. In turn, it was understood that a peaceful order is possible only insofar as there is cooperation among the Great Powers.

In the veto power the principle of sovereign unanimity was applied to the five major powers. Elsewhere—in decisions of the Security Council, the General Assembly (where all member states were represented with one vote apiece), and the specialized agencies—the principle of decision making by simple majority was the general rule. This marked a significant, although not complete, change in international organization.

The Charter omitted a critical element that the League Covenant had attached to collective security: a provision for general disarmament. As the political analyst Inis Claude has observed, the system of collective security could be employed only if the risk of war were not catastrophic. In that respect, the UN system was incomplete: "collective security cannot work unless states disarm, but states will not disarm until collective security has clearly shown that it merits confidence. . . . The maintenance of national military strength . . . , born of lack of confidence in collective security, prevents the development of an effective collective security system."[11]

In other respects, however, the United Nations Charter institutionalized ideas of peace that had developed through the first half of the twentieth century. An array of measures had become available for the peaceful settlement of disputes—negotiation, inquiry, mediation, conciliation, arbitration, and judicial settlement. These were put at the disposal of the General Assembly and Security Council (Articles 14, 33–39).

Beyond political security, moreover, the UN Charter pledged its members to promote human rights, international law, and economic and social advancement. Assuming that "conditions of stability and well-being" are required for peace, the UN created an Economic and Social Council to advance economic and social well-being, health, cultural co-operation, and human rights (Articles 55–72). A Trusteeship Council was established to administer territories formerly under the League mandate system, as well as those taken over from the Axis powers, and to guide them toward self-government (Articles 73–91). The established International Court of Justice was made "the principal judicial organ of the United Nations," and all UN members were members of it (Articles 92–96). The international secretariat was charged with maintaining liaison between the UN and other international agencies with specialized functions in the fields of relief and reconstruction, food, health, economic development, commerce, monetary policy, and cultural cooperation.

In the United Nations and related organizations were institutionalized many of the ideas of peace that had evolved over the course of western civilization: the pacific settlement of disputes, international law and organization, collective security, peaceful change, social and economic justice, and fundamental human rights. Other historic ideas of peace were also manifested during World War II: disarmament, world federation, and nonviolence as inner tranquility and ethical duty or as a form of direct action. As war had become more worldwide and total, the search for peace had become more varied and universal: it was conducted on official and popular levels, through organizations and networks among governments and peoples. Even as the mass destruction of modern warfare made peace essential, the variety of approaches raised difficult, probing questions beyond the settlement of disputes or even security—issues of the rights and duties of nations, the human rights of individuals, social justice, and the process of orderly change: questions, in sum, about the fundamental principles of international life and collective purpose.

Document 5.21

Léon Blum: Peace Based on Universal Values

From *For All Mankind*, 1943

It will not be difficult to convince the peoples of the world that true peace can be built up only on the threefold foundation of political democracy, social democracy, and international order. It is, indeed, almost mathematically certain that the work of social construction will move toward that goal, for its starting point will be the destruction of the totalitarian dictatorships and it will be controlled by the two greatest democracies in the world. Nor do I think that nations will take long, in the face of the overwhelming evidence, to realize that history is offering them a chance of a fresh start. . . . The winds of history are favorable, and everywhere the workers are conscious of being carried by the tide. But this is where the real difficulty arises. Will they be worthy of their destiny? Will they be able to play the parts for which history has cast them? Will they understand, or can they be made to understand . . . that if, to seize power, they will need both the force and the authority that come from being in harmony with the nature and the trend of economic evolution, they will have no less need of dignity, of the ascendency, in a word, that comes from moral superiority and efficiency? For a transfer of power to be consolidated and established before history, it must be acceptable to the conscience of mankind no less than to human emotion and to human reason. It must call forth from every sincere man the spontaneous tribute, "It had to be," but not that alone. He must also say, "It is right, it is good, and it is beautiful." . . .

That is what we should be preaching. This is the task we ought now to be undertaking, and we may have only a short time in which to accomplish it. In human affairs new roads must be taken boldly and quickly. . . . Above all, it must be borne in mind that the effort will be incomplete and fruitless if it is limited to the sum of individual *examens de conscience*. The ethics of the group—of political, social, and moral groups—are no less real than individual ethics, and it is precisely the organs of collective life that need thorough moral renewal. It is evident, for example, that national democracy would undergo a sea change if the interplay of forces within the nation were not in the future to be judged according to the criteria of good faith, integrity, and honor. Democracy everywhere presupposes freedom of action and, consequently, political conflict. But it does not follow that there are no rules in this civil conflict, that no holds are barred or that its ends justify any means, and this is as true of parties, social groups, and the press as it is of individuals. No advantage won, no plea of necessity, can justify lies, slander, dishonesty, the abuse of force, failure to fulfill obligations or to keep one's word. The argument becomes even stronger if we turn to the international order, for its foundations *must* be the belief in the validity and the sacredness of contracts; if that foundation is lacking, it is built on sand and must collapse. No doubt contracts will be violated in the international sphere, just as crimes are still committed in civil society. What is essential is that the injured nation shall at least be able to count with certainty on the support of others against the offender. In other words, morality must remain the law and the offending nation the exception.

Moreover, at every stage of this collective life subordination of private interests to those of the community must be recognized as an inescapable obligation and treated as such. . . . The difficulty is to secure from political and social groups what is required of the individual— namely, voluntary subordination to the general and permanent interests of humanity. . . . This renunciation of rivalry and of claims arising from the divergence of immediate interests, this spontaneous surrender to a higher will, this consciousness of permanent contact with and dependence on a higher order of reality . . . is what Socrates and Plato meant by wisdom and what a Christian thinker like Pascal called humility. But humility of this kind should be a source of strength, and then men should be proud to feel it. In the past men felt that it implied faith and obedience. We must see that it leads to faith and action.

Document 5.22

Emery Reves: Universal Peace Protected by Law

From *The Anatomy of Peace*, 1945

We believe that the progress of science and industry have rendered national authorities powerless to safeguard the people against armed aggression or to prevent devastating wars.

We believe that peace in any country of the world cannot be maintained without the existence of an effective universal government organization to prevent crime in the inter-national field.

We believe that independence of a nation does not mean untrammeled and unrestricted freedom to do whatever it wants, and that real independence can be created only if no nation is free to attack another, to drag it into war, and to cause such devastating loss of life and wealth as has been wrought twice in our lifetime.

We believe that security of a nation, just as security of an individual, means the co-operation of all to secure the rights of each.

We believe that the relations between nations, just as the relations between individuals in a community, can be peaceful only if based upon and regulated by Law.

We believe that the only way to prevent future world wars is through regulation of the interrelationship of nations, not by unenforceable treaty obligations, which sovereign nations will always disregard, but by an enforceable legal order, binding all nations, giving all nationals equal rights under the established law, and imposing equal obligations upon each.

We believe that peace and security can be established and assured only if we, the sovereign people, who, for our own safety and well-being have delegated parts of our sovereignty to cities to handle our municipal affairs, to departments, countries, provinces, cantons or states to take care of departmental, county, provincial, cantonal or state issues, to our national governments to attend to our national problems—to protect ourselves against the danger of inter-national wars, now delegate part of our respective sovereignty to bodies capable of creating and applying Law in inter-national relations.

We believe that we can protect ourselves against inter-national wars only through the establishment of constitutional life in world affairs, and that such universal Law must be created in conformity with the democratic process, by freely elected and responsible representatives. Creation, application and execution of the Law must be rigorously controlled by the democratic process.

We believe that only a world-wide legal order can insure freedom from fear, and make possible the unhindered development of economic energies for the achievement of freedom from want.

We believe that the natural and inalienable rights of man must prevail. Under twentieth century realities they can be preserved only if they are protected by Law against destruction from outside forces. . . .

The task is by no means easy. The deceptions caused by rationalism are real and understandable. Yet, to try to escape the complexities of life revealed to us by reason by seeking refuge in irrationalism and to let our actions be determined by superstitions, dogmas and intuition, is sheer suicide. We must resign ourselves to the fact that there is no other fate for us than to climb the long, hard, steep and stony road guided by the only thing that makes us different from animals: reason. . . .

Sovereignty of the community and regulation of the interdependence
of peoples in society by universal law are the two central pillars upon
which the cathedral of democracy rests.

Document 5.23

Robert H. Jackson: The International Military Tribunal

From his report to the president, 1945*

The Legal Position of the United States

The legal position which the United States will maintain, being
thus based on the common sense of justice, is relative simple and non-
technical. We must not permit it to be complicated or obscured by
sterile legalisms developed in the age of imperialism to make war
respectable. . . .

The Nature of International Law

International Law is more than a scholarly collection of abstract and
immutable principles. It is an outgrowth of treaties or agreements between nations and of accepted customs. But every custom has its origin
in some single act, and every agreement has to be initiated by the action
of some state. Unless we are prepared to abandon every principle of
growth for International Law, we cannot deny that our own day has its
right to institute customs and to conclude agreements that will themselves become sources of a newer and strengthened International Law.
International Law is not capable of development by legislation, for there
is no continuously sitting international legislature. . . . It grows, as did
the Common-law, through decisions reached from time to time in adapting settled principles in new situations. Hence I am not disturbed by the
lack of precedent for the inquiry we propose to conduct. After the shock
to civilization of the last World War, however, a marked reversion to the
earlier and sounder doctrines of International Law took place. By the
time the Nazis came to power it was thoroughly established that launching an aggressive war or the institution of war by treachery was illegal.
. . . It is high time that we act on the juridical principle that aggressive
war-making is illegal and criminal.

---

* Jackson was Chief of counsel for the United States in the prosecution of Axis war
criminals. In this report he outlined his plan for prosecution.

The Principle of Unjustifiable War

The reestablishment of the principle of unjustifiable war is traceable in many steps. One of the most significant is the Briand-Kellogg Pact of 1928, by which Germany, Italy, and Japan, in common with ourselves and practically all the nations of the world, renounced war as an instrument of national policy, bound themselves to seek the settlement of disputes only by pacific means, and condemned recourse to war for the solution of international controversies. . . .* In 1932, Mr. [Henry L.] Stimson, as Secretary of State, gave voice to the American concept of its effect. He said, "War between nations was renounced. . . . It is no longer to be the source and subject of rights. It is no longer to be the principle around which the duties, the conduct, and the rights of nations revolve. It is an illegal thing."

Charter of the International Military Tribunal

I. Constitution of the International Military Tribunal

ARTICLE 1. . . . there shall be established an International Military Tribunal . . . for the just and prompt trial and punishment of the major war criminals of the European Axis.†

II. Jurisdiction and General Principles

ARTICLE 6. The Tribunal . . . shall have the power to try and punish persons who, acting in the interests of the European Axis countries, whether as individuals or as members of organizations, committed any of the following crimes.

The following acts, or any of them, are crimes coming within the jurisdiction of the Tribunal for which there shall be individual responsibility:

(a) Crimes against peace: Namely, planning, preparation, initiation or waging of a war of aggression, or a war in violation of international

---

* Jackson cited the Briand-Kellogg pact as "only one in a series of acts" renouncing war as an instrument of policy, mentioning also the Geneva Protocol of 1924 for the Pacific Settlement of International Disputes, the Eighth Assembly of the League of Nations (1927), and the Sixth Pan-American Conference (1928).

† The Charter of the International Military Tribunal was part of the "Agreement for the Establishment of an International Military Tribunal," signed in London, 8 August 1945, on behalf of the United States of America, the Provisional Government of the French Republic, the United Kingdom, and the Union of Soviet Socialist Republics. Articles 2–5 define the composition and procedures of the Tribunal.

treaties, agreements or assurances, or participation in a common plan or conspiracy for the accomplishment of any of the foregoing;

(b) War Crimes: Namely, violations of the laws or customs of war. Such violations shall include, but not be limited to, murder, ill-treatment or deportation to slave labor or for any other purpose of civilian population of or in occupied territory, murder or ill-treatment of prisoners of war or persons on the seas, killing of hostages, plunder of public or private property, wanton destruction of cities, towns or villages, or devastation not justified by military necessity;

(c) Crimes against humanity: Namely, murder, extermination, enslavement, deportation, and other inhumane acts committed against any civilian population, before or during the war, or persecutions on political, racial or religious grounds in execution of or in connection with any crime within the jurisdiction of the Tribunal, whether or not in violation of the domestic law of the country where perpetrated.

Leaders, organizers, instigators and accomplices participating in the formulation or execution of a common plan or conspiracy to commit any of the foregoing crimes are responsible for all acts performed by any persons in execution of such plan.

ARTICLE 7. The official position of defendants, whether as heads of state or responsible officials in government departments, shall not be considered as freeing them from responsibility or mitigating punishment.

ARTICLE 8. The fact that the defendant acted pursuant to order of his government or of a superior shall not free him from responsibility, but may be considered in mitigation of punishment if the Tribunal determines that justice so requires.

ARTICLE 9. At the trial of any individual member of any group or organization the Tribunal may declare . . . that the group or organization of which the individual was a member was a criminal organization.*

---

* The remainder of this article concerns rules of fair trial and establishes an investigating committee. The rest of the charter relates to the conduct of trials, sentences, and expenses.

Document 5.24

The Four Power Declaration: General Security

From "The Moscow Declaration on General Security," * 1943

The Governments of the United States of America, the United King-dom, the Soviet Union and China:

United in their determination, in accordance with the Declaration by the United Nations of January 1, 1942, and subsequent declarations, to continue hostilities against those Axis powers with which they respectively are at war until such powers have laid down their arms on the basis of unconditional surrender;

Conscious of their responsibility to secure the liberation of themselves and the peoples allied with them from the menace of aggression;

Recognizing the necessity of ensuring a rapid and orderly transition from war to peace and of establishing and maintaining international peace and security with the least diversion of the world's human and economic resources for armaments;

JOINTLY DECLARE:

1. That their united action, pledged for the prosecution of the war against their respective enemies, will be continued for the organization and maintenance of peace and security.

2. That those of them at war with a common enemy will act together in all matters relating to the surrender and disarmament of that enemy.

3. That they will take all measures deemed by them to be necessary to provide against any violation of the terms imposed upon the enemy.

4. That they recognize the necessity of establishing at the earliest practicable date a general international organization, based on the principle of the sovereign equality of all peace-loving States, and open to membership by all such States, large and small, for the maintenance of international peace and security.

5. That for the purpose of maintaining international peace and security pending the re-establishment of law and order and the inauguration of a system of general security, they will consult with one another and as occasion requires with other members of the United Nations with a view to joint action on behalf of the community of nations.

6. That after the termination of hostilities they will not employ their

* This statement was issued in Moscow on 30 October 1943 as the Declaration of Four Nations on General Security.

military forces within the territories of other States except for the purposes envisaged in this declaration and after joint consultation.

7. That they will confer and co-operate with one another and with other members of the United Nations to bring about a practicable general agreement with respect to the regulation of armaments in the postwar period.

Document 5.25

The United Nations Charter

From the United Nations Conference on International
Organization, 1945

WE THE PEOPLES OF THE UNITED NATIONS determined
to save succeeding generations from the scourge of war, which twice in our lifetime has brought untold sorrow to mankind, and
to reaffirm faith in fundamental human rights, in the dignity and worth of the human person, in the equal rights of men and women and of nations large and small, and
to establish conditions under which justice and respect for the obligations arising from treaties and other sources of international law can be maintained, and
to promote social progress and better standards of life in larger freedom, and for these ends
to practice tolerance and live together in peace with one another as good neighbors, and
to unite our strength to maintain international peace and security, and
to ensure, by the acceptance of principles and the institution of methods, that armed force shall not be used, save in the common interest, and
to employ international machinery for the promotion of the economic and social advancement of all peoples,
have resolved to combine our efforts to accomplish these aims.

Accordingly, our respective Governments, through representatives assembled in the city of San Francisco, who have exhibited their full powers found to be in good and due form, have agreed to the present Charter of the United Nations and do hereby establish an international organization be known as the United Nations.

Chapter I. Purposes and Principles

ARTICLE 1 The purposes of the United Nations are:

1. To maintain international peace and security, and to that end: to take effective collective measures for the prevention and removal of threats to the peace, and for the suppression of acts of aggression or other breaches of the peace, and to bring about by peaceful means, and in conformity with the principles of justice and international law, adjustment or settlement of international disputes or situations which might lead to a breach of the peace;

2. To develop friendly relations among nations based on respect for the principle of equal rights and self-determination of peoples, and to take other appropriate measures to strengthen universal peace;

3. To achieve international co-operation in solving international problems of an economic, social, cultural, or humanitarian character, and in promoting and encouraging respect for human rights and for fundamental freedoms for all without distinction as to race, sex, language, or religion; and

4. To be a center for harmonizing the actions of nations in the attainment of these common ends.

ARTICLE 2 The Organization and its Members, in pursuit of the Purposes stated in ARTICLE 1, shall act in accordance with the following Principles.

1. The Organization is based on the principle of the sovereign equality of its Members.

2. All Members, in order to ensure to all of them the rights and benefits resulting from membership shall fulfil in good faith the obligations assumed by them in accordance with the present Charter.

3. All Members shall settle their international disputes by peaceful means in such a manner that international peace and security, and justice, are not endangered.

4. All Members shall refrain in their international relations from the threat or use of force against the territorial integrity or political independence of any state, or in any other manner inconsistent with the Purposes of the United Nations.

5. All Members shall give the United Nations every assistance in any action it takes in accordance with the present Charter, and shall refrain from giving assistance to any state against which the United Nations is taking preventive or enforcement action.

6. The Organization shall ensure that states which are not Members of the United Nations act in accordance with these Principles so far

as may be necessary for the maintenance of international peace and security.

7. Nothing contained in the present Charter shall authorize the United Nations to intervene in matters which are essentially within the domestic jurisdiction of any state or shall require the Members to submit such matters to settlement under the present Charter; but this principle shall not prejudice the application of enforcement measures under Chapter VII.

Chapter II. Membership

ARTICLE 3 The original Members of the United Nations shall be the states which, having participated in the United Nations Conference on International Organization at San Francisco, or having previously signed the Declaration by United Nations of 1 January 1942, sign the present Charter and ratify it in accordance with Article 110.

ARTICLE 4

1. Membership in the United Nations is open to all other peace-loving states which accept the obligations contained in the present Charter and, in the judgment of the Organization, are able and willing to carry out these obligations.

2. The admission of any such state to membership in the United Nations will be effected by a decision of the General Assembly upon the recommendation of the Security Council.*

Chapter III. Organs

ARTICLE 7

1. There are established as the principal organs of the United Nations: a General Assembly, a Security Council, an Economic and Social Council, a Trusteeship Council, an International Court of Justice and a Secretariat.

2. Such subsidiary organs as may be found necessary may be established in accordance with the present Charter.

ARTICLE 8 The United Nations shall place no restrictions on the eligibility of men and women to participate in any capacity and under conditions of equality in its principal and subsidiary organs.

---

* A member state against which the UN has taken action may be suspended (Art. 5), and a member state which "persistently" violates the Charter may be expelled (Art. 6).

Chapter IV. The General Assembly

Composition

ARTICLE 9

1. The General Assembly shall consist of all the Members of the United Nations.

Functions and Powers

ARTICLE 10 The General Assembly may discuss any question or any matters within the scope of the present Charter or relating to the powers and functions of any organs provided for in the present Charter, and, except as provided in Article 12, may make recommendations to the Members of the United Nations or to the Security Council or to both on any such questions or matters.

ARTICLE 11

1. The General Assembly may consider the general principles of cooperation in the maintenance of international peace and security, including the principles governing disarmament and the regulation of armaments, and may make recommendations with regard to such principles to the Members or to the Security Council or to both.

2. The General Assembly may discuss any questions relating to the maintenance of international peace and security brought before it by any Member of the United Nations, or by the Security Council, or by a state which is not a Member . . . and may make recommendations. . . .

3. The General Assembly may call the attention of the Security Council to situations which are likely to endanger international peace and security.

4. The powers of the General Assembly set forth in this Article shall not limit the general scope of Article 10.*

ARTICLE 13 The General Assembly shall initiate studies and make recommendations for the purpose of:

a. promoting international co-operation in the political field and encouraging the progressive development of international law and its codification;

b. promoting international co-operation in the economic, social, cultural, educational, and health fields, and assisting in the realization of

---

* The Assembly shall not make recommendations on a dispute which is under the purview of the Security Council (Art. 12.a), and the Secretary-General shall notify the Assembly or Members when a dispute ceases to be under consideration (Art. 12.2).

human rights and fundamental freedoms for all without distinction as to race, sex, language, or religion.

ARTICLE 14 Subject to the provisions of Article 12, the General Assembly may recommend measures for the peaceful adjustment of any situation, regardless of origin, which it deems likely to impair the general welfare or friendly relations among nations, including situations resulting from a violation of the provisions of the Charter setting forth the Purposes and Principles of the United Nations.*

Voting

ARTICLE 18

1. Each member of the General Assembly shall have one vote.

2. Decisions of the General Assembly on important questions shall be made by a two-thirds majority of the members present and voting. These questions shall include: recommendations with respect to the maintenance of international peace and security, the election of the non-permanent members of the Security Council, . . . the Economic and Social Council, . . . the Trusteeship Council . . . , the admission of new Members . . . , the suspension of the rights and privileges of membership, the expulsion of Members, questions relating to the operation of the trusteeship system, and budgetary questions.

3. Decisions on other questions, including the determination of additional categories of questions to be decided by a two-thirds majority shall be made by a majority of the members present and voting.†

Procedure

ARTICLE 20 The General Assembly shall meet in regular annual sessions and in such special sessions as occasion may require. Special sessions shall be convoked by the Secretary-General at the request of the Security Council or of a majority of the Members of the United Nations.§

---

* The Assembly receives and considers reports from the Security Council and other organs of the UN (Art. 15), performs assigned functions relative to the international trusteeship system (Art. 16), and approves a budget borne by member states (Art. 17).

† Voting rights of members failing to make their financial contributions to the Organization may be suspended (Art. 19).

§ The Assembly adopts its rules of procedure, elects a president for each session (Art. 21), and may establish subsidiary organs (Art. 22).

Chapter V. The Security Council

Composition

ARTICLE 23

1. The Security Council shall consist of fifteen Members of the United Nations. The Republic of China, France, the Union of Soviet Socialist Republics, the United Kingdom of Great Britain and Northern Ireland, and the United States of America shall be permanent members of the Security Council. The General Assembly shall elect ten other Members of the United Nations to be non-permanent members of the Security Council, due regard being specifically paid, in the first instance to the contribution of Members of the United Nations to the maintenance of international peace and security and to the other purposes of the Organization, and also to equitable geographical distribution.

2. The non-permanent members of the Security Council shall be elected for a term of two years. . . .

Functions and Powers

ARTICLE 24

1. In order to ensure prompt and effective action by the United Nations, its Members confer on the Security Council primary responsibility for the maintenance of international peace and security, and agree that in carrying out its duties under this responsibility the Security Council acts on their behalf.*

ARTICLE 26 In order to promote the establishment and maintenance of international peace and security with the least diversion for armaments of the world's human and economic resources, the Security Council shall be responsible for formulating . . . plans to be submitted to the Members of the United Nations for the establishment of a system for the regulation of armaments.

Voting

ARTICLE 27

1. Each member of the Security Council shall have one vote.

2. Decisions of the Security Council on procedural matters shall be made by an affirmative vote of nine members.

3. Decisions of the Security Council on all other matters shall be

---

* The Security Council acts under specific powers and in accordance with the Charter, and it submits annual and special reports to the Assembly (Art. 24.2–3); member states agree to carry out decisions of the Security Council (Art. 25).

made by an affirmative vote of nine members including the concurring votes of the permanent members; provided that, in decisions under Chapter VI, and under paragraph 3 of Article 52, a party to a dispute shall abstain from voting.

ARTICLE 28

1. The Security Council shall be so organized as to be able to function continuously.*

Chapter VI. Pacific Settlement of Disputes

ARTICLE 33

1. The parties to any dispute, the continuance of which is likely to endanger the maintenance of international peace and security, shall, first of all, seek a solution by negotiation, enquiry, mediation, conciliation, arbitration, judicial settlement, resort to regional agencies or arrangements, or other peaceful means of their own choice.

2. The Security Council shall, when it deems necessary, call upon the parties to settle their dispute by such means.

ARTICLE 34 The Security Council may investigate any dispute, or any situation which might lead to international friction or give rise to a dispute, in order to determine whether the continuance of the dispute or situation is likely to endanger the maintenance of international peace and security.

ARTICLE 35

1. Any Member of the United Nations may bring any dispute . . . to the attention of the Security Council or of the General Assembly.†

ARTICLE 36

1. The Security Council may, at any stage of a dispute . . . recommend appropriate procedures or methods of adjustment.§

---

* Each member of the Council shall be represented at all times, the Council shall meet periodically, and may meet elsewhere than at the seat of the Organization (Art. 28. 1–3); the Council may create subsidiary organs (Art. 29) and shall adopt its own rules of procedure (Art. 30). A UN member state which is not a member of the Council may be invited to participate without vote on issues affecting its interests (Art. 31), and a state not a member of the UN shall be invited if it is party to a dispute (Art. 32).

† A non-member state may bring to the attention of the UN any dispute to which it is a party if it accepts in advance the Charter's obligation for pacific settlement (Art. 35.2)

§ The Council should consider procedures already adopted by the parties, and as a general rule should refer legal disputes to the International Court of Justice (Art. 36.2–3). Parties failing to resolve a dispute shall refer it to the Security Council, which may act under Article 36 or recommend a pacific settlement (Art. 37.1–2), and it shall make such a recommendation upon the request of all parties to a dispute (Art. 38).

Chapter VII. Action With Respect to Threats to the Peace,
Breaches of the Peace, and Acts of Aggression

ARTICLE 39 The Security Council shall determine the existence of
any threat to the peace, breach of the peace, or act of aggression and
shall make recommendations, or decide what measures shall be taken
. . . to maintain or restore international peace and security.

ARTICLE 41 The Security Council may decide what measures not
involving the use of armed force are to be employed to give effect to its
decisions, and it may call upon the Members of the United Nations to
apply such measures. These may include complete or partial interruption
of economic relations and of rail, sea, air, postal, telegraphic, radio,
and other means of communication, and the severance of diplomatic
relations.

ARTICLE 42 Should the Security Council consider that measures provided for in Article 41 would be inadequate or have proved to be inadequate, it may take such action by air, sea, or land forces as may be
necessary to maintain or restore international peace and security. Such
action may include demonstrations, blockade, and other operations by
air, sea, or land forces of the Members of the United Nations.

ARTICLE 43

1. All Members of the United Nations, in order to contribute to
the maintenance of international peace and security, undertake to make
available to the Security Council, on its call and in accordance with a
special agreement or agreements, armed forces, assistance and facilities,
including rights of passage, necessary for the purpose of maintaining
international peace and security.*

ARTICLE 48

1. The action required to carry out the decisions of the Security
Council for the maintenance of international peace and security shall be
taken by all the members of the United Nations or by some of them, as
the Security Council may determine.†

ARTICLE 51 Nothing in the present Charter shall impair the inherent

---

* Agreements shall govern the make-up and deployment of forces and facilities of
member (Art. 43.2–3) and non-member states (Art. 44). Members agree to hold forces
available for international application of armed force (Art. 45), which is planned by the
Security Council and its Military Staff Committee (Arts. 46–47). The Military Staff Committee is defined as the Chiefs of Staff of the permanent members of the Council and other
member states that are invited.

† Article 48.2 and Articles 49 and 50 elaborate on this point and provide for consultation in the event that mutual assistance would be an economic hardship for a state.

right of individual or collective self-defense if an armed attack occurs against a Member of the United Nations, until the Security Council has taken measures necessary to maintain international peace and security. Measures taken by members in the exercise of this right of self-defense shall be immediately reported to the Security Council and shall not in any way affect the authority and responsibility of the Security Council . . . to take at any time such action as it deems necessary. . . .

Chapter VIII. Regional Arrangements

ARTICLE 52

1. Nothing in the present Charter precludes the existence of regional arrangements or agencies for dealing with such matters relating to the maintenance of international peace and security as are appropriate for regional action, provided that such arrangements or agencies and their activities are consistent with the Purposes and Principles of the United Nations.

2. The Members of the United Nations entering into such arrangements or constituting such agencies shall make every effort to achieve pacific settlement of local disputes through such regional arrangements or by such regional agencies before referring them to the Security Council.

3. The Security Council shall encourage the development of pacific settlement of local disputes through such regional arrangements or by such regional agencies. . . .

ARTICLE 53

1. The Security Council shall, where appropriate, utilize such regional arrangements or agencies for enforcement action under its authority. But no enforcement action shall be taken under regional arrangements or by regional agencies without the authorization of the Security Council.*

Chapter IX. International Economic and Social Co-operation

ARTICLE 55 With a view to the creation of conditions of stability and well-being which are necessary for peaceful and friendly relations among nations based on respect for the principle of equal rights and self-determination of peoples, the United Nations shall promote:

a. higher standards of living, full employment, and conditions of economic and social progress and development;

---

* An exception is made for measures against states which during the Second World War were enemies of any signatory of the UN Charter (Art. 53.2–3; 54).

b. solutions of international economic, social, health, and related problems; and international cultural and educational co-operation; and

c. universal respect for, and observance of, human rights and fundamental freedoms for all without distinction as to race, sex, language, or religion.

ARTICLE 56 All Members pledge themselves to take joint and separate action in co-operation with the Organization for the achievement of the purposes set forth in ARTICLE 55.

ARTICLE 57

1. The various specialized agencies, established by intergovernmental agreement and having wide international responsibilities, as defined in their basic instruments, in economic, social, cultural, educational, health, and related fields, shall be brought into relationship with the United Nations in accordance with the provisions of Article 63.

2. Such agencies . . . are hereinafter referred to as specialized agencies.*

ARTICLE 60 Responsibilities for the discharge of the functions of the Organization set forth in this Chapter shall be vested in the General Assembly and, under the authority of the General Assembly, in the Economic and Social Council. . . .

Chapter X. The Economic and Social Council Composition

Functions and Powers

ARTICLE 62

1. The Economic and Social Council may make or initiate studies and reports with respect to international economic, social, cultural, educational, health, and related matters and may make recommendations with respect to such matters to the General Assembly, to the Members of the United Nations and to the specialized agencies concerned.

2. It may make recommendations for the purpose of promoting respect for, and observance of, human rights and fundamental freedoms for all.

3. It may prepare draft conventions for submission to the General Assembly. . . .

4. It may call . . . international conferences. . . .†

* The UN shall recommend ways to coordinate policies and activities of special agencies (Art. 58) and shall initiate negotiations for the creation of new ones (Art. 59).

† Article 61 specifies the membership and electoral procedure of the Economic and Social Council (ECOSOC), and Arts. 63–70 and 72 describe its relationship to specialized agencies.

ARTICLE 71 The Economic and Social Council may make suitable arrangements for consultation with non-governmental organizations which are concerned with matters within its competence. Such arrangements may be made with the international organizations and, where appropriate, with national organizations after consultation with the Member of the United Nations concerned.

Chapter XI. Declaration Regarding No-Self-Governing Territories

ARTICLE 73 Members of the United Nations which have or assume responsibilities for the administration of territories whose peoples have not yet attained a full measure of self-government recognize the principle that the interests of the inhabitants of these territories are paramount, and accept as a sacred trust the obligation to promote to the utmost, within the system of international peace and security established by the present Charter, the well-being of the inhabitants of these territories, and, to this end:

a. to ensure, with due respect for the culture of the peoples concerned, their political, economic, social, and educational advancement, their just treatment, and their protection against abuses;

b. to develop self-government, to take due account of the political aspirations of the peoples, and to assist them in the progressive development of their free political institutions, according to the particular circumstances of each territory and its peoples and their varying stages of advancement;

c. to further international peace and security;

d. to promote constructive measures of development, to encourage research, and to co-operate with one another and, when and where appropriate, with specialized international bodies with a view to the practical achievement of the social, economic, and scientific purposes set forth in this Article; and

e. to transmit regularly to the Secretary-General for informational purposes, subject to such limitation as security and constitutional considerations may require, statistical and other information of a technical nature relating to economic, social, and educational conditions in the territories for which they are respectively responsible other than those territories to which Chapters XII and XIII apply.

ARTICLE 74 Members of the United Nations also agree that their policy in respect of the territories to which this Chapter applies, no less than in respect of their metropolitan areas, must be based on the general principle of good-neighborliness, due account being taken of the interests and well-being of the rest of the world, in social, economic, and commercial matters.

Chapter XII International Trusteeship System

ARTICLE 75 The United Nations shall establish under its authority an international trusteeship system for the administration and supervision of such territories as may be placed thereunder by subsequent individual agreements. These territories are hereinafter referred to as trust territories.

ARTICLE 76 The basic objectives of the trusteeship system, in accordance with the Purposes of the United Nations laid down in Article 1 of the present Charter, shall be:

a. to further international peace and security;

b. to promote the political, economic, social, and educational advancement of the inhabitants of the trust territories, and their progressive development towards self-government or independence as may be appropriate to the particular circumstances of each territory and its peoples and the freely expressed wishes of the peoples concerned, and as may be provided by the terms of each trusteeship agreement;

c. to encourage respect for human rights and for fundamental freedoms for all without distinction as to race, sex, language, or religion, and to encourage recognition of the interdependence of the peoples of the world; and

d. to ensure equal treatment in social, economic, and commercial matters for all Members of the United Nations and their nationals, and also equal treatment for the latter in the administration of justice. . . .

ARTICLE 77

1. The trusteeship system shall apply to such territories in the following categories as may be placed thereunder by means of trusteeship agreements:

a. territories now held under mandate;

b. territories which may be detached from enemy states as a result of the Second World War; and

c. territories voluntarily placed under the system by states responsible for their administration.*

---

* Art. 77.2 leaves for subsequent agreement the terms upon which territories were brought into the system; Article 78 excludes territories which are members of the UN, since they are accorded sovereign equality; Articles 79–84 specify terms and conditions for the operation of the trusteeship system in relation to UN organs.

ARTICLE 85

1. The functions of the United Nations with regard to trusteeship
. . . shall be exercised by the General Assembly.

2. The Trusteeship Council, operating under the authority of the
General Assembly, shall assist the General Assembly in carrying out these
functions.*

Chapter XIV. The International Court of Justice

ARTICLE 92

The International Court of Justice shall be the principal judicial
organ of the United Nations. It shall function in accordance with the
annexed Statute, which is based on the Statute of the Permanent Court
of International Justice and forms an integral part of the present Charter.

ARTICLE 93

1. All Members of the United Nations are *ipso facto* parties to the
Statute of the International Court of Justice.

2. A state which is not a Member of the United Nations may become
a party to the Statute of the International Court of Justice on conditions
to be determined in each case by the General Assembly upon the recommendation of the Security Council.

ARTICLE 94

1. Each Member of the United Nations undertakes to comply with
the decision of the International Court of Justice in any case to which it
is a party.

2. If any party to a case fails to perform the obligations incumbent
upon it under a judgment rendered by the Court, the other party may
have recourse to the Security Council, which may . . . make recommendations or decide upon measures to be taken or give effect to the judgment.†

Chapter XV. The Secretariat

ARTICLE 97 The Secretariat shall comprise a Secretary-General and
such staff as the organization may require. The Secretary-General shall

---

* Chapter XIII, Arts. 86–91, defines the membership of the Trusteeship Council, its
functions, voting, procedure, and cooperative relationship to specialized agencies.

† The Charter does not prevent Members of the UN from taking disputes to other
tribunals (Art. 95). It authorizes all UN organs and specialized agencies to request advisory
opinions from the International Court of Justice on any legal question within the scope of
their activities (Art. 96).

be appointed by the General Assembly upon the recommendation of the Security Council. He shall be the chief administrative officer of the Organization.

ARTICLE 98 The Secretary-General shall act in that capacity in all meetings of the General Assembly, of the Security Council, of the Economic and Social Council, and of the Trusteeship Council, and shall perform such other functions as are entrusted to him by these organs. The Secretary-General shall make an annual report to the General Assembly on the work of the Organization.

ARTICLE 99 The Secretary-General may bring to the attention of the Security Council any matter which in his opinion may threaten the maintenance of international peace and security.

ARTICLE 100

1. In the performance of their duties the Secretary-General and the staff shall not seek or receive instructions from any government or from any other authority external to the Organization. They shall refrain from any action which might reflect on their position as international officials responsible only to the Organization.

2. Each Member of the United Nations undertakes to respect the exclusively international character of the responsibilities of the Secretary-General and the staff and not to seek to influence them in the discharge of their responsibilities.*

Chapter XVI. Miscellaneous Provisions

ARTICLE 102

1. Every treaty and every international agreement entered into by any Member of the United Nations after the present Charter comes into force shall as soon as possible be registered with the Secretariat and published by it.†

---

* Article 101 provides for the appointment of staff, particularly on the criteria of competence and integrity, with consideration also for geographical distribution.

† No party to a non-registered treaty or agreement may invoke it before any organ of the UN (Art. 102.2). Obligations under the Charter supersede all other international obligations (Art. 103). The UN has legal status and, with its staff, diplomatic privileges and immunities in each Member territory (Arts. 104–105). Article 106 empowers the signatories of the Moscow Declaration of 30 October 1943 and France to make transitional security arrangements, and Article 107 exempts actions by signatory states during the Second World War from the provisions of the Charter. Chapter XVIII, Articles 108–111, provides for amendment and ratification.

Notes

Document Sources

Index

Notes

Introduction

1. Ipatyev Chronicle Code of the Twelfth Century, *Complete Collection of Russian Chronicles*, (St. Petersburg, 1908; Moscow, 1962), vol. 2, years: 364 (1148), 444 (1151).

2. Address of Vladimir and Izyaslav Davidovich, Svyatoslav Olegovich and Vsevolod Svyatoslavovich in 1148 to the Great Prince of Kiev, Izyaslav Mstislavovich, in Kiev Chronicle, ibid.

3. This phrase comes from the American antiwar movement of 1969 and its chant, "all we are saying is, give peace a chance."

4. Alexander I. Solzhenitsyn, *Mir e nasiliye. Publitsystika* (Paris: YMCA-PRESS, 1989), 125–26.

1. Premodern Ideas of Peace, 800 B.C.–A.D. 1815

1. From Pindar, "For Aristomenes of Aegina," "Pythian Odes," 8, in *The Odes of Pindar*, trans. John Sandys (Cambridge, Mass: Harvard Univ. Press, Loeb Classical Library [hereinafter LCL], 1915), 261. Aristomenes won the wrestling match of 446 B.C. at the Pythian games, which were held at Delphi.

2. Anonymous Hellenic fragment, quoted in Gerardo Zampaglione, *The Idea of Peace in Antiquity*, trans. Richard Dunn (Notre Dame: Univ. of Notre Dame Press, 1973 [original published as *L'Idea della pace nel mondo antico*, in Turin, Italy: 1967]), 40.

3. The large body of Stoic writings, like the works of Pythagoras, is lost and known only through contemporaneous descriptions.

4. Seneca, *Epistola ad Lucilium,* quoted in Zampaglione, *The Idea of Peace in Antiquity*, 158.

5. Seneca, "On Leisure," in *Seneca: Moral Essays*, trans. John W. Basore (LCL, 1922, rev. 1935), 2: 187–89 and passim. This was practical wisdom, too, because after gaining wealth and influence as the teacher of the emperor Nero, Seneca lost it upon a change in power. He committed suicide when threatened with assassination.

6. For a discussion of the terms of peace in English, Greek (*eirene*), Hebrew (*sha-*

lom), and Latin (*pax*), see Ronald G. Musto, *The Catholic Peace Tradition* (Maryknoll, N.Y.: Orbis Books, 1986), 7–13. Musto references scholarly sources.

7. Herodotus, *History of the Persian War*, in *Herodotus*, trans. A. D. Godley (LCL, 1929), 1: 113. Herodotus attributed the remark to Croesus, king of Lydia, who after his defeat by Cyrus of Persia explained that the gods must have willed the war since no man would desire it.

8. Fragment 110, "Dulce bellum inexpertis," in *The Odes of Pindar*, trans. John Sandys (LCL, 1915), 577 (language modernized by editors). See also Erasmus, document 1.37.

9. This refrain is repeated three times in the opening chorus of "Agamemnon," lines 121, 139, and 159. *Aeschylus*, trans. Herbert Weir Smith (LCL, 1952), 2: 121, 139, 159.

10. Prometheus, in "Prometheus Bound," in *Aeschylus*, trans. Herbert Weir Smith (LCL, 1952), 1: 241.

11. Isocrates, "Areopagiticus," in *Isocrates*, trans. George Norlin (LCL, 1929), 2: 113. This oration probably was written in 355 B.C., at the end of a disastrous war between Athens and the strongest members of her own Confederacy.

12. Plato makes extended use of this distinction in *Laws*, trans. R. G. Bury (LCL, 1926), 13–23. "Civil strife" is the translation used by Grube in document 1.8; Paul Shorey used "faction" in his edition of *Plato: The Republic* (LCL, 1930, rev. 1937).

13. *Aristotle: Politics*, trans. H. Rackham (LCL, 1932), 37. This attitude also characterized Aristotle's defense of slavery.

14. Elavius Arrianus, "Anabasis Alexandri," in *Arrian*, trans. E. Iliff Robson (LCL, 1929), 179–80.

15. Polybius, *The Histories*, trans. W. R. Paton (LCL, 1926), 333. Editor's italics.

16. Tacitus, *Life of Agricola*, cited in Zampaglione, *The Idea of Peace in Antiquity*, 136. Tacitus attributed the saying to the tribal commander Calgacus in A.D. 85.

17. The poem elevates Hesiod's quarrel with a brother over an inheritance into a treatise on strife, justice, and peace.

18. Hesiod, *Theogony*, line 903, in *Hesiod: Theogony, Works and Days, Shield*, trans. Apostolos N. Athanassakis (Baltimore, Johns Hopkins Univ. Press, 1983), 35.

19. "Jew" (Yehudi) technically refers to the descendents of Judeans, occupants of Judah after the nation of Israel was divided (922 B.C.). They gave continuity to the nation and culture of Israel, which had been formed by the Hebrew followers of Moses, so that the whole tradition may be called Judaic.

20. In ancient Hebrew: YHWH, vowels not being designated. *Yahweh* is the widely accepted approximation of the original pronunciation.

21. Yehezkel Kaufmann, "The Biblical Age," in *Great Ages and Ideas of the Jewish People*, ed. Leo W. Schwarz, (New York: Random House, 1956), 12.

22. Martin Buber, *The Prophetic Faith* (New York: Macmillan, 1949), 215.

23. Gregory of Nazianzus, from *Oratorio 22*, and *De pace 2*, quoted in Zampaglione, *The Idea of Peace in Antiquity*, 269–70. Gregory wrote in 379, when the empire was contested by the Franks, Goths, Lombards, among northern tribes, and by the rising power of Persia in the east.

24. See the 1527 Schleitheim Confession of Anabaptist leaders, reproduced in full and discussed in Peter Brock, *Pacifism in Europe to 1914* (Princeton, N.J.: Princeton Univ. Press, 1972), 69–71.

25. Urban II, speech at Clermont, 27 Nov. 1095 (account of Robert the Monk), trans. James A. Brandage, in Brandage, *The Crusades: A Documentary Survey* (Milwaukee

Wis.: Marquette Univ. Press, 1961), 19. Brandage gives "milk and money," a typographical error that is true to Urban's intent.

26. The image of "phantom" empire is aptly used by Frances A. Yates in *Astraea: The Imperial Theme in the Sixteenth Century* (London: Routledge & Kegan Paul, 1975), 1–2.

27. See, for example, Robert of Courson, Roland of Cremona, Peter Abelard, Peter Lombard, and William of Ockham, all mentioned in Ronald G. Musto's discussion of the subject, *The Catholic Peace Tradition*, 104–09.

28. Papal bull "Sublimis Deus" (2 June 1537), quoted in Lewis Hanke, *The Spanish Struggle for Justice in the Conquest of America* (Philadelphia: Univ. of Pennsylvania Press, 1949), 72–73. Las Casas explicitly studied and interpreted the just war tradition in his condemnation of wars against the Indians. See especially Angel Losada, "The controversy between Sepuúlveda and Las Casas in the Junta of Valladolid," in *Bartolomé de Las Casas in History*, ed. Joan Friede and Benjamin Keen, (DeKalb, Ill.: Northern Illinois Univ. Press), 279–307.

29. See Vitoria (1492–1546), *De Indis et De Jure Belli Relectiones*; Suarez (1548–1617), various works; Ames (1576–1633), *Conscience, with the Power and Cases Thereof*; Locke (1632–1704), *Two Treatises of Civil Government*; and Grotius (1583–1645), *De Jure Belli ac Pacis*. All are perceptively discussed in James Turner Johnson, *Ideology, Reason, and the Limitation of War: Religious and Secular Concepts, 1200–1740* (Princeton: Princeton Univ. Press, 1975).

30. Ibid., 254.

31. For a brief summary, see Ronald G. Musto, *The Catholic Peace Tradition*, 85–86.

32. Jean Jacques Rousseau, "Judgment on Perpetual Peace," in *A Project of Perpetual Peace*, trans. Edith M. Nuttall (London: Richard Cobden-Sanderson, 1927), 131; reprinted in *Peace Projects of the Eighteenth Century* (New York: Garland, 1974).

2. Citizen Initiatives and Official Agreements, 1815–1914

1. Sandi E. Cooper, *Patriotic Pacifism: Waging War on War in Europe, 1815-1914* (New York: Oxford Univ. Press, 1991), 60. Cooper notes that the word *pacifism* was first used in 1901 by Emile Arnaud, president of the Ligue International de la paix et de la liberté [International League of Peace and Freedom]. During World War I the word was narrowed in English and American usage to exclusively *absolute* pacifism, the refusal to sanction any violence, and it remained somewhat ambiguous thereafter.

2. The Interparliamentary Union and International Peace Bureau still exist.

3. David Starr Jordan, "A Blind Man's Holiday," speech from Jordan, *Imperial Democracy* (New York: Appleton, 1899; reprint, New York: Garland, 1972). 179. President of Stanford University, Jordan was a natural scientist whose studies documented the biological degradation of societies as a result of war.

4. Ladd's classic work was *An Essay on a Congress of Nations for the Adjustment of International Disputes Without Resort to Arms* (1840); reprint as *An Essay on a Congress of Nations* (New York: Oxford Univ. Press, 1916).

5. *Uncle Tom's Cabin*, by Harriet Beecher Stowe, had greatly stimulated the campaign against slavery in the United States before the Civil War.

6. An alternative interpretation is that the Tsar was influenced by advisors anxious

to avoid a new round of expensive investment in military technology. If so, his motive was in keeping with de Bloch's economic analysis.

7. Karl Marx and Friedrich Engels, preface to the German edition of 1872, repeated almost verbatim by Engels in the 1888 English edition: *Birth of the Communist Manifesto,* ed. Dirk J. Struik (New York: International Publishers, 1971), 129–30, 133–37.

8. Friederick Engels, "Can Europe Disarm" (*Vorwärts,* Mar. 1893), in *Karl Marx, Frederick Engels: Collected Works* (New York: International Publishers, 1990), 27: 371.

9. William Edgerton, introduction to *Memoirs of Peasant Tolstoyans in Soviet Russia,* trans. and ed. William Edgerton (Bloomington: Indiana Univ. Press, 1993), and "The Artist Turned Prophet: Leo Tolstoj after 1880," *American Contributions to the Sixth International Congress of Slavists,* Prague, 7–13 Aug. 1968, vol. 2: Literary Contributions (The Hague: Mouton, 1969).

10. Henry Dunant, born Jean-Henri Dunant (1828–1910), was the founder of the International Red Cross and co-winner with Frédéric Passy of the 1901 Nobel Peace Prize. The Red Cross has been known in Muslim countries as the Red Crescent since 1906.

11. Raymond L. Bridgman, *The First Book of World Law* (Boston: Ginn, 1911).

12. The British refused Washington's request to detain the Confederate ship the *Alabama,* which did immense damage to Northern shipping. Following the Civil War, relations between the U.S. and Great Britain reached a crisis until the British agreed to arbitration. Britain complied with the arbitration judgment and paid the prescribed fine, although its representative never signed the Geneva award.

13. Pauncefote to the Marquess of Salisbury, 31 July 1899, *British Documents on the Origins of the War, 1898–1914,* ed. G. P. Gooch and Harold Temperley (London: His Majesty's Stationery Office, 1927), 1: 232.

3. World War I and Peace, 1914–1919

1. Quoted in Sandi E. Cooper, *Patriotic Pacifism: Waging War on War in Europe, 1815–1914* (New York: Oxford Univ. Press, 1991), 196.

2. The name was adopted at a 1919 postwar conference in Zurich, but the 1915 meeting had expressly provided that an organizing conference should be convened at the war's end. The Women's Congress at The Hague did feel the impact of wartime nationalism, French women not being present, for example.

3. Such societies were the American Friends Service Committee and its British counterpart, the American Civil Liberties Bureau, the British No Conscription League and (as a part of its work) the Union of Democratic Control.

4. Liebknecht, an active Social Democrat and antimilitarist before the war, was imprisoned May 1916–October 1918. A leader of the Spartacus League, he was arrested and murdered in the midst of the uprising of January 1919.

5. "The Failure of the International," statement from the *Socialist Review,* in *The Socialists and the War,* ed. William E. Walling (New York: Henry Holt, 1915), 311. MacDonald resigned the leadership of the ILP, which he had held since 1906. He returned to leadership in 1922 and was Prime Minister in 1924 and 1929–1935.

6. The meeting included representatives from Italian party and eastern European ones as well as individuals from Germany, France, and some neutrals. It sought to align dissident socialists in all countries in an international campaign for peace. See document 3.26.

7. See V. I. Lenin, "Report on Peace" ("Decree on Peace") of the All-Russia Con-

gress of Soviets of Workers' and Soldiers' Deputies, 26 Oct. (8 Nov.), in Lenin, *Collected Works*, (Moscow: Progress Press, 1977), 26: 249–52. The proposal annulled secret agreements and called for an international settlement without annexations or indemnities. It was in some measure an offer to suspend international civil war for peace, but the invitation was not accepted by the western allies.

8. 3 March 1918. Ironically, the very harshness of German peace terms, and their clearly aggressive designs, contributed to workers' rebellions in Austria and Germany in 1918. In the following year there were significant rebellions throughout central Europe, but they were overwhelmingly responses to national conditions, including military defeat, rather than to communist ideology.

9. Kautsky was a leader in the German Social Democratic party and a member of the International Socialist Bureau. He opposed the war policy of the party's leadership but was loyal to the party as the instrument of future social reform.

10. *Militarism versus Feminism: An Enquiry and a Policy Demonstrating that Militarism Involves the Subjection of Women* (London: Allen & Unwin, 1915), 3–4.

11. Maude Royden was active in the postwar Women's International League for Peace and Freedom, though she reluctantly supported World War II. She was the first woman licensed as a minister in England and the first to earn a doctor of divinity (Glasgow 1931).

12. The Nobel Peace Prize was awarded to Wilson in 1919, to Bourgeois in 1920, when he presided over both the French Senate and the League Council, and to Cecil in 1937. The first official draft of a League was produced (20 Mar. 1918) by a committee formed by the British government and headed by Lord Walter G. F. Phillimore. Four Wilson drafts were produced thereafter.

13. Jan Christiaan Smuts, "The League of nations: A Practical Suggestion" [16 Dec. 1918], in David Hunter Miller, *The Drafting of the Covenant* (New York: Putnam, 1928), 2: 38. It must be added that Smuts never recognized the right of political consent of the African population in the South African state of which he was so much the architect.

14. Ibid., 40, 60. The Smuts document was a pamphlet about the nature of an appropriate international order, not a draft treaty. It was published while the official governmental drafts were still secret.

4. Alternatives to War, 1919–1939

1. The League of Nations Assembly first met on 15 November 1920. At that time the United States, the Soviet Union, and Germany were not members. Germany was admitted in 1926, but withdrew seven years later along with Japan. By that point the League had ceased to be a significant international actor. It collapsed as a political factor with German reoccupation of the Rhineland and Italian victory over Ethiopia in 1936.

2. The League Covenant, adopted by the Peace Conference on 28 April 1919 and signed by 32 nations two months later, came into force on 10 January 1920.

3. Inis L. Claude, Jr., *Swords into Plowshares: The Problems and Progress of International Organization* (New York: Random House, 1956), 59–60.

4. People of 26 nationalities were repatriated. The League authorized Nansen to issue international identification cards for displaced persons, which were accepted as the equivalent of passports by over fifty countries.

5. Quoted from Nansen's address upon receiving the 1922 Nobel Peace Prize, in J. M. Scott, *Fridtjof Nansen* (Geneva: Heron Books, 1971), 237–38.

6. Regarding the concept of interdependence in international law, notably in the thought of James Brierly and Nicolas Politis, see Dorothy V. Jones, *Code of Peace: Ethics and Security in the World of the Warlord States* (Chicago: Univ. of Chicago Press, 1991), 83–112.

7. The mandate principle was proposed by General Jan C. Smuts and others before the peace conference as an alternative to the annexation, international supervision, or restoration of territories formerly controlled by Germany, Austria-Hungary, Turkey, and, in some versions, Russia. Woodrow Wilson applied the principle to the non-European world and negotiated its acceptance. The mandate system was innovative because it was subject to the authority of an international agency. *Mandates Under the League of Nations* (Chicago: Univ. of Chicago 1930), 1–43, passim.

8. Francis P. Walters, *A History of the League of Nations* (London: Oxford Univ. Press, 1952), 200.

9. The organizational base included the Paneuropean Union (1926), the International Committee for a European Customs Union (1924), and the League for European Cooperation (1926), with allied groups in the peace movement.

10. Carl H. Pegg, *Evolution of the European Idea, 1914–1932* (Chapel Hill: Univ. of North Carolina Press, 1983), 165.

11. In addition, the League's section on Communications and Trade continued as the UN Transport and Communications Commission, its committee on Traffic in Opium became the UN Commission on Narcotic Drugs, and its committee on child welfare was expanded to become UNICEF.

12. E. D. Morel, *The Black Man's Burden: The White Man in Africa from the Fifteenth Century to World War I* (London: National Labour Press, 1920; New York and London: Monthly Review Press, 1969), 230.

13. The Genoa Conference, 10 April–19 May, included Germany and Russia in negotiations to regularize relations with the Soviet Union and stabilize the world economy. It stalled over French demands that the Soviet Union recognize the pre-war Russian debt. Litvinov was chosen to represent the USSR in the League's Preparatory Commission on Disarmament because he was inclined to work within the world community, and he became Commissar for Foreign Affairs in July 1930. His 1927 plan was submitted on 30 November. His 1928 plan was supported by Germany, China, and Turkey but was rejected by the Commission on 19 March. Soviet proposals often and understandably were spurned as propaganda devices. They were not unique on that score, and the issue here their merit, not their motive.

14. The Washington Conference was held from 12 November 1921 to 6 February 1922. Under the naval treaty, which expired in 1936, U.S. and British naval construction was constrained for a decade and a half, though Japan built up in absolute and relative terms. The Treaty of London did not cover Italy or France.

15. A Four Power Treaty obligated the United States, Britain, Japan, and France to respect one another's insular possessions in the Pacific. A Nine Power Treaty obligated those powers plus the Netherlands, Portugal, Belgium, and China to respect the so-called Open Door principle of unrestricted trade and investment.

16. Although not League members, the United States, Germany, and the Soviet Union were represented on this Preparatory Commission.

17. League of Nations General Assembly resolution of 1925, quoted in Elly Hermon, "The International Peace Education Movement, 1919–1939," *Peace Movements and Political Cultures*, ed. Charles Chatfield and Peter van den Dungen (Knoxville: Univ. of Tennessee Press, 1988), 129. Initiatives by groups in the nongovernmental sector, such as the

International Bureau of Education (1926, Geneva) tended to become intergovernmental until the mid-thirties when, with the collapse of the League, they became nongovernmental again.

18. Caroline E. Playne, "Le désarmement moral," *Le Mouvement Pacifiste* (July 1923), 81, trans. and quoted by Elly Hermon in "The International Peace Education Movement, 1919–1939," in *Peace Movements and Political Cultures*, 130. Playne was a member of the council of the International Peace Bureau.

19. Gerald Heard, "The Significance of the New Pacifism" (1936), in *The New Pacifism*, ed. Gerald K. Hibbert (London: Allenson & Company, 1936), 18. Heard was an organizer for the Agricultural Cooperative Movement and a science commentator for the British Broadcasting Corporation whose writing on pacifism influenced especially author Aldous Huxley.

20. Romain Rolland, *Mahatma Gandhi* (Paris, 1924), 113, quoted in David James Fisher, *Romain Rolland and the Politics of Intellectual Engagement* (Berkeley: Univ. of California Press, 1988), 124.

21. Barthelemy de Ligt, *The Conquest of Violence: An Essay on War and Revolution* (English edns. London: Headley Brothers, 1937; New York: Dutton, 1938), 2–7. For his strategy of civilian defense, see his *Plan of Campaign Against All War and All Preparation for War*, published in 1939 as a pamphlet by the Peace Pledge Union.

22. Manifesto of the "Clarté" Group, published in the occasional periodical, *L'Humanité*, Paris, 1919.

23. Speech of M. Noblemaire to the 1921 League Assembly, from the League of Nations *Official Journal*, in *The League of Nations*, ed. Ruth B. Henig (Edinburgh: Oliver & Boyd, 1973), 44–45.

24. Maurice Bourquin, "Final Report to the Conference," *Peaceful Change* [Proceedings of the Tenth International Studies Conference: Paris, June 28–July 3, 1937], vol. 1 (Paris: International Institute of Intellectual Cooperation, 1938), 588.

25. Negotiations for a treaty renouncing war were opened by Briand in April 1927; the Pact was signed by 15 governments on 27 April 1928; it became effective on 2 March 1929, and was subsequently endorsed by most states.

26. This argument was developed especially in the United States, where it reflected mistrust of European politics and a view of the League as dominated by victor states.

27. Statement by the minister of foreign affairs of Sweden, M. Sandler, on behalf of the Oslo conference of Scandinavian states at the third Meeting of the XIXth Ordinary Session of the Assembly of the League of Nations on 13 September 1938 (League of Nations, *Official Journal, Special Supplement* no. 183, Geneva, 1938, p. 38). The Oslo group was determined not to be again led into the application of sanctions that would not be fully applied by Britain and France.

28. "Paix Immédiate!", facsimile of a tract of which 100,000 copies were distributed in early September 1939, in Nicolas Faucier, *Pacifisme et antimilitarisme dans l'entre-deux-guerres* (Paris: Spartacus, 1983), 193. Trans. Sandi Cooper.

5. World War II and Peace, 1939–1945

1. The Congress of Racial Equality, founded in 1942–43 and originally sponsored by the Fellowship of Reconciliation, experimented with direct nonviolent action for civil rights from the 1940s to the 1960s.

2. The Spanish town of Guernica was subjected to fascist bombing on 28 April 1937. Picasso's large, evocative painting was completed two months later.

3. Laurence Housman, "From the Chair of the W.R.I.," in Houseman et al., *Autarchy, Internationalism and Common Sense* (Enfield, Eng.: WRI, 1940), 4.

4. The Four Freedoms were defined by President Franklin Roosevelt in his message to the Congress of 6 January 1941.

5. The term "United Nations" was coined by President Roosevelt to give the anti-Axis alliance a universal quality. The alliance evolved into the United Nations Organization.

6. The original British draft explicitly called for "effective international organization." This was struck out by Roosevelt, despite the objections of senior staff members, and was replaced with the ambiguous "system of general security" in deference to American sensitivity about the League of Nations. Robert A. Divine, *Second Chance: The Triumph of Internationalism in America During World War II* (New York: Atheneum, 1967), 44–45.

7. Amid futile attempts to locate the Polish soldiers captured by the USSR in 1939 there were rumors, later confirmed, that several thousands of them had been massacred in the Katyn forest on the order of Soviet security officers.

8. These Italians were Altiero Spinelli, Ernesto Rossi, and Eugenio Colorni.

9. The 1943 Declaration of Four Nations was issued on 30 October 1943 by the foreign ministers of the United States, the United Kingdom, and the USSR, and the Chinese Ambassador to Moscow. At Dumbarton Oaks in 1944, because the Soviet Union was not then at war with Japan, its delegation met with the Americans and British, who subsequently met with the Chinese.

10. China, France, the Soviet Union, the United Kingdom, and the United States.

11. Inis L. Claude, Jr., *Swords into Plowshares: The Problems and Progress of International Organization* (New York: Random House, 1956), 267.

Document Sources

Document numbers correspond to those used in the list of Documents and throughout the volume. Inclusive page numbers or line numbers refer to the passage from which a document has been excerpted.

The following abbreviations are used in the source notes: LCL, for the Loeb Classical Library of Harvard University Press, Cambridge, Massachusetts; RSV, for *The Holy Bible: Revised Standard Version;* and GPO, for the United States Government Printing Office.

1.1. Aristophanes, *The Peace.* In *The Complete Greek Drama,* edited by Whitney J. Oates and Eugene O'Neill, Jr., 2: 693. New York: Random House, 1938.

1.2. Albius Tibullus, "Against War," in *Tibullus, Catullus, Tibullus, Pervigilium Veneris,* translated by J. P. Postgate, 244–47. LCL, 1913.

1.3. *Virgil's Georgics: A Modern English Verse Translation,* translated by Smith Palmer Bovie, bk. 1, 505–14; bk. 2, 458–74, 490–98. Chicago: Univ. of Chicago Press, 1956.

1.4. Aeschylus, *The Seven Against Thebes.* In *Aeschylus,* translated by Herbert Weir Smith, 1: 320–56. LCL, 1952.

1.5. Xenophon, "Ways and Means." In *Xenophon: Scripta Minora,* translated by E. C. Marchant, 225, 229. LCL, 1925.

1.6. Thucydides, *History of the Peloponnesian War,* translated by Charles Forster Smith, 2: 143–49. LCL, 1930.

1.7. *Aristotle: The Nicomachean Ethics,* translated by H. Rackham, 615. LCL 1934.

1.8. *Plato's Republic,* translated by G. M. A. Grube, 130–31. Indianapolis: Hackett, 1974.

1.9. Isocrates, "On the Peace." In *Isocrates,* translated by George Norlin, 2: 17. LCL, 1929.

1.10. Lucius Annaeus Florus, *Epitome of Roman History,* translated by E. S. Forster, 2: 349, 351. LCL, 1929.

1.11. *Polybius: The Histories,* translated by W. R. Paton, 5: 281, 283. LCL, 1926.

1.12. Horace, "Augustus," (Ode 15). *Horace: The Odes and Epodes,* translated by C. E. Bennett, 345, 346. LCL, 1952.

1.13. Cassius Dio Cocceianus, in *Dio's Roman History,* translated by Earnest Cary, 8: 85–86. LCL 1925.

1.14. Hesiod, *Works and Days,* in *Hesiod: Theogony, Works and Days, Shield,* translated and edited by Apostolos Athanassakis, 11–24, 110–19. Baltimore: Johns Hopkins Univ. Press, 1983.

1.15. Amos 5: 4, 21–24; Isaiah 1: 11, 16–17, 19–20; Isaiah 2: 2–4; Isaiah 11: 1–4, 6, 9; 32: 17; Isaiah 42: 5–7. In RSV.

1.16. Matthew 5: 3–11 ("The Beatitudes"), and Luke 27–38 (The New Law). In RSV.

1.17. Romans 12: 9, 12–14, 17–21. In RSV.

1.18. Clement of Alexandria, *Miscellanies* and *Cohortatio ad Gentes.* Quoted in *The Idea of Peace in Antiquity,* by Gerardo Zampaglione, translated by Richard Dunn, 251. Notre Dame, Ind.: Univ. of Notre Dame Press, 1973.

1.19. Lactantius, *The Divine Institutes* (bks. 6–10), translated by Sister Mary Francis McDonald, 452. *The Fathers of the Church,* vol. 49. Washington, D.C.: Catholic Univ. of America Press, 1964.

1.20. A sermon, based on the Laurentian text. In *The Russian Primary Chronicle,* edited by Samuel H. Cross, 146–48. Harvard Studies and Notes in Philology and Literature, vol. 12. Cambridge, Mass.: Harvard Univ. Press, 1930.

1.21. Gregory of Nyssa, "On Perfection," in *Ascetical Works,* translated by Virginia Woods Callahan, 102–3. *The Fathers of the Church,* vol. 58 Washington, D.C.: Catholic Univ. of America Press, 1966.

1.22. "First Rule of the Third Order" [A.D. 1221], arts. 15–17. In *St. Francis of Assissi: Writings and Early Biographies,* edited by Marion A. Habig, 4th ed., rev., 168–75. Chicago: Franciscan Herald, 1975. "The Peace Prayer of St. Francis." In ibid., 1930–31.

1.23. Menno Simons, *Das Fundament des Christelycken Leers,* (The foundation of Christian doctrine [1539–40]). Quoted in Peter Brock, *Pacifism in Europe to 1914,* 107–8. Princeton: Princeton Univ. Press, 1972. Simeon Friderich Rues. *Aufrichtige Nachrichten von dem gegenwartigen Zustande der Mennoniten . . . in den vereinigten Niderlanden* (Sincere information on the present state of the Mennonites in the United Netherlands [1743]). Quoted in ibid., 199–200.

1.24. "A Declaration from the harmless and innocent people of God called Quakers." In *The Journal of George Fox,* edited by John L. Nickalls, 398–404. Cambridge: Cambridge Univ. Press, 1952.

1.25. Eusebius Pamphili. *Ecclesiastical History,* translated by Roy J. Deferrari,

287–88. *The Fathers of the Church*, vol. 29. New York: Fathers of the Church, 1955.

1.26. "The Testament of Vladimir Monomakh." App. 1 of *The Russian Primary Chronicle*, edited by Samuel H. Cross, 301–9. Harvard Studies and Notes in Philology and Literature, vol. 12. Cambridge, Mass.: Harvard Univ. Press, 1930. Cross notes that the Testament *(Pouchenie)* is found only in the Laurentian chronicle and probably dates from ca. 1117–26, though it was introduced to the Chronicle as late as the fourteenth century.

1.27. Letter of 796 from Charlemagne to Pope Leo III in *Christianity through the Thirteenth Century*, edited by Marshall W. Baldwin, 119–20. New York: Harper & Row, 1970. Letter of 799 from Alcuin to Charlemagne. In ibid., 120.

1.28. Dante Alighieri, *Il Convito* (The banquet), translated by Elizabeth Price Sayer, 173–74. London: George Routledge & Sons, 1887. Dante, *Monarchy and Three Political Letters*, translated by Donald Nicholl and Colin Hardie, 14, 17–18, 23–25, 93–94. London: Weidenfeld & Nicolson, 1954. Reprint, New York: Garland, 1972.

1.29. Thomas Aquinas. *Summa of Theology*. In *An Aquinas Reader*, edited by Mary T. Clark, 381–82. Garden City, N.Y.: Image Books, Doubleday, 1972.

1.30. Honoré Bonet. *The Tree of Battles*, translated by G. W. Coopland, 81, 118, 120, 188. Cambridge, Mass: Harvard Univ. Press, 1949.

1.31. "Peace of God at Charroux" [989]. In *A Source Book for Medieval History*, edited by Oliver J. Thatcher and Edgar H. McNeal, 412. New York: Scribners, 1905.

1.32. "Truce of God, Made for the Archbishopric of Arles, 1035–41." In *A Source Book for Medieval History*, edited by Oliver J. Thatcher and Edgar H. McNeal, 414–16. New York: Scribners, 1905.

1.33 "Peace of the Land Established by Henry IV, 1103." In *A Source Book for Medieval History*, edited by Oliver J. Thatcher and Edgar H. McNeal, 419. New York: Scribners, 1905.

1.34. Bartolomé de Las Casas, *Declaration of the Rights of the Indians* [1546]. Quoted in *A Cultural History of Spanish America*, by Mariano Picón-Salas, translated by Irving A. Leonard, 48. Berkeley: Univ. of California Press, 1962.

1.35. Account of the Lyubech Congress. In *The Russian Primary Chronicle*, edited by Samuel H. Cross, 279. Harvard Studies and Notes in Philology and Literature, vol. 12. Cambridge, Mass.: Harvard Univ. Press, 1930.

1.36. Hugo Grotius. *The Law of War and Peace* [1623], translated by W. S. M. Knight, 35–84. London: Sweet and Maxwell, 1922. Reprint in *Peace Projects of the Seventeenth Century*, edited by J. R. Jacob and M. C. Jacob. New York: Garland, 1972.

1.37. Desiderius Erasmus. "Dulce Bellum Inexpertis" and "Spartum Nactus Es, Hanc Orna." In *The 'Adages' of Erasmus: A Study with Translations*, edited by Margaret Mann Phillips, 300–301, 308–48. Cambridge: Cambrige Univ. Press, 1964. Reprint, New York: Garland, 1972.

1.38. Eméric Crucé, *The New Cyneas* [1623], translated by C. Frederick Farrell, Jr., and Edith Farrell, 44–60. New York: Garland, 1972.

1.39. William Penn. *An Essay towards the Present and Future Peace of Europe* [1693–94], 1–20. Washington, D.C.: American Peace Society, 1912. Reprint in *Peace Projects of the Seventeenth Century*, edited by J. R. Jacob and M. C. Jacob, 35–84. New York: Garland, 1972. Modern English adaptation for this volume.

1.40. Jean Jacques Rousseau. *A Project of Perpetual Peace* [1761], translated by Edith M. Nuttall, 21–95. London: Richard Cobden-Sanderson, 1927. Reprint in *Peace Projects of the Eighteenth Century*, edited by Sandi E. Cooper. New York: Garland, 1974.

1.41. Immanuel Kant. *Perpetual Peace: A Philosophical Essay* [1795], translated by M. Campbell Smith, 107–83. London: Allen & Unwin, 1903. Reprint, New York: Garland, 1972.

1.42. Anarcharsis Cloots, *La République Universelle ou adresse aux tyrannicides* (The universal republic, or address to those who would end tyrany), 8–21, 39–43, 59. Paris: Chez les Marchands de Bouveautés, n.d. [1793]. Reprint, New York: Garland, 1973. Edited and translated by Sandi E. Cooper.

2.1. Noah Worcester. *A Solemn Review of the Custom of War*, 4–6, 8, 14, 17, 20. Hartford, Conn.: N.p., 1815. Reprint in *The First American Peace Movement*, edited by Peter Brock. New York: Garland, 1972.

2.2. Angelo Umiltà, "L'oeuvre de la ligue internationalé de la paix et de la liberté" (The work of the International League of Peace and Freedom). A printed lecture, Neuchatel, 1891, 21 pp., edited and translated by Sandi E. Cooper for this work.

2.3. Margarethe Leonore Selenka. *Die internationale Kundgebung der Frauen zur Friedenskonferenz* (The international women's demonstration for the peace conference): 15 mai 1899, 1–9. Munich: Schupp, 1900. Translated by Emily Darby for this work.

2.4. Lucia Ames Mead. *Patriotism and Peace: How to Teach Them in Schools*, 7–18. Boston: International School of Peace, 1910.

2.5. "Ustav Obshchestva mira v Moskve" (The charter of the Moscow Peace Society [13 June 1909]). *Obshchestvo mira v Moskve*, issue 1 (Moscow, 1913): 85–86.

2.6. Pavel N. Miliukov. *Vooruzhennyi mir i ogranichenie vooruzenii* (The armed peace and the limitations of arms), excerpts from chaps. 10 and 12. St. Petersburg: B. M. Wolf for the Peace Society of St. Petersburg, 1911.

2.7. Vasily F. Malinovsky [Vasilii F. Malinovskii]. "Rassuzhdeniye o mire y voyne" (Deliberations on peace and war). In *Tractaty o vechnom mire* (Treatises on perpetual peace [1803]). Reprint, Moscow: Nauka, 1963.

2.8 Elihu Burritt, "Address at Brussels on the Propriety of Convoking a Congress of Nations. . . ." In *The Peace Congress at Brussels on the 20th, 21st, and 22nd September, 1848*, 24–34. London: Thomas Ward and Son, 1848.

2.9. Victor Hugo. Presidential address of 22 Aug. 1849, to the International Peace Congress, Paris. In *Douze Discours* (Twelve addresses). Paris: N.p., 1851. Reprint, Boston: World Peace Foundation, 1914.

2.10. Jacques Novicow. "Orientation a donner au mouvement pacifique pour accroitre son efficacité: Mémoire au Congrès Universel de la Paix, 1901" (An orientation for a more effective peace movement). Reprinted in *Peace and Civilization: Selections from the Writings of Jacques Novicow*, edited by Sandi E. Cooper, 315–25. New York: Garland, 1972. Translated by Sandi E. Cooper.

2.11. Bertha von Suttner, "The Evolution of the Peace Movement" [Nobel Lecture, 18 Apr. 1906]. In *Nobel Lectures: Peace*, edited by Frederick W. Haberman, 1: 84–90. Amsterdam: Elsevier, 1972.

2.12. Alfred Fried. *Die Grundlagen des revolutionaren Pacifismus* (The basis of revolutionary pacifism). Published in French as *Les Bases du Pacifisme; le pacifisme réformiste et le pacifisme révolutionnaire*, translated by Jean Lagorgette. Paris: A. Pedone, 1909. Excerpted and translated from the French edition by Sandi E. Cooper.

2.13. William James. "The Moral Equivalent of War," *McClure's Magazine* 35 (Aug. 1910): 463–68. Reprinted in William James, *Memories and Studies*, 167–96. New York: Longmans, Green, 1912.

2.14. Richard Cobden. Speech in *Report of the Proceedings of the Second General Peace Congress, Held in Paris, 22, 23, 24 August 1849*, 78–79. London: Gilpin, 1849.

2.15. Jean de Bloch [Ivan Bliokh]. "Author's Preface." In *The Future of War in Its Technical, Economic and Political Relations*, translated by R. C. Long, [a 1-vol. summary of the original 6 vols. (1898)], lxix–lxxix passim. Boston, 1902. Reprint, New York: Garland, 1972.

2.16. George H. Perris, "Industries de la guerre" (War industries [a speech in English to the Universal Peace Congress]). In *Bulletin officiel du XXe Congrès Universel de la Paix, La Haye, 18 août au 22 août, 1913*, 44–51. Berne: N.p., 1913. Reprint in *Internationalism in Nineteenth-Century Europe: The Crisis of Ideas and Purpose*, edited by Sandi E. Cooper. New York: Garland, 1976.

2.17. Victor Considérant. *La Dernière Guerre et la paix définitive en Europe* (The last war and permanent peace in Europe), 13 pages. (Paris: Librairie Phalanstérienne, 1850. Reprint in *Five Views on European Peace*, edited by Sandi E. Cooper. New York: Garland, 1972. Excerpted and translated by Sandi E. Cooper.

2.18. Karl Marx and Friedrich Engels. "The Manifesto of the Communist Party" [1888 edition, translated by Samuel Moore and Friedrich Engels]. In *Capital, The Communist Manifesto and Other Writings by Karl Marx*, edited by Max Eastman, 334, 340. New York: Modern Library, 1932.

2.19. Resolutions presented to the Zurich Congress of the Second International. In *Protokoll des Internationalen Sozialistischen Arbeiterkongresses in der Tonhalle,* (Proceedings of the Socialist Workers International in the city hall) *Zurich, 6 bis 12 August 1893,* 20–31. Zurich: Organistionskomitee, 1894.

2.20. George [Georgii] Plekhanov, "Sila y nasilie" (Power and violence, [1893]). In *Obraniye sochineniy* (Collected works), 2d ed., 4: 56–57. Moscow: Gosizdat, 1925.

2.21. Jean Jaurès. *Democracy and Military Service* [1916 abbreviated translation of *L'Armée Nouvelle* (1911)], edited by G. G. Coulton, 1–5, 8, 10 [as paraphrased by Coulton], 58, 61, 98, passim. Reprint, New York: Garland, 1972.

2.22. "Resolution of the VII International Socialist Congress at Stuttgart, August, 1907: on Militarism and International Conflicts." In *History of the International, Volume I: 1864–19141,* by Julius Braunthal, translated by Henry Collins and Kenneth Mitchell, 361–63. New York: Praeger, 1967.

2.23. Alexandra Kollontai. *The Autobiography of a Sexually Emancipated Communist Woman,* translated by Salvator Attanasio and edited by Irving Fetscher, 22–23. New York: Herder and Herder, 1971.

2.24. Jean Jacques, comte de Sellon. "Lettre sur la Guerre" (Letter on the war), July 1830, Sellon Papers, Bibliothèque universitaire et publique, Geneva. Translated by Sandi E. Cooper.

2.25. Frédéric Passy,. Speech in the French Chamber of Deputies. In *Journal Officiel,* 23 Dec. 1885. Translated by Sandi E. Cooper.

2.26. David Starr Jordan, *"The Question of the Philippines," Address before the Graduate Club of Leland Stanford Junior University, 14 February 1899,* 1–11. Palo Alto, Calif.: J. J. Ballantine, 1899.

2.27. William T. Stead. "On the British Refusal to Use Arbitration in South Africa." Speech in *Proceedings of the Tenth Universal Peace Congress, Glasgow, September 10—13, 1901,* 527–31. London and Bern: N.p., 1902.

2.28. Henry David Thoreau. "Resistance to Civil Government" [1849]. In *Civil Disobedience in America: A Documentary History,* edited by David R. Weber, 86–89. Cornell Univ. Press, 1978.

2.29. Leo Tolstoi, "Patriotism" [1896] and "On the Peace Conference at the Hague" [1899]. In *On Civil Disobedience and Non-Violence* [excerpted from *The Novels and Other Works of Lyof N. Tolstoi,* translated by Aylmer Maude (New York: Thomas Y. Crowell, 1899)]. New York: Mentor, 1967.

2.30. Victor Theodor Homén, "Passive Resistance" [20 Sept. 1900, an essay distributed in the resistance papers *Fria Ord* and *Vapaita Sanoja*]. Reprint in Homén's collected writings, *Passiiven vastarintamme: poliitillisia kirjoituksia 1899–1904* (Our passive resistance: Political essays 1899–1904), 8–21. Helsinki: Otava, 1906. Translated by Steven Huxley for this work.

2.31. "Convention for the Amelioration of the Wounded in Armies in the Field, 22 August 1864." In *Documents Relating to the Program of the First Hague Peace Congress*, 25–27. London: Clarendon, 1921.

2.32. "The Declaration of St. Petersburg: On Weapons." In *Documents Relating to the Program of the First Hague Peace Congress*, 30–31. London: Clarendon, 1921.

2.33. "Rescript of the Russian Emperor," 24 Aug. 1898 (12 Aug., O.S.) and "Russian Circular," 11 Jan. 1899 (30 Dec. 1898, O.S.), diplomatic notes from Foreign Minister Count Mouravieff to the diplomatic representatives accredited to the court at St. Petersburg. In *The Hague Peace Conferences, of 1899 and 1907*, by James Brown Scott, vol. 2 (documents), 1–5. Baltimore: Johns Hopkins Univ. Press, 1909.

2.34. "Final Act of the International Peace Conference," and "Convention Respecting the Laws and Customs of War on Land." In *The Hague Peace Conferences, of 1899 and 1907*, by James Brown Scott, vol. 2, 77–79, 111–41. Baltimore: Johns Hopkins Univ. Press, 1909.

2.35. "Convention for the Pacific Settlement of International Disputes." In *The Hague Peace Conferences, of 1899 and 1907*, by James Brown Scott, vol. 2, 81–109. Baltimore: Johns Hopkins Univ. Press, 1909.

2.36. "The Final Act of the Second International Peace Conference." In *The Hague Peace Conferences, of 1899 and 1907*, by James Brown Scott, vol. 2, 287–91. Baltimore: Johns Hopkins Univ. Press, 1909.

3.1. Henri Marie La Fontaine, "What Pacifists Ought to Say" [Nov. 1914], 4 pp. Papers of Henri La Fontaine, Mundanum (Brussels), box 40, and International Peace Bureau, Geneva.

3.2. Bertrand Russell. "An Appeal to the Intellectuals of Europe" [Apr. 1915]. In *Justice in War Time*, 2–5, 11–13, 17–18. London: Open Court, 1917. Reprint in *The Ethics of War*, edited by Charles Chatfield. New York: Garland, 1972.

3.3. "Appeal to Democratic Workingmen" [resolution of the Conference of Socialists from Sweden, Norway, Denmark, and Holland, Copenhagen, 17–18 Jan. 1915]. In *Toward an Enduring Peace: A Symposium of Peace Proposals and Programs, 1914–1916*, edited by Randolph S. Bourne, 261–63. New York: American Association for International Conciliation, 1916. Reprint, New York: Garland, 1971.

3.4. Resolutions 1–4 of the Women's International Peace Congress at the Hague, 28–30 Apr. 1915. In *Toward an Enduring Peace: A Symposium of Peace Proposals and Programs, 1914–1916*, edited by Randolph S. Bourne, 253–54, 258–59. New York: American Association for International Conciliation, 1916. Reprint, New York: Garland, 1971.

3.5. Pope Benedict XV, "Allorche Fummo; To the Belligerent Peoples and to Their Leaders" [28 July 1915, official translation]. In *The Teachings of the Church*, edited by Anne Fremantle, 74. New York: Mentor-Omega, 1963.

3.6. The Basis of the British Fellowship of Reconciliation, 1914. In *The Rebel Passion: A Short History of Some Pioneer Peace-Makers,* by Vera Brittain, 35. Nyack, N.Y.: Fellowship of Reconciliation, 1964.

3.7. Evan Thomas, private letter to Norman Thomas, 12 Apr. 1917. In *The Radical "No": The Correspondence and Writings of Evan Thomas on War,* edited by Charles Chatfield, 106–7, 109, 111–12. New York: Garland, 1974.

3.8. Bol'shevistskaia fraktsiia IV Gosudarstvennoi dumy (The Bolshevik faction of the Fourth States Duma), edited by M. L. Lour'e, 507–8. Leningrad: Gosudarstvennoi sotsial'no-ekonomicheskoe izdatel'stvo (State Social-Economic Publishing House), 1938. Translated by Tatiana Telyukova and Charles Chatfield.

3.9. Karl Liebknecht, statement of 2 Dec. 1914 [as reported in *Vorwaerts*]. In *The Socialists and the War,* edited by William E. Walling, 285–86. New York: Holt, 1915.

3.10. "Déclaration d'Hélène Brion lors de son procès, le 29 mars 1917" (Statement of Hélène Brion at her trial, 29 March 1917). In *Revue des causes célèbres politiques et criminelles, Jeudi 2 Mai 1918—N° 5,* 111–17. Translated by Judith Wishnia for this work. The date cited is in error; it was 1918.

3.11. The Majority Report of the St. Louis Convention of the Socialist Party of America. In *The American Socialists and the War,* by Alexander Trachtenberg, 39–43. New York: Rand School of Social Science, 1917.

3.12. Rosa Luxemburg, Draft of the Junius Theses [Dec. 1915]. In *Rosa Luxemburg Speaks,* edited by Mary-Alice Waters, 328–31. New York: Pathfinder, 1970. This translation follows that of the *Fourth International* (Amsterdam, winter 1959/60), and is published with the full text of the "Junius Pamphlet."

3.13. The Zimmerwald Manifesto ["French and German (Socialists) Put Forward a Joint Declaration," *Labour Leader,* no. 40, (7 Oct. 1915), p. 9]. In *The Bolsheviks and the World War,* by Olga Hess Gankin and H. H. Fisher, 329–33. Stanford, Calif.: Stanford Univ. Press, 1940.

3.14. Vladimir Ilyich Lenin, *Socialism and War* [1915], 9, 23–24. Reprint, Moscow: Progress, 1975. "Appeal to the Soldiers of All the Belligerent Countries" [*Pravda,* no. 37, 4 May (21 Apr. O.S.) 1917]. In Lenin, *Collected Works* 24: 186–88. Moscow: Progress, 1977.

3.15. Karl Kautsky. *Die Internationalität und der Krieg* (Internationalism and war), 22, 31, 39. Berlin: Buchhandlung Vorwärts Paul Ginger, 1915. Translated by Timothy Bennett for this work.

3.16. Jane Addams, "Pacifism and Patriotism in War Time" [speech of 16 June 1917]. Reprint in Addams, *Peace and Bread in Time of War,* 1–22. New York: Garland, 1971.

3.17. Maude Royden. "War and the Woman's Movement." In *Towards a Lasting Settlement,* edited by Charles Roden Buxton, 133–46. London: Allen & Unwin, 1915.

3.18. Randolph Bourne. "The State" [1919]. In *War and the Intellectuals: Essays by Randolph Bourne 1915–1919*, edited by Carl Resek, 65–104. New York: Harper Torchbooks, 1964.

3.19. "Resolutions of the International Congress of Women, The Hague, 28–30 April 1915." In *Toward an Enduring Peace: A Symposium of Peace Proposals and Programs, 1914–1916*, edited by Randolph S. Bourne, 254–58. New York: American Association for International Conciliation, 1916. Reprint, New York: Garland, 1971.

3.20. Resolutions of the League to Enforce Peace. In *The Framework of a Lasting Peace*, edited by Leonard S. Woolf, 61–62. London: Allen & Unwin, 1917.

3.21. Woodrow Wilson. Speech of 8 Jan. 1918 [The Fourteen Points]. In *Congressional Record* (8 Jan. 1918), 56: 691.

3.22. Jan Christiaan Smuts. "The League of Nations: A Practical Suggestion" [16 Dec. 1918]. In *The Drafting of the Covenant*, by David Hunter Miller, 2: 23–60. New York: Putnam, 1928.

3.23. "Covenant of the League of Nations, with amendments in force January 1 1927." App. 3 of *From Versailles to Locarno* by Harold S. Quigley, 90–105. Minneapolis: Univ. of Minnesota Press, 1927. For the English and French texts of the Covenant in the Treaty of Versailles, see *The Drafting of the Covenant*, by David Hunter Miller, 2: 721–43. New York: Putnam, 1928.

4.1 Salvador de Madariaga. *Disarmament*, 339–60. New York: Coward-McGann, 1929. Reprint, Port Washington, N.Y.: Kennikut, 1967.

4.2. James L. Brierly. *The Law of Nations*, rev. ed., 39, 44–45, 60–61, 65–66. London: Oxford Univ. Press, 1938.

4.3. "The Protocol of Signature and Statute Establishing the Permanent Court of International Justice." App. 4 of *From Versailles to Locarno*, by Harold S. Quigley, 106–20. Minneapolis: Univ. of Minnesota Press, 1927.

4.4. "The Constitution of the International Labor Organization" [extracts from Part 13 of the Treaty of Versailles, 28 June, 1919 (United States, 66th Cong. 1st sess., S. Doc. 49, Treaty of Peace with Germany, 1919)], in *From Versailles to Locarno*, by Harold S. Quigley, 152–67. Minneapolis: Univ. of Minnesota Press, 1927.

4.5. League of Nations, Secretariat. *The League of Nations and Minorities*, 11–13, 29–30. Geneva, 1923.

4.6. "The League of Nations Mandate for Palestine (including the Territory Known as Trans-Jordan)" [signed at London, 24 July 1922]. In Great Britain, *Parliamentary Papers*, 1923, vol. 25, Cmd. 1785, pp. 2–4, 8.

4.7. Aristide Briand. Speech of 11 Sept. 1930. In *League of Nations Official Journal, Special Supplement No. 84*, Records of the Eleventh Ordinary Session of the Assembly (Geneva, 1930), 37–39.

4.8. "The Protocol Prohibiting the Use in War of Asphyxiating, Poisonous or Other Gases and of Bacteriological Methods of Warfare, Geneva, 17 June 1925." In *League of Nations Treaty Series, Disarmament and Security*, doc. 29. Reprinted in *A Documentary History of Arms Control and Disarmament*, edited by Trevor N. Dupy and Gay M. Hammerman, 125. New York: R. R. Bowker, 1973.

4.9. "Statement by M. Litvinov, Head of the Soviet Delegation, at the First Meeting of the Fourth Session of the Preparatory Commission for the Disarmament Conference in Geneva" [30 Nov. 1927]. In *The USSR Proposes Disarmament 1920s–1980s*, 32–36. Moscow: Progress, 1986.

4.10. The Message of President Hoover to the Disarmament Conference, 22 June 1932. In *Minutes of the General Commission,* League Document, 1932, p. 122. Reprinted in *Documents on International Affairs 1932,* edited by J. W. Wheeler-Bennett, 169–71. London: Royal Institute of International Affairs, 1933.

4.11. Resolution of the WILPF at Executive Committee meeting at Lille, Apr. 1931. Quoted in *Women's International League for Peace and Freedom 1915–1965,* by Gertrude Bussey and Margaret Tims, 96. London: Allen & Unwin, 1965.

4.12. Statement by Secretary of State Charles Evans Hughes, Washington, D.C., 12 Nov. 1921, in his acceptance of the permanent chairmanship of the Conference on Limitation of Armament. Text in the *New York Times,* 13 Nov. 1921, p. 2. Treaty provisions from U.S. Department of State, *U. S. Treaty Series,* no. 671.

4.13. Draft text adopted by the Committee for Moral Disarmament of the League of Nations International Committee on Intellectual Co-operation, 17 Nov. 1933, and submitted to the General Commission of the Conference for the Reduction and Limitation of Armaments. In "Report of the Committee on the Work of Its Sixteenth Plenary Session." *League of Nations Publications,* XII A.2 (Geneva, 1934), 9.

4.14. Kirby Page. *If War is Sin.* (New York: Fellowship of Reconciliation, 1935). Reprinted in *Kirby Page and the Social Gospel: An Anthology,* edited by Charles Chatfield and Charles DeBenedetti, 181–88. New York: Garland, 1976.

4.15. Maria Montessori. "Educate for Peace" [1937]. In *Education and Peace,* by Maria Montessori, translated by Helen R. Lane, 33–37. Chicago: Regnery, 1972.

4.16. Martin Buber, "The National Home and National Policy in Palestine." In *A Land of Two Peoples: Martin Buber on Jews and Arabs,* edited by Paul Mendes-Flohr, 86–87. New york: Oxford Univ. Press, 1983.

4.17. Caroline E. Playne. *The Neuroses of the Nations,* 18–20, 58–62. New York: Thomas Seltzer, 1925.

4.18. Sigmund Freud. *Civilization and Its Discontents* [1930], translated by James Strachey, 92. Reprint, New York: Norton, 1961. Letter from Freud to Albert Einstein, Sept. 1932. In *Einstein on Peace,* edited by Otto Nathan and Heinz Norden, 196–202. New York: Schocken, 1968.

4.19. Mohandas Gandhi. "The Doctrine of the Sword" [*Young India,* 11 August 1920]. In *War and the Christian Conscience,* edited by Albert Marrin,

218–20. Chicago: Regnery, 1971. "War or Peace" [20 May 1926], in *Gandhi: Essential Writings*, edited by V. V. Ramana Murti, 424–25. New Delhi: Gandhi Peace Foundation, 1970.

4.20. Richard Gregg. *The Power of Non-Violence*, 125–27. Philadelphia: Lippincott, 1934.

4.21. Yakov Dragunovsky. "Address to the Soviet Government" [1936]. English translation from *Memoirs of Peasant Tolstoyans in Soviet Russia*, translated, edited, and with an introduction by William Edgerton, 240–41. Bloomington: Indiana Univ. Press, 1993.

4.22. Simone Weil. "Reflections on War." From *La Critique Sociale* [1933], in *Instead of Violence*, edited by Arthur and Lila Weinberg, 186–89. Boston: Beacon, 1971.

4.23. War Resisters' International. "Statement of Principles" [1925]. In *An Encyclopedia of Pacifism*, by Aldous Huxley. 95–96. New York: Harper, 1937.

4.24. Harold Laski. "The Economic Foundations of Peace." In *The Intelligent Man's Way to Prevent War*, edited by Leonard Woolf, 543–47. London: Victor Gollancz, 1934.

4.25. Rudolf Hilferding. "The Struggle of Workers Against the Military Menace" [report to the Congress of the Socialist Workers International, Marseilles, 22–27 Aug. 1925]. From *Zweiter Kongress der Sozialistishen Arbeiter-Internationale in Marseille 22 bis 27 August 1925* (Berlin, 1925). Translation by Timothy Bennett for this work. The report is also available in *Capitalism, Socialism and Social Democracy*, 100–108. Moscow-Leningrad: Moskovskiy Rabochiy, 1928.

4.26. "The World Political Situation and the International Labour Movement" [the Manifesto of the Third Congress of the Labour and Socialist International, Brussels, 5–11 Aug. 1928]. Reprinted in *History of the International, Volume II: 1914–1943*, by Julius Braunthal, translated by Henry Collins and Kenneth Mitchell, 548–52. New York: Praeger, 1967.

4.27. *The Struggle Against War and the Task of the Communists* [a resolution in pamphlet form of the Sixth World Congress of the Communist International, Moscow, July-Aug. 1928], 3–63. New York: Workers Library, 1932.

4.28. "The Tasks of the Communist International in Connection with the Preparations of the Imperialists for a New World War" [from the resolution on the report of Comrade Ercoli (Toliatty Palmiro), adopted by the Seventh Communist International, Moscow, 25 June–21 Aug. 1935]. In *Seventh World Congress, Communist International: Full Text of the Resolutions Adopted at the Seventh Congress*, 23–26. London: N.p. 1935.

4.29. John Foster Dulles. *War, Peace and Change*, 137–40, 156. New York: Harper, 1939.

4.30. "Protocol for the Pacific Settlement of International Disputes" [1924]. League of Nations, *Official Journal, Special Supplement No. 23*, Records of the Fifth Assembly, Annex II to A. 135, 1924, pp. 498–502.

4.31. U.S., Department of State. *The General Pact for the Renunciation of War, Text of the Pact as Signed, Notes and Other Papers,* 1–3. Washington, D.C.: GPO, 1928.

4.32. Convention of 4 July 1933. In *The Balkan Conferences and the Balkan Entente, 1930–1935,* by Robert Joseph Kerner and Harry Nicholas Howard, 228–30. Berkeley: Univ. of California Press, 1936.

4.33. Rassemblement Universel pour la Paix. "Le Premier Appell du R.U.P.: La Paix en Danger" (International Peace Campaign, first Appeal: Peace in danger). Special edition of the news agency Telegrafic of the R.U.P., 2d ser., doc. N 3, Comité France du R.U.P., Paris, 1936. Translated by Sandi E. Cooper.

4.34. Maxim Litvinov, speech of 1 July 1936 to the League Assembly. League of Nations, *Official Journal, Special Supplement No. 151,* Records of the Sixteenth Ordinary Session of the Assembly, Plenary Meetings, Part II (Geneva, 1936), 35–38.

4.35. Position of the Swedish government on the proposed system of mutual guarantees. *League of Nations Documents,* A. 35, 1923, IX (Part I), 46, and M. Undén, remarks of 1930. In *Records of the Committees of the Assembly,* 11A.1C., pp. 39–41. Quoted in *The Scandinavian States and the League of Nations,* by S. Shepard Jones, 228, 242. Princeton: Princeton Univ. Press, 1939.

4.36. Léon Blum. Speech to his followers on 6 Sept. 1936. In *L'Exercise du pouvoir,* Discours prononcés de mai 1936 à janvier 1937 (The exercise of power, addresses from May 1936 to Jan. 1937), 3d ed., 176–81 (condensed). Paris, Librairie Gallimard, 1937. Translated in *Readings in Twentieth-Century European History,* by Alexander Baltzly and A. William Salomone, 400–401. New York: Appleton-Century-Crofts, 1950.

4.37. Neville Chamberlain. Speech of 10 June 1936 to the 1900 Club. Reported in the *Times,* 11 June 1936. Remarks of 21 Feb. 1938 in the House of Commons. In Great Britain, *Parliamentary Debates, Commons,* 5th ser., vol. 332, pp. 53–54, 64. National broadcast of 27 Sept. 1938. From *In Search of Peace,* by Neville Chamberlain, 173–75. New York: Putnam, 1939.

4.38. Resolution of 29 September 1938 in the Nineteenth Ordinary Session of the Assembly of the League of Nations. In League of Nations, *Official Journal, Special Supplement No. 183* (Geneva, 1938), 94–95.

5.1. Virginia Woolf. "Thoughts on Peace in an Air Raid" [1940]. In *The Death of the Moth and Other Essays,* 243–48. New York: Harcourt, 1942.

5.2. A. J. Muste. "The World Task of Pacifism," [1941]. In *The Essays of A. J. Muste,* edited Nat Hentoff, 219–28. New York: Simon & Schuster, 1970.

5.3. The White Rose Leaflets [1942]. In *The White Rose: Munich 1942–1943,* by Inge Scholl, 73–74, 78–79, 82–84. Middletown, Conn.: Wesleyan Univ. Press, 1983.

5.4. André Trocmé. "Mise au point concernant mon attitude en temps de guerre" (A note about my attitude in time of war), personal testimony of 5 Sept. 1939. In the André and Magda Trocmé Papers. Swarthmore College Peace Collection, Swarthmore, Pa.

5.5. Diderich Lund. *Resistance in Norway*, 1–7. Enfield, England: War Resisters' International, 1954.

5.6. Vera Brittain. *Seed of Chaos: What Mass Bombing Really Means*, 7–13. London: New Vision, 1944.

5.7. James Franck et al. "A Report to the Secretary of War" [June 1945]. In *The Atomic Age,* edited by Morton Grodzins and Eugene Rabinowitch, 19–20, 26–27. New York: Basic, 1963.

5.8. Leo Szilard. "A Petition to the President of the United States" [17 July 1945]. Folder "201 (Szilard, Leo)," Manhattan Engineering District records, National Archives.

5.9. Norman Cousins. "Modern Man Is Obsolete." *Saturday Review of Literature* 28 (18 Aug. 1945): 5–9.

5.10. Henry A. Wallace. "The Price of Free World Victory: The Century of the Common Man," speech delivered to the Free World Association, New York City, 8 May 1942. Reprinted in *Vital Speeches of the Day,* 8, no. 16 (June 1, 1942).

5.11. W. E. B. Du Bois. "Democracy and Peace" [paper delivered in Haiti, summer 1944]. Reprinted in *Against Racism: Unpublished Essays, Papers, Addresses, 1887–1961, by W. E. B. Du Bois,* edited by Herbert Aptheker, 239–44. Amherst: Univ. of Massachussetts, 1985.

5.12. The "United Nations Conference on Food and Agriculture. Hot Springs, Virginia. Final Act" [3 June 1943]. In *Documents on American Foreign Relations,* July 1942–June 1943 (Washington, D.C.: GPO, 1943), 5: 302–37.

5.13. Herbert Lehman. Address on Relief and Rehabilitation before the Foreign Policy Association, New York City, 17 June 1943. *Department of State Bulletin* 8 (1943): 539. Reprinted in *War and Peace Aims of the United Nations,* compiled and edited by Louise W. Holborn, 2: 220–25. Boston: World Peace Foundation, 1948.

5.14. *The UNESCO Constitution and Basic Law,* 1–10. Washington, D.C.: GPO, 1952.

5.15. "The Atlantic Charter," joint declaration of President Franklin Delano Roosevelt of the United States and Prime Minister Winston S. Churchill of Great Britain, signed 14 Aug. 1941 on board the warship *Prince of Wales* in the Atlantic near Newfoundland. *Yearbook of the United Nations 1946–1947,* 2. New York: United Nations, 1947.

5.16. "Declaration of Friendship and Mutual Assistance" signed in Moscow by General Sikorski and Marshal Stalin, 4 Dec. 1941. Translated from Polish in *Documents on Polish-Soviet Relations 1939–1945* 1 (1939–1943): 246–47. London: Heinemann, 1961.

5.17. "The Declaration of the United Nations," 1 Jan. 1942, signed by twenty-six states in Washington, D.C. In *Yearbook of the United Nations 1946–47*, 2. New York: United Nations, 1947.

5.18. "Per un Europa libera e unita. Progetto d'un manifesto" (For a united Europe: plan of a manifesto [1941]). In *Problemi della Federazione Europea*, by A. Spinelli and E. Rossi, 9–23. Rome N.p. 1944. Translated by Alexander de Grand for this work.

5.19. Henry Noel Brailsford. *Our Settlement with Germany*, 126–30. New York: John Day, 1944.

5.20. Leonard Woolf. *The War for Peace*, 220–24. London: Routledge, 1940.

5.21. Léon Blum. *For All Mankind* (*A l'Echelle Humaine* [1943]), translated by W. Pickles, 173–76. New York: Viking, 1946.

5.22. Emery Reves. *The Anatomy of Peace*, 255–57, 272–75. New York: Harper, 1945.

5.23. "Report of Robert H. Jackson to the President" [released on 7 June 1945] and "Agreement for the Establishment of an International Military Tribunal." The full text of these documents is in *Department of State Bulletin*, 12 (10 June 1945): 1071 et seq.

5.24. "The Moscow Declaration on General Security." *Yearbook of the United Nations, 1946–47*, 3. New York: United Nations, 1947.

5.25. "Charter of the United Nations." In *The United Nations Conference on International Organization, San Francisco, California, April 25–June 26, 1945. Selected Documents*, 943–65, U.S., Department of State, Publication 2490. Washington, D.C.: GPO, 1946.

Index

PEACE/MIR

was composed in 10 on 12 Sabon on a Mergenthaler Linotron 202,
with display type in Radiant Extra Bold Condensed,
by Dix Type, Inc.;
printed by sheet-fed offset on 50-pound, acid-free Natural Smooth,
bound over binder's boards in Holliston Roxite B,
and notch bound with paper covers printed in 2 colors
by Braun-Brumfield, Inc.;
and published by
Syracuse University Press
Syracuse, New York 13244-5160

Syracuse Studies on Peace and Conflict Resolution
Harriet Hyman Alonso, Charles Chatfield, and Louis Kriesberg, *Series Editors*

A series devoted to readable books on the history of peace movements, the lives of peace advocates, and the search for ways to mitigate conflict, both domestic and international. At a time when profound and exciting political and social developments are happening around the world, this series seeks to stimulate a wider awareness and appreciation of the search for peaceful resolution to strife in all its forms and to promote linkages among theorists, practitioners, social scientists, and humanists engaged in this work throughout the world.

Other titles in the series include:

An American Ordeal: The Antiwar Movement of the Vietnam Era. Charles DeBenedetti;
  Charles Chatfield, assisting author
Building a Global Civic Culture: Education for an Interdependent World. Elise Boulding
The Eagle and the Dove: The American Peace Movement and United States Foreign Policy,
  1900–1922. John Whiteclay Chambers II
From Warfare to Party Politics: The Critical Transition to Civilian Control.
  Ralph M. Goldman
The Genoa Conference: European Diplomacy, 1921–1922. Carole Fink
Give Peace a Chance: Exploring the Vietnam Antiwar Movement. Melvin Small and
  William D. Hoover, eds.
Intractable Conflicts and Their Transformation. Louis Kriesberg, Terrell A. Northrup, and
  Stuart J. Thorson, eds.
Israeli Pacifist: The Life of Joseph Abileah. Anthony Bing
Mark Twain's Weapons of Satire: Anti-imperialist Writings on the Philippine-American
  War. Mark Twain; Jim Zwick, ed.
One Woman's Passion for Peace and Freedom: The Life of Mildred Scott Olmsted.
  Margaret Hope Bacon
Peace as a Women's Issue: A History of the U.S. Movement for World Peace and Women's
  Rights. Harriet Hyman Alonso
Plowing My Own Furrow. Howard W. Moore
Polite Protesters: The American Peace Movement of the 1980s. John Lofland
The Road to Greeham Common: Feminism and Anti-Militarism in Britain since 1820.
  Jill Liddington
Timing the De-escalation of International Conflicts. Louis Kriesberg and Stuart Thorson,
  eds.
Virginia Woolf and War: Fiction, Reality, and Myth. Mark Hussey, ed.